The Research Mission of Higher Education Institutions Outside the University Sector

HIGHER EDUCATION DYNAMICS

VOLUME 31

SCOPE OF THE SERIES

Higher Education Dynamics is a bookseries intending to study adaptation processes and their outcomes in higher education at all relevant levels. In addition it wants to examine the way interactions between these levels affect adaptation processes. It aims at applying general social science concepts and theories as well as testing theories in the field of higher education research. It wants to do so in a manner that is of relevance to all those professionally involved in higher education, be it as ministers, policy-makers, politicians, institutional leaders or administrators, higher education researchers, members of the academic staff of universities and colleges, or students. It will include both mature and developing systems of higher education, covering public as well as private institutions.

For further volumes:
http://www.springer.com/series/6037

Svein Kyvik · Benedetto Lepori
Editors

The Research Mission of Higher Education Institutions Outside the University Sector

Striving for Differentiation

 Springer

Editors
Dr. Svein Kyvik
Norwegian Institute for Studies
 in Innovation, Research and Education
 (NIFU STEP)
Wergelandsveien 7
0167 Oslo
Norway
svein.kyvik@nifustep.no

Dr. Benedetto Lepori
University of Lugano
Faculty of Economics
Centre for Organizational Research
Via Giuseppe Buffi 13
6904 Lugano
Switzerland
blepori@unisi.ch

ISSN 1571-0378
ISBN 978-1-4020-9243-5   e-ISBN 978-1-4020-9244-2
DOI 10.1007/978-1-4020-9244-2
Springer Dordrecht Heidelberg London New York

Library of Congress Control Number: 2010928325

Printed on acid-free paper

Springer is part of Springer Science+Business Media (www.springer.com)

Preface

Even if in most countries, higher education institutions outside the university sector originally did not have a research mandate, it is well known that many of these institutions, which in the English language variably are named 'universities of applied sciences', 'university colleges', 'institutes of technology' or 'polytechnics', have subsequently developed some research activities. In general, governments have begun to recognise the research role of these institutions, to provide them with research funding and to initiate various measures for enhancing research activities.

However, despite the importance of this issue, only a handful of papers and reports have been published on the research mission of these institutions, and except for Norway and Switzerland, very few in-depth studies have been undertaken. These studies show that higher education institutions outside the university sector are faced with many challenges in their efforts to develop research as an ordinary activity alongside teaching. Moreover, the enhancement of this activity leads to quite complex interactions with universities, both in the sense of differentiation based on a specific research mandate oriented towards the regional economy and in the improvement of teaching and professional practice, and convergence related to the drift of research towards traditional academic standards. Thus, we believe that there would be substantial interest in Europe for a book that focuses on the research mission of this sector.

This book is organised into four parts: The first part is constituted by an introductory chapter (by Svein Kyvik and Benedetto Lepori) which provides a general overview of this sector in a European context and the issues that are discussed in the various chapters. This chapter also presents an analytical framework aimed at improving the understanding of the processes driving the development of research in these institutions.

The second part contains four chapters which analyse a number of transversal issues related to the research mission: the regional relevance of research (by Ben Jongbloed), the relevance of research for the improvement of education and professional practice (by Kristin Heggen, Berit Karseth and Svein Kyvik), funding of research (by Benedetto Lepori) and the human resource challenge (by Ellen Hazelkorn and Amanda Moynihan).

The third part consists of eight chapters which gives an overview of the state of the art in each of the countries included in this study: Belgium (by Jef Verhoeven), the Czech Republic (by Petr Pabian), Finland (by Jussi Välimaa and Marja-Liisa Neuvonen-Rauhola), Germany (by Marianne Kulicke and Thomas Stahlecker), Ireland (by Ellen Hazelkorn and Amanda Moynihan), The Netherlands (by Egbert de Weert and Frans Leijnse), Norway (by Svein Kyvik and Ingvild Marheim Larsen) and Switzerland (by Benedetto Lepori).

Finally, a concluding chapter (by Benedetto Lepori and Svein Kyvik) summarises the main findings in this book and discusses some challenges and dilemmas related to the further development of research in this sector.

The intention of the joint effort of the 16 contributors to this project has been to produce a book that will become a reference work for the further discussion of the role of research in European higher education institutions outside universities.

We would like to thank Peter Bentley and Peter Maassen for their valuable comments on a draft version of this book.

Oslo, Norway   Svein Kyvik
Lugano, Switzerland   Benedetto Lepori
November, 2009

Contents

Part I   Introduction

  **1 Research in Higher Education Institutions Outside
the University Sector**   3
Svein Kyvik and Benedetto Lepori

Part II   Thematic Studies

  **2 The Regional Relevance of Research in Universities
of Applied Sciences** 25
Ben Jongbloed

  **3 The Relevance of Research for the Improvement
of Education and Professional Practice** 45
Kristin Heggen, Berit Karseth, and Svein Kyvik

  **4 Funding for Which Mission? Changes and Ambiguities
in the Funding of Universities of Applied Sciences and
Their Research Activities** 61
Benedetto Lepori

  5 Transforming Academic Practice: Human Resource Challenges . 77
Ellen Hazelkorn and Amanda Moynihan

Part III   National Case Studies

  6 Research in University Colleges in Belgium 97
Jef C. Verhoeven

  7 Czech Republic: Research Required but Not Supported 115
Petr Pabian

  **8 'We Are a Training and Development Organisation' –
Research and Development in Finnish Polytechnics** 135
Jussi Välimaa and Marja-Liisa Neuvonen-Rauhala

9   **The Role of Research in German Universities of Applied Sciences**   155
    Marianne Kulicke and Thomas Stahlecker

10 **Ireland: The Challenges of Building Research in a Binary
    Higher Education Culture**   175
    Ellen Hazelkorn and Amanda Moynihan

11 **Practice-Oriented Research: The Extended Function
    of Dutch Universities of Applied Sciences**   199
    Egbert de Weert and Frans Leijnse

12 **Norway: Strong State Support of Research in University Colleges**   219
    Svein Kyvik and Ingvild Marheim Larsen

13 **Striving for Differentiation: Ambiguities of the Applied
    Research Mandate in Swiss Universities of Applied Sciences** . . .   237
    Benedetto Lepori

Part IV   Conclusion

14 **Sitting in the Middle: Tensions and Dynamics of Research
    in UASs**   259
    Benedetto Lepori and Svein Kyvik

Author Index   273

Subject Index   277

Contributors

Ellen Hazelkorn Higher Education Policy Research Unit (HEPRU), Dublin Institute of Technology, Dublin, Ireland, Ellen.Hazelkorn@dit.ie

Kristin Heggen Faculty of Medicine, University of Oslo, Oslo, Norway, k.m.heggen@medisin.uio.no

Ben Jongbloed Centre for Higher Education Policy Studies (CHEPS), University of Twente, Enschede, The Netherlands, b.w.a.jongbloed@utwente.nl

Berit Karseth Faculty of Education, University of Oslo, Oslo, Norway, berit.karseth@ped.uio.no

Marianne Kulicke Fraunhofer ISI, Karlsruhe, Germany, Marianne.Kulicke@isi.fraunhofer.de

Svein Kyvik Norwegian Institute for Studies in Innovation, Research and Education (NIFU STEP), Oslo, Norway, svein.kyvik@nifustep.no

Ingvild Marheim Larsen Faculty of Social Sciences, Oslo University College, Oslo, Norway, Ingvild.M.Larsen@sam.hio.no

Frans Leijnse Hogeschool Utrecht, Open University, Utrecht, The Netherlands, frans.leijnse@hu.nl

Benedetto Lepori Faculty of Economics, Centre for Organizational Research, University of Lugano, Lugano, Switzerland, blepori@unisi.ch

Amanda Moynihan Higher Education Policy Research Unit (HEPRU), Dublin Institute of Technology, Dublin, Ireland, amanda.moynihan@dit.ie

Marja-Liisa Neuvonen-Rauhala Innovation Centre, Lahti University of Applied Sciences, Lahti, Finland, Marja-Liisa.Neuvonen-Rauhala@lamk.fi

Petr Pabian Department of Social Sciences, University of Pardubice, Pardubice, Czech Republic, petr.pabian@upce.cz

Thomas Stahlecker Fraunhofer ISI, Karlsruhe, Germany, Thomas.Stahlecker@isi.fraunhofer.de

Jussi Välimaa Finnish Institute for Educational Research, University of Jyväskylä, Jyväskylä, Finland, jussi.p.valimaa@jyu.fi

Jef C. Verhoeven Centre for Sociological Research, Catholic University of Leuven, Leuven, Belgium, Jef.Verhoeven@Soc.Kuleuven.be

Egbert de Weert Centre for Higher Education Policy Studies (CHEPS), University of Twente, Enschede, The Netherlands, e.deweert@utwente.nl

Part I
Introduction

Chapter 1
Research in Higher Education Institutions Outside the University Sector

Svein Kyvik and Benedetto Lepori

Introduction

In many European countries, higher education institutions outside the university sector now have a formal mandate to perform research related to regional needs and the improvement of education and professional practice. In addition, in the wake of the Lisbon strategy aiming to make the European Union the most competitive and dynamic knowledge economy in the world, the role of these institutions has been put on the European political agenda. There is, however, a general lack of knowledge on the extent of research in this sector, on research conditions and research capability and on the results of this activity. Apart from a few national case studies, this issue has not received much attention in the scholarly literature so far. However, the European Network for Universities of Applied Sciences recently initiated a report on research in these institutions, aimed at identifying good practices of research activities relevant for professional education (de Weert & Soo, 2009).

The purpose of this chapter is to give a general account of the state of the art of research in higher education institutions outside the university sector through focusing on eight selected European countries: Belgium, the Czech Republic, Finland, Germany, Ireland, The Netherlands, Norway and Switzerland.

Most European countries now have a wide range of institutions that offer short-cycle professional and vocationally oriented programmes. However, from a historical perspective, the status of these establishments as higher education institutions is relatively new. Prior to 1960, most European higher education systems were university-dominated. Schools offering short-cycle professional programmes, such as teacher training, engineering, nursing and social work, were not considered as higher education establishments. However, in the ensuing years, most Western European countries gradually developed dual and later binary systems by

S. Kyvik (✉)
Norwegian Institute for Studies in Innovation, Research and Education (NIFU STEP),
Oslo, Norway
e-mail: svein.kyvik@nifustep.no

S. Kyvik, B. Lepori (eds.), *The Research Mission of Higher Education Institutions Outside the University Sector*, Higher Education Dynamics 31,
DOI 10.1007/978-1-4020-9244-2_1, © Springer Science+Business Media B.V. 2010

upgrading professional schools, by establishing new types of colleges and by formalising a division between universities and other higher education institutions (OECD, 1991; Scott, 1995; Kyvik, 2004; Taylor, Ferreira, Machado, & Santiago, 2008; Kyvik, 2009a). In the dual systems, there were a large number of different professional colleges with distinct cultures and they were subject to different public regulations. This functional organisation principle, with many small and specialised institutions that offered 2- or 3-year vocational courses in a limited number of subjects, was common during the 1960s and 1970s. The binary system was first established in the UK in the mid-1960s by organising higher education outside universities into polytechnics based on mergers of specialised colleges according to geographic location. In the 1980s and 1990s, the majority of other Western European countries also established binary systems, while the UK in 1992 created a unified system by upgrading polytechnics and some colleges of higher education into universities (Pratt, 1997). So far, only Iceland has followed in the footsteps of the UK (Jónasson, 2004). In Western Europe, Spain already created a unified system in the 1970s by incorporating vocational post-secondary institutions into universities as separate schools (Bricall & Parellada, 2008). In Eastern and Central Europe, higher education systems have also been subject to substantial reforms. During the 1990s, many countries made efforts to create dual or binary systems, in some countries by upgrading professional schools to higher education institutions and in other countries by merging specialised higher education institutions into multi-faculty colleges (Scott, 2006). Thus, most European countries today have two distinct higher education sectors, although there are large variations between countries with respect to the relative size of the two sectors and the relationship between them.

In the English language, comprehensive higher education institutions outside the university sector are variably called 'universities of applied sciences', 'university colleges', 'institutes of technology' or 'polytechnics'. In some countries, the professional higher education sector also encompasses specialised institutions, such as 'colleges of education'. Several attempts have been undertaken to find a common English term for this sector which could be used in comparative contexts: 'the non-university sector', 'the polytechnic sector', 'the college sector' and 'the alternative higher education sector' are labels that have been applied, but a consensus never has emerged on how these institutions should be termed in international contexts (Teichler, 2008). For matters of convenience, we have chosen to use the term 'university of applied sciences' (abbreviated UAS), even though this term is contested. In four of the countries included in this study, Finland, Germany, The Netherlands and Switzerland, this term is now officially recognised as the name of the comprehensive institutions to be used in international contexts. In Belgium and Norway, university college is the official translation of the national name. In three of the countries, Czech Republic, Germany and Ireland, specialised colleges of education are also part of this sector, but only the comprehensive institutions are referred to in this study as UASs.

Even though in all countries many were critical to the development of research activity in the UAS sector, research has gradually come to play a larger role in these institutions. The OECD report *Redefining Tertiary Education* (1998) thus stated that the policy intention to exclude research from designated non-research institutions seldom succeeds over time, but the reason for this is not that the staff see research as an important condition for good teaching. Rather, the issue is the status of research in tertiary education and the value that staff see in some kind of creative knowledge quest, whether in the form of basic or applied problem-solving research. The institutions themselves have usually wanted to develop a research mission, supported by the regional political community, but often resisted by the traditional universities and sceptical state authorities. However, the large and increasing size of this sector and the increasing number of research qualified institutional staff seem to have convinced many governments and regional stake-holders that these institutions should have an important role to play in the national R&D system, though there should be differentiation of emphasis from the role of universities.

In this chapter, after portraying the eight countries included in this study, we will present an analytical framework which puts us in a position to discuss and interpret the development of research in the UAS sector. Thereafter, we will give a brief overview of the sector's research mission and show how the notion of research is interpreted and used to characterise a wide variety of activities. Furthermore, we will give an overview of central issues related to the implementation of the research mission in this sector, both at the state and the institutional level.

The Countries Included in This Book

Eight European countries have been subject to analysis of research in the UAS sector: Belgium, the Czech Republic, Finland, Germany, Ireland, The Netherlands, Norway and Switzerland. Other European countries have also established a UAS sector where research has long been a mission in addition to teaching, for example, Sweden, Greece, Portugal and Austria. Thus, the selection of countries is not representative in the sense that they portray the general situation in Europe. Some countries have been selected because they have a UAS sector where research plays an important role (like Norway and Switzerland). Other countries are included because research in this sector is a relatively new activity (like in Belgium and the Czech Republic), while the remaining countries have been selected because they have a large UAS sector in which applied research and development have become tasks of growing importance. These differences between individual countries are in themselves of interest in the analysis of the development of research in these institutions.

All these countries have binary systems, but the UAS sector varies considerably between individual countries in terms of (a) types of institution included, (b) programmes provided, (c) degrees given, (d) the size of the sector, and (e) its status and relation to the university sector.

Types of Institution

The dominant type of non-university higher education institutions in each country is comprehensive multi-faculty establishments, termed *fachhochschulen* in Germany and the German speaking part of Switzerland, *hogeschoolen* in The Netherlands and the Flemish speaking part of Belgium, *hautes écoles* in the French speaking part of Belgium, *hautes écoles spécialisées* in the French speaking part of Switzerland, *institutes of technology* in Ireland, *ammatikorkeakoulu* in Finland, *vysoké školy neuniverzitního typu* in the Czech Republic and *statlige høgskoler* in Norway (Table 1.1). In addition, Germany and the Czech Republic have a wide range of specialised professional colleges, and Ireland has a number of colleges of education. Moreover, most countries have some specialised colleges in arts, design and music. In this chapter, only the comprehensive UAS-type institutions have been included as a basis for comparison.

Table 1.1 Terminology and number of UAS-type institutions by country in 2009

	National terms	English terms	Number
Belgium	*Hogescholen Hautes écoles*	University colleges	64
Czech Republic	*Vysoké školy neuniverzitního typu*	Non-university higher education institutions	43
Finland	*Ammattikorkakoulu*	Universities of applied sciences	30
Germany	*Fachhochschulen*	Universities of applied sciences	164
Ireland	*Institutes of technology*	Institutes of technology	14
The Netherlands	*Hogescholen*	Universities of applied sciences	45
Norway	*Statlige høgskoler*	University colleges	24
Switzerland	*Fachhochschulen Hautes écoles spécialisées*	Universities of applied sciences	9

The number of UAS-type institutions varies greatly between countries; from only 9 in Switzerland to 164 in Germany. These differences reflect not only population size and national topography, but also regional political considerations and the political will to merge small institutions into larger entities.

Types of Study Programme

Engineering and economics/business studies are the two major disciplinary areas in which commonly the UAS institutions in all involved countries provide study programmes. Other fields in which study programmes are typically offered by the UAS sector institutions are information technology, various types of health education, arts and design and social work. Teacher training for elementary schools is provided by UASs in Belgium, The Netherlands, Norway and Switzerland; by specialised colleges in Ireland and the Czech Republic; by the universities in Finland;

and in Germany, these teacher training programmes are offered both by the universities and by specialised professional colleges. In Norway, the university colleges also offer a range of disciplinary study courses usually confined to universities.

However, there are large differences between countries in terms of the relative size of these programmes. Engineering has a strong position in Germany, Ireland and Switzerland, while in Norway this programme area enrols only a minor part of the students.

Types of Degree

Although the Bologna Process has had a strong impact on the degree system in many European countries, there is a long way to go before a truly common system is realised (Kehm & Teichler, 2006). Nevertheless, the bachelor degree is introduced as the final qualification for students in most countries and in most professional UAS programmes, although with different length of study programmes. In Germany and The Netherlands, the UAS bachelor degree programmes take 4 years; in the Czech Republic, Belgium, Finland, Ireland, Norway and Switzerland the dominant length of study is 3 years.

In Norway, the university colleges recently have introduced a wide range of 2-year research-oriented master degree programmes in a selection of subjects. Such degrees also are offered by UASs, although on a smaller scale, in the Czech Republic, Germany, Belgium (1 or 2 years), Finland, Ireland, The Netherlands and Switzerland.

Ph.D. programmes have so far only been introduced in a few Norwegian university colleges and a few institutes of technology in Ireland. Also in the Czech Republic, a non-university higher education institution can obtain accreditation for a doctoral programme, but in that case it will also achieve university status.

Size of the UAS Sector

There is considerable variation in the size of the UAS sector in relation to the university sector in these countries, as measured by the proportion of students in higher education. However, a precise comparison of countries is difficult to make due to differences in classification and the inclusion of private colleges and a number of smaller educational institutions, in particular those covering arts and design. As an indicator, the percentage of first-year students in the two sectors has been used. This is a better indicator than the proportion of the total number of students because UAS education is generally of shorter duration than university education; a comparison with the entire student population would thus result in a lower 'score' than a comparison with all freshmen.

Table 1.2 displays the large differences between the various countries. The figures for the UAS sector also include students in specialised colleges. Figures have been rounded to the nearest 5%. The percentage of first-year students in the UAS

Table 1.2 Percentage of
first-year students in 2007 in
the UAS and university
sectors in selected European
countries

	UAS sector	University sector
The Netherlands	70	30
Belgium	65	35
Finland	60	40
Norway	50	50
Ireland	45	55
Switzerland	45	55
Germany	30	70
Czech Republic	25	75

sector is largest in The Netherlands and Belgium. Germany is the only country with
a long-established binary system that has a relatively low proportion of first-year
students in the UAS sector. The main trend in countries with a binary system has
been that student numbers have increased stronger in the UAS sector than in the
university sector. Moreover, the former sector has expanded more than anticipated
(OECD, 1998).

The Development of Research
in the UAS Sector – An Analytical Framework

In order to improve our understanding of the development of research in the UAS
sector and the challenges that these institutions are facing in this respect, we have
developed an analytical framework that places this sector in each country within
a wider context constituted by four principal external actors – state authorities,
supranational organisations, societal stakeholders and academia (see Fig. 1.1). The
figure indicates that the UAS sector is structurally subordinated to the policies and

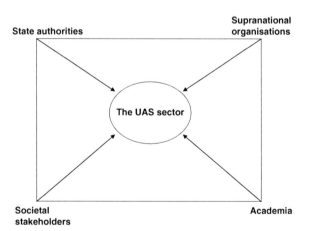

Fig. 1.1 The relationship
between the UAS sector
and state authorities,
supranational organisations,
societal stakeholders and
academia

expectations of state authorities and supranational organisations, societal needs and demands, and the requirements of the universities and the academic community at large. The institutions in the UAS sector had to adapt to the expectations of these four groups of actors, but have also contributed in shaping their own trajectory of development. We will argue that the development of research in the UAS sector can be regarded as a special case of academic drift, though different from what is usually meant by this notion, and choose to use the term *research drift* to characterise this process.

But before proceeding with our new term, we will briefly discuss what the notion of academic drift implies. The term academic drift was originally coined to describe the tendency of non-university higher education institutions to orient their activities in ways that bring them closer to the university image (Burgess, 1972). The role of research in academic drift processes has, however, received relatively little attention in the literature on academic drift, which has largely concentrated on the introduction of more theory in the curriculum at the expense of practice, on the vertical extension of study programmes and on the introduction of university courses in non-university institutions. Horta, Huisman, and Heitor (2008) indicate that drift processes are also visible in the research context, but they argue that one has to be careful in determining this solely as a case of drift. With reference to Gibbons et al. (1994), they argue that the gradually disappearing traditional differences between basic and applied research and the fact that the higher education institutions outside the traditional university sector contribute to the dispersion of knowledge in their own particular way should be largely interpreted as semi-autonomous processes. We agree that the reasons for the development of research in these higher education institutions are more complex than a mere imitation of traditional university practice, or are mainly due to a desire of these institutions to bring them closer to the university image. There are other very good reasons why these institutions should develop research activities, for instance, to strengthen the scientific basis of professional practice in occupations in which universities do not train people for a career and to take part in regional innovation processes in collaboration with industry and local authorities. In this sense, we will argue that in many of these institutions, there is a drift towards developing research as an ordinary activity alongside teaching, but this drift is not necessarily motivated by a desire to become more similar to a traditional university.

We will further argue that research drift, in addition to taking place within the UAS sector itself, is impacted by the relationship between these institutions and each of the four external actors: state authorities, supranational organisations, societal stakeholders and the academic community at large. The state affects, directly and indirectly, the development of research in the UAS sector. Supranational organisations, such as the EU and the OECD, not to mention the Bologna and Lisbon processes, have profound influence on national discussions on the role of this sector in the research system. Societal stakeholders, such as local industry, have requested a stronger research commitment by the UASs in regional development, and universities and the academic community at large have great impact on the research practice in these institutions.

Research Drift as the Outcome of Internal Processes in the UAS Sector

The reasons why research drift takes place within individual UASs are complex. As an analytical approach to enhance our understanding of this process, we will look at the interplay between research-oriented staff members and entrepreneurial programme managers and institutional leaders, as well as at the role of students in these drift processes (see Kyvik, 2007).

Most staff members have traditionally performed their teacher role according to the expectations of their institution and profession, but many also have taken up research as a more or less regular work task. The majority of those who are recruited to these institutions have been trained in universities or specialised university institutions, many of them have some experience from research during their master level studies and increasing numbers of staff members hold a doctoral degree and expect to have the possibility to pursue their research interests. A theoretical explanation for such individual drift processes can be deduced from reference group theory (Merton, 1968). The basic idea is that people frequently compare themselves with individuals within groups other than their own when assessing their own situation. For UAS staff, their counterparts in universities are a most relevant reference group in assessments of working conditions, status and salary.

The UAS sector is constituted by programmes and courses which were developed to serve the needs of industry and the public sector and which initially were strictly profession-oriented with few links to the universities. A common trend for many programmes is a drift towards developing research activity. The reason for this drift is basically found in professionalisation strategies by entrepreneurial leaders and professional associations. Elzinga (1990) argues that professionalisation is characterised by the scientification of the knowledge core through the establishment of a research capability, as well as new career patterns based on research and research training, while the role of tacit knowledge in the training process is downplayed. Several arguments have been used to justify the necessity of doing research in professional and vocational programmes, and these will be discussed in Chapter 3.

At the institutional level, the basic mechanism behind research drift is much the same as for research drift at the programme level, but still different. While programme drift is driven by professionalisation processes, institutional drift is driven by status competition. Many institutional leaders regard the development of research as an important way of increasing the status of their institution. An adequate theoretical explanation for research drift at the institutional level can be drawn from organisation theory. There seems to be a universal tendency for organisational leaders to try to imitate other organisations they regard as more successful (DiMaggio & Powell, 1983), and polytechnics are no exception in their drive to enhance research activity.

Finally, students may have an indirect effect on research drift processes. According to the theory on *credentialism* developed by Collins (1979), students compete for credentials in the form of college and university degrees in order to enhance their competitive advantage in the labour market and their social and cultural capital. This theory is of relevance to our subject, because if increasing numbers of UAS graduates want to extend their lower degree with a higher university degree and this alternative does not exist within the UASs, these institutions might try to develop higher degrees in order to sustain or advance their position in the higher education market. But to be able to establish higher degrees, UASs need to develop their research capability. Student drift towards universities might therefore indirectly enhance research drift in the UAS sector.

Thus, research drift in the UAS sector can be regarded as the combined effects of intertwined processes taking place at different levels within the UASs themselves. But in order to fully grasp the development of research activity in these institutions, we also have to include the role of state authorities, supranational organisations, societal actors and academia in these processes.

The Impact of External Actors on Research Drift in the UAS Sector

In regard to the research mission of the UAS sector, the state is not a single body, but is constituted by a ministry for research affairs, the government, parliament, as well as ministries for industrial and regional affairs. In addition, most countries have one or more national research councils or other agencies that implement state policy for funding of research in this sector. Over time, state policy for research in higher education outside the traditional university sector has in many countries changed from being very restrictive to encouraging. In this respect, the concept of 'policy drift' (Neave, 1979) can be used to describe the process whereby state authorities gradually change their views on the role of research in the UAS sector and the rights and obligations of its academic staff. This policy change may be due to pressure from the UAS sector and regional stakeholders, or to a shift in attitudes regarding the mission of these institutions.

International organisations also have had an impact on the research mission of the UAS sector, though more indirectly. The OECD regularly conducts reviews of the higher education systems in its membership countries, where recommendations for an enhanced research activity in higher education institutions outside the traditional university sector have been put forward. In its report on tertiary education, the OECD (1998) recommended that all higher education should take place in a research culture. Furthermore, the Bologna and Lisbon processes have each in its own way had an effect on the thinking about the status of higher education outside the traditional universities and the role of research in these institutions.

External stakeholders, such as regional political and administrative authorities and industry, may encourage, or even pressure, the local UASs to develop research activities as part of a policy effort to develop the region. The argument is that it is important to carry out research on regional problems and issues and that this research should be undertaken by researchers living in the region. They have better knowledge about local conditions and may more easily identify with the problems of their region.

Finally, the development of research in the UAS sector has been influenced by the dynamics of research in the universities and the knowledge production in the academic community, as well as by the attitudes of universities to other higher education institutions. Academic knowledge production takes place predominantly within disciplinary communities and in the intersection between related disciplines (Clark, 1983; Becher & Trowler, 2001), and universities are the host institutions of disciplinary research, teaching and education and are, as such, centres of academic authority and power. In addition, many staff members in the UAS sector have been trained in universities and have brought with them norms and values on proper research conduct, and many also collaborate in research with colleagues in universities.

The Dynamics of Research Drift in the UAS Sector

According to the model presented above, the development of research in the UAS sector should be regarded as the outcome of mutually reinforcing processes taking place within the sector itself and between the UASs and state authorities, supranational organisations, societal stakeholders and academia. The state has affected the research conditions of institutions in the UAS sector, but the internal development in these institutions and their articulated demands have also affected state policy. Governmental reforms, like the introduction of reward structures emphasising research and publishing, may encourage research drift at the staff level, the programme level and the institutional level. Societal stakeholders, like local industry, have requested a stronger commitment by UASs in regional development, but UASs also have asked for a stronger engagement by local industry in joint research efforts. Universities set standards in research that UASs have to live up to, they train the doctoral students that have a career in the UAS sector and their staff collaborate with colleagues in the UAS sector, affecting research priorities and research practice.

The underlying theoretical assumption is that research-oriented staff, programme leaders and their professional associations, entrepreneurial institutional leaders, state authorities and external stakeholders take part in mutually reinforcing research drift processes. Research-oriented staff may, for instance, want to raise their status and pay through copying the research practice of their university colleagues. They put pressure on the institution to obtain better research conditions. In turn, institutional leaders and programme leaders, inspired by research achievements of parts of the staff, may put pressure on all staff members to do more research. Accordingly, the essence of this theoretical assumption is that research drift on one of the levels, which has been triggered by research drift on another level, may have a reverse effect on drift processes on the initial level, leading to mutually reinforcing and self-sustaining drift processes.

The Problematic Notion of Research

In all the countries, the government has stated that there should be a division of labour in research between universities and UASs. Basic research and research training are the responsibility of the universities, while the UASs should engage in applied research and development. In addition to the role of state authorities in this context, supranational organisations, regional stakeholders and universities have all played a role in the process of defining the research mission. There seems to be a relatively strong consensus among these stakeholders that there should be a division of labour in research between universities and UASs. The EU and the OECD have advocated a concentration of basic research in strong research environments. Universities want to keep research resources for basic research for themselves, while regional stakeholders are primarily interested in the contribution of UASs in the form of applied research, development and knowledge transfer to local industry and business enterprises.

However, there is no common perception of which scholarly activities constitute research in this sector, neither across countries nor within individual countries and individual institutions. Research is frequently used as a synonym for research and development (R&D) as defined by the OECD (2002) for statistical purposes. But the notion of research also often includes activities which are not part of the R&D concept as applied in national and international R&D statistics. Which activities should be encompassed by this concept is, however, not only a semantic discussion, but has consequences for the distribution of resources for research as well as for the evaluation of the outcome of this activity. Defining research and measuring its output has therefore become a controversial issue in higher education (Hazelkorn, 2005).

Research and development is a fairly imprecise term used for activities within relatively undefined boundaries. In order to be able to make international comparisons of contributions to R&D by various nations, the OECD has prepared guidelines for what should be included. The OECD's R&D concept comprises two main components: *research* and *experimental development*. The definition of research which was formulated by the OECD in the 1960s, and which has since formed the basis for its research statistics, has two sub-categories: *basic research* and *applied research*. The 'Frascati Manual' (OECD, 2002) emphasises that the boundary between basic research, applied research and experimental development is difficult to determine for all domains, partly because the concepts are difficult to operationalise and partly because the same research project frequently encompasses more than one type of activity. Still, these definitions are used by the OECD as a basis for the compilation of R&D statistics.

The terminology used in R&D statistics is, however, challenged by other concepts. For instance, in The Netherlands, various public documents refer to the distinction between Mode 1 and Mode 2 type of knowledge production (Gibbons et al., 1994), arguing that the UASs should concentrate on Mode 2 research (see Chapter 11). Terms widely used are 'design and development' and particularly 'practice-oriented research' or 'design research', rather than 'applied research'.

'Innovation' is another concept that is common terminology in this sector, but which clearly is not part of the statistical R&D term of the OECD. In Germany, 'technology transfer' and 'knowledge transfer' between UASs and industry are regarded as important objectives (see Chapter 9), and in the Finnish case the term 'training and development' is suggested as an alternative concept to R&D to pinpoint that most of this activity is undertaken in the context of student projects in cooperation with industry and other external actors (see Chapter 8). In the Czech Republic, virtually all polytechnic institutions extend the boundaries of research to include activities excluded from the definition of research used by state authorities and the universities (see Chapter 7). Thus, they include activities such as training and consultancy programmes, course development within the framework of the EU education programmes, as well as consultancy to private companies.

Similarly, in a study of new universities with a predominantly applied mission, not very different from many large UASs, Hazelkorn (2005, pp. 60–61) found that these institutions define research and scholarly activities in broad terms, including

- traditional academic investigation (whether basic, applied or strategic, and whether using quantitative, qualitative, practice-based or other methodologies);
- professional and creative practice (including architecture, visual, performing and media arts, and consultancy and related activities, etc.);
- knowledge and technology transfer (including development projects and other forms of innovation, commercialisation, software, prototypes, including evaluation and other externally commissioned contracts, etc.).

The point is that the terms 'research' and 'R&D' are used in various manners and often comprise activities other than those originally included in the concepts, even though it is clear that parts of this activity lie beyond the research concept as defined for statistical purposes and beyond those kinds of scholarly activities that are traditionally funded by research councils. This means that in practice the concept has two definitions: a narrow one for statistical purposes and a wider one for description of scholarly activities that go beyond the definition in the Frascati Manual. For matters of simplicity, in this book we will apply the concept of research as a denominator for all these activities.

National Strategic Measures

Even though higher education institutions have been granted greater autonomy by the central state authorities, the institutions can still be viewed as agencies in a state hierarchical structure. Accordingly, the development of a research strategy at the national level can be regarded as a new way of governmental steering of the institutions' scholarly activities. The most important strategic measures at a national level are (a) the formulation of the research mandate, (b) the funding of research over the state budget, and (c) the design of career structures. In addition, national strategic measures include to a varying extent special programmes for academic staff to raise their research competence, demands for cooperation with universities in specific programmes and instructions to UASs to establish strategic plans for the further development of research.

The Research Mandate

Generally, governments have formulated two main objectives for research activities in the UAS sector: (a) research should be of relevance for regional development and (b) research should aim at improving education and professional practice. Obviously, the emphasis on each of these objectives varies between countries.

The relevance of UASs for the region and their role in regional innovation systems have long been emphasised by state authorities in all countries included in this book. The extent to which these institutions undertake research that supports these aims is examined in Chapter 2.

The relevance of research for the improvement of education and professional practice is discussed in Chapter 3. The authors distinguish between four arguments that have been used to introduce research in professional programmes: (a) Teaching will improve if the staff engage in research (research-based teaching), (b) students will learn more if they come into contact with research (research-based learning), (c) professional practice will improve if professional workers in their training learn how to base their work on research-based knowledge (research-based practice), and (d) professional programmes have an obligation to improve the knowledge basis of professional work through research (research-based knowledge production).

Funding of Research

In most countries higher education institutions outside the universities were created without a research mandate; and subsequently without funding for research. Gradually, however, some staff members started to undertake research, partly within the frames of their teaching positions and partly with funding from external sources. While research is stressed more than before, governments have not provided much money for research, and extra resources usually can only be provided through reducing the time for teaching or through the provision of third-party research grants. The national case studies reveal large variation in state policy, the extent of research funding and type of funding sources. In the development of research in the UAS sector, some topical questions are as follows: Should extra resources for research be transferred from teaching activities or through additional funding from the state? Should the UASs compete for grants and contracts with the universities, or would ring-fenced schemes be an option? To what extent should research funding of UAS research be targeted towards specific purposes according to some public goals? Answers to these questions are likely to profoundly shape the configuration of research in UASs, and Chapter 4 provides a comparative perspective on different national choices in this respect.

Career Structures

In all countries included in this book, the state decides on the career structure in the UASs. In the universities, most academic staff members are entitled to and even required to spend time on research. These rights and demands are reflected in the names of positions and in the incentive structure; research output is the primary indicator of status and the main promotion criterion. In the UAS sector, with the exception of Norway, the career structure is quite different from that of the universities, reflecting the role of the UASs as primarily teaching institutions. Thus, the state is a key actor in defining the role of research in UASs through the design of career structures, through limiting the number of positions with a research mandate and through deciding on promotion criteria. Accordingly, an effective state measure to enhance research in UASs would be to introduce academic positions and career paths similar to those of universities. On the other hand, the main objective of the UASs is to train students for various professions. Thus it might be more important that staff have some practical experience from professional work than that they possess formal research qualifications. It has been argued that it is not reasonable to educate preschool teachers, nurses and physiotherapists with staff unfamiliar with the practice of their profession and unable to teach students technical, professional and social skills in working with children, patients and clients (Stjernø, 1999). As will be shown in the various country chapters, in this respect, national policies vary greatly. This issue is also addressed in Chapter 5.

Research Strategy at the Institutional Level

Over the last two decades, a common tendency in higher education systems in Europe is a development towards greater institutional autonomy (Maassen & Olsen, 2007). This development has been followed by the expectation of governments that individual institutions shall generate a larger share of their funding from external sources and undertake strategic planning through goal-setting and priority-making. But the institutions themselves have, for a variety of reasons, also become motivated to engage in such planning. In this respect, we may distinguish between strategic processes that aim at adapting to external expectations (state policy, international trends, regional demands and the knowledge production in academia) and processes that reflect the needs of leaders to change institutional behaviour (Presley & Leslie, 1999). However, the purpose of the strategic plan can be restricted to comply with external expectations through formal statements on the further development of research, rather than to provide a platform for institutional action (Larsen, 2000).

In general, the idea of an institutional strategy is part of what is usually called the managerial revolution in higher education, emphasising the need of a more coherent and purposeful institutional policy (Amaral, Meek, & Larsen, 2003; Hazelkorn, 2005). Over time, planning, reporting and allocation systems have become increasingly sophisticated, also in the field of research. Today, most UASs undertake some kind of strategic planning of their research activity, but relatively little is known about such processes in this sector, apart from a few studies of individual countries (Lepori & Attar, 2006; Kyvik, 2008), as well as a comparative study of research strategy in new universities aiming at developing their research capacity (Hazelkorn, 2005).

In broad terms, a research strategy at the institutional level could be defined as a plan defining the main institutional goals to be achieved in research by an institution as a whole, as well as the measures to reach them. In principle, a strategy should be stated in an official document approved by some institutional authority, but in a broader sense a strategy can also exist in a less formalised way, where some elements are more or less implicitly accepted in the institutions. A research strategy can be developed at different organisational levels: the state level, the institutional level, the faculty or school level and the department level. In recent years, we observe an increasing tendency to consider the level of the *individual institution* as a major strategic level, where key decisions concerning the portfolio of activities, the regulatory framework and the internal organisation are taken and then implemented (Amaral et al., 2003; Bonaccorsi & Daraio, 2006). In principle, the development of a research strategy is a hierarchical process where state guidelines direct institutional strategy, which set the boundaries for planning at the faculty level, which in turn constrain the strategy process in the basic units, ending up with guidelines for research activities which should be followed by individual staff members.

In reality, however, such strategy processes are much more complex; strategic development usually takes place simultaneously at these levels. In fact, instead of top-down planning, the development of a research strategy may take the form of a bottom-up process, where the strategy of a basic unit is a collation of individual plans, the strategy of a faculty is a summary of the plans of basic units and the institutional strategy is a list of faculty or school priorities.

We can distinguish between two major elements in a research strategy: (a) the definition of the research mission and positioning of the institution inside the wider national and international research system and (b) a plan or strategy for how the objectives should be achieved. With regard to the latter element in the research strategy, every analysis of strategies in new research institutions comes to a more or less similar list of issues which should be addressed (Hazelkorn, 2005):

- The organisation of research activities and the management of research.
- Policies concerning the allocation of funds and fund-seeking from external sources.
- Policies concerning the recruitment and development of human resources.
- Finally, cooperation with other research institutions and with stakeholders.

The national case studies indicate large differences between countries and institutions to the extent that research strategies are developed and implemented in the UAS sector.

Management and Organisation of Research

There seem to be large variations between individual UASs in all the countries involved, to the extent that they have established an administrative body to attend to research matters. These tasks typically include being a secretariat for research governing bodies, drafting strategy plans, suggesting rules and regulations for the allocation of internal resources among units and individuals, coordinating institutional policy, advising academic staff on proposal preparation, assisting with project administration and compiling statistics. The larger UASs may have set up a separate research office headed by a director of research, while in the smaller institutions these tasks are handled by the general administrative staff on a part-time basis.

There are also large variations between individual UASs in the extent that they have formalised research groups as part of the organisational structure, set up research centres and established research programmes in order to concentrate and profile research activities. Differences between UASs are typically related to their size and engagement in research, more so than to the national context.

Allocation of Funds and Work Time for Research

With the shift from a direct to a more indirect steering approach in the public sector, the UASs now have more room for making their own policy within the frameworks set by their government. However, institutions in the UAS sector generally have scarce resources for research, and an important part of a research strategy is to prioritise between research areas and define guidelines for the distribution of resources for research among academic staff (Kyvik, 2009b). The most important resource is staff time. Because resources for research are much more limited in these institutions than in the universities, and because there are large differences in research qualifications, priority making is necessary. This fact creates some dilemmas within the individual institutions. First, if institutions with low research activity wish to use more resources for research, this will subsequently result in a reduction of the time used for teaching. The question is whether a transfer of resources from teaching to research is desirable and appropriate in the light of profession-oriented education as the prime function of these colleges. Second, institutional leaders face the dilemma of how big a share of research resources should be allocated based on expected quality or relevance of the research and how much should go towards improving the research competence of the institution's staff. The various country studies show that these resources are distributed in various ways – also within individual institutions.

Recruitment and Development of Research Competence

Human resources are of course a central concern in a research strategy, and there are significant challenges for UASs whose academic staff are often hired to teach, without consideration of research skills or future research activities in mind. Many staff members lack a postgraduate qualification and/or research experience and have limited capacity to attract or compete for funding or produce the requisite outcomes. In most countries relatively few staff members in these institutions have doctoral level qualifications. In addition to recruiting new staff qualified for doing research, an important part of a research strategy would then be to develop research competence with the existing staff, either through formal research training in doctoral programmes or through the participation in research projects headed by experienced researchers. In addition, for institutions without traditions in research, the development of a sustainable research culture is of fundamental importance. These issues are discussed in Chapter 5.

Collaboration with Universities, Research Institutes and Industry

Finally, a research strategy should consider how the institution should enhance closer cooperation with other higher education establishments, research institutes and industry. Cooperation is a central concern in European higher education and research policy, and it is even of greater importance for UASs given their size and limited research capability. Thus development of cooperation at all levels should be a central concern for research strategies. In some domains, forms of cooperation could even be the only possibility for developing or maintaining research in an institution. As shown in the national case studies, forms of collaboration with other research establishments, industry and regional stakeholders vary greatly between countries and between domains.

Conclusion

In this chapter, we have provided an overview of the main issues related to the research mission of higher education institutions that are not part of the university sector. For matters of convenience, we have used the term 'the UAS sector' as a common label for this part of the education system because 'universities of applied sciences' is the official English name of these institutions in four of the countries included in this book (Germany, Switzerland, Finland and The Netherlands).

The binary divide between a university sector and a UAS sector has in itself been the basic premise for the different roles research is supposed to play in the two sectors: as a major task for universities and as a minor activity compared to education in UASs. In addition, universities should have a major responsibility for fundamental research and the training of new researchers, while UASs should concentrate on applied research with relevance for the region and professional practice in those occupations for which they educate students for a future career.

In order to better understand the increasingly important role of research in the UAS sector, we introduced the notion of *research drift* and developed an analytical framework which places this sector within a context constituted by state authorities, supranational organisations, societal stakeholders and academia. We argue that there is a drift towards developing research as an ordinary activity alongside teaching and that this development is driven by mutually reinforcing processes consisting of activities taking place within the UAS sector itself and decisions, initiatives and pressures by the four external actors mentioned above.

As will be demonstrated in this book, there are differences between countries included when it comes to how far the process of research drift has come. However, in all countries there is a political concern to further develop UASs as research institutions, though with a different mission and with less resources than the traditional universities. The various chapters in this book also demonstrate that UASs face large challenges in their efforts to enhance research activities and that national and institutional research strategies vary greatly between countries. Research drift in the UAS sector implies challenges and dilemmas that have no simple solutions, and the various countries included have chosen different paths. In the concluding chapter, we will discuss the main open issues and options which are likely to shape the future of research in these institutions.

References

Amaral, A., Meek, V. L., & Larsen, I. M. (Eds.). (2003). *The higher education managerial revolution?* Dordrecht: Kluwer.

Becher, T., & Trowler, P. R. (2001). *Academic tribes and territories. Intellectual enquiry and the cultures of disciplines.* Milton Keynes: Society for Research into Higher Education & Open University Press.

Bonaccorsi, A., & Daraio, C. (Eds.). (2006). *Universities as strategic units. Productivity and efficiency patterns in the European university system.* Cheltenham: Edward Elgar.

Bricall, J. M., & Parellada, M. (2008). The non-university sector in the Spanish system of higher education. In J. S. Taylor, J. B. Ferreira, M. L. Machado, & R. Santiago (Eds.), *Non-university higher education in Europe* (pp. 215–230). Dordrecht: Springer.

Burgess, T. (1972). *The shape of higher education.* London: Cornmarket Press.

Clark, B. R. (1983). *The higher education system. Academic organisation in cross-national perspective.* Berkeley, CA: University of California Press.

Collins, R. (1979). *The credential society: An historical sociology of education and stratification.* New York: Academic Press.

de Weert, E., & Soo, M. (2009). *Research at universities of applied sciences in Europe. Conditions, achievements and perspectives.* Enschede: CHEPS, University of Twente.

DiMaggio, P. J., & Powell, W. W. (1983). The iron cage revisited: Institutional isomorphism and collective rationality in organizational fields. *American Sociological Review, 48,* 147–160.

Elzinga, A. (1990). The knowledge aspect of professionalization: The case of science-based nursing education in Sweden. In R. Torstendahl & M. Burrage (Eds.), *The formation of professions. Knowledge, state and strategy* (pp. 151–173). London: Sage Publications.

Gibbons, M., Limoges, C., Nowotny, H., Schwartzman, S., Scott, P., & Trow, M. (1994). *The new production of knowledge. The dynamics of science and research in contemporary societies.* London: Sage Publications.

Hazelkorn, E. (2005). *University research management. Developing research in new institutions.* Paris: OECD.

Horta, H., Huisman, J., & Heitor, M. (2008). Does competitive research funding encourage diversity in higher education? *Science and Public Policy, 35,* 146–158.

Jónasson, J. T. (2004). Higher education reforms in Iceland at the transition into the twenty-first century. In I. Fägerlind & G. Strömqvist (Eds.), *Reforming higher education in the Nordic countries – Studies of change in Denmark, Finland, Iceland, Norway and Sweden* (pp. 137–188). Paris: International Institute for Educational Planning.

Kehm, B., & Teichler, U. (2006). Which direction for Bachelor and Master programmes? A stocktaking of the Bologna process. *Tertiary Education and Management, 12,* 269–282.

Kyvik, S. (2004). Structural changes in higher education systems in Western Europe. *Higher Education in Europe, 29,* 393–409.

Kyvik, S. (2007). Academic drift – A reinterpretation. In J. Enders & F. van Vught (Eds.), *Towards a cartography of higher education policy change. A festschrift in honour of Guy Neave* (pp. 333–338). Enschede: CHEPS.

Kyvik, S. (2008). *FoU-strategi ved statlige høgskoler.* Oslo: NIFU STEP.

Kyvik, S. (2009a). *The dynamics of change in higher education. Expansion and contraction in an organisational field.* Dordrecht: Springer.

Kyvik, S. (2009b). Allocating time resources for research between academic staff: The case of Norwegian university colleges. *Higher Education Management and Policy, 21,* 109–122.

Larsen, I. M. (2000). Research policy at Norwegian universities – Walking the tightrope between internal and external interests. *European Journal of Education, 35,* 385–402.

Lepori, B., & Attar, L. (2006). *Research strategies and framework conditions for research in Swiss universities of applied sciences.* Lugano: KTI/CTI.

Maassen, P., & Olsen, J. P. (Eds.). (2007). *University dynamics and European integration.* Dordrecht: Springer.

Merton, R. K. (1968). *Social theory and social structure.* New York: The Free Press.

Neave, G. (1979). Academic drift: Some views from Europe. *Studies in Higher Education, 4,* 143–159.

OECD. (1991). *Alternatives to universities.* Paris: OECD.

OECD. (1998). *Redefining tertiary education.* Paris: OECD.

OECD. (2002). *The measurement of scientific and technological activities. Frascati Manual 2002: Proposed standard practice for surveys on research and experimental development.* Paris: OECD.

Pratt, J. (1997). *The polytechnic experiment 1965–1992.* London: The Society for Research into Higher Education.

Presley, J. B., & Leslie, D. W. (1999) Understanding strategy: An assessment of theory and practice. In J. C. Smart (Ed.), *Higher education: Handbook of theory and research* (Vol. XIV, pp. 201–239). New York: Agathon Press.

Scott, P. (1995). Unified and binary systems of higher education in Europe. In A. Burgen (Ed.), *Goals and purposes of higher education in the 21st century* (pp. 37–54). London: Jessica Kingsley Publishers.

Scott, P. (2006). Higher education in Central and Eastern Europe. In J. J. F. Forest & P. G. Altbach (Eds.), *International handbook of higher education* (pp. 423–441). Dordrecht: Springer.

Stjernø, S. (1999). Planning, co-ordination and academic drift – From 4 to 36 universities in Norway? Paper for the CHER Conference, Oslo.

Taylor, J. S., Ferreira, J. B., Machado, M. L., & Santiago, R. (2008). *Non-university higher education in Europe.* Dordrecht: Springer.

Teichler, U. (2008). The end of alternatives to universities or new opportunities? In J. S. Taylor, J. B. Ferreira, M. L. Machado, & R. Santiago (Eds.), *Non-university higher education in Europe* (pp. 1–13). Dordrecht: Springer.

Part II
Thematic Studies

Chapter 2
The Regional Relevance of Research in Universities of Applied Sciences

Ben Jongbloed

Introduction

In 1611, Thomas Sagittarius, a learned man from the German town of Jena, explored the question of what impact a university can have on its surrounding region. He found that universities had an important regional function, because they normally improve the level of health care, lead to better marriage opportunities for girls and induce more piety among the local population (Buursink, 2002). Nearly 400 years after Sagittarius, universities still are seen as regional boosters. However, it is the region's socio-economic development that is the centre of attention these days (Florax, 1992; OECD, 2007). Universities not only are expected to provide education and conduct fundamental research, but also are to play an active role in the development of their economic, social and cultural surroundings. In other words, they are entrusted with a regional mission (Arbo & Benneworth, 2007).

This chapter is not about research universities. It is about *Fachhochschulen*, *hogescholen*, polytechnics, university colleges, institutes of technology and universities of applied sciences. This type of higher education institution – which we from now on will denote by the term 'university of applied sciences' (UAS) – is primarily focused on the training of students for particular professions in the labour market. As indicated in the country studies contained in this volume, many of these UASs are also increasingly active in carrying out applied research geared to the professional fields covered in their degree programmes. In this respect, UASs are distinct from research universities, because these are very much into fundamental research and a more academic type of programs as well as the training of researchers. Compared to the research universities, UASs are explicitly expected to make regional engagement and regional innovation part of their mission. In the majority of the countries represented in this book, UASs are more evenly spread across the country compared to the research universities. This implies that, by their very nature, UASs will have close ties to business and industry and their staff will be oriented on the needs of the

B. Jongbloed (✉)
Centre for Higher Education Policy Studies (CHEPS), University of Twente, Enschede,
The Netherlands
e-mail: b.w.a.jongbloed@utwente.nl

S. Kyvik, B. Lepori (eds.), *The Research Mission of Higher Education Institutions*
Outside the University Sector, Higher Education Dynamics 31,
DOI 10.1007/978-1-4020-9244-2_2, © Springer Science+Business Media B.V. 2010

workplace, providing courses that have direct relevance for the regional economy and the needs of the regional communities.

Because it would go too far to present examples from all countries represented in this book, the sections that follow will focus mostly on three countries when we discuss the connection between the research taking place in the national UAS sector and the regions where this sector's institutions are situated. The three countries are Switzerland, Norway and The Netherlands. As we will see, the three cases are quite distinct and represent interesting examples of the ways in which UASs interact with regional business and other regional stakeholders. We are primarily interested in the role that the research activities of UASs play in regional development, but will also discuss to what extent the teaching activities in UASs are affected by – and affect – the region.

We are aware that there is no accepted definition of a region (Siegfried, Sanderson & McHenry, 2008). For the time being it will be defined here as a sub-national special entity, 'an administrative division of a country' (Cooke & Leydesdorff, 2006, p. 6). Where once it may have been possible to identify the territory of an institution – say its catchment area or its sphere of immediate influence – new technologies and globalisation have changed all that and made borders much less relevant. The audiences, communities and clients – in short: the *stakeholders* – of a research university or a UAS are nowadays multi-faceted, ranging in scale and scope from local to regional, to national and international. However permeable and virtual the geographic boundaries may be these days, the immediate surroundings of a university will still feel a direct effect because of the proximity of a knowledge institution. Proximity still matters (Morgan, 2004). This effect extends beyond the direct economic impact resulting from an institution's expenditure and includes the impact of a knowledge institution on the regional innovation system. Such effects are often presented when higher education institutions have to justify their claims on the public purse. Universities frequently make claims about the number of jobs they create locally and how much a city or state benefits from their presence in terms of purchasing power or tax revenues. Siegfried et al. (2008) quote a number of economic-impact studies that boast regional multipliers of well over 1, meaning that a Euro spent on the local university will increase the wealth of a regional community with much more than that single Euro.

There is a renewed interest in regionalism in almost all EU countries, leading some to proclaim a 'Europe of regions' (Harvie, 1994). Regional and local authorities take on an active role in the enhancement and promotion of innovation and regional development. In fact, regions compete for skills, investment, infrastructure, tourism and so on. In this competitive climate, regional authorities see their university as a 'booster', 'engine', 'powerhouse', 'driver' or 'lever' for regional growth and prosperity (Arbo & Benneworth, 2006, p. 6). These metaphors suggest that the university is the place where the pace is set for the region's progress. Another type of metaphor is the biological: Higher education represents a 'breeding ground' or 'catalyst' for new economic activity in the region, producing spin-offs and entrepreneurial activity. Thus universities are looked to as the place for innovation and reinvigoration.

In this chapter we explore in particular what role UASs play in contributing to the regional development agenda. We will highlight the distinctive role (if any) that the UAS has in comparison to its 'big brother', the research university. We will argue that the contribution that UASs make to their regional communities differs across the three countries that we cover. The way they play out their role depends on the institutional arrangements that are present in the country and the different development trajectories that the UAS sectors in Europe have so far experienced. We will argue that the contribution that research by UASs can make to the region will be higher, depending on the institutionalisation of the linkages ('partnerships') between UASs and regional businesses. The relevance of UASs for their region can be further improved if there are mechanisms that encourage UASs to put in place an 'entrepreneurial curriculum' that can further enhance the region's human capital. Our conclusion is that research undertaken by UASs – whether it is applied research, consultancies or a more design and development type of activity – can help to intensify UAS–regional partnerships and make the UAS curriculum more entrepreneurial. Thus a UAS's research activity may have an added value for the UAS's teaching and the quality of its staff.

The Regional Mission of the UASs in Europe

From the various country chapters contained in this volume it has become clear that research, or indeed research that is carried out in collaboration with the regional environment, is not present in equal amounts across the different UAS sectors in Europe. The question to what extent the research by UASs has relevance for the region will be answered differently, depending on the country at stake. The mere fact that the UASs are larger in number than the research universities does not automatically mean that their research has a larger impact on their region. The fact is that the functions and missions awarded by the public authorities to the UAS sector differ across countries. Among other things, this translates into different funding streams made available for UAS research and it leads to different evaluation criteria for judging the UAS performance. In most countries, UASs have been given responsibilities for local and regional research, but there are clear distinctions between national policies.

Located at one of the extreme ends of the spectrum is the Czech Republic. Among the eight countries represented in this volume, it is the least developed when it comes to a research portfolio for the UAS sector. The vast majority of UASs in the Czech Republic align themselves closely to the region, but in doing so, UASs focus less on research and much more on the provision of training courses. The research carried out by Czech UASs stands very much in the shadow of research carried out by public research universities that have significantly higher research capacities.

Ireland is a case where the UAS institutions are also at a disadvantage compared to the research universities. The Institutes of Technology are expected to educate 'for trade and industry over a broad spectrum of occupations'. Compared to the Czech Republic they have more access to research funds, but at present Irish

UASs are in a state of transition that sees them struggling to compete with universities and secure a distinctive identity. It is difficult to predict whether and how the Irish Institutes of Technology will become the 'gateways' and 'hubs' for social and economic development around the country.

Turning to Belgium and The Netherlands, we observe that research in UASs is on the rise, mostly thanks to dedicated government programmes to enhance the UASs' role in meeting demands from industry and strengthening innovation in the region. The two low countries follow different routes in this respect. The Belgium case is seeing this transition taking place alongside a policy of consolidation and academisation, where UASs are expected to join up with other UASs, respectively research universities, in order to secure their individual place in the research landscape. In the Dutch case, UASs are also in a transition process and, helped by targeted research subsidies, well underway towards becoming important players in the regional innovation systems.

In Germany and Finland, the *Fachhochschulen* and the polytechnics respectively have been carrying out regionally related research and development activities for some time already. This UAS activity is supposed to be supporting the region's educational needs and its innovation climate. Technology transfer, in particular to small and medium-sized enterprises (SMEs), is an explicit part of the UAS mission in Finland and Germany. Next to the national government, regional authorities play an important part in supplying the resources to enable this role.

The cases of Norway and Switzerland are different from either of the above. In both countries the UAS sector, next to its teaching mission, has an officially recognised research mission that is funded through a recurrent funding stream. In Norway, UAS research is expected to be connected to specific occupational fields and to problems in the regions. However, the way in which this objective is met is left to the university colleges themselves and, on top of the block grant, very little in terms of targeted public funding for research is made available. In Switzerland, such dedicated targeted funding streams do exist, and have led to a situation where UASs play distinctive roles in the research and innovation system.

Throughout the remainder of this chapter we will present examples from three countries only (Switzerland, Norway, The Netherlands) to illustrate our argument that institutional arrangements in a particular country will have implications for the ways in which and the extent to which UASs engage in research that is relevant for their region. However, in all eight cases included in this book, UASs indeed play a prominent role in their region. Apart from their role in providing professional education – often to meet regional needs – they also are to a varying extent engaged in research-based services to regional business and regional authorities. Certainly, there are differences across the various systems, some of which can be explained by referring to the (sometimes short, sometimes longer) history of the UAS sector and the ways in which its sometimes uneasy relationship with the research university sector has been delineated. For the three countries we will highlight some of the policy instruments in place for addressing research in the UAS sector. As always, funding policies are important instruments for steering applied research activity in UASs.

If the UAS sector is charged with an explicit research task right from its creation – as is the case for Swiss UASs – this will make a difference compared to a UAS system that only later on saw a research task being added to its education task, as is the case in The Netherlands, Belgium and – to a lesser extent – Germany. In the latter case, the staff of UASs are less likely to have research skills – let alone possess a PhD. This is why some countries are much less active than others in having their UASs carry out R&D projects for local business. On the same note, if public funding for research is provided as part of the lump sum for the UAS (as is the case for Norway and Switzerland) this is likely to make a difference compared to UAS systems where research funds are only provided in the form of earmarked project funds that the UASs have to compete for (as is the case in Belgium, The Netherlands, Ireland and Finland). In other words, institutional differences and lock-in effects will cause wide differences across Europe when it comes to explaining the impact of UASs on their regions.

The Rise and Decline of the Region: The Triplet of Hardware, Software and Mindware

Now that we have looked briefly at the UAS side of the UAS–region link, it is time to take a look at the other side, the region. An important question here is what makes a region economically more (or less) prosperous and what potential role does the UAS have in this? In recent decades, major shifts took place in regional economic fortunes in the face of internationalisation and globalisation of the world economy. The 1970s and 1980s have seen the demise of 'smoke-stack' industries and a growth in service-oriented companies. The industrial regions in Europe where textiles, coal, steel, shipbuilding and other heavy industries were concentrated have experienced a spiral of decline. Some examples of these 'rustbelt regions' are the Ruhr Area, Tyne and Wear, Nord-Pas-de-Calais and Northern-Jutland (Cooke, 1995). To revive these regions, and to find ways in which they might break out from their path dependency, a prominent role is awarded to higher education.

For understanding a region's economic development trajectory the triplet of *hardware*, *software* and *mindware* may be used (Benneworth, Hospers, & Jongbloed, 2006). The term *hardware* refers to the visible and tangible (hence 'hard') aspects of the regional economic structure. Traditionally, economists have stressed the importance of the production factors labour, natural resources and capital for regional economic dynamics (Barro & Sala-i-Martin, 1995). However, in recent decades regional scientists have pointed to the role of infrastructure (roads, airports, harbours and digital infrastructure) and knowledge (human capital) as additional ('hardware') factors of regional development (Vickerman, 1991). The assumption is that if a region has a high concentration of high-tech firms, knowledge-based industries and a stock of creative human capital (Florida, 1995, 2002), the region is most probably doing well in economic terms. Together with research universities and other education institutions, the UASs contribute to the development of human capital.

A region's *software* refers to its institutional set-up. Geographers and sociologists see regional economic development as being first and foremost about people, the way they interact and their norms and values. This institutional perspective stresses networks, enabling structures (e.g. business support, technology-diffusion programmes) and their processes to enhance a region's development. However, clustering and networking, combined with a concentration of knowledge-based firms and a stock of creative human capital (Florida, 2002), is seen by scholars as not enough to explain regional development. The literature on social capital (Putnam, 1993, 2000), trust (Fukuyama, 1999) and learning regions (Maskell, Eskelinen, & Hannibalsson, 1998) suggests that local networks and mutual trust between the actors in the regional network will lower transaction costs and contribute to regional dynamics. Successful local economies are said to depend on complex local processes of integration, built on trust, reciprocity and loyalty that create social capital. The UASs can have a facilitating role here in helping to build networks and facilitating the exchange of information, ideas and innovation through collaborations of various sorts (Garlick, Taylor, & Plummer, 2008). In the case of The Netherlands, an important initiative is the creation of a new senior staff position in the UAS, the *lector*. The *lector* is required to build a network of professionals from within the UAS and the business sector (in particular SMEs). The *lector* is expected to work on stimulating the external orientation of the UAS and engaging in knowledge transfer between the UAS and its regional environment.

Apart from the tangible assets of a region in terms of its 'hardware' and 'software', also the image of a region – its 'mindware' – plays a role in regional development. Regions increasingly compete to attract residents, entrepreneurs and visitors. Areas with a good image will attract more businesses, residents and tourists than areas suffering from a bad image. The image that the outside world may have of a region can be very one-dimensional and indeed may even be entirely wrong. If research universities or UASs are successful in producing well-known scholars, inventions, spin-off companies or leading businessmen, this success can contribute to painting a more favourable picture of a region, enhancing the region's 'mindware'. By helping in the creation of new businesses, the UAS can produce a 'buzz' in the region – also because of their role in the cultural/arts community. In turn, this may attract investments to the region.

The UASs are potentially key actors in developing the regional community in which they are located (Goddard, 1997; Garlick, 2000). They play multiple roles in regional environments, providing access points to global academic and commercial knowledge networks, embedding knowledge in students and employees and upgrading regional business life (OECD, 1999). However, it would be too simple to suggest that a combination of the three attributes of hardware, software and mindware will automatically bring economic prosperity to the region. The Silicon Valley model (the combination of Stanford university, high-tech firms, informal networks, venture capital providers, business incubator facilities) is not a simple recipe for regional development (Saxenian, 1994) and it is still unclear to what extent the economic success of the region can be attributed to the role played by Stanford University (Gibbons, 2000; Moore & Davis, 2004). This suggests that something else may be needed to achieve the wished-for benefits of the interaction between the UAS/university and its region. However, before discussing this, we will turn to the various modes of interaction between a knowledge institution and its region.

Interactions Between Knowledge Institutions and Their Region

There is increasing recognition of the extensive and multi-faceted contribution that universities and UASs make to the economic, social and cultural development of their regions, and the multiple links they have with businesses and other regional partners (e.g. OECD-CERI, 1982; Goddard, Charles, Pike, Potts, & Bradley, 1994; OECD, 2007; Jongbloed & Van der Sijde, 2008). In fact, one can see an emergence – or a reaffirmation – of a *third mission* of higher education institutions (HEIs) next to their traditional missions of teaching and research (Laredo, 2007). Third mission activities are concerned with the generation, use, application and exploitation of knowledge outside academic environments. This third mission is about the interactions between knowledge institutions and the various communities, firms, etc., situated in their external environment. HEIs are expected to be *engaged* with the community through their teaching and research. The regional communities are an important subset of the communities that feature in this third mission agenda. HEIs, and in particular UASs, enrol a large part of their students from the region in which they are located. Many SMEs often will first look at nearby UASs when seeking advice on matters of technological and organisational innovation. Many businesses and local SMEs employ students and graduates from their local universities and UASs – with some students doing internships or thesis work and others being employed on a more permanent basis. Regional authorities as well as public organisations also will often call on local higher education institutions to provide policy advice and help in the solving of social and environmental issues in the community.

UASs have the capacity to engage in partnerships and different forms of knowledge exchange with regional businesses and regional communities in many ways. Before we go to some of the country cases, let us first look at the channels of interaction presented in Table 2.1. The table distinguishes various types and channels of interaction, some of them of a formal character, others of a more informal kind. The table also distinguishes the exchange of 'on the shelf' knowledge (e.g. education activity; communicating research outputs; renting out of equipment) from newly created and tailor-made knowledge (original research in response to demands from business, either produced by academics, or in close collaboration with the contracting firm). Although the table looks at interactions between a HEI and its external (mostly business) community in general, the table can also serve to illustrate that many examples of the interaction will involve regional communities and businesses.

For the UAS, the regional stakeholders will constitute the most important subset of external 'clients'. The partners of UASs include businesses of various

Table 2.1 Typology of knowledge interactions between higher education institutions and business/local communities

Type of knowledge transfer	Medium	Character	Examples
Transfer of already existing knowledge	Meetings	Informal	Situations and occasions where academics and business/community representatives meet by chance, such as during special events (fairs) or festivities, manifestations, open days, networking events; meetings with alumni
		Formal	Organisation of (formal/official) meetings between academics and business/community: excursions, seminars, conferences, visits to laboratories and companies
	Databases		Transfer of information through internet, newsletters and libraries
	Staff	Oral	Knowledge transfer through (formal/informal) conversations, presentations, training courses; platforms
		Written	Knowledge transfer (formal/informal) through e-mail or publications in an academic or popular journal/medium/newspaper; patents
	Students		Internships, placements, company visits; bachelor and master's thesis work
Provision of 'embedded' knowledge	Infrastructure and equipment, manuals		Giving private businesses and start-ups access to laboratories and research equipment owned by the higher education institution (facility sharing)
Transfer of modified knowledge	Staff		Courses, advisory activities (consultancy – also to spin-offs); secondment of academics
	Students		Bachelor and master's thesis work where the student works in/for a business/organisation
Development and transfer of newly created knowledge	Contract		Commissioned research projects, spin-offs
Joint development and transfer of new knowledge	Collaborative research (joint research)	Pre-competitive	University–industry collaboration encouraged by national/regional/European government to create knowledge that precedes a commercial application
		Competitive	Joint research programmes (in public–private partnerships; strategic alliances)

Source: Jongbloed and Van der Sijde (2008).

types (SMEs, specific industries), regional/provincial government agencies, non-governmental organisations (non-profits, charities), health institutes, vocational schools, special interest groups, etc. Many studies on university–regional interaction tend to focus very much on the 'top of the iceberg' – looking at quantifiable manifestations such as the number of spin-offs, income from contract research, joint labs and licensing income. However, the table illustrates that much of the interaction between a UAS and regional partners is of an informal kind, less visible and probably the biggest part of the iceberg. While quantitative measures of formal interactions between UASs and regional businesses are frequently used, a key element of knowledge transfer is through the interaction and learning that comes about from direct personal contact. Much of this is connected to the UASs' mainstream teaching activities, but there are other forms such as student placements and exchange of staff. It is a huge challenge to make any sort of quantification and assessment of the more informal kinds of interaction. As Mowery, Nelson, Sampat, and Ziedonis (2004) have argued, 'any assessment of the economic role of universities must recognize the numerous, diverse channels through which university research influences industrial innovation and vice versa'.

Examples of interaction between a UAS and the communities/businesses in their region may be grouped into the following categories:

1. Alignment of curricula with demand
2. Student internships and thesis work
3. Staff mobility
4. Supporting graduate entrepreneurs
5. Contract research and consultancy
6. Including regional representatives in UAS governance structures

We will now discuss these six categories and give examples from our case studies.

Alignment of Curricula with Demand

The first category of interactions concerns regional interest in (or enrolment in) courses provided by UASs. This includes enrolment in the regular (bachelor, master, diploma) programmes, as well as in UAS programmes in the continuing professional training (or lifelong learning) activities. The quality of higher professional education – specifically, its accreditation status – is heavily dependent on the connection between the programmes on offer and the demands emerging from the professions in the labour market. This is why, for instance, the UASs in The Netherlands have set up a national structure to ensure this is the case. For each programme, at a national level a professional profile and professional qualifications are formulated under the responsibility of the world of work. Some 70% of the so-called programme qualifications are nationally uniform. The other 30% can be filled in (profiled) by the individual UAS, and, subsequently, by the student in question (electives, etc.). This programme profile may be elaborated with an eye upon the characteristics and needs of regional labour market. In the Dutch UASs, every group of bachelor programmes in a broad field has a *field committee* from the world of work that represents the professional field. The field committee provides information on relevant trends in the profession in order to improve and update the content of the programmes. Course programmes are discussed with supervisory boards, with field committees, in regional networks, and aligned with the regional labour market.

UASs in countries like The Netherlands and Switzerland regularly carry out tailor-made education programmes for individual companies or institutions. They offer such tailor-made programmes at both bachelor and post-bachelor level. These are organised as demand-driven programmes and paid for by the participants on the basis of a cost-covering fee. Because master's programmes in Dutch UASs are not funded by the government there is a need to keep strong links with the professional sector in order to make these programmes profitable. Apart from their external earning potential, one of the aims of such tailor-made programmes and courses is to strengthen the relations with the region and the business sector.

Student Internships and Thesis Work

It is often stated that knowledge exchanges will be mainly person-embodied. 'The best tech transfer is a pair of shoes' is a statement that expresses the belief that skilled graduates are the key mechanism of knowledge transfer. The interaction taking place through UAS students doing an internship or thesis work in a private firm or public organisation is an essential part of the knowledge exchange between a UAS and its regional communities. Apart from the student, the UAS and the student's host organisation will benefit (i.e. learn) from the interaction. This exchange of knowledge and the experience of students will indirectly feed into UAS curricula. A related type of knowledge exchange is on-the-job training or work-based learning of students. The phenomenon of sandwich students is an example here. A sandwich student works in an organisation, for instance, a hospital or school, for part of the time and spends the rest in the UAS. In this way, the knowledge and experience gained by the sandwich student feeds back into the UAS and – the other way around – the student's hosting organisation takes advantage of the knowledge brought in by the student.

Staff Mobility

Bringing in external (i.e. guest) lecturers or appointing 'outsiders' for part of the working week as a staff member in a UAS will also bring about knowledge exchange. The secondment of UAS lecturers to industry or government is another, less frequently found example and usually differs across disciplinary fields. For instance, in the Swiss UASs many of the senior academics in the technological domains come directly from private companies, whereas in the social sciences more come from research universities.

Supporting Graduate Entrepreneurs

Increasingly, HEIs are paying attention to graduates that wish to start their own business. Apart from offering office space, some UASs also provide legal advice and share their knowledge with the start-up entrepreneur. Connected to this, some UASs have set up programmes to enhance the students' capacity to be enterprising. Teaching students entrepreneurial skills is gradually becoming a part of many UASs' curricula. As part of their training, students can choose to do courses on becoming self-employed entrepreneurs, writing business plans or learning other skills connected to setting up and running one's own company. The attention paid to stimulating start-up companies extends to the academics as well. In The Netherlands one sees the emergence of *Centres for Entrepreneurship and Innovation* that function as a broker and information source for newly established firms as well as students and staff that wish to start a company. In Switzerland some UASs have created a service facility where UASs, research universities and industry jointly operate a technology transfer office.

Contract Research and Consultancy

UASs and research universities provide both formal and informal technical support, as well as specialised expertise and facilities for R&D activities in the private sector and provide firms with access to the worldwide pool of knowledge. Many UASs actively engage in contract research and advisory services for regional businesses. Certainly, as was indicated above, not all UASs are equally active in such activity, as this will also depend on the UAS's strategy, its funding and the research skills of its staff. The knowledge exchange and interaction that takes place between UASs and regional partners is dependent also on whether rewards and incentives exist for UAS staff (see below). The Norwegian case shows that only 6% of academic staff in the UAS sector collaborated with industry during the past 3 years. In Switzerland, despite the fact that UASs receive a quite substantial part of their research funds as core funding from public sources, about a fifth of Swiss UAS research income is from the private sector. For the year 2006, the Dutch UAS revenues from contract research represent 2% of UAS revenues, while income from contract teaching and continuous professional education amounts to 4%. Although most of this income will be from sources located in the region, there are no precise data on this.

External Representatives in UAS Governance

UASs also have contacts with regional stakeholders on a structural basis by including 'external personalities', 'laymen' or 'regents' in their various governing bodies (Rhoades, 1983; Trow, 1997). This is the case for Norway, where UASs have board members from the region. Also in Switzerland regional industry is represented in the UAS council. In The Netherlands, representatives from the world of work do not formally form part of the executive board of a UAS. However, they may have seats in the supervisory boards and advisory councils. Programme committees also may have representatives of businesses, not-for-profit organisations and local authorities as members.

Encouraging UAS–Regional Interaction

In all European countries the national and regional governments stimulate the co-operation between UASs and industry through various programmes, funding instruments and regulatory arrangements. National and regional innovation policies as well as initiatives undertaken by the UAS and business sector itself are trying to bring about a fruitful interaction between knowledge producers and knowledge users. Governments often feel that firms and organisations do not utilise the knowledge produced by UASs and research universities to the full extent possible. The set of rules, regulations, quality assessment procedures, accountability standards and incentive (e.g. funding) schemes that shape the framework conditions within which UASs operate may not be very conducive to UAS–regional interaction. There are still barriers that stand in the way of an effective interaction between regional actors and higher education institutions. Figure 2.1 below addresses the issue of how to encourage knowledge flows between UASs and private sector institutions. Attention is paid in particular to the policies and measures for encouraging the knowledge transfer between UASs and business. The instruments included in the figure's call-out boxes are addressing distinctive parts of the chain. Some are targeting the UASs, others the business sector (often SMEs) and the knowledge flows between the two. Another set of instruments address the capacity of either UASs or businesses to articulate their demands to the other party, while there may also be measures that assist an actor to more effectively disseminate its knowledge.

Looking at three countries – Switzerland, Norway and The Netherlands – in particular, one may observe wide differences with respect to the funding flows made available to ensure the interaction between UASs and regional businesses. The Swiss case is one where, due to the strong research mandate that UASs have, UASs have access to funding from federal sources as well as regional sources. Core funds from the Confederation and Cantonal governments ensure that the UASs have a firm research basis that can be exploited by regional firms. On top of that the CTI (Swiss Innovation Promotion Agency) makes project funds available for bottom-up projects that are a co-operation between UASs and industry partners, in particular SMEs. Compared to this, Norwegian UASs do have an explicit research mission as well as core funding for research, but access to project funding for regional co-operation is more limited. The Research Council of Norway funds a programme targeted towards a closer interplay and mutual competence development between SMEs and the university colleges, with the aim of improving the regional innovative capabilities in both the SMEs and the university colleges. However, the Research Council plans to make Norwegian UASs compete more with research universities when it comes to project funding. Norwegian UASs consequently have forged fewer well-developed ties to the local business sector than the Swiss UASs.

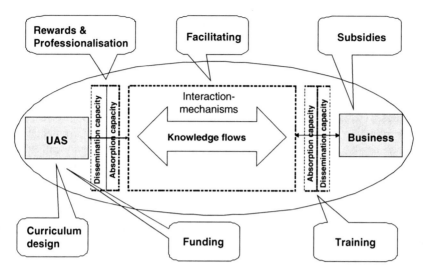

Fig. 2.1 Knowledge flows between UAS and business

Funding for research, let alone regional research collaboration is much less abundant in Dutch UASs compared to Switzerland and Norway. This has led to a situation where the UAS research capacity is relatively underdeveloped. To develop a regional research function, the RAAK (Regional Attention and Action for Knowledge Circulation) programme was set up by the Dutch government in 2005. RAAK aims to improve knowledge exchange between SMEs and UASs and comprises two schemes: one aimed at SMEs and the other aimed at not-for-profit institutes. RAAK subsidies are awarded to consortia of one or more UASs and one or more businesses.

The reward structure of academics in UASs is another enabling factor in UAS–regional interactions. In research universities, the salary of scientists and lecturers will often largely be determined by the academic's research production in terms of refereed publications or the volume of competitive grants brought in from research councils. In many of the UAS sectors in Europe, such as in The Netherlands, it is the lecturer's workload and responsibilities in terms of teaching that define terms of employment, salary and promotion opportunities. Publishing in media that concentrates on professionals working in industry and public sector organisations is not affecting the salary of the average academic in a Dutch UAS. However, with the emergence of the *lector* a change is underway to encourage and reward research activity. In Swiss and Norwegian UASs, there are professor positions where part of the job description and remuneration is tied to carrying out of research.

The presence of an entrepreneurial culture in a UAS not only depends on human resources policy but also on the fact that UAS staff are often unaware of the commercial potential of their findings. They may be lacking the required business attitude to develop their concepts and ideas further into products or prototypes. Assisting UAS academics in commercialising their ideas may help. Another option is to set up, like research universities have done, dedicated technology transfer offices or professionalising the staff in such units to assist in disseminating UAS knowledge to business. Examples of such units are found in Switzerland and are starting to appear also on the Dutch scene. Such initiatives belong to the 'facilitating' and 'professionalization' instruments shown in Fig. 2.1. In Norway, half of the university colleges have close relationships to a regional research institute. These institutes were established partly on the initiative of the colleges themselves, partly on the initiative of the county council, local industry and the governmental ministry responsible for regional affairs. Some of these institutes are co-localised with a university college, and in these cases there is an intimate relationship between the institute and the UAS in terms of collaboration on projects and exchange of personnel.

For research universities in most European national settings, several instruments to promote university–industry relationships have been in operation since the middle of the 1990s. Policies range from research programmes (and funding opportunities) that require university–industry collaboration, subsidies for university spin-offs, researcher mobility grants, etc. When it comes to policies to stimulate the regional relevance of research in UASs, governments often show a preference for policies that focus on the demand (that is: business) side, rather than the supply side (the UAS side) of the relationship between the UAS and the business/community. In The Netherlands, the government has initiated policies to stimulate the interaction between UASs and industry, especially SMEs, by making 'knowledge vouchers' available. Knowledge vouchers allow companies to buy research services from knowledge institutions. They represent a modest value still (€7,500 or €2,500), but proved quite popular among businesses to acquaint themselves with UASs and research universities.

Another set of instruments relates to the training of businesses in order to increase their potential to communicate more effectively with academics and to absorb knowledge provided by UASs and research universities. Often, representatives of SMEs have difficulty articulating their questions and would have to be supported by intermediary organisations or trained by universities. For this, some UASs provide short training courses, clinics and workshops 'on demand'. Such courses exist in Switzerland and The Netherlands, with UAS courses often addressing demands expressed by associations of firms in a particular industry sector. The latter represents an example of the bundling of demand.

From these examples it becomes clear that the economic development of the local region is of continuing importance to UASs. However, many barriers – financial as well as cultural – still exist on both sides of the relationship between the UAS and the region. The degree of regional engagement still differs between countries due to national systemic features, local institutional characteristics and availability of financial resources.

In addition to the national and regional policy instruments, there are initiatives undertaken by the UASs themselves to strengthen their regional engagement. Being multi-actor, multi-purpose organisations, these initiatives are situated on three levels:

- Macro: constructing a strategic vision for the institution as a whole that expresses the intention to contribute to regional development and mobilising institutional networks and resources to this end.
- Meso: developing new institutional constellations that encourage departments to engage in new types of multi-disciplinary co-operation with regional counterparts and to support new, regionally relevant types of knowledge development.
- Micro: encouraging UAS staff to enact new kinds of behaviour alongside teaching that help underpin the flow of societally useful knowledge and research into the region.

UASs may help to configure responses to regional problems and add value by linking between the levels, for example, by developing new multi-disciplinary sub-units which improve regional impact through constructing practice-led research partnerships which create viable solutions to regional problems. The Dutch case of the *lector* position, and the 'knowledge circle' that this *lector* is supposed to build, provides an example of such an initiative. In many Dutch UASs, the knowledge circle involves representatives from different disciplines as well as from regional business. The knowledge circle helps the region identify where improvements can be made and often engages in regional planning exercises and assessments.

UASs can play a range of roles in regional governance networks along a variety of dimensions. On the macro level one can distinguish two roles. First, UASs may provide institutional leadership to identify regional challenges and place them on socio-political agendas. Thus, they become involved in regional governance. This is a *leading* role. Second, recognising that many of today's challenges are of a multi-dimensional kind, UASs could become the places where different actors (state/UAS/industry/society) and disciplines come together. This is an *integrating* role. UASs in that sense 'join up' between the different roles in places where there are no strong existing actors able to perform that joining up role (Arbo & Benneworth, 2006, p. 76). Part of this role is to encourage co-operation between firms and other institutions to generate technological, commercial and social benefits. As discussed earlier in this chapter, regional collaboration and learning between organisations are important in regional success. UASs can promote the application of knowledge through regional partnerships, and encourage networking and the building of trust.

The Engaged UAS

Becoming regionally engaged is a multi-level challenge. We now turn to the meso and micro level to explore what UASs may do to increase their contribution to regional development and to become more engaged in the region. As shown above, the UAS sector is tailoring educational programmes to areas of regional need and – to varying degrees – is engaging in collaborative research with local business and communities. An additional area where engagement may be intensified is through the design of the curriculum (see Fig. 2.1). Building enterprising skills into the curriculum may have the potential to strengthen regional impact of the UAS. As we will argue, such initiatives are closely connected to the role and place of research in UASs.

At first sight, enterprising skills are about the (individual's) ability to perceive opportunities and set up a business plan to realise them. Such skills also include the ability to analyse and solve problems and communicate effectively in teams. In many UASs, entrepreneurship programmes are in place, or being put in place. Students learn about developing a business plan that includes a marketable product, a resource plan, a marketing plan, and is founded on a sound legal basis. UASs, thanks to their links with regional business and local communities, are well-placed to organise and provide such learning in practical hands-on situations. Such programmes are mostly confined to UAS fields such as engineering and business studies, because graduates from these fields find employment in the private sector. However, one may argue that the teaching of entrepreneurial skills should not be confined to these fields alone and may very well extend to fields like social sciences, cultural studies and health-related professions.

We argued above that any skills development strategy of a regionally engaged UAS starts with the observation that human capital is key for regional development. To have the UAS provide the human capital that can support a region's prosperity, one needs to realise that this is not just about the *numbers* of graduates provided by UASs, but just as much about the *type* of human capital. A regionally engaged UAS therefore will have to put in place an entrepreneurial curriculum and equip students with the capacity to transform an idea into an outcome. Such a curriculum pays attention to students' abilities to analyse problems, to synthesise, to propose solutions and to communicate about various challenges in a multidisciplinary environment. Entrepreneurial skills are actually close to some of the skills required to do research. However, they are not only important for those working in research environments. Analytical skills and communicative skills are increasingly becoming important also for workers in industry and in society at large. A region's innovative power is heavily dependent on the quality and skills of its workforce. Thus, UASs will need to pay attention not just to the professional skills of students, but also their students' research skills.

One may argue that if UAS lecturers possess the skills to carry out research themselves, they are also better placed to instil an enterprising spirit into their students. 'Teaching-only' institutions and teaching-only staff are more likely to behave in a reactive way when responding to a local/regional demand for graduates in particular professions. This means they are always one step behind when it comes to providing the skills and graduates necessary for the future development of the region. Our proposition is that UAS institutions can make a significant contribution to regional development if they are active in research themselves and use this research to enhance their education. The UAS's students, through UAS lecturers that are actively involved in research, will thus be educated to become professionals with a sufficient dose of research attitude. Such students will be familiarised with the skills required to solve multi-faceted problems in real-life situations and learn how their solution can be integrated into an organisation's business process.

The crucial thing to realise here is that research skills and attitudes are not only useful in addressing already well-articulated problems and the pressing problems of today, but that those skills are also relevant in identifying future opportunities, innovations and less-well articulated problems. Some businesses may not be aware of potential innovations, and only by interacting with academics and properly trained graduates can they hope to benefit from ideas and capacity existing in UASs. Many SMEs employ only few degree holders and, as a consequence, will often not be aware of the potential benefit that can be achieved through research co-operation in UAS-led projects. This refers to the articulation problems identified in connection to the right-hand side of Fig. 2.1 above. SMEs often claim to be seeking professional skills in their employees, rather than a research attitude. We already gave examples of initiatives from Switzerland and The Netherlands, where this lack of interaction is tackled through collaborative research projects that are funded by innovation agencies, research councils or through innovation vouchers.

In countries with a less research intensive UAS sector, the UAS institutions are more likely to be focusing on upgrading the existing industry and are less well-equipped to cater to the needs of new knowledge-intensive firms. The Swiss case exemplifies that UASs that strive to be regionally relevant may want to become more pro-active and creative in their strategic relationships with regional business. In doing so, they will have to reassess their strategy, budgeting and internal reward systems. In their region, the UASs often will possess a critical mass that potentially can make a difference in the regional development process. Given their role in the education and training of professionals, their links to regional businesses – many of them SMEs – and their links to the secondary education system as well as the research universities, the UASs are better placed than other tertiary education institutions to become regionally engaged.

Conclusion

As argued by the OECD (2007, p. 11) in a recent study on higher education and regions:

> ...with the parallel processes of globalisation and localisation, the local availability of knowledge and skills is becoming increasingly important. OECD countries are thus putting considerable emphasis on meeting regional development goals, by nurturing the unique assets and circumstances of each region, particularly in developing knowledge-based industries. As key sources of knowledge and innovation, higher education institutions can be central to this process.

This illustrates that the interaction between higher education institutions and their regional partners is becoming increasingly important for a region's innovation potential. This chapter presented some of the ways in which this interaction takes place and highlighted the prominent role played here by the UAS sector as well as the theoretical perspectives that may shed some light on the factors that contribute to a region's social and economic success.

The economic impact of a UAS extends to the enhancement of the region's human capital through its education of professionals and the creation of wealth through the spill-over effects from its (mostly applied) research activities to the public sector and businesses. We have argued that a UAS that implements an entrepreneurial curriculum that is sufficiently research-based is more likely to be regionally relevant. This also contributes to a situation where there is a better chance to keep talented young people in the region or attract talent and new businesses to the region. Moreover, an entrepreneurial UAS also makes contributions to the regional community in terms of service in social and cultural development.

In a knowledge-based society it may be argued that a firm's competitive position is very much determined by its capacity to undertake research itself. In this sense, the capacity for learning of firms in a region is a critical variable in successful innovation. A competitive region will have human resources that enable its firms to absorb new technologies and create new knowledge itself. Successful firms therefore will need workers that possess high-level skills and new capabilities. It was argued in this chapter that such capabilities include professional skills, entrepreneurial skills and – connected to the main topic of this volume – a healthy dose of 'research attitude'. This suggests a key task for UASs in providing the region's labour market with graduates that possess such capabilities. In order to properly carry out this task, UASs require academic staff with sufficient capacities to do research as well as incentives to engage in research partnerships with regional business. The distinct cases of Switzerland and The Netherlands – with their respectively high and low research intense UAS sectors – can serve as an illustration that the presence of a strong research mandate, together with UAS staff having a research degree (or PhD), makes a difference.

Because of their different development trajectories, the different UAS sectors in Europe have so far experienced different degrees of success in realising their contribution to regional development. Government policies (and funding streams) may be helpful in strengthening the regional relevance of UAS research, but it is equally the UAS's own strategy and internal institutional arrangements that contribute to the UAS's regional engagement. We have pointed at the need to reassess the UAS curriculum and to align it closely to the needs of modern private and public employers by paying more attention to the students' entrepreneurial skills and research attitudes.

The message of this chapter is that, because of its links to industry and its focus on job-specific education, the UAS is very well placed to foster regional development in two ways: First, the education role the UAS can play is an important part in developing enterprising skills, knowledge and cultures to ensure that regional human capital is used to its full potential. Second, through using its close connections with business, the UAS can contribute to regional development by building regional coalitions and linkages. Many of these networks are forged through research and consultancy services for regional business and involve students doing graduate work or placements.

In observing these options, the UAS can become a key asset for the economic development of their region.

References

Arbo, P., & Benneworth, P. (2007). *Understanding the regional contribution of higher education institutions: A literature review*. Paris: OECD/IMHE.

Barro, R., & Sala-i-Martin, X. (1995). *Economic growth*. New York: McGraw-Hill.

Benneworth, P., Hospers, G. J., & Jongbloed, B. (2006). New economic impulses in old industrial regions. The case of the University of Twente. In A. Prinz, A. E. Steenge, & J. Schmidt (Eds.), *Innovation: Technical, economic and institutional aspects* (pp. 1–24). Berlin: Lit.

Buursink, J. (2002). Regionale impact universiteiten overschat. *Geografie, 11*, 36–39.

Cooke, P. (Ed.). (1995). *The rise of the rustbelt*. London: UCL Press.

Cooke, P., & Leydesdorff, L. (2006). Regional development in the knowledge-based economy: The construction of advantage. *Journal of Technology Transfer, 31*, 5–15.

Florax, R. (1992). *The university: A regional booster?* Ashgate: Aldershot.

Florida, R. (1995). Towards the learning region. *Futures, 27*, 527–536.

Florida, R. (2002). *The rise of the creative class*. New York: Basic Books.

Fukuyama, F. (1999). *Trust: The social values and the creation of prosperity*. London: Penguin Books.

Garlick, S. (2000). *Engaging universities and regions. Knowledge contribution to regional economic development in Australia*. Canberra: DETYA.

Garlick, S., Taylor, M., & Plummer, P. (2008). *An enterprising approach to regional growth. Implications for policy and the role of vocational education and training*. Adelaide: National Centre for Vocational Education Research (NCVER).

Gibbons, J. F. (2000). The role of Stanford University: A dean's reflections. In C. M. Lee, W. F. Miller, M. Gong Hancock, & H. S. Rowen (Eds.), *The Silicon Valley edge: A habitat for innovation and entrepreneurship* (pp. 200–217). Stanford: Stanford University Press.

Goddard, J. (1997). Managing the university/region interface. *Higher Education Management, 9*, 7–27.

Goddard, J. B., Charles, D., Pike, A., Potts, G., & Bradley, D. (1994). *Universities and communities*. London: CVCP.

Harvie, C. (1994). *The rise of regional Europe*. New York: Routledge.

Jongbloed, B., & van der Sijde, P. (2008). *Interacties tussen universiteit en MKB*. Report for the Ministry of Economic Affairs. Enschede: CHEPS & NIKOS.

Laredo, P. (2007). *Toward a third mission for universities*. Paper presented at UNESCO Forum. 'Globalizing Knowledge'. Available at http://unesdoc.unesco.org/images/0015/001578/157815e.pdf

Maskell, P., Eskelinen, H., & Hannibalsson, I. (1998). *Competitiveness, localized learning and regional development: Specialization and prosperity in small open economies*. London: Routledge.

Moore, G. E., & Davis, K. (2004). Learning the Silicon Valley way. In T. Bresnahan & A. Gambardella (Eds.), *Building high-tech clusters: Silicon valley and beyond* (pp. 190–228). Cambridge, UK: Cambridge University Press.

Morgan, K. (2004). The exaggerated death of geography. Learning, proximity and territorial innovation systems. *Journal of Economic Geography, 4*, 3–21.

Mowery, D. C., Nelson, R. R., Sampat, B. N., & Ziedonis, A. A. (2004). *Ivory tower and industrial innovation: University-industry technology transfer before and after the Bayh-Dole Act*. Stanford: Stanford Business Books.

OECD (1999). *The response of higher education institutions to regional needs*. Paris: OECD.

OECD (2007). *Higher education and regions: Globally competitive, locally engaged*. Paris: OECD.

OECD-CERI (1982). *The university and the community. The problems of changing relationships*. Paris: OECD.

Putnam, R. D. (1993). *Making democracy work. Civic traditions in modern Italy*. Princeton: Princeton University Press.

Putnam, R. (2000). *Bowling alone*. New York: Simon & Schuster.

Rhoades, G. A. (1983). Conflicting interests in higher education. *American Journal of Education, 91*, 283–327.

Saxenian, A. (1994). *Regional advantage: Culture and competition in Silicon Valley and Route 128*. Cambridge, MA: Harvard University Press.

Siegfried, J. J., Sanderson, A. R., & McHenry, P. (2008). The economic impact of colleges and universities. *Change, 40*, 25–29.

Trow, M. (1997). The development of information technology in American higher education. *Daedalus, 126*, 293–314.

Vickerman, R. W. (1991). *Infrastructure and regional development: Vol. 1. European Research in Regional Science*. London: Pion.

Chapter 3
The Relevance of Research for the Improvement of Education and Professional Practice

Kristin Heggen, Berit Karseth, and Svein Kyvik

Introduction

The purpose of this chapter is to discuss the relevance of research for the improvement of professional education in universities of applied sciences (UASs) and
professional practice in the relevant occupations. Higher education institutions outside the universities provide study programmes in a wide range of professional
education areas, of which engineering, teacher training (for elementary school and
preschool) and nursing generally are the most important in terms of number of
staff and students. In addition, these institutions offer many other professional programmes, e.g. social work, arts and design, and different types of health education,
as well as studies in economics, business and information technology. So far, the
number of master's degrees in the UAS sector is low in most countries, and the number of PhD programmes, with the exception of Norway, is negligible. Accordingly,
in this chapter, the discussion on the relevance of research for the improvement of
teaching will be confined to bachelor programmes. The question on the relevance of
research for the improvement of professional work applies, however, to professional
programmes in general.

These programmes represent different historical traditions and cultures related
to practice and working life. Some of the programmes were originally founded
on an apprenticeship model where the education was organised within working-
life institutions. Others were established within the secondary vocational education
sector, and as a consequence, there is a strong traditional pedagogy for schooling.
Common for these programmes is the tendency towards professionalisation through
the development of a scientific knowledge base and extended use of abstract vocab-
ularies (Brint, 2002, p. 238), and the movement from a 'vocational' to an 'academic'
education (Smeby, 2007).

In this chapter, *engineering*, *teacher training* and *nursing* will be specifically
examined, but the discussion is relevant for all types of professional programmes.
In the countries included in this book, engineering is the only programme that

K. Heggen (✉)
Faculty of Medicine, University of Oslo, Oslo, Norway
e-mail: k.m.heggen@medisin.uio.no

S. Kyvik, B. Lepori (eds.), *The Research Mission of Higher Education Institutions
Outside the University Sector*, Higher Education Dynamics 31,
DOI 10.1007/978-1-4020-9244-2_3, © Springer Science+Business Media B.V. 2010

is provided by most UAS-type institutions. Also, teacher training for elementary school is mainly provided by institutions outside the traditional university sector. This applies to Belgium, the Czech Republic, Ireland, The Netherlands, Norway and Switzerland, while in Germany this programme is offered both by universities and teacher training colleges, and in Finland by universities only. Nursing is mainly provided by UASs in countries like Finland, The Netherlands, Norway and Switzerland.

The introduction of research as a task for teaching staff in these programmes has been contested, and the extent of research varies much between countries. Still, it has become more commonly accepted that research-based teaching can be important in order to improve the quality of education and subsequently the practice of professionals. The rationale for this development has been excellently summarised by Pratt, based on his study of the development of the former British polytechnics (1997, p. 326):

> The critical argument is that those teaching future professionals cannot do so without reflecting on the implications of professional and educational practices. Moreover, they need experience and understanding of current developments in theory and practice. The graduates, too, need to have a firm understanding of investigative methods appropriate to their future careers. Most non-university institutions also have an important task of offering advisory and consultancy services to firms of all sizes. This activity is itself investigative; much research arises in this way. Staff need research skills to undertake this task and they (and students) can further develop these skills by doing it.

The call for a stronger research orientation of professional programmes comes from different groups (see the model presented in Chapter 1). Staff members who are competent and interested in undertaking research, as well as programme leaders and institutional leaders, actively work to create a research culture and to increase the resource basis for this type of scholarly activity. National authorities, professional associations and working-life institutions argue that research is important to improve the quality of professional programmes and the knowledge basis of professional work. Similarly, the OECD and the European Commission support the enhancement of research activity in these programmes.

Nevertheless, many are sceptical to this development and argue that too much emphasis on research in professional programmes might in fact be detrimental to the vocational orientation of the courses and the employability of the graduates (Skoie, 2000). Furthermore, there is not much evidence in the research literature that increased focus on research in professional programmes at a bachelor's level will increase the quality of teaching and learning and improve the preparation of students for a professional career. To the extent that this issue has been addressed in this literature, it is the relationship between teaching and research within disciplinary university programmes that have been examined.

In this chapter, we will discuss four arguments that have been used to introduce research in professional programmes:

1. Teaching will improve if the staff engage in research (research-based teaching).
2. Students will learn more if they come into contact with research (research-based learning).

3. Professional practice will improve if professional workers in their training learn how to base their work on research-based knowledge (research-based practice).
4. Professional programmes have an obligation to improve the knowledge basis of professional work through research (research-based knowledge production).

The first three arguments focus on the importance of basing professional programmes on research, while the fourth argument concerns the importance of doing research to enhance 'evidence-based' knowledge. Although these arguments are closely related, they are analytically distinct and will be examined separately.

National Policies

In the countries included in this book, national policies vary in the extent to which research in professional programmes is regarded as important for improving education and professional practice. In most countries, state authorities have expressed that teaching in professional programmes should have a basis in research as well as in practical knowledge, but the implications of rather diffuse statements are unclear. The second purpose – that research should contribute to improved professional practice in the relevant occupations – is not visible in the official mandate of the UASs in all of the countries.

Norway is the country where state authorities most clearly pronounce that research is important to improve the quality of these programmes and that research should contribute to better teaching in elementary school, to better kindergartens and to improved health care and social care. Furthermore, in order for professional programmes to obtain accreditation, research-based teaching is one of the criteria. National evaluations of nursing (2005), teacher training (2006) and engineering (2008) have recommended that the extent of research and the research competence of their staff should be enhanced. Similarly, a national commission set up to propose reforms in the higher education system (Stjernø Committee, 2008) argued that the quality of professional programmes should be improved and that a stronger research-orientation was needed to improve professional education and professional work. Based upon the recommendations by this commission, the Minister of Education and Research stated that elementary school teachers should have a research-oriented approach to their teaching practice, have access to research and be competent to apply research results in his/her teaching. Thus, during teacher training, students should come in contact with research and get experience with research (Aasland, 2008).

In The Netherlands, the act on higher education states that the UASs can undertake research to the extent that this activity is related to the education at the institutions. What this statement actually implies for the relationship between research, teaching, learning and professional practice is not quite clear, but other policy documents state that research in UASs should contribute to improving the quality of education as well as improving professional practice in society.

Because professional work is to an increasing extent supposed to be evidence-based, research and knowledge transfer should play an important role in the education of professionals and in the societal mission of the UASs.

In Finland, the Polytechnic Act says that the tasks of the UASs are to provide teaching which is based on scientific or artistic foundations aiming to produce high expertise in the related fields, to support the professional development of students and to conduct applied research and development which supports both the development of teaching, working life and regional development. The Development Plan for Education and Research for the years 2007–2012 similarly states that the primary mission of the UASs is to provide and develop professional higher education closely connected with working life and to conduct R&D which serves working life and regional development as well as teaching.

In Germany, the role of application-oriented research in the education of students in the UASs is emphasised, because research among the teaching staff establishes the relationship to work practice via cooperation with industry and supervision of the students' bachelor and master theses in firms.

In the other countries, the role of research in the education of students and in the development of evidence-based professional practices is not very visible in policy documents. This does not necessarily mean that research is regarded as unimportant for these purposes, but the awareness that research should play an important role in the enhancement of teaching, learning and professional practice is not very well developed at the state level. To some extent, this situation is probably due to fact that national authorities regard the role of research in UASs primarily as a tool in the regional innovation processes.

In the following, we will critically examine arguments for research in professional programmes in terms of a *teaching* perspective, a *learning* perspective and a *knowledge-production* perspective by briefly reviewing relevant literature and by comparing practices across the major professional programmes.

Research-Based Teaching

The notion 'research-based teaching' is ambiguous and is interpreted in different ways, of which we will analytically distinguish between two interpretations: (a) all staff should undertake research and (b) teaching should take place in a research culture.

An argument for introducing research as a task for academic staff in professional study programmes is that the teaching of students needs to be done by teachers who are themselves engaged in research. It is important that teachers keep being informed on recent research in their own field. In this respect, reading the literature is not regarded as sufficient; teachers have to undertake research themselves. Such activity may develop passion for the subject which in turn is communicated to students, and engagement in research may develop thinking abilities, knowledge and skills that can be reused in teaching (see Trowler & Wareham, 2008). A strong interpretation of this proposition is that teaching should only be provided by staff members who have themselves done research related to their lectures. In practice, this interpretation is not sustainable (not even in research universities) because staff are required to offer lectures in areas and subjects where they themselves have not undertaken research.

Others argue that the requirement of research-based teaching will be fulfilled if the teaching takes the form of dissemination of research-based knowledge by teachers who are well-informed on established scientific knowledge in their domain. This means that all staff members do not need to undertake research themselves; it will be sufficient that they keep themselves up-to-date with the essential literature in the field. This seems to be the message in the OECD report on tertiary education (1998, p. 58), which states that 'a culture of research and scholarship implies not that all teachers are current, active researchers but that all understand and experience the ethos of critical, reflective inquiry and efforts to explore, construct and create knowledge'. Embedded in this debate is the question about what should be the minimum level of academic qualifications in order to be a teacher in a permanent position in the UASs.

The argument that teaching in professional programmes will improve if the teachers are engaged in research is however contested. It is commonplace knowledge that there are good researchers who are excellent teachers, but also that there are research-oriented teachers who use too little time for their students. It is also well-known that there are "teaching-only staff" who lack engagement for teaching or have great difficulties in communicating the curriculum to their students. How we perceive the relationship between research and teaching also depends on our notions of what research is (Brew, 2006). A broad conception of research seems to be needed for this activity to have an impact on education at a bachelor's level. Furthermore, the meaning of research-based teaching is dependent on the nature of the field of knowledge or discipline (Neumann, Parry, & Becher, 2002).

In the scholarly literature the extent to which there is a positive relationship between research and teaching has been discussed over a very long time, but for the most part, confined to university teaching. Numerous studies have been undertaken to examine and discuss the relationship between research and teaching, but the results are inconclusive (see Hattie & Marsh, 1996 for a review). Marsh and Hattie (2002, p. 635) conclude that good researchers are neither more nor less likely to be effective teachers than are poor researchers, and that good teachers are neither more nor less likely to be productive researchers than are poor teachers. Based on these results, Marsh and Hattie argue that personnel selection and promotion decisions must be based on separate measures of teaching and research.

But even though the general evidence for such a relationship is inconclusive, it seems to be a common belief among academics and societal stakeholders that teaching in higher education, including professional education at a bachelor's level, should take place in a research atmosphere (OECD, 1998; Barnett, 2005; Brew, 2006). Still, few studies support the argument that teaching in professional programmes at this level will improve if the teachers engage in research.

There is not much information from the various countries about the extent of, forms of and experiences with research-based teaching in professional programmes.

Table 3.1 Percentage of academic staff in Norwegian university colleges in 1998 who reported that their teaching was influenced by their research

	To a large extent	To some extent	Not at all/not relevant	Sum	N
Engineering	6	17	77	100	(376)
Nursing	15	33	52	100	(267)
Teacher training	14	29	57	100	(808)

An obvious reason is that the share of teachers who undertake some kind of research themselves is relatively low.

A survey of Norwegian university colleges undertaken in 1998 show that only a small share of the academic staff reported that their teaching was influenced by their research 'to a large extent' (Table 3.1). In nursing and teacher training programmes more than half of the staff stated that there was no relation at all between their research and their teaching, or that this issue was not relevant to them, while in engineering programmes this applied to three quarters of the staff. However, if we confine the results to those who were research active, about 30% of the teacher training staff, and about 20% of the engineering and nursing staff reported that their teaching was influenced by their research 'to a large extent'. In total, approximately three quarters of those who were research active said that their teaching to a large or some extent was influenced by their research (Karseth & Kyvik, 1999).

Another survey among academic staff in Norwegian university colleges found large differences between programmes with regard to the purpose of their research. Of those teachers who reported that they undertook applied research and development work, 58% of the teacher training staff, 47% of the nursing staff and 34% of the engineering staff answered 'to a large extent' on the question whether the purposes of the research was to improve teaching (Larsen & Kyvik, 2006).

Research-Based Learning

The notion of 'research-based learning' is ambiguous and comes in different versions. In this chapter, we will analytically distinguish between two interpretations: (a) Learning should take place in a research culture and (b) learning should take place through student participation in research. The former interpretation implies that the students do not necessarily need to participate in or undertake research themselves. It is sufficient that they are taught scientific theory and methodology in such a way that they understand what science is and how research is undertaken. The latter interpretation implies that students should do some project work under the supervision of an experienced researcher. The collecting and analysing of data, even at a simple level, promotes a critical understanding of the nature of research.

The OECD report on tertiary education (1998, pp. 57–58) argues that 'all students, whether enrolled in university or non-university institutions would benefit from an active research and scholarly culture in which they participate both directly and indirectly'. According to the report, a reason for this is that 'students need to understand that knowledge ... is the fruit of inquiry, that it is constructed and reconstructed through criticism, analysis and reflection and that being a student means being an active, reflective, critical inquirer'. The OECD report (1998, p. 58) furthermore states that 'engagement in small group projects directed at solving practical problems is a valid way of introducing students to research conceived as structured critical inquiry'. This interpretation has clear parallels to the notion of project-based learning.

The OECD report (1998, p. 58) also proposes that students themselves, as part of their studies, should undertake projects and field work in which they assume some responsibility for formulating research questions, designing studies and evaluating results. This can be done by integrating students as assistants in research projects undertaken by academic staff or by introducing bachelor theses which should be founded on research or some kind of investigation.

There is some scattered evidence for the argument that students at a bachelor's level will learn more if they come into contact with research. Cousin, Healey, Jenkins, Bradbeer, and King (2003) point to students perceiving research-based learning as an invitation to be part of a research community of practice. Although they saw themselves as peripheral participants, they appreciated to have a legitimate position in research. Neumann (1994) conducted in-depth interviews with students in a range of disciplines and concluded that there were benefits to students of staff research. Students perceived the teaching as up-to-date and reported excitement about the enthusiasm demonstrated in courses taught by researchers. Healey (2005) argues that there is an increasing amount of evidence that one of the most effective ways in which students might benefit from research is through active engagement in the research process. Finally, Lucas (2007) maintains that in teacher education, engagement in research can have positive impacts on student learning.

Turner, Wuetherick, and Healey (2008) report evidence of the effectiveness of problem-based and inquiry-based learning with undergraduate students, both of which encourage students to be engaged with learning in a research mode. On the other hand, they also report that many students identify negative impacts of research on their learning, e.g. lack of interest in teaching and lack of availability of teachers. Similarly, Jenkins, Blackman, Lindsay, and Paton-Saltzberg (1998) found that many students did not perceive themselves as stakeholders in staff research and they saw research as quite separate from their own learning activities. In a study of research-led teaching and learning among undergraduate students, Zamorski (2002) reports that students, as well as lecturers, described research-led teaching and learning in practice in a variety of ways. The students' engagement with research varied to a large extent and occurred in a number of forms and levels of learning. Most students saw it as important to develop research skills as part of the undergraduate curriculum and saw research skills as important for their future career and job applications. They clearly valued being part of a research community and expressed commitment to the academic ethos. On the other hand, they expressed frustration over the lack of access to research activities as well as feelings of being excluded from research and were irritated by the lack of availability to researchers/teachers. Zamorski (2002) underlines the students' ambivalence; they appreciate being part of a research active community and consider engaging with research as a useful learning experience, but at the same time they lack understanding of the nature of academic work and experience a lack of access to research.

The studies cited above mostly report on students' *perceptions*, and Jenkins (2004) argues that there are few studies analysing the impact of student *learning* related to teachers' engagement in research. The study conducted by Cousin et al. (2003), however, reported that students who participated in research became more confident as learners and that it made them more capable of thinking independently.

In all three programmes, research-based learning takes place through the engagement of students in projects, although there is not much available information on the share of the students who actually participate in research projects. A survey among academic staff in Norwegian university colleges in 2006 shows that about 20% of those who undertook applied research in each of the programmes for engineering, nursing and teacher training reported that students participated 'to a large extent' in these projects (Larsen & Kyvik, 2006).

The extent to which students undertake some kind of research related to bachelor theses varies between countries and programmes. The bachelor thesis is common in engineering programmes, and generally it is regarded as an important part of the learning process. In many of the countries, an important aim of the bachelor thesis is to support the link to local industry. Critical analysis of information, problem-solving, reasoning and argumentation skills and development of work practices and clear written communication skills are important objectives of the thesis. The assumption is that through their thesis work, students can enhance their expertise and relations with working life. However, there seems to be a tension in the engineering programmes between the importance of ensuring that the students learn some core competence with a strong emphasis on mathematics and natural sciences on the one hand and a more application-oriented approach on the other hand (Maffioli & Augusti, 2003).

The rationale behind the bachelor thesis in nursing can be seen in the light of the argument of professionalisation. This holds true at least for Norway and Sweden where the purpose of the thesis is for the students to gain more in-depth knowledge of the scientific methodology and theoretical structures of nursing. The meaning of 'research-based' is closely linked to the disciplinary content of what is defined as nursing science. However, in the curriculum of nursing we also find arguments that emphasise the employability of students. By basing the curriculum and teaching on current research and developments in the nursing field, the students should develop professional attitudes towards continually updating their knowledge and practice. A Norwegian study shows, however, that in nursing programmes there are doubts about whether the students at a bachelor level are competent to participate in research projects undertaken by employees within health institutions (Larsen, Heggen, Carlsten, & Karseth, 2007).

In teacher training, the rationale behind the bachelor thesis is not easy to grasp. Meeus, Van Looy, and Libotton (2004) argue that the thesis in teacher education in most cases is a derivative of the master thesis. They draw on data from a Flemish university college and conclude that the thesis was subject to fierce criticism. They argue in favour of a more practice-oriented approach with the portfolio as a model. A needed connection to research is not clearly stated. Neither the employability argument nor the argument of professionalisation seems to be advocated.

Research-Based Practice

Another argument for introducing research in professional programmes is that professional practice will improve if professional workers in their training learn how to apply research-based knowledge in their work. Said differently, in order to become well-qualified workers, and thereby guarantee optimal employability in the knowledge society, the education must be based on research (see Simons & Elen, 2007). In a world of rapid change, students must be motivated and enabled to engage in life-long learning, and learning to do research is the best way of acquiring the competence and motivation to do so. Furthermore, in a knowledge society, professional workers are encouraged to continuously upgrade and broaden their skills (Peters & Humes, 2003). A knowledge society is run by expert settings and expert processes and in such a society, '... effective participation and power increasingly rests on access to scientifically legitimated knowledge (expert knowledge) and the capacity to apply such knowledge productively, individually and collectively' (Jensen, 2007, pp. 55–56). Similarly, Scott (2005, p. 64) argues that there are good reasons to associate research and teaching, also at a bachelor's level:

> If one of the goals of mass higher education systems within a 'knowledge society' is to produce knowledge workers – who are 'more' than simply graduates with expert academic or professional skills and who have an active 'enquiry capacity', but are 'less' than professionalized researchers – the significance of the teacher-researcher (and even the teacher-researcher-practitioner) as a role model (and intellectual leader) is correspondingly enhanced.

This kind of argumentation has been used also in a report published by the Commission of the European Communities, and which does not distinguish between undergraduate and graduate education (2002, p. 40):

> When taking a close look at the type of core competencies that appear central to employability (critical thinking, analysing, arguing, independent working, learning to learn, problem-solving, decision-making, planning, co-ordinating and managing, co-operative working, etc.), it appears quite clearly that the old Humboldtian emphasis on the virtues of research-teaching cross-fertilisation remain surprisingly relevant in the current context. It is very striking that the list of 'employability' competencies overlaps quite largely with the competencies involved in the exercise of the modern research activity.

However, the discourse advocated by the Commission is in sharp contrast with the Humboldtian premise of academic freedom which indicated that the pursuit of knowledge should be protected from the rest of the society. The importance of research-based education according to the Commission is its potential to develop students' capacity to apply scientific knowledge to solve practical problems. A similar argument is visible in the communiqué from the Minister meeting of the Bologna

Process in Leuven (28–29 April 2009). It is stated that 'Higher education should be based at all levels on state of the art research and development thus fostering innovation and creativity in society' (p. 4).

In other words research-based education is seen as an instrument to produce knowledge workers who have intellectual and innovative skills necessary for taking a leading position in the development of their professional practice. Following this argument professional programmes have to involve students in research in order to gain the key competences pointed to above by the Commission.

Research-Based Knowledge Production

The final purpose of introducing research in the UAS sector is that professional programmes have an obligation to improve the knowledge basis of professional work in their relevant occupations through research-based knowledge production. Many professional programmes are not provided by universities; subsequently the scientific basis for competent professional practice as well as for the production of text books is insufficient. Applied research and development work in professional programmes is assumed to communicate directly with stakeholders in the field.

The importance of the interaction with the users or practitioners in order to define the research question, as well as professional goals and research design, has been highlighted in the argument for a practice-driven research approach. Close cooperation and partnership between the research institutions and schools, companies or hospitals is seen as a way to improve the knowledge base of professional work. Action research is a well-known label used to underline the importance of participation, involvement and the processes of innovation and change with a strong focus on the local context (see Hollingsworth, 1997; Dick, 2004). Research undertaken across professional boundaries during the previous three decades has articulated the qualities of thorough professional work and emphasised the significance of the individual practitioner's experience, contextual sensitivity and ability to exercise skilful discretionary judgement in various situations (Schön, 1983; Lave & Wenger, 1991; Nielsen & Kvale, 1999). Furthermore, the emphasis on change and innovation corresponds with the paradigm of Mode 2 research (Gibbons et al., 1994), where a new form of knowledge production is distinguished by its close proximity to the context for problem-solving and to the user. Groups that traditionally are separated from the processes of knowledge production are integrated into the definition of, and solution to a problem, and in the evaluation of performance and quality.

Evidence-based practice is another argument used to emphasise the importance of the role of professional programmes in the research-based knowledge production. 'Evidence-based' is one of the most used adjectives in health care today indicating the need to inform patient treatment and care by scientific evidence. It was previously applied almost exclusively to medicine in the term 'evidence-based medicine', but terms like 'evidence-based practice' and 'evidence-based nursing' are becoming more widespread and stress that nursing practice ought to be based on reliable and valid proof for the effects of nursing care. Academic nurses and clinicians advocate strongly for the necessity of improving the quality of patient care by updating nurses on research findings and making them able to utilise research in the assessment and interpretation of patients' health and illness problems. This movement towards professional practice based on new scientific knowledge is also supported by health politicians who aim at increasing the quality of health care.

Also in teacher training, evidence-based teaching has gained ground. In elementary school teaching and preschool teaching, the emphasis of evidence teaching entails a need to strengthen educational research (see, for instance, Hargreaves, 1999; Davies, 1999). There is a call for increased research activity which might produce a better knowledge base, which in turn might lead to more research-informed educational policies and practices (see OECD, 2003).

A third argument underlines both a strong user orientation and a strong scientific orientation in knowledge production. The principle of user-inspired basic research, as introduced by Stokes (1997), has influenced OECD's (2003) strategy for research in the field of education. Research on education is recommended to focus on problem areas in the educational sector, while also contributing to overall development of knowledge. This argumentation reflects the belief that research can improve professional practice; furthermore, that the interaction between researchers and practitioners should be intensified, practices should adapt to research and research should adapt to practices. The success criteria are related to those of action-oriented research, in which the purpose of the research is to generate new opportunities for action to the same extent as producing new knowledge.

In the arguments about research-based knowledge production in professional programmes, such as nursing, teacher training and engineering, all three approaches are observable and they all emphasise the user. However, while the user is placed as a co-producer in an action research approach, the user's position within an evidence-based framework and a user-inspired basic research approach is restricted to be taken into account in defining research questions.

A recent issue of *Educational Researcher* (2008) – the official journal of the American Educational Research Association – illustrates the tension between these different approaches to knowledge production within the field of education research. Bulterman-Bos (2008) asks for a clinical approach to make research more relevant for practice where teachers and researchers can be reconciled in the context of clinical research practice. She argues that 'in clinical education research practice, the proof of success is not whether arguments are sound or ideas are interesting but whether the arguments and ideas contribute to better practice' (Bulterman-Bos, 2008, p. 419). On the other hand, Labaree (2008), one of the four commentators on Bulterman-Bos article, argues that the attempt to make educational research more relevant is counterproductive. Teachers and researchers have different orientations towards education based on different institutional settings, occupational constraints, daily work demands and professional incentives. Furthermore, the issue of relevance is difficult, and he argues that what seems to be of little relevance may turn out to be highly useful at a later time and in a different place (Labaree, 2008, p. 421).

Furthermore, we may question whether these different approaches to the production of research-based knowledge mentioned above, take place according to different sets of criteria (Hammersley, 2002; Rasmussen, Kruse, & Holm, 2007). Scientific knowledge defined as basic research is assessed on the basis of the valid/non-valid. On the other hand, we may argue that practice-oriented research is guided by the criterion of useful/useless, or the criterion professional improvement/no professional improvement. This argumentation conflicts with the views of Gibbons et al. (1994) and the idea of a new paradigm where the production of knowledge transcends and interacts with research contexts and practical contexts. Rasmussen et al. (2007) point to the risk that this will dilute research and claim that research will not become more indicative of action by renouncing their scientific criteria. Research which is not produced on the basis of scientific criteria loses its credibility among practitioners and politicians alike.

The criticism that academic staff in professional programmes produce research mainly to promote the vested interests of professions, and less often with the intention to enhance the quality of the services that are provided to users, is also well-known (Elzinga, 1990). Nursing science represents a good illustration of professionalisation through the development of a scientific knowledge base. As an academic discipline, nursing science has evolved in stages (Martinsen, 1986; Elzinga, 1990). Until 1950, the knowledge of nursing can be described within a humanistic tradition based on practical knowledge where caring was the central concept. In the second phase nursing drew heavily upon medical and technical knowledge. According to Elzinga (1990), a 'technification' was taking place. The third period which started in the middle of the 1960s is characterised by the establishment of a research capability. The aim of the nursing education that developed at this stage was to educate independent and reflective professionals who showed responsibility in the use of scientific knowledge and acquired a critical ability in assessing the practice of nursing. Furthermore, the student should learn the history of nursing as a discipline, its main models, concepts and theoretical frame of references (Karseth, 2004). However, the success of this professionalisation strategy can be questioned. The rapid shifts in knowledge and culture undermine the ability to root professional practice in a stable base of collective knowledge legitimised by references to the past. This creates a climate in which any foundation or authorising centre of knowledge is subject to question (Karseth & Nerland, 2007). According to Kessl and Otto (2006), traditional systems of knowledge production and knowledge reception are subjected to a steady loss of legitimacy. Paradoxically, however, the current trends of incredulity and doubt are accompanied by a strong call for increased research activity which may produce authoritative knowledge, which in turn may lead to a more research-informed nursing practice. This call challenges the approach advocated in the universities which argues in favour of theory-oriented and researcher-driven approaches that emphasise academic freedom. But it also challenges the approach defined by the UAS sector which embraces case-oriented and action-based research.

For academic staff within professional programmes the contesting arguments presented above are challenging. However, as we will point to below, the practical relevance aspect is of primary importance in how to define the research project.

A survey undertaken among academic staff in Norwegian university colleges provided information on various aspects of the applied research in the university

Table 3.2 Characteristics of applied research among academic staff in Norwegian university colleges in 2006. Percentage of staff who answered 'to a large extent'

	Engineering	Nursing	Teacher training
Inspired by practical problems	67	62	56
Based upon own experience in the field of practice	27	38	36
The initiative came from the field of practice	26	14	9
Developed in cooperation with the field of practice	31	32	23
(N)	(110)	(380)	(490)

colleges (Larsen & Kyvik, 2006). Table 3.2 shows that practical problems are an important point of departure for the staff members in their research. The most apparent importance is the role of practical problems as an inspiration for research. The findings support the significance of a close connection between research and practical problems. Furthermore, almost one third of the academic staff in engineering and nursing answered that their research is to a large extent developed in cooperation with the field of practice, while this holds true for less than one quarter in teacher education. Although there is a strong rhetoric in the field of teacher education about the necessity of a close relationship with the field of practice, such a relationship is unusual.

In another Norwegian study conducted in 2007 on nursing and other health courses provided by university colleges (Larsen et al., 2007), a questionnaire-based survey was combined with a qualitative interview study, in which a small sample of employees in nursing programmes were requested to describe research that transcended the distinction between university colleges and various clinical fields. The respondents were furthermore asked to reflect on the distinctive character of the research efforts they themselves were undertaking. Nursing staff orient their research towards improvement of practices, while at the same time being concerned with making contributions to the overall development of knowledge. The researchers were reluctant to use the label basic research, but were concerned that their efforts should contribute to production of knowledge and extend the research frontier within their own discipline. However, they were clearly and primarily motivated by, and oriented themselves towards, the practical importance that their research would entail for patients, healthcare workers and to improvements in treatment and care for patients.

Taken together, close partnership between research institutions and schools, companies or hospitals, is a central argument in order to improve the knowledge base of professional work. User involvement is seen as one of the key features of knowledge production and knowledge is generated in the context of application. Still, there are different approaches and contesting views of how research-based knowledge is constituted. There is a tradition of regional knowledge development and cooperation in all the three professions as well as an increased emphasis on a more cumulative knowledge production based on rigorous scientific procedures. This challenges the different programmes within the UASs and calls for redefining their research profiles.

58   K. Heggen et al.

Conclusion

In this chapter we have discussed the relationship between research, education and professional practice within bachelor degree programmes in engineering, nursing and teacher training. This review shows that there are different arguments advocating the importance of research-based teaching and learning in professional education at a bachelor's level. It is also clear that these arguments differ among the various professional programmes.

Both academic staff and students welcome a research-based approach to teaching and learning. However, the studies presented reveal doubts, barriers and challenges related to the development of a research culture that facilitates research activities by academic staff as well as by students. To build a professional programme on research-based knowledge is not a straightforward process. As this chapter shows there are many contesting views on the nexus between research and teaching, as well as the meaning of the concepts of scientific knowledge and research.

UASs, as well as politicians, have expressed the wish that their research should have an applied profile, and thereby better serve the interests of professional training. Through this discussion, we arrive at a point of view inspired by Rasmussen et al. (2007), where we show how the criteria for production and assessment of knowledge are different within research compared to practical, professional work. Recognising this difference may represent a favourable basis for maintaining high quality in both professional training and research, and it also points to the need for transcendence and linkages between research and education. The needs and opportunities for linkages are present, and in these efforts to achieve transcendence and linkages, the opportunities for utilisation of research as a means to improve undergraduate professional education are likely to be found.

While professional programmes offered by UASs were established within educational institutions with a knowledge culture related to practical knowledge and working life, the professionalisation of these programmes has to a large extent relied on the development of a scientific knowledge base. As a consequence, these programmes are embedded in different value and reward structures, creating tensions concerning what counts as valuable knowledge and appreciated competences and skills. These tensions have to be recognised in higher education policy aiming at making research relevant for the improvement of professional education and professional practice.

References

Aasland, T. (2008). Lærerutdanning for framtida. *Utdanning, 17,* 34.
Barnett, R. (Ed.). (2005). *Reshaping the university. New relationships between research, scholarship and teaching.* Maidenhead: Society for Research into Higher Education & Open University Press.
Brew, A. (2006). *Research and teaching. Beyond the divide.* Hampshire: Palgrave Macmillan.
Brint, S. (2002). The rise of the 'practical arts'. In S. Brint (Ed.), *The future of the city of intellect. The changing American university* (pp. 231–259). Stanford: Stanford University Press.

Bulterman-Bos, J. A. (2008). Will clinical approach make education research more relevant for practice? *Educational Researcher, 37*, 412–420.
Commission of the European Communities. (2002). *Developing foresight for the development of higher education/research relations in the perspective of the European research area (ERA).* Strata-Etan Expert Group. Brussels: European Commission, Directorate General for Research.
Cousin, G., Healey, M., Jenkins, A., Bradbeer, J., & King, H. (2003). Raising educational research capacity: A discipline-based approach. In C. Rust (Ed.), *Improving student learning. Theory and practice – 10 years on* (pp. 296–306). Oxford: Oxford Brookes University.
Davies, P. (1999). What is evidence-based education? *British Journal of Educational Studies, 47*, 108–121.
Dick, B. (2004). Action research literature. Themes and trends. *Action Research, 4*, 435–444.
Educational Researcher. (2008). *Educational Researcher, 37*, 412–445.
Elzinga, A. (1990). The knowledge aspect of professionalization: The case of science-based nursing education in Sweden. In R. Torstendahl & M. Burrage (Eds.), *The formation of professions. Knowledge, state and strategy* (pp. 151–173). London: SAGE Publications.
Gibbons, M., Limoges, C., Nowotny, H., Schwartzman, S., Scott, P., & Trow, M. (1994). *The new production of knowledge. The dynamics of science and research in contemporary societies.* London: SAGE Publications.
Hammersley, M. (2002). *Educational research, policymaking and practice.* London: SAGE Publications.
Hargreaves, D. H. (1999). The knowledge-creating school. *British Journal of Educational Studies, 47*, 122–144.
Hattie, J., & Marsh, H. W. (1996). The relationship between research and teaching: A meta-analysis. *Review of Educational Research, 66*, 507–542.
Healey, M. (2005). Linking research and teaching: Exploring disciplinary spaces and the role of inquiry-based learning. In R. Barnett (Ed.), *Reshaping the university. New relationships between research, scholarship and teaching* (pp. 67–78). Maidenhead: Society for Research into Higher Education & Open University Press.
Hollingsworth, S. (1997). *International action research. A casebook for educational reform.* London: Falmer Press.
Jenkins, A. (2004). *A guide to the research evidence on teaching-research relations.* The Higher Education Academy. Online resource http://www.heacademy.ac.uk/resources/detail/a_guide_to_the_research_evidence
Jenkins, A., Blackman, T., Lindsay, R., & Paton-Saltzberg, R. (1998). Teaching and research: Student perspectives and policy implications. *Studies in Higher Education, 23*, 127–141.
Jensen, K. (2007). Commenting on Nel Nodding's key-note. Knowledge in post-traditional society. *Nordisk Pedagogik, 1*, 54–58.
Karseth, B. (2004). Curriculum changes and moral issues in nursing education. *Nurse Education Today, 24*, 638–643.
Karseth, B., & Kyvik, S. (1999). *Undervisningsvirksomheten ved de statlige høgskolene.* Delrapport nr. 1, Evaluering av høgskolereformen. Oslo: Norges forskningsråd.
Karseth, B., & Nerland, M. (2007). Building professionalism in a knowledge society: Examining discourses of knowledge in four professional associations. *Journal of Education and Work, 20*, 335–355.
Kessl, F., & Otto, H. U. (2006). Pedagogic professionalism Defi(l)es the knowledge economy? Some preliminary notes. *Policy Futures in Education, 4*, 256–264.
Labaree, D. F. (2008). The dysfunctional pursuit of relevance in education research. *Educational Researcher, 37*, 421–423.
Larsen, I. M., Heggen, K., Carlsten, T. C., & Karseth, B. (2007). *Praksisrettet FoU? En undersøkelse av høgskolesektorens forsknings- og utviklingsarbeid innen helse- og sosialfag.* Oslo: NIFU STEP.
Larsen, I. M., & Kyvik, S. (2006). *Tolv år etter høgskolereformen – en statusrapport om FoU i statlige høgskoler.* Oslo: NIFU STEP.

Lave, J., & Wenger, E. (1991). *Situated learning: Legitimate peripheral participation*. New York: Cambridge University Press.

Lucas, L. (2007). Research and teaching work within university education departments: Fragmentation or integration? *Journal of Further and Higher Education, 31*, 17–29.

Maffioli, F., & Augusti, G. (2003). Tuning engineering education into the European higher education orchestra. *European Journal of Engineering Education, 28*, 251–273.

Marsh, H. W., & Hattie, J. (2002). The relation between research productivity and teaching effectiveness: Complementary, antagonistic, or independent constructs? *Journal of Higher Education, 73*, 603–614.

Martinsen, K. (1986). Omsorg og profesjonalisering. *Nytt om kvinneforskning*, Issue 2, 21–31.

Meeus, W., Van Looy, L., & Libotton, A. (2004). The Bachelor's thesis in teacher education. *European Journal of Teacher Education, 27*, 299–321.

Neuman, R. (1994). The teaching-research nexus: Applying a framework to university students' learning experiences. *European Journal of Education, 29*, 323–339.

Neumann, R., Parry, S., & Becher, T. (2002). Teaching and learning in their disciplinary context: A conceptual analysis. *Studies in Higher Education, 27*, 405–417.

Nielsen, K., & Kvale, S. (Eds.). (1999). *Mesterlære. Læring som sosial praksis*. Oslo: Gyldendal Norsk Forlag.

OECD. (1998). *Redefining tertiary education*. Paris: OECD.

OECD. (2003). *New challenges for educational research*. Paris: OECD.

Peters, M. A., & Humes, W. (2003). Education in the knowledge economy. *Policy Futures in Education, 1*, 1–19.

Pratt, J. (1997). *The polytechnic experiment 1965–1992*. London: The Society for Research into Higher Education.

Rasmussen, J., Kruse, S., & Holm, C. (2007). *Viden om uddannelse. Uddannelsesforskning, pædagogik og pædagogisk praksis*. Copenhagen: Hans Reitzels Forlag.

Schön, D. (1983). *The reflective practitioner. How professionals think in action*. New York: Basic Books.

Scott, P. (2005). Divergence or convergence? The links between teaching and research in mass higher education. In R. Barnett (Ed.), *Reshaping the university. New relationships between research, scholarship and teaching* (pp. 53–66). Maidenhead: Society for Research into Higher Education & Open University Press.

Simons, M., & Elen, J. (2007). The 'research-teaching nexus' and 'education through research'. An exploration of ambivalences. *Studies in Higher Education, 32*, 617–631.

Skoie, H. (2000). Faculty involvement in research in mass higher education: Current practice and future perspectives in the Scandinavian countries. *Science and Public Policy, 27*, 409–419.

Smeby, J. C. (2007). Connecting to professional knowledge. *Studies in Higher Education, 32*, 207–224.

Stjernø Committee. (2008). *Sett under ett. Ny struktur i høyere utdanning. NOU 2008:3*. Oslo: Departementenes servicesenter.

Stokes, D. E. (1997). *Pasteur's quadrant: Basic science and technological innovation*. Washington: The Brookings Institution Press.

Trowler, P., & Wareham, T. (2008). *Tribes, territories, research and teaching. Enhancing the teaching-research nexus*. York: The Higher Education Academy.

Turner, N., Wuetherick, B., & Healey, M. (2008). International perspectives on student awareness, experiences and perceptions of research: Implications for academic developers in implementing research-based teaching and learning. *International Journal for Academic Development, 13*, 199–211.

Zamorski, B. (2002). Research-led teaching and learning in higher education: A case. *Teaching in Higher Education, 7*, 411–427.

Chapter 4
Funding for Which Mission? Changes and Ambiguities in the Funding of Universities of Applied Sciences and Their Research Activities

Benedetto Lepori

Introduction

In most countries, universities of applied sciences (UASs) have been originally created without a research mandate (see Chapter 1), and thus their funding mechanism did not automatically include resources for research, unlike universities where it was assumed that a substantial share of a professor's time should be devoted to their own research. In fact, excluding research from UAS activities and funding was seen as a means to avoid increases in expenditures for higher education and thus to cope with the growth in student numbers without providing additional resources in the same proportion (OECD, 2005).

The implication of this policy is that, when they began to develop research activities, UASs had to find additional resources, either from the state or from private sources, since their core budget was usually devoted only to educational activities. In almost all countries considered in this book, getting resources for research has been a major issue at stake in the development of research and, at least when the extent of research exceeds some threshold, resources can quickly become a limiting factor as competition for resources between education and research can emerge (as in the case of Switzerland). Considering that, on the average, UASs account for between one third and two thirds of the first-year enrolments in higher education, it is easy to understand the sheer size of financial issues borne by the development of research in these institutions.

However, funding of research raises wider issues than just the predisposition of financial resources for these activities. First, it is an indicator of the role and the policy of the state towards research in the non-university sector, beyond official declarations. While practically all countries considered in this volume did introduce some specific support measures, there has been strong variation in the extent of these policies from country to country, thus distinguishing situations where state

B. Lepori (✉)
Faculty of Economics, Centre for Organizational Research, University of Lugano,
Lugano, Switzerland
e-mail: blepori@unisi.ch

S. Kyvik, B. Lepori (eds.), *The Research Mission of Higher Education Institutions Outside the University Sector*, Higher Education Dynamics 31,
DOI 10.1007/978-1-4020-9244-2_4, © Springer Science+Business Media B.V. 2010

intervention was largely reactive – accepting the willingness of UASs to develop research – from more explicit and proactive policies.

Second, allocation of funding can be a powerful means to direct UAS research towards specific goals, for example, focusing on applied research and cooperation with private companies through specific funding schemes. Moreover, in the wake of the redefinition of the binary divide related also to the new research mission, funding schemes can contribute to the convergence of the two sectors or to distinguish UAS research from universities. The choice to rely on the same or on different funding mechanisms for universities and UASs is thus relevant to shape the future of the binary system.

Third, looking to the funding streams and their composition might yield useful information on the role of UASs in the overall landscape of public research, for example, on their competition with other performers for project funding, as well as on the institutional strategies to develop research. In turn, these choices are likely to have an impact on the future configuration of higher education and on the position of non-university institutions in it, both concerning specific research activities and the nature of the binary divide overall.

This chapter pursues two main aims. First, it provides a comparative overview of research funding mechanisms and streams in the considered countries, based on documentary information and on the information available in the national chapters of this book (section 'How Much Research and How Is It Funded?'). Second, I discuss the wider implications of these funding schemes for public policies, the configuration of research in UASs and the future of the binary divide (section 'Funding Systems and Role of UASs in Public Research'). Beforehand, section 'Funding Models, Higher Education Steering and Research in the Non-university Sector' provides a framework for the analysis of research funding, as well as a discussion of some of their underlying conceptual issues.

Funding Models, Higher Education Steering and Research in the Non-university Sector

We may basically distinguish between the following four main funding sources for research:

(1) *General government allocations* are contributions from the state (national, as well as regional, in federal countries like Germany and Switzerland) which are attributed to higher education institutions (HEIs) as a whole for their normal functioning, like paying permanent staff and most current expenditures. While these funds are attributed globally, there are strong variations concerning the degree of autonomy in the use of these resources by the institutions, the allocation criteria adopted and the activities for which funds can be used; education; and/or research (Benninghoff, Perellon, & Leresche, 2005; Kaiser, Vossensteyn, & Koelman, 2001). Overall, there has been a shift in the last two

decades from line-item budgets, where funding was attributed as reimbursement of specific costs, to global budgets which are either negotiated between state and higher education institutions (possibly on the basis of some performance measure) or calculated through a formula (Strehl, 2007).

(2) *Public grants and contracts from the government* are attributed for specific activities – mostly research, but to some extent also service – for a limited period of time and directly to institutional subunits (institutes and laboratories). Examples are competitive grants from research councils, European framework programmes and contracts from the government. Most European countries possess a variety of funding agencies and programmes, pursuing different goals (from investigator-driven research to applied research and service to public policies); attribution is in most cases decided on the basis of competitive bids open to different research providers (even if some target measures might be reserved to some of them). Project funding has been in the recent years an instrument to finance research activities selectively and its share of total research funding has increased in all European countries (Lepori et al., 2007b). Earmarked funds in the general government allocation are largely an intermediate case between the two categories (depending on the specific features of their allocation and use).

(3) *Grants and contracts from private companies* are usually attributed for specific research purposes through bilateral contracts between the company and the research performer (usually at the institute and laboratory level). There has been a wide debate on the increase of private funding to higher education and in its consequences on research activities (for example, on the risk of focusing on short-term research and of private appropriation of research results), but overall this source accounts for a limited share of resources, except in some specific domains and institutions (for example, business schools and technological universities; Lepori et al., 2007a).

(4) *Funding coming from the students* in the form of tuition fees for attendance to curricula or different types of courses is an additional source. It is useful to distinguish between fees for undergraduate students, which are in most cases fixed by the state, and fees for postgraduate education where institutions have a larger freedom to set the level. In all countries these fees are to some extent subsidised by the state especially for lower income people. The introduction or the increase of tuition fees has been one of the most widely debated issues in higher education funding (Teixeira, Johnstone, Rosa, & Vossensteyn, 2007), but empirical work shows that, with the exception of the UK, undergraduate fees do not yet cover a substantial share of educational costs in European countries (Lepori et al., 2007a).

Beyond this description, there are a number of underlying issues which are relevant also for the development of research in UASs and which I shortly discuss in the following paragraphs. As it shall become clear later, most of them are related to the future configuration of the binary system; an issue which I discuss more in-depth later in this chapter.

Funding and Steering of Higher Education

From the viewpoint of the state, allocation of funding has always been a choice instrument to direct higher education towards policy goals. While in the past this took place through detailed regulations and line-item budgeting, with precise control on expenditures, new approaches in public management emphasise an arms length approach where, through allocation rules, the state sets incentives for higher education institution (HEI) behaviour to reach certain goals, leaving it to the HEI themselves a wider strategic and operational autonomy (Ferlie, Musselin, & Andresani, 2008; Amaral, Meek, & Larsen, 2003). Thus, increasingly funding policies reflect wider policy goals like increasing efficiency of HEI, promoting institutional differentiation and targeting research to some specific objectives (Geuna, 2001). A relevant example is provided by the UK, where a system of incentives has been set up by the government to promote institutional specialisation and concentration of the research activities in the best universities, through a combination of project funding and selective core funding for research (Stiles, 2000; Naidoo, 2008).

Moreover, beyond economic incentives, funding instruments have also a normative role, embedding conceptions on the mission and function of HEIs, for example, on the relationship between research and education and the type of research which should be performed (Lascoumes & Le Gales, 2000). Even if not legally binding, these norms tend to diffuse also to internal allocation rules, where a tendency to follow the national incentive system has been documented (Jongbloed, 2009).

When looking to the development of research in UASs, it is thus relevant to take a closer look at the system of incentives set out by the state for these institutions and to understand the underlying conceptions of research and the specific role of UASs in the national research system. Moreover, it is relevant to examine whether the state provides specific instruments to promote UAS research.

The Role of the State and the Autonomy of Individual Institutions

Funding systems also shape to a large extent the relationship between the state and the institutions themselves and to which extent they are able to develop their own strategies (for example, concerning the orientation and organisation of research). Funding systems thus embody different conceptions of state steering, as well as of institutional autonomy (Jongbloed, 2007).

Thus, even if most countries have moved to global budgets and detailed line-item budgeting has become the exception, the remaining level of state control and regulation strongly differs across countries (OECD, 2003), and this impacts on the possibility of institutional strategies and their implementation. This includes, for example, the degree of state control over the costs of activities, of funding between domains and activities and of the level of tuition fees. More technical aspects are also relevant, such as the possibilities of getting loans, amortisement policies and flexibility concerning salaries and hiring policies. Both formal duties and soft controls, related to social norms, are at stake here.

A further issue concerns the share of core versus project funding for research and their relationships. Since project funding is usually attributed directly to institutional units, a high share is likely to reinforce the autonomy of these units and weaken the establishment of a coherent organisational strategy. However, different institutional strategies are possible in this respect, including attributing core funding in proportion to external funding (overhead) or rather allocating core funding based on strategic considerations at the institutional level.

Thus, an analysis of funding allocation mechanisms is also likely to provide some indications on the relative power of the state, of UAS directions and of departments and institutes in determining the extent and orientation of UAS research.

Education and Research: Jointly or Separated Funding?

A central issue in higher education funding lies in the existence of separate funding channels for research and educational activities, respectively of separated accounting of costs for the two activities. This seemingly technical question is rooted in different conceptions of the relationship between education and research in HEIs.

The traditional Humboldtian model assumed a direct connection between education and research in universities at the level of individual teachers, and thus their salary included also time for research. Joint funding and no separated accounting of research costs are a consequence of this model, which dominated European higher education until the 1970s. In contrast, UAS teachers were assigned a much higher number of teaching hours since they were not supposed to do research.

Also in universities, research and education have become less strongly connected during the recent years, with research activities concentrating on some parts of the system, either on few institutions or on specific departments and research centres, even if national systems strongly differ in the extent and forms of this process (Clark, 1995; Schimank & Winnes, 2000). This impacted also on funding: first, the widespread introduction of project funding of research since the Second World War introduced a specific channel for research funding, largely used to hire additional personnel specialised in research. More recently, most countries introduced a model for general allocation to universities with components for education and research respectively, calculated using different criteria. However, in principle universities are still free to decide how to use these resources, even if splitting allocation might impact also on use of funds. With the exception of UK and of some research centres, separated accounting of research and educational activities (through the use of timesheets) is still the exception in European universities.

Of course, core funding for UASs was at the beginning devoted only to educational activities and, where formula-based allocation has been introduced, it was based only on education (for example, the number of students). With the development of research within the UAS sector, two main questions emerge: first, to what extent is the state introducing a research component in the general funding allocation for UASs and, second, to what extent have UASs themselves some freedom (explicit or implicit) to decide how to use financial resources and to move them from one activity to the other? Both are closely connected to the mission of the UAS, to the importance of research versus education, as well to the representation of their relationship.

Competing for Project Funding and for Private Sources

Most Continental European countries possess a dual research funding system, with a large core funding component directed to universities and public research organisations alongside an important share of project funding attributed through a highly differentiated system of funding agencies and programmes (Lepori et al., 2007b). Empirical analysis shows that project funding markets are highly differentiated according to the agency and funding instrument, the type of research, the subject and the discipline. I basically distinguish in this respect between research councils, largely devoted to academic investigator-driven research (Slipersaeter et al., 2007), technological programmes and innovation agencies, contracts from different ministries and, finally, private contracts. These different streams are related to different policy goals, finance different research activities and are characterised by quite different selection processes and allocation criteria.

Once UASs begin to develop their research activities, the issue of their positioning in the project funding market becomes unavoidable, especially if core funding for research is not provided. Except in case of ring-fenced project funding schemes, UASs have to compete directly with universities and public research organisations, having a much stronger research tradition and infrastructure (thanks also to their large core budget). It is then relevant to look at the extent to which UASs are able to get project funding and from which sources, and if they show distinct specialisations towards some kind of sources – like technological agencies or private contracts. This is a relevant indicator of their future ability to stand up to competition in the wider research system, for example, if the binary divide is weakened or abolished, but also of their future trajectory, either towards a research model similar to universities or focusing on a specific niche.

How Much Research and How Is It Funded?

In this section, I present an overview of research funding in the non-university sector in the eight countries considered in this book, focusing on the level of funding and its composition, on the presence or absence of a research component in the general allocation, on the competitive position of UASs in contract funding and, finally, on the extent of specific measures to promote research in UASs and their orientation.

Beforehand, it is important to notice that the quality of information concerning UAS funding – for research, but also in general – is much lower than for universities. Practically, all comparative studies on higher education funding are limited to the university sector only (see, for example, Strehl et al., 2007, Lepori et al., 2007a), while information from national documents and reports on funding mechanisms for

UASs is also rather limited (see, for example, the OECD national reviews of tertiary education).

Available quantitative data are also scarce and display major methodological problems. First, the definition of the non-university higher education sector is in most countries imprecise and changing across time, due to the progressive integration of existing tertiary education institutions and on-going reform processes (Kyvik, 2004). Second, in most countries data on universities and UASs are collected and managed separately and thus are hardly comparable and, in general, the collection of data for the non-university sector is more recent and less systematic than for universities. Third, R&D statistics paid historically little attention to the non-university sector, which is usually not shown as a distinct performing domain in the R&D statistics. Also the correct identification of R&D expenditures in UASs is often difficult for conceptual reasons (see Chapter 1), but also because they account for a low share of total expenditures. The data presented in this chapter should thus be considered in most cases as a rough approximation and are not always comparable, having been collected from different data sources.

Low Level of Resources, Mostly from External Sources

Table 4.1 presents an overview of the level of research expenditures in the non-university sector, as well as the main funding sources.

Sources include the reference in the table and the country chapters in this volume, as well as information from the authors themselves. They were complemented with information on funding schemes from the ERAWATCH inventory of the European Commission. German data refer to *Fachhochschulen* and *Verwaltungsfachhochschulen*. No data is available for the Czech Republic, but R&D expenditures are probably very low.

The table displays some interesting patterns. Thus, in the countries where the level of development of research in UASs is lower – Belgium, Ireland and The Netherlands – funding comes essentially from third-party sources, and mostly from

Table 4.1 Funding of research activities in UASs

	R&D exp. Mill Euro	Percent R&D funding from general allocation (%)	Year	Sources
Belgium	58	20	2005	Ministry of Education and Training 2006
Czech Republic	Very low			
Ireland	33	0	2006	Forfás 2008
Netherlands	82	19	2005	Boezerooy 2003
Germany	674	45	2005	German Statistical Office
Norway	157	79	2007	Norwegian R&D statistics
Finland	100	25	2005	Ministry of Education 2004
Switzerland	217	62	2007	Swiss National Statistical Office

specific measures to promote research in UASs. The situation in the Flemish region of Belgium strongly changed in the most recent years because of large academisation credits (see Chapter 6); these credits increased from €15 million in 2006 to €25 million in 2008 and were attributed as earmarked funds to the whole UAS sector. In countries where research is more developed, there is a substantial contribution from the core budget, like in Norway, Switzerland and Germany. In particular, Norway stands out from the countries considered since most research funding comes from the general budget.

General Allocation: Different Rules and Limited Research Support

Table 4.2 presents the rules for the general allocation of funding from the state to the UASs. This table shows first that formula-based allocation has become by far the most widespread mechanism and additional countries are moving towards this mechanism, like Belgium, Ireland and to some extent Germany and Switzerland (with wide regional differences). We can distinguish in this respect two opposite situations:

(a) Countries where allocation for UASs is based on distinct rules and budgetary lines different from universities and, in almost all cases, allocation is attributed for education only and, essentially, on the number of students. This is the case in Belgium, Ireland, The Netherlands and Finland. Switzerland also belongs to this group, but there is a specific budgetary line for research owing to the fact that, from the beginning, the state indicated (applied) research as a major objective of UASs (Lepori, 2008). Some limited core funding is available also to Finnish UASs through their performance contracts (mostly earmarked to specific objectives).

(b) Countries where UASs basically follow the same funding rules as universities and have the right to get core research funding if they fulfil the required criteria. In our sample, this is the case of the Czech Republic and of Norway. The Czech Republic illustrates the implications of this choice in a context of very competitive research funding for universities: formally, UASs can compete with universities for research plans – being the main source of core funding (Sima, 2008), but in reality they do not have any chance to stand up competition with universities and de facto receive very little funding. A similar situation is shown by the former UK polytechnics, which since 1992 are subject to the same funding rules as universities, but receive very low core funding for research because they hardly satisfy the quality criteria set by the Research Assessment Exercise (RAE). The introduction of the RAE can thus be interpreted also as a means to avoid providing additional funding for research to the polytechnics in the transition from a binary to a unitary system (Stiles, 2000). Norway displays a milder variant: Norwegian university colleges have a stronger research tradition, and also the funding system is less competitive compared to the UK, and the allocation criteria have been slightly differentiated to owe for specificities of

Table 4.2 General allocation of funding for UASs

	Core funding for research		Allocation mechanisms
	Legal right to use for R&D	Specific R&D allocation	
Belgium	Yes	No	UASs are funded through a separate mechanism based on historical criteria and number of students (with different rates by domains), the last component being now the dominant one. In the Flemish community a new allocation model is foreseen where education allocation is the same as universities, but UASs do not receive a core grant for research
Czech Republic	Yes	No	Non-university institutions receive core funding through the same mechanism as universities. In fact, they receive an extremely limited amount through specific research and no funding through competitive research plans since they do not meet the criteria of these instruments
Ireland	No	No	Block grant from the Department of Education and Science based on history. Since 2007, funding from the Higher Education Agency has been based on number of students (same as universities), but without allocation for research
The Netherlands	No	No	General funds calculated on a formula based on enrolments and an incentive factor to decrease time to graduation. The scheme is separated from universities. No core funding for research, except own funding to the *lectorates* (20% of the total costs, €19 million)
Germany	Yes	Yes	Due to the federal organisation of the country, core funding is attributed through different mechanisms according to the *Länder*. Where formulas are used, these are mostly based on the number of students, but with a share calculated on research activities (mostly third-party funding). In some *Länder* the same funding scheme is adopted for universities and UASs, while in others, schemes and streams are separated. See Leszczensky and Orr (2003) for a detailed discussion
Norway	Yes	Yes	Core funding is calculated with a similar mechanism as universities. A specific component of core funding is devoted to R&D (about 6% of the core funding volume against 22% for universities). It is calculated with a formula based on number of professors, credit points and third-party funding
Finland	No	No	General allocation is based on standard rates and on an agreed number of study places set in performance contracts between State and Polytechnics. The contracts include also some very limited funding for research purposes (earmarked to specific activities)
Switzerland	Yes	Yes	Funding for UASs is through a channel and mechanism separate from universities. Most funding is based on standard costs per students. The Confederation has a specific budgetary line for research distributed on the basis of third-party funding and of research personnel, while Cantons include research funding in the core budget of individual UASs (with very large differences between Cantons and between individual UASs)

UAS research, including all contract research (instead of just research council and EU funding) and credits (instead of master's and doctoral degrees). Thus university colleges receive a substantial amount of core funding for research, although much lower than universities (6% against 22%).

The German situation is the most complex one because of the federal structure of the country. Existing information shows that, also for *Fachochschulen*, the general allocation is attributed both for education and research and, where formulas have been introduced, a specific research component is present also for *Fachhochschulen* (Leszczensky & Orr, 2003). We notice that also in universities this component accounts for a low share of core public funding (well below 10%) and thus it is assumed that research is funded largely through the educational component of the budget, corresponding to the Humboldtian model. In this respect, there is little differentiation between universities and *Fachhochschulen*: the different shares of education and research seem to be essentially due to differences in the teaching duties of professors between the two sectors, rather than through splitting financial allocations for education and research. However, the German data are rough estimates, since they are based on the assumption that on the average UAS staff member devotes 5% of their working time to R&D activities and this is just a rule-of-thumb calculation.

Pushing the Development of Research Through Specific Support Measures

Practically, all countries have introduced some specific support programme for UAS research, but there are variations in their size, importance and orientation. We can broadly distinguish among the considered countries three different situations (see the national chapters for full details):

(a) *Countries where specific support measures account for most of research funding in UASs* of which the most relevant case is The Netherlands. In this country, the *lectorate* programme covers at least half of the research expenditures of *hogescholen* and, indirectly, steers probably an even large share (since lectors are supposed also to acquire third-party funds). Belgium seems to be a similar case, especially in Flemish Community where academisation credits account for a large share of the funding volume. Additionally, in both linguistic regions there are specific programmes to promote research in UASs. Both academisation credits and *lectorates* are supposed to be transitory measures, to be replaced in the next years with core funding.

(b) *Countries where specific support measures – devoted only to UASs – are important, but do not constitute the core of research funding* include Ireland, with its specific Technological Sector Research programme reserved for UASs (about one third of total funding volume in 2006), Germany, with the BMBF specific programmes for *Fachhochschulen*, with however a limited funding volume (€16 million in 2006), to which we should however add some programmes in the *Länder*, and Switzerland. In this country, the Swiss Innovation Agency had a specific programme to develop research in UASs in the period 1997–2007, which accounted for a substantial share of funding (26 million CHF in 2005), while the Swiss National Science Foundation has a programme to support practice-oriented research in social sciences (Do-RE programme; 4.5 million CHF in 2005), which shall continue until 2011. In all these cases these are ring-fenced competitive schemes with a strong focus in promoting technological research and cooperation with private companies. In Finland, UASs also receive project funding for a number of targeted activities and programmes, defined in the performance agreement with the state.

(c) *Countries where specific support programmes play a very limited role* include the two extreme cases in our sample concerning the development of research; the Czech Republic and Norway. In the latter country, the Research Council of Norway has targeted programmes for supporting research in the university colleges, but its amount is very limited compared to total expenditures.

Competing for Project Funding

All existing studies show that UASs receive a much lower amount of project funding than universities. However, this overall view has to be made precise by looking at different segments of project funding, which also cover different types of research and quality requirements.

Unfortunately, the data situation is quite difficult since there is no detailed international statistics on project funding (Lepori et al., 2007a) and, in many countries where data are available, the UAS sector is included in the general statistics for the whole higher education sector. The Table 4.3, based on different data sources, provides some estimates of the total volume of project funding in the UAS sector, the percent of UAS R&D expenditures financed through third-party means, and information on the composition of project funds.

The table displays that in two countries UASs are strong in getting third-party funding, namely Finland and Switzerland. Both are countries where public policies strongly emphasise the service function of UASs towards regional economy and private companies, what we could call a customer-oriented approach to UAS research. UASs in these countries account for about 10% of the total volume of third-party funding for research in the higher education sector, but a much higher proportion when looking at research funding oriented to technology and regional economic development. In both cases, strong specialisation are also apparent; thus, Swiss UASs receive by now about one third of the total funding volume of the Swiss Innovation Agency and are particularly strong also in getting private contracts, while in Finland, European structural funds have provided a specific niche for UASs.

In the other countries considered, UASs are weak competitors for all third-party funding schemes. This is striking, especially in Norway, where the extent of research in university colleges is relatively high, but these institutions get much lower shares of their research income than universities, whose average share of third-party

Table 4.3 Third-party funding for research in UASs (2005)

	€ Million	% R&D exp.[a]	Composition of third-party funding	Source
Belgium	30	82%	6.5% enterprises, 88.4% other ministries, 0.2% private non-profit, 4.8% international programmes	Commissie Federale Samenwerking, Overleggroep CFS/STAT
Ireland	32	100%	34% TSR programme (specific for UAS), 24% enterprise Ireland, 18% programme for research in third level institutions, 24% other funding	Hazelkorn and Moynihan (see Chapter 10)
The Netherlands	80	80%	50% for the *lectorates* plus 30% from the RAKK programme	De Weert and Leijnse (see Chapter 11)
Germany	200	55%	40% private funding, 22% federal state, 16% international programmes, 22% other funding	Statistiches Bundesamt (2007)
Norway	22	18%	45% research council, 27% ministry contracts, 9% EU funding, 8% private contracts, 11% other funding	NIFU STEP R&D statistics (2005)
Finland (2004)	67	75%	32% EU funding (structural funds), 24% project funding from the education ministry, 13% innovation agency, 9% private companies, 22% other funding	Marttila and Kautonen (2006)
Switzerland	45	40%	49% private contracts, 37% Swiss innovation agency, 14% other funding	Lepori (2007)

[a]Percent of UAS R&D expenditures financed through third-party means.

funding is about 35% (Source: Norwegian R&D statistics). A similar situation is shown in Germany, with *Fachhochschulen* having a profile more oriented towards private funding, but with a weak position in terms of their ability to attract third-part funding and, especially, public competitive funds.

Overall, even if UASs nowadays generally have access to research council funding and to European Framework Programmes, they are weak competitors on both funding markets, owing in the first case to its focus on academic research and, in the second case, to the lack of a well-structured and wide international network.

Funding Systems and Role of UASs in Public Research

The Table 4.4 provides a summary overview of the comparative analysis done in the preceding section. It clearly displays the wide differences in the funding structures of research and the position of UASs in the public funding system, which can also be related to different state policies and understanding of the role of UASs in the public research system.

Even if, of course, each classification scheme does not cover all cases found in the reality, it seems that most countries in our sample can fit in two main models, which are closely related to the overall configuration of research in the UAS sector (see Chapter 14).

In the first one, there is a strong state intervention to direct UAS research towards specific policy goals, especially cooperation with regional actors, transfer of knowledge and technology and cooperation with private companies. Of course, these rationales are present in almost all countries where UASs are developing their own research activities, but the uniqueness of these countries is that this policy has been embodied in specific and targeted support instruments, which comprised, at least in the first phase of research development, the bulk of available resources. At the same time, core funding has been reserved for educational purposes and limited transfers of the core budget towards research activities have occurred.

The typical examples of this model are The Netherlands, through the *lectorate* scheme, and Switzerland, through the specific measures of the Swiss Innovation Agency launched in late 1990s. Finland also to some extent seems to follow this model, even if state steering has been realised more through the performance contracts with the UASs, rather than with direct funding. In all these cases, one witnesses also a strong sense of collective action of UASs towards developing research and a relevant role of their collective organisations in promoting research funding and, to some extent, also contributing to managing these schemes (as the HBO-Raad in The Netherlands). One could argue that the ideas of a knowledge society and of Mode 2 research, strongly connected to society and economy, have provided an underpinning to identify a specific role of the UAS also concerning research, much

Table 4.4 Summary of UAS research funding

	Core funding	Specific support measures and programmes	Project funding
Belgium	No (but right)	Important	Weak
Czech Republic	No (but right)	No	Very weak
Ireland	No	Yes	Weak
The Netherlands	No	Important	Weak
Germany	Yes	Yes	Weak
Norway	Prevalent	Not important	Weak
Finland	Limited	Yes	Strong
Switzerland	Yes	Yes	Strong

like the distinction between professional and academic programmes for education. Belgium displays a similar approach, but with a different policy goal since (in the Flemish region) most of research funding is now specifically attributed through academisation credits meant to improve the qualifications of staff teaching in the academic track.

The cases of Finland and Switzerland, where the development of research started already some years ago, display some relevant implications and evolutions of this model. First, specific support measures are considered as provisional and it is assumed that after a while UASs will have to get their funding from the general third-party funding market, competing with universities and public research organisations. In these two countries this strategy has been quite successful since, thanks to their orientation towards regional economy and SMEs, UASs have built a strong position in specific niches of the competitive funding market, especially in the schemes to support regional development, technological agency programmes and contracts from private companies. In turn, this tends to build stable interactions between UASs, users of their research (regional communities; private companies) and funders (the companies and regional authorities, but also technological agencies and state programmes) which define their position in the competitive funding market. Thus, this positioning can be stable even after the end of the specific state support measures.

Second, in this model core funding is in fact driven by specific support measures and third-party funding since, once these exceed some threshold, core funding is required to maintain the general research infrastructure, to stabilise research units and to hire senior researchers to lead research groups. In the Swiss case, core funding nowadays covers about 60% of R&D expenditures, even if the original assumption was that research activities should be completely financed through external means. However, letting research activities emerge and be selected through external funding is likely to push towards some institutional concentration and some separation between teaching and research activities. The Swiss case, with its strong differences in research intensity between technology and their other UAS activity domains, clearly displays this pattern (Lepori, 2008).

In the second model, the development of research took place mostly by using the UAS core budget, either comprising a specific allocation for research activities (Norway), or since it was tacitly assumed that the core budget is meant for both activities (Germany). In a sense, it seems that the state has no strong representation in the specific role of UAS research, but is accepting and recognising that these institutions are allowed to perform research by their own means and are allowed to use part of their funding for that purpose. These countries (including also the Czech Republic) display a much stronger convergence of public funding allocation between universities and UASs, as well as a low share of specific support measures for research. The data show that in these countries UASs are weak competitors for third-party funding and, actually, get a lower share of their research budget than universities from these sources (especially in Norway). It seems that in these countries the sheer size and reputation effects come to full weight since UASs do not develop a specific profile on the funding market (and are not actively supported by the state for this purpose). However, this model is likely to promote a stronger integration between research and education, a pattern which is very evident in Norway, but seems also to emerge in Germany.

In these countries, the resources available to UASs for research are largely dependent upon the overall configuration of the core funding allocation to higher education institutions: weakly competitive models like in Germany and in Norway, where some incentives are introduced but core funding for research includes also a basic component and is spread throughout most institutions, allow UASs to get some level of core funding and to develop their research activities. On the contrary, strongly competitive systems de facto exclude UASs from research funding and tend to segregate them in the teaching-only part of the higher education system, as shown by the Czech Republic and the UK. The UK case shows that segregation through competitive core funding is quite stable across time and very limited upward mobility is possible (Stiles, 2000), while in countries where core funding is less competitive one could foresee some great opportunities for change.

References

Amaral, A., Meek, V. L., & Larsen, I. M. (Eds.). (2003). *The higher education managerial revolution*. Dordrecht: Kluwer.

Benninghoff, M., Perellon, J. F., & Leresche, J. P. (2005). *L'efficacité des mesures de financement dans le domaine de la formation, de la recherche et de la technologie. Perspectives européennes comparées et leçons pour la Suisse*. Lausanne: Les cahiers de l'Observatoire.

Boezerooy, P. (2003). *Higher education in the Netherlands. Country report*. Twente: CHEPS.

Clark, B. R. (1995). *Places of inquiry: Research and advanced education in modern universities*. Berkeley: University of California Press.

Ferlie, E., Musselin, C., & Andresani, G. (2008). The steering of higher education systems: A public management perspective. *Higher Education, 56*, 325–348.

Geuna, A. (2001). The changing rationale for European university research funding: Are there negative unintended consequences? *Journal of Economic Issues, 35*, 607–632.

Jongbloed, B. (2007). Creating public-private dynamics in higher education funding: A discussion of three options. In J. Enders & B. Jongbloed (Eds.), *Public-private dynamics in higher education: Expectations, developments and outcomes* (pp. 113–138). Bielefeld: Transcript Verlag.

Jongbloed, B. (2009). Steering the Dutch academic research enterprise: *Universities responses to project funding and performance monitoring*. In P. Clancy & D. Dill (Eds.), *The research mission of the university* (pp. 95–132). Rotterdam: Sense Publishers.

Kaiser, F., Vossensteyn, H., & Koelman, J. (2001). *Public funding of higher education. A comparative study of funding mechanisms in ten countries*. Zoetermeer: Ministerie van Onderwijs, Cultuur en Wetenschappen.

Kyvik, S. (2004). Structural changes in higher education systems in Western Europe. *Higher Education in Europe, 29*, 393–409.

Lascoumes, P., & Le Gales, P. (2000). Introduction: Understanding public policy through its instruments – from the nature of instruments to the sociology of public policy instrumentation. *Governance, 20*, 1–21.

Lepori, B. (2007). *Funding models of universities of applied sciences. International experiences and options for the Swiss case*. Report to Rector's conference of Swiss Universities of Applied Sciences, Bern.

Lepori, B. (2008). Research in non-university higher education institutions. The case of the Swiss universities of applied sciences. *Higher Education, 56*, 45–58.

Lepori, B., Benninghoff, M., Jongbloed, B., Salerno, C., & Slipersaeter, S. (2007). Changing models and patterns of higher education funding: Some empirical evidence. In A. Bonaccorsi & C. Daraio (Eds.), *Universities and strategic knowledge creation. Specialization and performance in Europe* (pp. 85–111). Cheltenham : Edward Elgar.

Lepori, B., van den Besselaar, P., Dinges, M., van der Meulen, B., Potì, B., Reale, E., et al. (2007). Comparing national research policies and their evolution over time. An empirical study on public project funding. *Science and Public Policy, 34*(6), 372–388.

Leszczensky, M., & Orr, D. (2003). *Staatliche hochschulfinanzierung durch indikatorgestützte mittelverteilung*. Hochschulinformationsystem HIS, A2/2004.

Marttlila, L., & Kautonen, M. (2006). *Finnish polytechnics as providers of knowledge-intensive services*. Paper for the XVI International RESER Conference, Lisbon, September 28–30, 2006.

Ministry of Education. (2004). *OECD thematic review of tertiary education. Country background report for Finland*. Helsinki: Ministry of Education.

Ministry of Education and Training . (2006). *OECD thematic review of tertiary education. Country background report – Flemish Community of Belgium*. Brussels: Ministry of Education and Training.

Naidoo, R. (2008). L'Etat et le marché dans la réforme de l'enseignement supérieur Royaume-Uni (1980–2007). *Critique internationale, 39*, 47–66.

OECD. (2003). *Education policy analysis 2003*. Paris: OECD.

OECD. (2005). Alternatives to university revisited. In *Education policy analysis 2005* (pp. 15–45). Paris: OECD.

Schimank, U., & Winnes, M. (2000). Beyond Humboldt? The relationship between teaching and research in European university systems. *Science and Public Policy, 27*, 397–408.

Sima. (2008). *Czech Republic country report. Research funding systems in Central and Eastern European countries*. PRIME-CEEC report, Olso.

Slipersaeter, S., Lepori, B., & Dinges, M. (2007). Between policy and science: Research councils responsiveness in Austria, Norway and Switzerland. *Science and Public Policy*: 34, 401–415.

Statistisches Bundesamt. (2007). *Bildung und kultur*. Bonn: Monetäre Hochsculstatistische Kennzahlen.

Stiles, D. (2000, October–December). Higher education funding patterns since 1990: A new perspective. *Public Money and Management, 20*, 51–57.

Strehl, F. (2007). *Funding systems and their effects on higher education systems*. Paris: OECD.

Teixeira, P. N., Johnstone, D. B., Rosa, M. J., & Vossensteyn, H. (Eds.). (2007). *Cost-sharing and accessibility in higher education: A fairer deal?* Dordrecht: Springer.

Chapter 5
Transforming Academic Practice: Human Resource Challenges

Ellen Hazelkorn and Amanda Moynihan

Changes in Academic Work

The emergence in the post-1960s of a higher education alternative to universities was a response to the pressures of socio-economic demand and new opportunities at a time of rapid economic change (Scott, 1995; Huisman, de Weert, & Bartelse, 2002; Taylor, Ferreira, Machado, & Santiago, 2008). In many cases their growth was facilitated by upgrading existing vocational training institutions which had a ready cohort of students while others were formed through merger, or occasionally, as ab initio institutions. Each country responded differently to the same challenges but essentially whether these higher education institutions (HEIs) were called poly-technics (UK), *fachhochschulen* (Germany), *hogescholen* (The Netherlands and Belgium), institutes of technology (Ireland), etc. they were established to provide vocational, career-oriented, technological and specialist programmes at certificate, diploma and/or bachelor level with a responsibility towards their region or the small and medium enterprise (SME) sector. Often branded today as 'universities of applied sciences' (henceforth UASs), their institutional mission has variously been described as 'carrying out applied research and development work' (Finland), 'scientific consultancy work and organised technology transfer activities' (Germany) or transmitting 'scientific knowledge that is both theoretical and practical in order to prepare students for professional life' (Portugal).

Over the years, the environment which generated these institutions has changed dramatically and the strategic focus of many of them has changed as a consequence. Even before the harmonising effects of the Bologna Process had begun to take full effect, the political and public climate was already changing (see Verhoeven, 2008, p. 56; Välimaa & Neuvonen-Rauhala, 2008, p. 94). As higher education came to be seen as vital to economic development and national innovation, these institutions

E. Hazelkorn (✉)
Higher Education Policy Research Unit (HEPRU), Dublin Institute of Technology, Dublin, Ireland
e-mail: Ellen.Hazelkorn@dit.ie

S. Kyvik, B. Lepori (eds.), *The Research Mission of Higher Education Institutions Outside the University Sector*, Higher Education Dynamics 31, DOI 10.1007/978-1-4020-9244-2_5, © Springer Science+Business Media B.V. 2010

began to offer higher level programmes and strengthened their research capacity and capability in order to support professional training and advances in knowledge. In recent years, these trends gathered pace under the influence of EU and national policy decisions, such as the strategy for a European Research Area, academisation in Belgium, competitive research opportunities in Ireland and re-designation of university colleges in Norway. They have all contributed to raising both the profile of research and the sense of urgency. In the process, they have impacted significantly on the roles and responsibilities of academic staff in UASs, their contractual arrangements and their working environment.

The academic literature, with notable exceptions (see the following), has however been largely silent on the particulars of this experience. Instead, it has chronicled the transformation of a relatively autonomous academic profession operating within a self-regulated code of 'collegiality' into an increasingly 'organizationally managed' workforce comparable to other salaried employees (Slaughter & Leslie, 1997; Rhoades, 1998; Farnham, 1999) as if this is the common and only experience – not just across national borders but across sectoral boundaries. Yet, it stands to reason that if massification results in a greater diversity of institutions, then these HEIs will recruit 'different kinds of staff to the academic profession, who, in turn, are more disparate in their professional and social origins' (Farnham, 1999, p. 21). Thus, not only is the 'ideal, and self-concept, of the professor' (Altbach, 2000, p. 13) no longer valid but the notion that there is a 'single academic profession' (Marginson, 2000, p. 23) with a common experience of academic work is no longer applicable. The 'diversification of institutions has meant diversification of the professoriate [and the professoriate experience] as well' (Altbach, 2000, p. 13).

At the time many UAS academic staff were initially employed, 'their principal role [was] as teachers' (Pratt, 1997) and their focus was on vocational/professional practice. Most held an undergraduate qualification with professional experience, but few had research credentials or practice. As the focus of attention has shifted towards more active engagement in the research enterprise, these academic staff have been asked to build up a sustainable research profile, participate in 'national and international scientific networks' and develop a presence in international publications. The sheer magnitude of this transformation – on a personal and collective level – cannot be underestimated; 'acquiring and/or developing research competences is a complex process of apprenticeship which requires time and resources' (Lepori & Attar, 2006, pp. 57, 64). Indeed, the particular characteristics of academic work and institutional culture in UASs may necessitate policy involvement in maximising research potential.

While this profile has changed over time, many new academic staff are still being recruited into institutions which retain many historic values and where 'academic work' is still contested. According to Bland and Ruffin (1992), building an active and prominent research portfolio is thus dependent upon changes in academic attitudes and behaviour, such as social and professional norms, what it takes to be successful, promotional opportunities and processes, and changes in organisational structures and environment (quoted in Pratt, Margaritis, & Coy, 1999, p. 46). The process of growing a research culture – of transforming an institution from a teaching to research-focused one – is complex, difficult and potentially lengthy, equivalent to a 'generational change among the academic staff . . .' which could take 20 years (Hazelkorn, 2008, p. 166). Studies on research culture have focused on the kind of environment that leads to research productivity among faculty members in HEIs. The process of building the appropriate environment can be theorised as a paradigm shift comprising 'three concentric circles of change' whereby academic staff are (1) transforming their own academic practice concurrently with a (2) revolution in the strategic focus and institutional culture at a time when (3) higher education nationally and globally is itself coming under pressure to modernise, be competitive, more accountable and efficient (Hazelkorn, 2008).

This chapter argues that there are particular characteristics of academic work and institutional culture in UASs across Europe. Divided into three sections, the first two sections describe (1) academic employment conditions across selected UASs and (2) the teaching and research environment. Finally, (3) discusses the tensions and challenges that arise as UASs attempt to develop a research culture. The chapter draws variously on a subset of country experiences, e.g. Belgium, the Czech Republic, Finland, Germany, Ireland, The Netherlands, Norway and Portugal, and explores the extent to which these developments transcend institutions and countries and should be considered part of a wider sectoral experience. Finally, because UASs – despite differences in origin and mission – are competing with universities for research funding and prestige, comparisons, where appropriate, between sectors will help contextualise the UAS experience.

Comparison of Academic Employment in UASs

For many UASs, research is a relatively new mission objective, and for most academic staff, research competence is a new condition of employment. 'Typically [they came] . . . from work experience in their profession rather than the traditional academic progression from doctoral student to apprentice academic' (Adams, 2000). Many had a taught (or non-research) master's degree in disciplines which were new, and often without a strong academic focus or research ethos (Gellert, 1994). In some disciplines such as nursing, media, art, design, architecture, social work and social care, postgraduate qualifications are only recently becoming the norm (Jones & Lengkeek, 1997), and the development of a research culture with internationally agreed academic outputs is still under discussion. As a consequence, many inherited academics – those associated with the original institutional mission – lack the appropriate research background or experience and/or have limited capacity to produce the obligatory outcomes at the requisite level or compete for funding.

Given their origin and mission, it is not surprising that research has not been a precondition for appointment. Most countries continue to require an undergraduate qualification supplemented with appropriate practical or professional experience. Only relatively recently has the master's degree become a prerequisite for career advancement in Portugal, the Czech Republic or Ireland. Candidates must produce verifiable evidence of publications or other scholarly activity, albeit institutions have discretion in most circumstances. This is similar for most senior positions in all countries, such as the *lector* who leads a 'knowledge circle' in The Netherlands or the senior lecturer in Ireland. Portugal's new funding formula (2006), which is tied to indicators such as the educational level or the percentage of academic staff holding a PhD, has contributed to changing the profile (Taylor, Graca, de Lourdes Machado, & Sousa, 2007). In Belgium, seniority combined with useful professional experience is required for promotion to most posts, albeit promotion to professor requires that the college itself must be actively involved in scientific research in co-operation with a university within the field of the vacancy and that the candidate must have been a lecturer, senior lecturer or assistant professor for 6 years at a college or university and, during that time, have been responsible for quality research (Verhoeven & Beuselinck, 1999; Verhoeven, 2008, p. 52). This trend is likely to accelerate under the academisation process now underway in Belgium, and similar processes in other countries.

Hence, the qualifications profile is changing, slowly and unevenly across the sector. While national differences and institutional self-reporting make direct comparison difficult, the percentage of academics with a PhD is still quite low (see Table 5.1). Yet even these levels are straining traditional collegial relationships and creating a culture clash between departments within the institutions and between staff. Departments offering vocational programmes are likely to recruit individuals with high levels of practical and professional skills whereas other departments, in the same institution, offering more academic or advanced level programmes, are likely to require a PhD and research experience. In these circumstances, it is not uncommon for different attitudes and assumptions about academic work to emerge, not just between individuals but also in discussions about priorities and academic procedures and policies.

Table 5.1 Indicative research competence of UAS academic staff

Country	Percentage of academic staff with a PhD	Comments
Belgium	10% (2004) (Estimation)	Based on total teaching staff
Finland	6.4% (2004)	Based on total teaching staff
Ireland	9–11% (2007)	IOTI (2008, p. 17)[a]
The Netherlands	3.7% (2007)	Based on total teaching staff
Norway	20% (2008)	Based on permanent academic staff
Portugal	11% (2005)	Public institutions only
Switzerland	16% (2008)	Includes only professors and researchers, excludes teachers (most of them external)

[a]This reflects the percentage of 'academic staff in research' which is the closest data available in Ireland.

Because reputation is often closely aligned to institutional and personal status, academic nomenclature is important. Many countries continue to use language which appears closer to the secondary sector from which many UASs emerged. Unlike the university sector which has been for further education subjected to greater globalising and homogenising processes over the decades, there is no agreed terminology, appointment process or criteria for appointment for most UASs. Portugal uses the generic term 'professor' to refer to all academic staff, but the Czech Republic and Germany use professorial or 'docent' – which often refers to teaching staff usually not holding a PhD – for higher grades, while entry grades are referred to as teacher and *lector*. Finland, The Netherlands and Ireland use the term lecturer, albeit in the latter there are different pre-noms to indicate the level, e.g. assistant or Lecturer 1, 2 or 3, respectively. There is no apparent correlation between qualification level and terminology, as the Finnish example illustrates, but there is arguably a perceived differentiated status being conferred upon UAS academics. These subtle distinctions can influence academic behaviour and institutional culture – and importantly how UAS academics are viewed by university peers.

Despite retaining many of the virtues of public or civil service employment, most countries lack a promotional or US-style tenure track process which provides a transparent career path with standardised procedures clearly indicating what it takes to be successful (Enders & de Weert, 2004, pp. 12–14). Many countries, e.g. Germany and the Czech Republic, have quite rigid systems which invest considerable professional status and benefits in professorial staff while restricting opportunities, including progression and promotion, to younger academics. In others, such as Portugal and Ireland, career grades and promotional processes are determined by the government and national negotiations. There are a restricted number of posts per institution, and new appointments or promotional opportunities only arise once a vacancy occurs. The new position is then advertised openly. In Ireland, promotion beyond senior lecturer requires stepping outside of teaching and research to take up a management type position, e.g. Head of Department or Head of School – in other words, there is no academic career path. These mechanisms have contributed to a structure with little opportunity to appraise and reward individual performance – contributing to difficulties recruiting and retaining ambitious academics (Taylor et al., 2007). In sharp contrast, Norway and Belgium both have career tracks. Norway's policy of treating universities and university colleges equally has resulted in a common career structure (1995) with promotion to professorship based on research competence (Olsen, Kyvik, & Hovdhaugen, 2005, see also Chapter 12). While the senior lecturer and lecturer are predominantly teaching positions with the possibility of doing some research, permanent academic positions are associate professor and professor, which combine teaching and research positions.

Permanent contracts appear to be quite common in most UASs. Two thirds of UAS academic staff in Belgium and Finland are permanent while the proportion is closer to 90% in The Netherlands and Norway (Enders, 2001, p. 14) and 94% in Germany (RIHE, 2008, p. 142). Portugal is exceptional in that only 6% of academic staff in polytechnics, compared to 59% in universities, are permanent (Taylor et al., 2007). In contrast, most Finnish junior academics work on short-term contracts because their funding comes from external sources (Välimaa, 2001, pp. 83, 85), while there has also been widespread use of temporary or contract appointments – some on a semester or hourly rate, in the Czech Republic and Ireland, respectively. Recent EU Directives on Part-time and Fixed Term employment have sought to eliminate the worst excesses by harmonising employment conditions between part-time, temporary and full-time permanent appointments (EU, 1997, 1999).

Traditionally, the participation of women in academic life has been low, particularly in the higher grades. According to Enders and de Weert (2004, p. 16), the overall

> percentage of women [in higher education] dwindles by career stages, particularly in the tenured positions. Their progress in a scientific career is slower compared to men and their numbers start to rarefy climbing the ladder of responsibilities. It is clear that much talent is getting lost.

This trend is apparent in the countries under consideration here but again the pattern is more complicated. In Norway, 46% of academic staff in the state colleges are female, but only 17% of the full professors and 30% of associate professors are women. The same pattern can be found in Belgium (Flanders): 49% of staff are female but only 8% of the full professors and 11% of the assistant professors. Comparable figures for the largest Institute of Technology (IoT) in Ireland show females comprise 34% of the total academic population but 24% at Head of Department/School and Director (VP) level. Yet, a recent survey of challenges to research at the same IoT also indicated that gender was not a prominent concern. Below the macro level, divergence is more apparent and discipline-related. With feminisation of disciplines, e.g. media, social sciences, nursing, art and design, languages, many UASs ironically have a positive track record. In Portugal, male academics constitute 58% of the total workforce (2002) with 78% of engineering academics while females are 65% of those in education faculties (Taylor et al., 2007).

The Teaching and Research Environment

Given the history and mission of UASs, the emphasis has been and continues to be on practice-based vocational/professional teaching and learning at the bachelor or sub-degree level although this is changing and more postgraduate programmes are being offered. Class-sizes have tended to reflect this, but student/staff ratios have usually been higher in UASs compared with universities. In Belgium, the ratio is broadly similar across all HEIs. Ireland is atypical, with a significantly lower student/staff ratio in UASs than universities, although the gap is likely to be reduced under new (2008) funding arrangements. At the same time, student contact levels and workloads have usually been higher across the UAS sector than in universities. Despite greater emphasis on research which has impacted on and altered promotional criteria, workload patterns have remained relatively static and/or grade-related. While university academic staff teach, on average, only 40% of the time, UAS academic staff can teach as much as 90% of the time (Belgium, Germany and Ireland). This represents approximately 16–18 plus teaching hours per week (Ireland) compared with research-oriented universities which average 6 h/week (Portugal); others teach somewhere between these two bands (see Enders & Teichler, 1997; Adams, 2000; Gellert, 1994).

While the level of interest in research and the time spent varies across countries, different institutions within each country and between different academics, the key distinction between universities and UASs is that the latter do not have an explicit allocation of research time. The Czech Republic allows teaching load to reduce with increasing academic rank whereas Finland, Ireland, The Netherlands and Belgium allow decisions to be made at institutional or sub-institutional level as long as the budget allows. This is not without problems; for example, Belgium trade union pressure to reduce the number of contract positions has discouraged academics temporarily swapping teaching or research time. The need for greater flexibility is increasingly manifest as institutions struggle to develop the appropriate research environment. Reforms in Finland introduced at the beginning of 1999 aimed to make the allocation of a teacher's time between academic tasks and duties more accommodating. In the Czech Republic, teaching time decreases with academic rank, while Dutch academic staff who belong to a knowledge (or research) centre can get reduced teaching loads (de Weert, 2001). Belgium provides opportunities for a professor to leave his/her position for some years to conduct research and come back later. It is also not uncommon for external research funds to be used to buy-out teaching time or make changes in the timetable.

Only the Norwegian government has stipulated that undertaking research is neither an individual duty nor right, but an institutional responsibility. Hence university colleges are required by law to determine the annual work programme for each individual in accordance with competences albeit all academics have a responsibility to keep 'themselves abreast of developments in their own field and those skills in which students are to be trained'. These guidelines were challenged in 1995 when a common career structure across the universities and state colleges was introduced. However, the Norwegian Parliament stated it was 'reasonable that academic staff who work within the same field and at the same level, over time shall have the same working conditions independent of institutional type' (see Chapter 12).

The combination of high student/staff ratios and teaching loads has been blamed for why UAS academics do not/cannot invest sufficient time in research. This may reflect different academic cultures and the way in which academic work is viewed. For example, colleagues in universities see themselves performing several interrelated tasks: teaching, research and service, but UAS academic staff do not always share this view. They were appointed originally to a teaching-only role in an institution which did not prioritise research or scholarship (see Berrell, 1998). And, because many older academic staff were hired at a time when their institution was predominantly or only focused on vocational education, the new environment represents a substantial change in their working conditions. Many have a trade union

Table 5.2 Indicative percentage of work time spent on teaching (average across all grades)[a]

	Percentage of work time spent on teaching	
Country	Universities	UASs
Belgium	40%	90%
Finland	43%	74%
Germany	40%	90%
Ireland	40%	80–90%
The Netherlands	40%	60–80%
Norway[b]	42%	58%
Portugal[c]	6–9 h/week	6–12 h/week
Switzerland	40%	51%

Source: Information provided by contributing authors to this book.
[a]The percentages are calculated using the following formula: (1 h teaching = 1 h preparation/40 h/week) × 100. This calculation was not deemed applicable to Portuguese institutions.
[b]These percentages are self-reported by academic staff in mail surveys. Teaching includes time for supervision of PhD students.
[c]Information on Portuguese polytechnics and universities refers to the public institutions only.

attitude towards their careers and workloads, and enjoy relatively long summer holidays. This is the case in Belgium and Ireland. In the former instance, the law guarantees each university college teacher at least 9 weeks holidays, and seniority might expand this, whereas in Ireland academics finish work on the 20 June and do not return until 1 September. In Germany, professors and academic staff at *fachhochschulen* work 40 h/week compared to university professors who work 52 h/week (RIHE, 2008, p. 139).While there has been a noticeable cultural shift among some academics, the holidays carry little or no stipulation or expectation that this non-teaching period should be used for research – unlike colleagues in universities.

Due to their history and mission, UASs have inevitably had limited resources for research but now find themselves competing directly with universities because of changed circumstances. As such, they have been less attractive to research-active scholars, and have tended to spend significant resources and time on staff development. This is due to the fact that many academic staff have neither the experience nor research prerequisites and require much greater institutional support than colleagues in universities would require or expect. The acquisition of a PhD, however, does not alone guarantee the transition to research active status – thereby raising questions about whether the time and resources spent on staff development represents value-for-money. Because of the arguably less favourable or more restrictive funding model under which UASs operate, there are also fewer resources available for research support, including sabbaticals. As the percentage of the government core grant declines across most European countries, academics are pressurised to earn a greater proportion or all of their research funding competitively. This is the case in Belgium, Germany, Ireland and Norway. In Ireland, because the government grant has (until 2008) been on the basis of teaching hours, there has been an institutional disincentive or penalty for encouraging too much research time.

Despite changes in policy and new demands on UAS institutions to develop research capacity and capability, there has been little additional or targeted funding given to them. German *fachhochschulen* were specifically excluded from competing for the Excellence Initiative. In contrast, Belgium *hogescholen* receive a special academisation grant, and targeted research funds have been available for Irish IoTs. UAS focus on teaching over research has also influenced the type and quality of the facilities which they have. Libraries, laboratories and office space are regularly cited as no longer fit-for-purpose (see Table 5.3). While it may seem reasonable to argue that if UASs want to devote resources to research, this must come from the teaching allocation, given their historic, mission, governance and funding circumstances this demand poses a particularly steep 'barrier to entry' at a time when competition is accelerating (Hazelkorn, 2005).

Table **5.3** Comparison of resources for research

Country	Research facilities	Research funding	Staff development
Belgium	No office accommodation; most academics work at home. Research units comparable to university labs but too few. Libraries small	'Envelope' of funds index-linked to unit costs and consumer prices. Lump sum plus other funding from competitive sources until 2013	Education/research programmes available through university associations. PhD programmes available in universities
Czech Republic	Disadvantage partially alleviated by focus on 'inexpensive' disciplines. Libraries not research focused	No dedicated research funding available. Competitive project funding open to all HEIs	National staff development framework, which leaves little leeway for institutions
Finland	Because there are few science fields, main requirement is library services but this is poorly resourced	Polytechnics receive project-based funding for joint ventures to gradually develop R&D	Depends upon and varies between institutions

Table 5.3 (continued)

Country	Research facilities	Research funding	Staff development
Germany	Less funding with comparably poorer facilities than universities	Public funds generally a lump sum; most *Länder* have small output-based funding budgets of 2–3% total public budget	No specific facilities in UASs
Ireland	Relatively poor quality facilities and libraries	Core grant based on teaching hours plus small dedicated head-start grant. Open competition for research funding with universities	In service training is matter for institution. Support for PhD programmes, and research and supervisor training
The Netherlands	Infrastructure for research very limited	Institutions funded via formula-based lump sum, but there are special schemes for research funding	Institutional responsibility within national collective labour agreement. Regulations for study facilities and staff development
Norway	Library and administration support good, but lab equipment poor	Research undertaken within core annual budget but engage in contract research to maintain level of operations	PhD and senior lecturer programmes. PhD programmes available in universities
Switzerland	Reasonably good laboratory equipment, facilities and informatics equipment, as well as administrative support	External funding through contract with companies and public institutions; UASs provide infrastructure and to some extent time for research	Mostly on-site training to research, limited offer of courses

Issues and Challenges

If massification and expansion in the 1960s differentiated the second stage in higher educational development from its elite origins, then the late 1990s marked the beginning of the third stage. By then, it was clear that a broadly educated population could no longer be formed by and within universities alone. Similarly, Europe's continuing aim to be a/the leader in the global knowledge economy has highlighted the necessity to involve all HEIs in research, development and innovation (RDI) if this ambition is to be realised. These challenges are huge, particularly for UASs which, as already discussed, have emerged from and with a different tradition. Some governments, such as Norway, have made research an institutional responsibility, while The Netherlands, Ireland and Belgium have targeted particular resources and/or policies to help give a head-start. But, the challenge is not just at the institutional level; more is expected of academic staff. The transition from vocational teaching to research-informed professional education requires a substantial transformation in academic culture.

Studies on developing a research culture have focused on the complex inter-relationship between attitudes and behaviour which is reinforced through the organisational culture. Pratt et al. (1999, p. 46) argue that it is not 'sufficient for a dean or department chair to try to change people's attitudes towards research ... rather, whole sets of beliefs must be changed'. A recent qualitative study in an Irish IoT questioned academic staff on performance measures and found the majority (9/17) cited student numbers as the main performance measure despite research (cited by 2/17) being a key element of the institutional strategy (Lillis, 2007, p. 3). To be successful in cultivating a research ethos requires alignment and shared beliefs across the organisation, concerning academic work and requirements for performance and success in order to create the kind of environment that leads to high research productivity.

Challenges for Staff and Institutions

Despite introducing new appointment and promotional criteria and procedures, the percentage of academic researchers with a PhD in the various UASs remains low. All UASs provide staff development opportunities but such processes may not be sufficient or always suitable to overcome these difficulties. Indeed, the time spent acquiring the appropriate research qualification – in other words a PhD – could be counterbalanced by a recruitment strategy both in terms of time spent and money. Even if UASs are successful in recruiting a significant number of younger, more active and internationally engaged researchers, the strategy could destabilise the organisation: older, existing staff may feel aggrieved that they have been overlooked or marginalised while the latter may feel restricted by the prevailing culture or critical of the pace of change, e.g. inadequate physical environment, the quality and/or quantity of research space. Many of the former may also be concerned about how the changes and new demands will impact on her/his own workload, position, promotional and career opportunities and the balance between teaching and research. This person is likely to be a product of the institution's history and a potential contributor to its future, but her/his willingness to engage in research may also be contingent upon the supports and rewards that the institution offers (Hazelkorn, 2005, 2008). The lack of sufficient resources restricts an institution's ability to respond appropriately and speedily – a situation often aggravated by perceived lower status of UASs vis-à-vis universities which has hampered their ability to earn funding via philanthropy or partnerships. But regardless, the real challenge is to find the appropriate balance between staff development and recruitment, without severely unsettling the body politic. This can be difficult as the requirements and expectations of the different academic staff can be in conflict.

The actual work environment is often cited as another constricting factor but the situation is not necessarily straightforward. According to Bland and Ruffin (1992) one factor present in high performance research environments is 'appropriate rewards' and peer recognition. While it is unclear the extent to which the lack of a clear career path or specific contractual arrangements actually discourage UAS academics to be research active, the work environment is generally perceived as being more restrictive and less welcoming and rewarding to openly ambitious individuals than would be the case in universities. Rigid career structures are also seen to contribute to difficulties recruiting and retaining ambitious and prolific academics. Ultimately, it may be the intangible reputational and status factors, which are associated with UAS positioning nationally and globally, which influence and impact most on institutional and academic behaviour.

Many UAS staff complain about the lack of esteem for research or sufficient research time. While there is little doubt that the resources available are more limited, the issue may be one of better use of resources and time management. As Pratt et al., 1999, p. 51) observe, 'it was possible, during the 26 weeks of the teaching year, to arrange their teaching in a way that left 1 day each week free of teaching commitments as a "research day"'. Likewise, the time spent on holidays by Irish IoT academics is peculiar to their historic position and would be more akin to secondary teachers than university colleagues. Some individuals have sought to resolve tensions between 'excessive' teaching workloads and research by seeking to buy themselves out of teaching through competitive grants or pursuing research-only positions. Ironically, this solution could be the Achilles heel of the

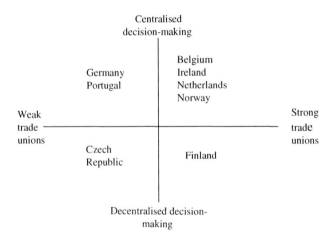

Fig. 5.1 Regulating employment relationships

teaching–research nexus, breaking the link between teaching and research by encouraging special arrangements for research-active staff.

The trend towards greater institutional autonomy, making institutions and academic staff more accountable, increasing academic productivity and creating greater flexibility in the academic workforce has been evident in the university sector for some time as a result of competitive and marketisation pressures but has been evolving more slowly in UASs (Kyvik et al., 2001). This is largely due to their governance model, which has emerged as part of a top-down binary structure of mission differentiation. Germany, Portugal, Belgium, Ireland, The Netherlands and Norway retain much of this tradition, with a strong centralised decision-making structure, albeit there is some variation in trade union strength. Fig. 5.1 illustrates the different models, drawing upon the work of Kahn-Freund (1977). This scenario has hindered the ability of these institutions to develop human resource strategies and policies appropriate to their institutional challenges. Changes could benefit academics who wish to excel not least because existing policies have tended to dampen down dynamism and personal ambition by treating all academics equally and rewarding seniority rather than merit. New policies challenge this notion. Resolution of these tensions could involve reaching a new understanding of what constitutes academic work, with the respective trade union, which could have implications for institutional mission. Yet, doing nothing is not an option because it is uncertain how new ambitions can be realised without such action.

While it is neither possible nor desirable to convert all academic staff into active researchers, it is vital to embed research activity as a professional norm within the institutional culture from the moment of appointment and certainly prior to promotion. Most UASs appear to be following this pattern, focusing on staff development initiatives developing appropriate facilities and other incentives in order to attain high performance. Organisationally they are preferencing interdisciplinary and collaborative teams in order to build sustainable critical mass. However, UASs struggle to attain the necessary balance of cultural coherence, not least because their governance structure retains many historically restrictive practices and comprise many inherited staff recruited for a different purpose with a different vision of the institution and their academic work. Their ability to present a clear, unfettered vision and mission is not always possible, contributing to confused and conflicting messages.

The challenge is to develop a research policy and agenda mapped against its own mission and competences, rather than sending mixed-messages to academic staff by seeking to ape the agenda of traditional universities. But this means making choices in ways they may not previously have encountered or anticipated. What is the best way to motivate, mentor and facilitate research-active faculty while ensuring that teaching-focused academic staff do not feel marginalised? What is the appropriate balance between recruiting new academic staff or helping existing academics develop research competence? Should research be a key criterion in appointment and promotion or would it be better to establish dual or parallel career paths, and if so, what impact would this have on the institutional mission? Because funding is limited, is it best to support research active staff or try to boost the performance of the greatest number?

Challenges for Government

Drawing on the experience of UASs across Europe, it seems clear that while there are distinct national contexts and circumstances which cannot be ignored, there are sufficient similarities to suggest that the experiences cross national boundaries and operate almost irrespective of the political party in power. UASs face many challenges associated with their status and their late entry into the research world. Creating the appropriate research environment and culture is dependent upon a cluster of factors and is not simply the result of a single aspect or condition of employment. A key ingredient is the role of policy, but it is not clear the extent to which governments fully understand what a strategy for diversity of mission actually entails. Many governments continue to use language which unwittingly confers differentiated status.

At its simplest, many governments have historically used regulatory mechanisms to enforce differentiation between vocational and academic education. When that model was no longer fit-for-purpose, some governments, e.g. the UK, sought to reconstruct a new binary between teaching and research institutions. Underpinning some of the indecisiveness is the realisation that global competition for research excellence – as exemplified by worldwide rankings – is pushing up the cost of the reputation race. Given mounting pressures on the public purse, governments are struggling with whether to concentrate research activity in a few universities or to recognise and support research excellence wherever it occurs. Another problem arises over confusion about what constitutes research. While advocating the importance of applied research, policy and evaluation language privileges expensive basic scientific discovery conducted in research-intensive universities and ignores the intellectual and strategic importance of collaborative and interdisciplinary work focused on useful application conducted by UASs with external partners including the wider community (Gibbons et al., 1994).

As higher education systems, nationally and internationally, become more competitive, barriers to entry are rising. Experience strongly supports the view that challenges experienced by UASs, and their staff, are not likely to be overcome by conventional means. In other words, without active and selective use of policy instruments, UASs will find it increasingly difficult if not impossible to overcome barriers to entry because 'the pecking order of research activities is not easy to change' (Hazelkorn, 2005, p. 138). Such actions should include removing many of the legislative and other constraints which currently curtail or restrict the operation and development of UASs. Finland stands out with the greatest percentage of PhDs, the most time for research and a legislative expectation that teachers and students participate in research while Norway has a common career structure with similar conditions of employment; UASs in The Netherlands have a distinctive research function supported by all major stakeholders with the capacity to award end of year bonuses, albeit they have the lowest number of academics with a PhD. National comparisons are complicated, but evidence suggests a strong correlation between institutional autonomy, performance pay, flexibility in salary negotiation and national support for research with research productivity. This would correspond with the conclusions of a recent report which argued that research productive institutions enjoy considerable institutional autonomy (Aghion, Dewatripont, Hoxby, Mas-Colell, & Sapir, 2008, p. 50) to define goals, allocate research time and resources and reward research performance.

Conclusion

Global competition has pushed higher education to the centre of national economic and innovation strategies. The OECD (2009) has reiterated the importance of research and innovation as key to sustainable recovery from the current economic recession, encouraging governments to channel stimulus funds to R&D, entrepreneurs and education. Building research capacity and capability is no longer optional, and human capital formation is critical to success. This refers to not just the graduates but also the academic staff. But developing a research culture is a complex and lengthy process, and considerable challenge. The experience of European UASs and their academic staff is not unique, and replicates that of colleagues in other jurisdictions, most notably the UK and Australia. It may be nuanced by national circumstance, level of maturity and cultural and political milieu, including party political and ideological perspectives, but UASs share a contested view of academic work and many characteristics of their employment conditions. The high teaching load and commitments plus basic facilities were appropriate when they were founded, but it is questionable whether they are fit for their new purpose. The situation is not, however, static. While university colleagues complain about research intensification and tighter regulation, UAS academic staff are moving towards greater flexibility under the auspices of institutional autonomy. Some governments and institutions have begun to tackle these deficiencies with greater alacrity than others – with anticipated results. This suggests that policy is critical – and that institutional action is not sufficient in itself to enable UASs to overcome the barriers to entry. At the macro level, UASs and universities are converging in their governance and management models, and are likely to meet somewhere in the centre between regulation and autonomy, between rigid and flexible structures and between research-intensive and teaching-intensive.

Acknowledgements Special thanks are due to colleagues from contributing countries for all their help assembling the comparative information, and to Brian O'Neill and Kevin Lalor for their helpful comments and suggestions during the course of writing this chapter. All errors remain ours.

References

Adams, D. (2000). Views of academic work. *Teacher Development, 4*(1), 68.
Aghion, P., Dewatripont, M., Hoxby, C., Mas-Colell, A., & Sapir, A. (2008). *Higher aspirations: An agenda for reforming European universities*. Brussels: Bruegel Blueprint Series.
Altbach, P. G. (2000). The deterioration of the academic estate: International patterns of academic work. In P. G. Altbach (Ed.), *The changing academic workplace: Comparative perspectives*

(pp. 1–33). Boston: Centre for International Higher Education, Lynch School of Education, Boston College.

Berrell, M. (1998). The place of teaching research and scholarship in newly established universities. *Higher Education Management, 10*, 77–93.

Bland, C., & Ruffin, M. (1992). Characteristics of a productive research environment: Literature review. *Academic Medicine, 67*, 385–397.

de Weert, E. (2001). The end of public employment in Dutch higher education? In J. Enders (Ed.), *Academic staff in Europe* (pp. 195–216). Westport: Greenwood Press.

EU. (1999). *European Council Directive 1999/70/EC of 28 June 1999 concerning the framework agreement on fixed-term work.* Retrieved January 29, 2008, from http://eurlex.europa.eu/smartapi/cgi/sga_doc?smartapi!celexapi!prod!CELEXnumdoc&lg=EN&numdoc=31999L0070&model=guichett.

EU. (1997). *European Council Directive 97/81/EC of 15 December 1997 concerning the Framework Agreement on part-time work.* Retrieved September 29, 2008, from http://eurlex.europa.eu/smartapi/cgi/sga_doc?smartapi!celexapi!prod!CELEXnumdoc&lg=EN&numdoc=31997L0081&model=guichett.

Enders, J. (2001). Between state control and academic capitalism: A comparative perspective on academic staff in Europe. In J. Enders (Ed.), *Academic staff in Europe* (pp. 1–23). Westport: Greenwood Press.

Enders, J., & de Weert, E. (Eds.). (2004). *The international attractiveness of the academic workplace in Europe.* Frankfurt am Main: Gewerkschaft Erzieung und Wissenschaft.

Enders, J., & Teichler, U. (1997). A victim of their own success? Employment and working conditions of academic staff in comparative perspective. *Higher Education, 34*, 347–372.

Farnham, D. (1999). Managing universities and regulating academic labour markets. In D. Farnham (Ed.), *Managing academic staff in changing university systems: International trends and comparisons* (pp.15–43). Buckingham: Society for Research into Higher Education.

Gellert, C. (1994). *Diversification in the tertiary sector – new developments in the EU's member states.* Introductory text for conference of the Federal Ministry of Education and Science, Bonn. Unpublished.

Gibbons, M., Limoges, C., Nowotny, H., Schwartzman, S., Scott, P., & Trow, M. (1994). *The new production of knowledge.* London: Sage.

Hazelkorn, E. (2005). *Developing research in new institutions.* Paris: OECD.

Hazelkorn, E. (2008). Motivating individuals: Growing research from a 'fragile base'. *Tertiary Education and Management, 14*, 151–171.

Huisman, J., de Weert, E., & Bartelse, J. (2002). A European perspective on academic careers. *Journal of Higher Education, 73*, 141–160.

IOTI – Institutes of Technology Ireland. (2008). *Framework for the development of research in the institutes of technology, 2008–2013.* Ireland: IOTI.

Jones, G., & Lengkeek, N. (1997). Research development: The experience of the new university'. *Research and the new tomorrow* (pp. 223–239). Auckland: UNITEC Institute of Technology.

Kahn-Freund, O., (1977) Labour and the Law. 2nd ed. London: Stevens.

Kyvik, S., Skodvin, O. J., Smeby, J. C., & Sundnes, S. L. (2001). Expansion, reorganization and discontent among academic staff: The Norwegian case. In J. Enders (Ed.), *Academic staff in Europe* (pp. 217–232). Westport: Greenwood Press.

Lepori, B., & Attar, L. (2006). *Research strategies and framework conditions for research in Swiss universities of applied sciences.* Lugano: KTI/CTI.

Lillis, D. (2007) Reconciling Organizational Realities with the Research Mission of the Irish Institutes of Technology. Paper presented to CHER conference. Dublin.

Marginson, S. (2000). Rethinking academic work in the global era. *Journal of Higher Education Policy and Management, 22*, 24–35.

OECD. (2009). Policy responses to the economic crisis: Investing in innovation for long-term growth. Paris. Retrieved October 23, 2009, from http://www.oecd.org/dataoecd/59/45/42983414.pdf

Olsen, T. B., Kyvik, S., & Hovdhaugen, E. (2005). The promotion to full professor – through competition or by individual competence? *Tertiary Education and Management, 11*, 299–316.

Pratt, J. (1997). *The polytechnic experiment: 1965–1992.* London: The Society for Research into Higher Education & Open University Press.

Pratt, M., Margaritis, D., & Coy, D. (1999). Developing a research culture in a university faculty. *Journal of Higher Education Policy and Management, 21*, 43–55.

Rhoades, G. (1998). *Managed professionals: Unionized faculty and restructuring academic labor.* Albany: State University of New York Press.

RIHE. (2008). *The changing academic profession in international comparative and quantitative perspectives.* Report on the international conference on the Changing Academic Profession Project, 2008. Hiroshima University, Hiroshima.

Scott, P. (1995). *The meanings of mass higher education.* Buckingham: Open University Press.

Slaughter, S., & Leslie, L. (1997). *Academic capitalism: Politics, policies, and the entrepreneurial university.* Baltimore: Johns Hopkins Press.

Taylor, J. S., Ferreira, J. B., Machado, M. L., & Santiago, R. (2008). *Non-university higher education in Europe.* Dordrecht: Springer.

Taylor, J. S., Graca, M., de Lourdes Machado, M., & Sousa, S. (2007). Portugal: Adapting in order to promote change (pp. 211–227). In W. Locke & U. Teichler (Eds.), *The changing conditions for academic work and careers in select countries.* Kassel: University of Kassel.

Välimaa, J. (2001). The changing nature of academic employment in Finnish higher education. In J. Enders (Ed.), *Academic staff in Europe* (pp. 67–89). Westport: Greenwood Press.

Välimaa, J., & Neuvonen-Rauhala, M. L. (2008). Polytechnics in Finnish higher education. In J. S. Taylor, J. B. Ferreira, M. L. Machado, & R. Santiago (Eds.), *Non-university higher education in Europe* (pp. 77–98). Dordrecht: Springer.

Verhoeven, J. C. (2008). Questioning the binary divide: Non-university higher education in Flanders (Belgium). In J. S. Taylor, J. B. Ferreira, M. L. Machado, & R. Santiago (Eds.), *Non-university higher education in Europe* (pp. 43–75). Dordrecht: Springer.

Verhoeven, J. C., & Beuselinck, I. (1999). Belgium: Diverging professions in twin communities. In D. Farnham (Ed.), *Managing academic staff in changing university systems: International trends and comparisons* (pp. 35–57). Buckingham: Open University Press.

Part III
National Case Studies

Chapter 6
Research in University Colleges in Belgium

Jef C. Verhoeven

Introduction

As in many other countries, university colleges in Belgium, are rather new, having developed mainly after the 1970s. The core business of the UCs was – and for many of the UC teachers still is – to train professionals such as accountants, industrial engineers, infant- and primary-school teachers and nurses. Scientific research was of minor importance, since it has long been considered the domain of universities. Nevertheless, in recent decades, policymakers and some UC managers and teachers have insisted that UCs should also conduct scientific research. This is expressed in the Decree of 13 July 1994 in Flanders and in the Decree of 9 September 1996 in the Francophone Community of Belgium. In spite of this definition of the responsibility of UCs, it would take a considerable amount of time to stimulate UCs to do applied scientific research.

Why did involvement in research come about so slowly? In addition to scientific research being traditionally seen to be the responsibility of the universities, the government provided little research funding for UCs. After the establishment of the federal state structure in Belgium in 1989, the federal government's responsibility for education and research changed totally: research promotion and funding became more the responsibility of the Communities and the Regions. Indeed, Belgium was split into three Communities (Dutch-speaking, French-speaking and German-speaking) and three Regions (the Flemish Region, the Walloon Region and the Brussels-Capital Region). Each of these institutions bore some responsibility for education and/or research. Before new areas of emphasis could be established, each of them wanted to establish new educational structures. One of the main objectives of the legislatures, both north and south, was to reduce the number of UCs in their Community in order to improve their organisational management. Before the decrees of the 1990s, there were hundreds of UCs spread out over the country. Flanders, the northern part of the country, established a funding system that was advantageous for large, consolidated UCs (Verhoeven, Devos, Smolders, Cools, &

J.C. Verhoeven (✉)
Centre for Sociological Research, Catholic University of Leuven, Leuven, Belgium
e-mail: Jef.Verhoeven@Soc.Kuleuven.be

S. Kyvik, B. Lepori (eds.), *The Research Mission of Higher Education Institutions Outside the University Sector*, Higher Education Dynamics 31,
DOI 10.1007/978-1-4020-9244-2_6, © Springer Science+Business Media B.V. 2010

Velghe, 2002). The policymakers of the southern part, the Francophone Community, were more lenient but also suggested consolidation. At present, Flanders has 22 UCs, while the Francophone Community finances 42. Although this merging was supposed to be advantageous for the organisation of UCs, the merging process absorbed much energy, so many did not assign research a high priority.

The legislator and UCs were also sensitive to the EU policy. The Lisbon strategy (March 2000) aims to make 'Europe, by 2010, the most competitive and the most dynamic knowledge-based economy in the world'. Education and research are key instruments for achieving this goal. Following the decision of the European Council, the Belgian government and the three Regions took measures to comply (Federaal Planbureau, 2006, p. 9), and the UCs are expected to contribute to the process. Since 2003–2004, the Bologna Process, has also greatly influenced because it was a reason for policymakers to reduce the ternary higher education system into a binary system: a professional track in the UCs of 3 years, and an academic track of 4 or more years in UCs and universities.

These European objectives have certainly given an impetus to scientific research in the UCs. Nevertheless, although UCs do more research than they did before, they still are rather modest players in this respect. To explain why they are in this position, we will describe three critical factors: first, the structure of the UCs themselves; second, the Community and Regional research policies in UCs; third, the research strategies in the UCs themselves. We will then review the research performance and conclude with some challenges for the UCs.

The Structure of the UCs

The federal structure of Belgium has put the political responsibility for the organisation of education and a large part of scientific research into the hands of the Communities and the Regions. Although the general structure of higher education in the Flemish and French-speaking Communities is rather similar, there are some differences.

In both Communities alike, UC education is divided into two tracks. Although each Community uses a different terminology, the structure is similar. One stream, the professional, offers education for a professional bachelor's degree, which is a one-cycle programme (3 years). No master programme is offered to these students. The other, the academic stream, offers training for the academic bachelor's degree (3 years) and the master's degree (1 or 2 years), which is a two-cycle programme. It is now possible for a student to move from one stream to another and also to the university, although he or she sometimes is required to pass an admission test to do so. Before the merging process, the UCs generally offered no more than one field of study. At present, they can offer different fields of study. In spite of these similarities between the two Communities, there are also important differences, one being the average size of the institutions: for the 2006–2007 academic year, there were 1,802 students per UC in the south and 4,810 in the north. Another is the structure for the collaboration between the UCs and the universities.

The Flemish Community has opted for a strong degree of harmonisation of the UC academic track with those of the universities. Policymakers expect that the two-cycle academic (bachelor's and master's) programmes of UCs will be 'academised' by 2012–2013. What does this mean? UCs should present a detailed planning to guarantee that all academic courses are based on scientific research. They have also to ensure that the teaching staff are engaged in scientific research. They should develop an evaluation system for this process and report on the use of the special funding for this process. The accreditation organisation NVAO (*Nederlands-Vlaamse Accreditatieorganisatie*: Netherlands-Flanders Accreditation Organisation) will determine whether this objective has been attained. To achieve this, the UCs can associate themselves with a university. Such an association is an independent body specially founded to realise this academisation process. All of the UCs belong to such an association, the meeting place for coordinating the education and research of all of its members. Five associations have been established, the largest of which accounts for about 70,000 students and the smallest for about 8,000. The rectors of the universities (unlike some years ago) speak of integrating the UCs into the universities. The Flemish government has also taken steps in that direction by supporting the establishment in 2007 of the HUB (*Hogeschool-Universiteit-Brussel*) in Brussels, for which some departments of two UCs and one university in Brussels merged. It offers academic master's degrees. Whether or not the accredited two-cycle programmes will become part of the university system has yet to be determined by law (Boon, 2007–2008).

The French Community also favours a rapprochement between the universities and the UCs although its approach has been less coercive than in Flanders. In the French Community, three 'academies' were established, each academy being composed of two or more universities. An academy is an independent legal entity with its own financial resources but without any personnel (they are provided by the member universities). Academies organise the PhD programmes, may grant a PhD degree, establish graduate schools, organise complimentary master's training and a centre for didactics. Moreover, they can take initiatives in order to organise education, research and social services in the academy. In addition to these academies, three 'poles' have been established in which UCs can enter into agreements with the university members concerning education and research, but the UC members of a 'pole' remain independent.

In 2005–2006, Belgian UCs enrolled 188,883 students and the universities 141,841. This number is still rising, though slowly. If the students in the academic stream would be removed from the UCs and counted as university students (which is not as yet the case), the number of enrolments in universities would be 185,383 and in the UCs 145,341 (Vlaams Ministerie van Onderwijs en Vorming, 2006; Ministère de la Communauté Française, 2006). Some policymakers in Flanders prefer (hope for) this development, but this cannot occur without new legislative steps. In the Francophone Community, policy makers are more hesitant.

National Research Policy with Regard to UCs

Strategic Goals and Guidelines for Research

About 27% of the national research budget in 2006 was in the hands of the federal government (CFS, 2007). The rest of the research budget was the responsibility of the Communities and the Regions. Consequently, most of the UCs' research funding is provided by the Communities and/or the Regions. Although the Communities and the Regions make their own policy, they share some common strategies. For instance, they agreed with the Lisbon strategy to allocate 3% of the GDP for research in 2010 (High Level Group 3% Belgium, 2005). Whether this will actually occur is, as yet, uncertain.

Although UCs do not enjoy much of the federal research funding, they follow the federal policy, which is supported by the Communities and the Regions (Federaal Wetenschapsbeleid, 2007), the main providers of funding. In order to meet the target of 3%, the federal government has opted for the following: the expansion of public expenditure for R&D, special support for collaboration between private entrepreneurs and public entities, collaboration between federal and regional advisory councils, the increase of research funding in institutions of higher education, the creation of networks of excellence, financial promotion for collaboration between private entrepreneurs and institutions of higher education, a decrease of taxes on salaries for researchers, programmes to attract young researchers and other measures (CFS, 2005).

Very important for the growth of research in Flemish UCs is the academisation policy (Vandenbroucke, 2006, p. 58), the increased funding by other ministries and the supportive advice for the UCs by the Flemish Council for Science policy (Vlaamse Raad voor Wetenschapsbeleid, 2004).

The Francophone Community of Belgium has a similar policy, although it has no explicit academisation policy as in Flanders. In this Community, the responsible Ministers created several programmes to expand the research capacity of the UCs. The idea behind the establishment of the university 'poles' (pôles universitaires) is to generate synergy between the UCs and the universities for research. Moreover, many of the sources for funding of research in UCs stress collaboration between UCs and industry (Région Wallonne, Communauté Française, 2005).

In both parts of the country, the collaboration between universities and UCs is supposed to contribute to the development of the professional expertise of established and young teachers in the UCs (Teachers in this chapter refers to UC statutory staff who might teach and conduct research). Whereas the emphasis in universities is more on fundamental research, UC researchers are more focused on applied research and collaboration with local industry.

Priority Setting Between Teaching and Research

Since the legislation passed in the 1990s, teaching, applied research and social service provision were stipulated by the government to be the core business of UCs, but in practice attention was mainly paid to teaching. Indeed, the government in both parts of the country did not provide much money to do research. At this time, while research was stressed more than before, the government did not want to make a list of priorities. How UCs use the available time for research or teaching is their responsibility, although the law in the Francophone Community determines how many hours each rank has to teach in a year. However, the academisation programme in Flanders has certainly put some pressure on the two-cycle programmes to invest more in research than they had been doing. Further, themes of research that deserve priority are proposed by the *Conseil de la politique scientifique de la Communauté Française* in Francophone Belgium and the *Vlaamse Raad voor Wetenschapsbeleid* (VRWB) in Flanders (VRWB, 2004). Both stress the importance of collaboration between the UCs and the universities and industry.

The Funding of Research

Within the framework of the Barcelona objectives, the member countries are expected to spend 3% of their GDP on R&D in 2010. In 2005, Belgium spent 1.86% of its GDP on R&D (Federaal Wetenschapsbeleid, 2007) and has still much to do to attain the 3% goal. Higher education provided a small part of it. Universities spent 0.4% of the GDP, and UCs 0.01% (CFS, 2005). The main contribution to R&D in Belgium comes from private enterprises. Higher education provides only 21.1% of the R&D expenditure in Belgium (2007), and only a small part of this is provided by UCs. In the year 2000, UCs spent only 2.4% of the research money spent by universities. In 2007, this percentage increased to 4.6%.

The UCs differ not only in having less money to spend for R&D than universities but also in the importance assigned to the domains of research (Federaal Wetenschapsbeleid, 2007). In UCs, no money is available for natural sciences, whereas natural sciences take 22.4% of the total budget in the universities. In the UCs, 45% of the expenditure is provided for engineering followed by the social sciences and the humanities. In universities, medical and natural sciences lead followed by engineering and the social sciences.

The positive picture is that the research budget of the UCs in comparison with 2002 increased by 83% in 2007. While the UCs could apply for more money than before, some of the resources could be used only conditionally.

For example, the Francophone Community has specially created for UCs the programme *FIRST Hautes Écoles* (1991), and 'mobilising programmes' that have to be shared with others. Applications have to be made in co-operation and/or in competition with others. Moreover, UC researchers can apply for funding from the FNRS (National Foundation for Scientific Research), which previously served only the universities (Graitson, 2006).

The Flemish Community offers also special funding for research in UCs. *Projectmatig Wetenschappelijk Onderzoek* (project-oriented research) and TETRA provide only or mainly funding for UCs, although for the latter a co-operation with the local industry is a condition (Van Looy et al., 2006). Moreover, since 2003, 17 out of the 22 UCs have been receiving a special academisation credit for the two-cycle programmes (gradually growing from about €15 million per year in 2006 to about €30 million in 2009) bringing the research budget from €33 million in 2005 to €45.5 million in 2006 and €57.7 million in 2007. Within the new financing system of the UCs, starting in 2008, these special credits will stop in 2012. From then on (if the two-cycle programme is accredited), many expect that the UCs will be able to rely on the much larger research grants for universities, but this has to be confirmed by a new law. Others fear that this might impair the critical mass necessary for fundamental research. In addition to these sources, the UCs can also apply for funding in collaboration with universities and/or industry within several other programmes. There is very little participation in European research programmes (Van Ryssen, Van Pelt, & Wuyts, 2007, p. 155, Debackere & Veugelers, 2007, p. 20).

The UCs are free to apply for research funding. No limits are determined by the governments, except that the Flemish UCs that provide two-cycle degrees will have to prove in 2012–2013 that they have a research output that meets the demands of the accreditation organisation NVAO. Until now, neither the law nor the NVAO has published clear standards for determining the academisation level. In order to have some guidance, associations refer to the advice of the *Werkgroep Academisering* (Dekelver, 2007; Gysen et al., 2006; Spruyt, Tan, & Van Dyck, 2005–2006).

The Research Strategies in UCs

Although research was not the primary concern of the UCs in the 1990s, the wish of some UC staff and also the Bologna Process has opened the prospects for more research in UCs. This was not an obvious objective, which is confirmed by the low figures of Table 6.1. Even though the legal structure had already been accepted by the parliaments in 2003 and 2004, the amount of research money spent by UCs is still low. In the meantime, this has changed for the better, more in the Flemish (because of the academisation policy) than in the Francophone Community. To check whether this new policy can introduce a change in the research behaviour of UCs, we conducted case studies (November 2007–January 2008) of one association in Flanders and one pole in the Francophone Community in which the universities are strongly research-orientated. In each, we studied two UCs. For an overview of the research strategy during the 1990s we rely on previous research.

The Flemish association with 12 UCs in this study is the largest in Flanders (about 70,000 students) and is involved with a research-oriented university. Two of these UCs were studied in some detail. One offers only professional bachelor degrees (later A1), and the second (later A2) offers two-cycle programmes in addition to professional bachelor's programmes. Each of these UCs has slightly fewer than 5,000 students enrolled. Unlike most of the other UCs, A2 has more than 25 years of research experience and accounts for a fifth of the about €26 million research money allocated to all of the UCs of the association in 2006. A1 had a research budget of €600,000 in 2007.

The Francophone pole (about 35,000 students) is linked to an *académie* composed of three universities, but the pole itself consists of one university, one

Table 6.1 R&D expenditure in UCs and universities in Belgium (2001–2007) by domain of research (in per cent and € million in current prices)

	2001		2003		2005		2007	
	UCs	Universities	UCs	Universities	UCs	Universities	UCs	Universities
Natural sciences	–	24.7	–	22.8	–	22.1	–	21.4
Engineering	54.1	16.0	47.6	16.0	48.1	16.0	45.3	17.5
Medical sciences	3.8	24.5	7.2	24.5	7.6	26.8	6.8	27.7
Agricultural sciences	17.5	10.9	11.9	11.2	7.9	10.7	6.5	9.6
Social sciences	15.4	16.2	20.0	17.6	20.4	16.8	26.1	15.8
Humanities	9.1	7.7	13.2	7.9	15.9	7.6	15.2	8.0
Sum	100	100	100	100	100	100	100	100
€ million	25.3	1,013.6	33.7	1,087.6	36.2	1,174.2	57.7	1,251.6

Source: Commissie Federale Samenwerking, Overleggroep CFS/STAT (CFS, 2009).

university institution, five UCs, two schools for architecture and four art schools. Two of the UCs, each with about 2,000 students, were examined. Both of the UCs offer professional bachelor's programmes and academic master's programmes. Although this pole mentions as one of its targets to 'guarantee and reinforce the complementarity of the research of the university and the UCs', it has hitherto focused more on educational co-operation. Therefore, the research collaboration between the university and the two observed UCs is on a personal basis. Between 2004 and 2007, P1 had a research budget of at least €800,000. One research unit of P2 has a research tradition that goes back to the nineteenth century. According to the director, his unit has at its disposal 50% (or about €2 million in 2006) of the research money provided by the Walloon Region to UCs for research. This unit had occupied its strong position already before the Bologna Process had begun.

This focus on more research-oriented UCs in these case studies reveals that many UCs cannot attain that level of research. Nevertheless, focusing on research-oriented colleges might unveil what UCs can do in the field of research if they act like the more experienced colleges.

In this section, we will discuss five issues: The institutional strategy of the UCs, the organisation and management of research, the collaboration with universities and industry, human resources and careers and the allocation of the research resources.

Institutional Strategy and Priority Setting

In many of the UCs, research was a choice made by individual researchers. While some of the more established research units had formulated an institutional strategy, most had not. This has changed now in Flanders because of the academisation process. Association A has set up a research council in which the university and UCs are integrated. This research council has formulated a 48-page strategic plan for 2007–2011, and each UC offers within the same framework a strategic plan of 8–20 pages. Agreements are made between faculties and departments of the university and the UCs. Some faculties integrated the faculty of the university and the UCs (e.g. linguistics) into one faculty, others, when the type of research was different, established an associated faculty (e.g. engineering). In 2008 this association announced the integration of the UC master programmes in the university in 2013. The interviewees in A2 stressed that even when the department had become part of an associated faculty, the strategic plan of the UC was formulated by themselves. Although Association A has adopted a strategic plan for the research provided in the professional track, there is less coherence in this research. Because of the modest budget for research in this track and the many fields of research, only a few applicants can be financed. In A1, three research projects can be granted each year, and in A2 the number is between 3 and 6.

The pole did not develop a strategic research plan and is still focused on collaboration for the organisation of education between universities and the UCs. In P2, some of the institutes and departments developed a strategic plan, and one of its established institutes had long one. Whether these strategic plans will have the desired effect, the future will show.

The Organisation and Management of Research

The organisation of research differs between the north and the south of the country. In Flanders, at present, associations are very important for research, but this is not the case for the poles in Francophone Belgium. Although there is co-operation between the universities and the UCs in the French Community, the UCs determine independently what research they do and how they go about it. The UCs do have a research council, but it is up to each teacher to apply for research funding and to manage his or her own research. Some research units of the academic track in P1 and P2 have an established management structure, but most research projects of the professional track are organised by an individual research director.

Since the establishment of the Association, the management of research in UCs has changed. Until then, whether or not to do research was the free choice of a teacher, but since the commencement of the compulsory academisation process, the academic track in the UCs cannot do without research. Moreover, the universities became important parties in this process. In Association A, this is apparent in its organisation, the advisory research councils for the association, the formulation of strategic plans, the integration or association of departments of UCs with faculties of the university, etc. But, after deliberation among the different parties, it is still the responsibility of each research director to search for money and to manage the project. Both A1 and A2 have a research council and one or two coordinators of research, but this does not diminish the responsibility of each research director. Within the framework of the academic track, A2 has a research institute in which seven sections are functioning. In an interview, a head of a department hopes that, in the future, the UCs will be able to organise their own PhD programmes because the type of research of the UCs differs from that of the universities. Up to the present, however, granting PhD degrees is the privilege of the university.

Collaboration with Universities and Industry

Research has shown that the academic drift was still not very pronounced in UCs at the end of the 1990s. On the contrary, teachers, students and employers saw a different type of students in UCs than in universities. The UC courses were supposed to teach students readily usable skills for particular occupations, whereas university courses are less application-oriented and lead to many kinds of occupations (De Wit & Verhoeven, 2003). In 2001, in a survey of UC teachers, we asked the question: 'To what extent does your UC collaborate with universities for doing research?' Few teachers recognised collaboration with universities (Verhoeven et al., 2002). No longer ago than 2000, Zwerts and Hollebosch (2000, p. 42) stated that UCs wanted to be more independent from universities as far as research is concerned.

This has changed now. The Bologna Process brought the UCs and the universities, willy-nilly, closer to each other in Flanders because it led to the establishment of associations and in the Francophone Community to the creation of opportunities to collaborate within the academies and/or poles. The UCs of the pole of our case studies, however, had not changed very much as far as their contact with universities is concerned.

The situation differed in Flanders. Associations were created by law and are the only route to academisation of the UCs. Therefore, Association A created a structure in order to bring not only the teaching but also the research of the university and the UCs closer to each other. This did not destroy the independence of the UCs, but opened for them new forms of collaboration. For instance, researchers of the UCs can become affiliated with the university; UC applicants may apply for research funding together with university colleagues; fields of research can be adapted to each specialty; and, in the near future, UC teachers may be appointed to an associate position at the university.

The industry in general, trading companies and social-profit organisations have long been the natural allies of the UCs. To offer their students practical training they needed these organisations. These contacts not only provided trainee posts but also opened opportunities for collaborating in research. The government supported this situation by creating special research programmes in which industry collaborates with UCs or universities. Association A was very entrepreneurial in this programme. Of the 234 TETRA projects from 1997 to 2006, Association A accounted for some 52% (Van Ryssen et al., 2007, p. 68). In 2004–2007, P1 was awarded 4 FIRST programmes, and P2 eight FIRST and five other projects, among which were three from the FNRS, a resource traditionally the privilege of the universities. In addition to such projects, UCs often do smaller projects for the industry.

Although the interviewees appreciate collaboration with industry, they mentioned some problems. First, research conducted for industry limits the opportunity for publication, as industry often considers the results as private property. Second, a research programme that makes the approval dependent on the collaboration with industry might hinder the application process as private companies are not always very eager to fill out the forms. An interviewee hoped that the academisation process would give more opportunities for research grants without being obliged to involve a private company.

Human Resources and Careers

When the legislatures enacted new laws in the 1990s, they changed the names and ranks of the teaching staff of UCs. The Francophone Community and the Flemish Community acted differently. In Flanders, three groups are distinguished (see Table 6.2). Group 3 is identical to the ranking system of the universities, and these positions may be granted in both the professional and the academic track. Most of these teachers teach in the academic track and should in principle have a PhD degree (bold in Table 6.2), but under some conditions these positions are also open to civil engineers. In the future, because of the academisation policy, most of them are supposed to have a PhD. These principles apply also to Rank 2 of the Francophone Community. Nevertheless, only the title of professor is the same as in universities; the two other titles do not have the same meaning as in the universities. The *chef de travaux* may be called a junior lecturer, and the *chef de bureau*

Table 6.2 Types of academic staff in UCs in Flanders and the Francophone Community

Flanders group 1	Francophone Community rank 1	Flanders group 2 (auxiliary staff)	Flanders group 3	Francophone Community rank 2
Junior practical lector (*Praktijklector*)	*Maître de formation pratique*	Research assistant (*Assistent*)	**Junior lecturer** (***Docent***)	*Chef de travaux*
Senior practical lector (*Hoofdpraktijklector*)	*Maître principal de formation pratique* (*rang 2*)	**Doctoral assistant** (***Doctor-assistent***)	**Senior lecturer** (***Hoofddocent***)	*Professeur*
Junior lector (*Lector*)	*Maître assistant*		**Assistant professor** (***Hoogleraar***)	***Chef de bureau d'études***
Senior lector (*Hoofdlector*)	***Chargé de cours***	Senior researcher (*Werkleider*)	**Professor** (***Gewoon hoogleraar***)	

d'études has the same position and salary as the assistant professor in universities (or in Flemish UCs) but spends most of his time managing the organisation of teaching.

Group 1 in Flanders and Rank 1 in the Francophone Community is composed of different ranks of teachers teaching the professional bachelor's courses. They teach professional practice and theory. Two positions in the Francophone Community are different from the Flemish situation. The *Maître principal de formation pratique* actually belongs to Rank 2, and the *chargé de cours* is supposed to have a PhD, but, as already noted, this is not necessary. For the first two positions in Group 1 and Rank 1, the candidate needs to have a bachelor's degree; the other positions require at least a master's degree.

Salaries vary according to the position of the teacher and seniority. There is no extra salary for teachers doing research, but they may receive part of the profits based on the inventions in which they are involved.

Most UCs were accustomed to selecting teachers solely on the basis of their teaching abilities. In the meantime, this has changed. Teaching abilities are still very important, but teachers for the two-cycle programme are, more than previously, being selected for their interest in research and the ownership of a PhD. This is not the case for the teaching staff of the one-cycle BA programmes.

Since research became more important, it could be expected that teachers who are also involved in research would have more opportunities for promotion. This is the case in A2 and P2, but much less in the other cases. Moreover, there is some hesitation also in A2. If a teacher without a PhD does a good job, he or she can also be promoted, a principle that is supported by the unions. Although the hierarchy shown in Table 6.2 varies considerably, there are few opportunities for promotion because of the modest budgets of the UCs and the age structure of the staff (Verhoeven, 2005; also in P1).

The equivalents of university positions, the first four rows of Table 6.3, 14.6% of the staff in Flanders and 12.8% in the Francophone Community, is the smallest group among the teachers. With these figures, one might expect that this is the proportion of teachers having a PhD. Nevertheless, information from the Association shows that not all bearers of these titles have a PhD. In Association A in most domains of study less than 55% of the teachers have a PhD (Gysen et al., 2006). The total number of teachers with a PhD in Flemish UCs is certainly less than 14.6%. How much less is hard to tell because teachers in the other ranks may also have a PhD. Nevertheless, based on a sample of 7 UCs where professional bachelors are trained, a much smaller proportion than 14.6% of PhDs among the teachers was reported. Only 5.7% of the teachers had a PhD. ETNIC calculated that in the Francophone Community 6.8% of their UC teachers have a PhD.

The small amount of funding for research (see Table 6.1) and the small number of staff of group 3 or rank 2 (see Table 6.3) is a foreshadowing of the small figures of the UCs in Table 6.4. UCs had only 2.7% (in FTE) of the number of researchers in universities in 2000, and 5.2% in 2007. In 2007, 40.2% of them were female (CFS).

Other research confirms that teachers of UCs did not invest very much effort in research in the 1990s. A survey conducted in 2000 in Flanders showed that about 9% of the teachers of the UCs ($N = 4,043$) reported that they did research. 68%

Table 6.3 Teaching staff (only main categories) in UCs in Flanders (FTE) and French-speaking community (persons; sample of UCs) by rank and tenure in 2007. Percentages

Rank	Flanders			French-speaking community		
	Provisional	Permanent appointment	Total	Provisional	Permanent appointment	Total
Professor	0.1	0.5	0.4	–	–	–
Assistant professor	0.1	3.8	2.3	–	4.5	2.7
Senior lecturer	0.4	2.5	1.6	–	–	–
Junior lecturer	8.8	11.4	10.3	0.2	17.0	10.1
Senior lector, senior researcher, doctoral assistant	2.1	6.1	4.4	19.5	10.7	14.4
Junior lector, research assistant	70.0	59.5	63.8	33.8	25.7	29.0
Senior practical lector	0.1	0.6	0.4	–	1.4	0.8
Junior practical lector	18.4	15.6	16.8	46.5	40.7	43.0
Sum	100	100	100	100	100	100
Number of staff	2,909	4,160	7,069	1,228	1,768	2,996

Source: Department of Education (Ministry of the Flemish Community) and ETNIC. Our own calculations.

Table 6.4 R&D personnel in UCs and universities in Belgium (2001–2007) classified as researchers, technical personnel and other personnel (FTE)

Year	UC			Universities		
	Total	Function	%	Total	Function	%
2001	489	Researcher	73.3	15,503	Researcher	74.3
		Technician	10.2		Technician	17.5
		Other	16.5		Other	8.1
2003	624	Researcher	82.5	15,630	Researcher	74.8
		Technician	8.1		Technician	16.6
		Other	9.4		Other	8.6
2005	702	Researcher	93.2	16,760	Researcher	77.3
		Technician	4.1		Technician	15.1
		Other	2.7		Other	7.6
2007	996	Researcher	94.2	18,206	Researcher	78.5
		Technician	2.6		Technician	13.0
		Other	3.2		Other	8.5

Source: Commissie Federale Samenwerking, Overleggroep CFS/STAT (Federaal Wetenschapsbeleid, 2009).

of this small group spent only 1 day a week on research in the first semester, and in the second semester between 2 and 5 h a week (Smolders, Velghe, & Verstraete, 2000, p. 75). Research was very often seen by the teachers as a burden that had to be done in addition to teaching (Zwerts & Hollebosch, 2000). Moreover, most of the research projects were rather brief in duration and did not deliver much satisfaction to the researchers. The consequence was that a research culture was not supported by a large part of the teachers in the UCs.

Nevertheless, in spite of the still low figures given in Table 6.1, we suggest that this picture is changing. Above we have seen that the Bologna Process pushed the policymakers to change the law and brought the two-cycle programmes in the UCs closer to those of the universities. The Associations are seen as the basic organisation for coordinating this academisation process and more money is being made available for research. A1 (33 contractuals in 2007) and A2 (65 contractuals) can, more than before, hire contractual researchers to do research in collaboration with the tenured teachers.

Although the policy in Francophone Belgium is different, the UCs there are also now being given more opportunities to do research than previously. But here, more than in Flanders, research is concentrated in a small group of established UCs. For instance, between 2004 and 2007, P1 had as many as seven additional contractual researchers. P2 hired 17 contractuals and one research institute of P2 has had a staff of about 20 appointed researchers for many years.

In 2000, of a sample of 4,043 UC teachers in Flanders, only 48 were working towards a PhD (Smolders et al., 2000, p. 76). This has changed now. In Association A: 14.7% of the staff in Economics, 11% in Applied Linguistics, and in Engineering 37 candidates are working towards a PhD (Gysen et al., 2006). This positive development is also supported by new programmes. TETRA, for instance, launched 30 PhD candidates (Van Ryssen et al., 2007, p. 191), who have yet to obtain their degrees. Whether this will come up to the criteria of academisation has to be proven.

The Allocation of Resources for Research

For the allocation of the resources for research, the general principle is that the applicant who received the contract is responsible for its implementation. This means that the money is at her/his disposal. Depending on the UC policy, the applicant can replace some of her/his teaching by working on a project or/and can hire contractuals to do the research. The special academisation grant, which most of the UCs of Association A receive, is used for the research projects of the PhD students and of teachers with a PhD doing research as part of the academisation process.

Although there is now a more positive attitude towards research, this was not the case in the 1990s. Research was considered as something to do in addition to teaching (Zwerts & Hollebosch, 2000), even though the Flemish law allowed the UCs themselves to decide about the division of labour. This was not so in the Francophone Community. Here the law prescribes the number of teaching hours per year.

In Flanders in 2001, the average weekly working load was 44 h. At average a teacher had to teach 14 h a week. This means that the average teacher used about 30 h weekly to prepare classes and/or to do research. However, about 60% of the teachers did no research at all. In relation to research, it is interesting to know that teachers having a PhD did not teach less than did teachers without a PhD (Verhoeven, 2005).

This has changed now in Association A. This Association has put the target that an 'active researcher' should spend at least 20% of a full-time position on research. A2 even decided to strive for 30%. In A1 and A2, a wide variety of measures are being taken to open more possibilities to do research. Nevertheless, this is not without problems. In A1, for instance, it is possible for a teacher to change teaching hours into research hours. The problem later on is that this teacher might have difficulties in returning to his/her former teaching position. Another problem is the pressure of the unions to reduce the number of contractuals because this position is less appreciated than a statutory position. The policy of P1 and P2 is partly different, partly similar. In P1, large projects are conducted mainly by professors. Other staff members have to teach 16 or more hours a week, and only a few of them do research. In P2, professors have to teach less than the law has determined. Instead of 360 h a year, they teach 200 h.

Research Performance

The Extent and Output of Research

It is not surprising that UCs publish less than universities, apply for fewer patents and establish fewer spin-offs. This is to be expected because the research budgets of UCs are so much smaller than those of the universities, and publishing is not part of the culture of the UCs. This attitude is sometimes supported by the demands of the private company with which they collaborate as such companies do not want the results to be published. Nevertheless, their output is visible in SCIE and SSCI. Bart Thijs (Steunpunt O&O Indicatoren, KU Leuven) calculated that, in 1992, the UCs published 1.3% of the 5,757 Belgian publications reported in these indexes, whereas the universities published 99.4%. In 2005, these figures were respectively 1.6 and 98.9% of the 11,897 publications. Between 1992 and 2005, the UCs published 1.2% and the universities 99.1% of the publications ($N = 118,416$). Only 0.9% was published by UC researchers alone. Moreover, research by Bart Van Looy (Steunpunt O&O Indicatoren, KU Leuven) found that a UC of Association A had applied for 2 patents of a total of 825 patents in Belgium between 1989 and 2004. He also stated that, in this period, 4 spin-offs were established by UCs, one of them by P2 (see also Debackere & Veugelers, 2007).

Nevertheless, although the small group of publishing teachers did not often publish in first rate journals, there is a wider publishing activity. Within the framework of TETRA (1997–2006), about 600 articles were published and about 200

websites, manuals, etc. Sixty-five per cent of the projects contributed to new calculation models or simulations. Ten patents were applied for by the collaborating
private company (Van Ryssen et al., 2007, pp. 189–198).

Because the academisation target has to be attained in 2012–2013, Association A
monitors some indicators, one being publications. Although the publication activity
is still small, there is some increase (Gysen et al., 2006, p. 31). For the publications
of books and papers in local journals the UCs approach the results of their university
counterparts.

The Relevance of Research for the Regional Community and for the Development of Professional Expertise

Until the 1990s, hundreds of small UCs were spread over the country. The distance
between the old UC and local business, government, schools and welfare organisations was small. This made contacts between UCs and the region easy, and after the
merger these links did not disappear. Research was often conducted in collaboration
with local industry. This more application-oriented research is the type of research
often practised by teachers of the professional track, and industrial research was
mostly a service to local SMEs (Van Ryssen et al., 2007, pp. 70, 190). The regional
community seems to appreciate this collaboration, a statement that is confirmed by
our four case studies.

All the interviewees also saw this type of research as contributing to the
professional expertise of teachers and students. Indeed, this type of research created opportunities to encounter the everyday practice of a profession. For the
Associations in Flanders, research is even more important because it is the basic
criterion for obtaining entrance into the system of academic education. Therefore,
Association A has created a system to determine whether the Association is making progress in the academisation process. This does not mean that the contact with
the regional environment should be reduced. The TETRA projects, for instance,
opened the road for about 400–450 researchers to move from UCs to companies
(Van Ryssen et al., 2007, p. 190). The same phenomenon was mentioned in our four
case studies.

Conclusion

Until the 1990s, Belgian UCs were not accustomed to investing much in research.
Research in UCs was the initiative of some individuals, and some were able to
establish research units. Nevertheless, the research resources available for the UCs
were only a small fraction of what universities got for research.

Since 2003–2004 the climate changed. During the 1990s small UCs were consolidated to bigger units, and under the influence of the Bologna Process policymakers
wanted to reinforce the link between UCs and universities by creating associations

and poles. These new organisations seem to be stronger in Flanders than in the French-speaking Community, although some 'academies' announced to make the collaboration stronger starting in 2010. This policy was accompanied by more funding for research, the obligation to participate in the academisation policy (only in Flanders), and more supervision (possible accreditation in 2012–2013 in Flanders). Nevertheless, because of the recent character of this policy, it is still too early to assess to what extent this policy will change the production of research in the UCs, or to what extent universities will benefit more from this policy compared to UCs, as some suggest.

Various scenarios are possible. In 2009, a special commission advised the Minister of Education to merge the training for academic degrees of the UCs and the universities. UCs were advised to offer only the professional degrees (Ministeriële Commissie, 2009). UCs may integrate in universities or not, and the academic master's programmes of the UCs may be accredited or not (only in Flanders). Each scenario will bring new challenges for the development of research in UCs.

Merging of UCs and universities might put an end to the binary system, but this will not happen for free. At the national level the laws should be adapted and funding should be brought at the level of the universities. At the university level, management and staff might face a lot of problems. For instance, how to consolidate the missions of UCs (composed of one-cycle professional and two-cycle academic programmes) and universities? How to integrate the different research and teaching culture? How to distribute the meagre research funding? How to keep the standards, etc.?

The second scenario, when there is no merging, does not leave the UCs untouched either. Unless the current policy is changing, they still will have to cope with very small research funding, and teachers who have to integrate a research culture with the predominant teaching culture. Moreover, research standards are made up by the international scientific community and have to be met.

The third scenario, the accreditation of the UCs, will not solve all problems either. One of them is the legal position of the association. Will the association structure be continued or will policymakers opt for the merger of UCs and universities? Will UCs (or only the two-cycle courses) become part of the university or will they keep their independence? Will the government expand the funding for research to satisfy the increased demands? Should accredited UCs be obliged to leave the applied research track?

What about institutions that did not earn the accreditation (the fourth scenario)? What will be their position after losing a provisional accreditation? What will be the consequences for the graduates of these UCs? Will the additional research funding offered during the academisation process still be available and can they try again to get accredited?

Whatever direction UCs are developing, our observations confirm that research is concentrated in some UCs, and that in each UC not all staff members share the research culture of their colleagues of strong research units. For many staff members, attention to research in the UCs came too late in their career, and investing in research did not always seem to be a guarantee for promotion. This might slow down the interest in research.

In Flanders, the attention has focused on the academisation process. Several experts doubt whether this is possible in the provided span, and with a much smaller budget than the universities. Although a ministerial assessment committee is moderately positive about the provisional results on the road to academisation, it warns in its report of 16 November 2008 that '... there still is the real danger that the academisation process might ultimately experience a little satisfactory result' (Erkenningscommissie, 2008). Some also feared that UCs would conduct research that was the privilege of the universities. This opinion is not shared by most of our interviewees. Both universities and UCs hope that the UCs will maintain the individuality of their research and do not move to types of research popular at the universities. They also wish one can obtain the right to apply for research funding from foundations that has been and still is the privilege of universities. This is different in one-cycle programmes. Here the available research funding is much less than for the two-cycle programmes. The interviewees expect that research will be able to maintain its own character but they also hope that more funding will be available and that research will become part of the job description of the teachers and subject of quality assurance.

But in spite of this new policy, scientific research in UCs is still modest and receives only a fraction of the research funding of the universities. Nevertheless, this new policy has given UCs a boost to do research. Whether this process will continue and even expand, only the future can tell.

Acknowledgements   I want to thank Kurt De Wit for his critical comment on this chapter.

References

Boon, A. (2007–2008). Associatie: quo vadis – waar ga je heen? *Tijdschrift voor Onderwijsrecht en Onderwijsbeleid* (1–2), 3–17.

CFS. (2005). *Bijdrage van de departementen Wetenschapsbeleid aan het Nationaal Actieplan ter uitvoering van de Lissabon-agenda*, Brussel. Retrieved November 1, 2007, from http://www.belgium.be/eportal/ShowDoc/chancellery/imported_content/pdf/Bijlage1_Onderzoek_en_ontwikkeling.pdf?co...

CFS (Commissie Federale Samenwerking van de Interministeriële Conferentie voor Wetenschapsbeleid/Commission Coopération Fédérale de la Conférence Interministérielle de la Politique Scientifique). (2007). *Budgettaire kredieten voor O&O van de overheden in België in de 1995–2006/Crédits budgetaires de R&D des autorités Belges au cours de la période 1995–2006.* Brussel: Federaal Wetenschapsbeleid – Politique Scientifique Fédérale

Commissie Federale Samenwerking van de Interministeriële Conferentie voor Wetenschapsbeleid (CFS) – Commission Coopération Fédérale de la Conférence interministérielle de la Politique scientifique. (2009). *Onderzoek en ontwikkeling door de non-profitorganisaties in België in 2006 en 2007. Recherche et développement dans les organisations du secteur non marchand en Belgique en 2006 et 2007.* Brussel: Federaal Wetenschapsbeleid – Politique Scientifique Fédérale. Retrieved September 3, 2009 from http://www.belspo.be/belspo/home/publ/pub_ostc/ind/OO_200607_2.pdf

Debackere, K., & Veugelers, R. (Eds.). (2007). *Vlaams Indicatorenboek 2007.* Brussel: Vlaamse Overheid/Steunpunt O&O Statistieken.

Dekelver, N. (2007, December). Academisering. Welke koers? *Delta. Tijdschrift voor Hoger Onderwijs*, 26–32.

De Wit, K., & Verhoeven, J. C. (2003). The context changes but the divisions remain. The binary education system in Flanders (Belgium). The case of information science. *Studies in Higher Education, 28*, 143–156

Erkenningscommissie. (2008) *Rapport van de Erkenningscommissie Hoger Onderwijs inzake de Voortgangstoets van de Academisch Gerichte Opleidingen van de Hogescholen in Vlaanderen* (55 pp). Brussel.

Federaal Planbureau. (2006). *Lisbon strategy. National reform programme 2005–2008 Belgium. More growth, more jobs . . . Progress report 2006.* Brussel: Federaal Planbureau.

Federaal Wetenschapsbeleid. (2007). *O&O-Activiteiten in België in 2005. Overzicht van de resultaten van de O&O-enquêtes 2006.* Brussel. Retrieved November 3, 2007, from http://www.belspo.be/belspo/home/pers/20070718_nl.pdf

Federaal Wetenschapsbeleid. (2009). *O&O-Statistieken.* Brussel: Federaal Wetenschapsbeleid. Retrieved September 3, 2009, from http://www.belspo.be/belspo/stat/index_nl.stm

Graitson, D. (2006). *La R&D en Wallonie: état des lieux et perspectives.* Liège: CESRW.

Gysen, M., Loosvelt, H., De Vuyst, J., Baert, F, Belmans, R., & Lambrecht, M. (2006). *Academisering ondersteunen en opvolgen.* Leuven: Associatie K.U. Leuven.

High Level Group 3% Belgium. (2005). *Research, technology and innovation in Belgium: The missing links.* Brussels: Belgian Science Policy.

Ministeriële Commissie Optimalisatie en Rationalisatie in het hoger onderwijs. (2009). Optimalisatie en rationalisatie van het hoger onderwijslandschap en -aanbod. Deel II van het vervolgrapport van de Ministeriële Commissie aan de heer Frank Vandenbroucke, Vlaams minister van Werk, Onderwijs en Vorming. Brussel, 2009.

Ministère de la Communauté Française. (2006). *Statistiques de l'enseignement de plein exercice et budget des dépenses d'enseignement. Annuaire 2004–2005. Volume I.* Bruxelles: ETNIC.

Région Wallonne, Communauté Française. (2005). *Les actions prioritaires pour l'avenir wallon.* s.l.: Région Wallonne, Communauté française.

Smolders, C., Velghe, J., & Verstraete, A. (2000). *De taakbelasting van het onderwijzend personeel in de Vlaamse Hogescholen.* Gent: Departement Handelswetenschappen en Bestuurskunde. Gent : Hogeschool Gent.

Spruyt, E., Tan, B., & Van Dyck, D. (2005–2006). Onderzoek binnen de academiseringsopdracht in de associaties met als casus de Associatie Universiteit & Hogescholen Antwerpen. *Tijdschrift voor Onderwijsrecht en Onderwijsbeleid* (4–5), 415–433.

Vandenbroucke, F. (2006). *Voortbouwen en vooruitzien. Beleidsbrief Onderwijs en Vorming 2006–2007.* Brussel: Ministerie van de Vlaamse Gemeenschap.

Van Looy, B., Lecocq, C., Belderbos, R., Faems, D., Veugelers, R., Van Haverbeke, W., et al. (2006). *Samenwerking universiteiten, hogescholen, onderzoeksinstellingen, intermediairen en bedrijven. Een studie van de internationale literatuur.* Brussel: VRWB.

Van Ryssen, S., Van Pelt, S., & Wuyts, A. (2007). *TETRA/HOBU Effect- en outputmeting.* Brussel: IWT.

Verhoeven, J. C. (2005). Hogescholen en Academisering. *Tijdschrift voor Onderwijsrecht en Onderwijsbeleid , 6*, 495–505.

Verhoeven, J. C., Devos, G., Smolders, C., Cools, W., & Velghe, J. (2002). *Hogescholen enkele jaren na de fusie.* Antwerpen/Apeldoorn: Garant.

Vlaams Ministerie van Onderwijs en Vorming. (2006). *Statistisch Jaarboek van het Vlaams Onderwijs, Schooljaar 2005–2006.* Brussel: Vlaams Ministerie van Onderwijs en Vorming.

Vlaamse Raad voor Wetenschapsbeleid (VRWB). (2004). W*etenschap en innovatie in Vlaanderen 2004–2010. Voorstellen voor een strategisch beleid.* Brussel: VRWB.

Werkgroep Academisering. (2005). *Advies van 29 juni 2005.* Brussel: Ministeriële Werkgroep Academisering.

Zwerts, E., & Hollebosch, B. (2000). *Inventarisatie van het projectmatig wetenschappelijk onderzoek en de maatschappelijke dienstverlening.* Brussel: Vlaamse Hogescholenraad.

Chapter 7
Czech Republic: Research Required but Not Supported

Petr Pabian

Introduction

The situation of the non-university higher education sector in the Czech Republic is particularly complex because, in addition to the distinction between universities and non-university institutions, the non-university sector is further differentiated. Two types of non-university institutions exist in the Czech Republic, each with a different mission, legal status, degree programmes and research involvement: first, the teaching-only professional education colleges that are legally not a part of higher education and second, non-university higher education institutions distinguished from universities by the degrees offered as well as by size and tradition. Indeed, the dividing line between these two types, i.e. *within* the non-university sector, is more firmly drawn than the one between universities and non-university institutions. The situation is further complicated by the fact that the non-university higher education segment has been almost entirely private, while the university segment has been until very recently exclusively public.

In the first section of this chapter, I will therefore offer both a diachronic and a synchronic description of the Czech non-university sector and discuss the data and methods used in this study. The second section will deal with national research policies in relation to the non-university sector, with public funding of research and with staffing policies inherent in the accreditation system. The third section reviews institutional strategies and practices in the area of research, while in the final section I will reflect on the dilemmas and challenges facing the future development of research in the Czech non-university sector.

P. Pabian (✉)
Department of Social Sciences, University of Pardubice, Pardubice, Czech Republic
e-mail: petr.pabian@upce.cz

S. Kyvik, B. Lepori (eds.), *The Research Mission of Higher Education Institutions Outside the University Sector*, Higher Education Dynamics 31,
DOI 10.1007/978-1-4020-9244-2_7, © Springer Science+Business Media B.V. 2010

Non-university Higher Education Sector in the Czech Republic

Historical Development

In the last two decades, the Czech sector of non-university higher education under-
went a series of loosely coordinated reforms that resulted in a highly complex
contemporary situation. During the first of these reforms, implemented in the
first years after the end of the communist regime, all the existing non-university
institutions were transformed into university-type institutions. This wave of de-
diversification changed the stratified state-socialist higher education system into one
dominated by public universities. Shortly after the first round of changes, another
set of reforms was set in motion, this time in an effort to create a new sector of
professional higher education out of the post-secondary courses already existing
at some upper-secondary schools. This wave, however, was pacified by the mid-
1990s by creating institutions higher than post-secondary but just short of the higher
education status: professional education colleges. Only at the end of the 1990s it
became possible to establish new non-university but genuinely higher education
institutions.

The higher education system of the late state-socialist period was stratified
beyond the simple binary divide, encompassing several types of institutions differentiated by degrees offered, legal status and governing authorities. Of the 28
higher education institutions (HEIs) existing at the end of the 1980s, only three
had university status. What might be called the non-university sector thus comprised the remaining 25 institutions. These included seven technical HEIs – two
of them multifield and five smaller institutions covering a narrower range of
fields; two agricultural HEIs and one veterinary institution; five teacher training
colleges; four institutions of creative arts; one institution specialised in economics; one in political studies; a police academy and three military academies.
Several of these institutions were under the supervision not of the Ministry of
Education but of the various sectoral ministries. However, the institutional differentiation was somehow counter-balanced by the fact that the mission of virtually
all higher education institutions was defined in vocational terms: to train experts
for the corresponding sectors of the centrally planned economy (Hartman & Drnka,
1987).

The situation changed after the end of the communist regime in 1989. The
most important new development was the abandonment of the formal differentiation between various types of institutions. As a result, within a few years all the
existing institutions acquired university status. Most of these new universities were
created by merging several single-field and single-purpose institutions located in
the same region, while others were created by adding new faculties to existing institutions. In one case, even an entire university was built from the scratch. Many
of the new universities acquired the new status without any significant disciplinary
expansion (e.g. the academies of creative arts). Within a few years, the Czech higher
education system was thoroughly transformed from a highly diversified, with a sizeable non-university sector offering professional degrees, to one dominated by public

universities dedicated to the Humboldtian vision of academic self-governance and offering predominantly academic long-cycle degrees (Čerych et al., 1992).

The first policy's effort to develop a new non-university sector arose already in the early 1990s as a counter-balance to this domination of public universities. The association of the Dutch *Hogescholen* provided the initial impulse that was welcomed both by the Czech Ministry of Education (with the expectation that the new sector would help to satisfy the large excess demand for higher education) and by the upper-secondary professional schools that were selected to become the foundation for the development of new professional HEIs. The first programmes were launched in 1992 at 21 institutions and the name of the policy project, 'Alternative Higher Education', clearly indicated the eventual goal of creating a non-university sector providing professional higher education degrees. However, public universities resisted this development from the beginning. In the mid-1990s, the ministry terminated the project before its completion by legislating that the transitional status of the new professional programmes – above post-secondary but below higher education – was to become permanent. This resulted in the creation of a new sector, precariously located between secondary and higher education, which has been the subject of policy debates since; this decision also effectively ended the initial expansion of this sector (Pabian, 2009).

A new policy opening for the expansion of the non-university higher education sector was created at the end of the 1990s, when the 1998 Higher Education Act brought about two significant legislative changes. First, for the first time in the post-communist period it formally established university and non-university HEIs as two distinct categories. Second, for the first time in the post-war period the act allowed the establishment of private HEIs. These two provisions paved the way for the establishment of almost 50 new non-university institutions over the following decade, the vast majority of them private, prompted to the market by the existence of a large surplus of student demand for higher education. These new institutions have very diverse backgrounds: some represent the upgrading of the existing tertiary professional colleges or other education institutions, others are trans-national institutions operating in the Czech Republic that seized the opportunity to acquire formal recognition, and yet others were created almost from the scratch.

Contemporary Situation

As a result of these developments, three types of tertiary education institutions exist in the Czech Republic: first, professional education colleges (*vyšší odborné školy*) that are formally not part of higher education; second, non-university HEIs (*vysoké školy neuniverzitního typu*); and finally, universities (*vysoké školy univerzitního typu*). For the purpose of this study, the non-university sector will be defined as comprising the two former types of institutions; I include into this definition also three HEIs that were originally established as non-university institutions and recently acquired university status. In this section, I will provide more detailed information first on the professional educational colleges and then on the non-university higher education institutions.

The professional education colleges offer programmes and degrees above the post-secondary level but below the bachelor level; on the ISCED scale, they are classified as ISCED 5B. As of 2008, there were 184 of these institutions with little more than 28,000 students. This means that these institutions are very small, with the average number of students per institution little more than 150. In the Czech education system, their position is precarious both in terms of their institutional status and in terms of degree programmes they offer. As institutions, they are part of the tertiary education sector but governed by secondary-school legislation; in terms of degrees, they are bound by law to offer programmes of the same length as bachelor programmes while granting degrees of lower status. This reflects the fact that they are the outcome of an experimental project that was politically frozen at a transitional stage.

Ever since the mid-1990s, there has been political debate aimed at overcoming this temporary solution. The provision of the 1998 Act that opened up the possibility to create non-university HEIs was at least partly intended to enable these colleges to acquire higher education status, but only nine private and three public colleges so far successfully completed this transformation. Since the efforts to deal with the situation at the level of individual institutions failed, the largest association of the colleges called for a system-wide upgrading of all professional programmes to the bachelor level at the end of 2006 (Association of Professional Education Colleges, 2006). This initiative, together with the OECD review of Czech tertiary education (File et al., 2006), elevated the future of the professional education sector to one of the hotly debated issues of Czech higher education policy.

Within the higher education sector proper, the principal difference between non-university and university HEIs is in the level of degree programmes they offer. Universities offer all degree programmes from the bachelor to the doctoral level, while non-university institutions offer bachelors and masters programmes (focusing on the bachelor level). The right to confer doctoral degrees thus constitutes the dividing line between non-university and university HEIs. However, this dividing line is permeable: every non-university institution that obtains accreditation for a doctoral programme is granted a university status and, presumably, every university that fails to accredit any would lose its status. It is important to note that the distinction between the two institutional types does not correspond to the distinction between academic and professional orientation: both universities and non-university HEIs carry out programmes of both kinds. In short, the difference is not of kind but rather of degree.

Since 1999, 50 new non-university HEIs were established, three of which so far succeeded in obtaining university status (two in 2007 and one in 2009), two merged with a public university (in 2005 and 2008) and two lost accreditation (one in 2008 and the other in 2009 immediately after receiving it) and ceased to exist as HEIs. Only 2 of the 43 currently existing non-university HEIs are public, the rest of them are private (as are the three new universities). The total number of students at these institutions in 2006 was more than 53,000, which means that the

Table 7.1   Tertiary education institutions and students in the Czech Republic

University sector		Non-university sector			
		Professional education colleges		Non-university HEIs	
Institutions	Students	Institutions	Students	Institutions	Students
24	321,247	184	28,027	48	53,528

Note: 'University sector' includes public universities only; new private universities
are included among 'Non-university HEIs'.
Source: Institute for Information on Education, data current as of December 2008.

average number of students per institution is more than 1,100. In other words, even
though the institutions are on average about seven times larger than the professional
colleges, they are still quite small and dramatically smaller than public universities,
which have more than 13,000 students per institution on average (Table 7.1).

The non-university sector as defined in this chapter comprises little more than
20% of the total size of the Czech higher education in terms of student numbers;
almost two thirds of this share is concentrated in the non-university higher education sector, which has also been rapidly expanding over the past decade in contrast
to the stagnating professional college sector. On the other hand, 90% of institutions
in Czech tertiary education belong to the non-university sector. This means that all
non-university institutions are rather small, ranging from less than a hundred students at the smallest professional colleges to several thousand students at the largest
non-university HEIs. This fact, as well as the focus of non-university institutions on
bachelor-level degrees, has important consequences for the research ambition and
capacity of these institutions.

Data and Methods

The institutional diversity and segmentation present considerable challenges for
data gathering and analysis. For example, national statistical data collection uses
completely different templates for collecting staff data about professional education
colleges from public HEIs, while staff data about private HEIs are not collected
at all. It has also proved impossible to collect reliable system-wide data about
institutional funding because many private HEIs consider this information confi-
dential. The peripheral position of the non-university sector in the Czech system
is also reflected in the fact that it has been excluded from surveys of academic
staff. Furthermore, the expanded definition of research as understood by the non-
university HEIs renders its funding sources and outcomes invisible to the national
system of research assessment and data collection.

This chapter thus complements the available statistical data on higher education
(collected by the Institute for Information on Education) and on research (collected

by the Research and Development Council) with information obtained from systematic analysis of the institutional documents and websites. For the same reason, it relies primarily on qualitative methods, especially on discourse approaches to documentary analysis.

Concerning 'research' as the central focus of this study, I adopt an 'ethnographic definition', i.e. I do not devise my own definition of research but report on whatever activities that are defined as research by the actors. This approach reflects the fact that 'research' is a socially constructed category and that different actors employ different definitions of research (this topic is futher developed in the section below). Throughout this report, I use the term 'research' (equivalent of the Czech *výzkum*) as the generic term for this category of activities.

Public Policies and Research in the Non-university Sector

Even though there is a distinction between university and non-university institutions in the Czech higher education system, research policy and funding make no distinction between the different types of institutions. There is no specific public research policy for the non-university sector that would set objectives and funding mechanisms different from those for universities; correspondingly, no funding sources or programmes are available specifically to non-university institutions. This means that in order to receive research funding, these institutions must fulfil the same criteria as universities and for most funding sources to compete directly with universities.

Non-university HEIs and Professional Education Colleges in National Research Policy

All legislative and public research policy documents treat the Czech higher education sector as unitary, making no distinction between university and non-university institutions with regard to strategic goals for research, allocation mechanisms and criteria for research evaluation. Closer analysis of the documents reveals that the existing public research policy has been formulated with *only* universities in mind, completely ignoring the existence of the non-university sector. The most visible example of this tendency is the use of the terms 'universities' and 'higher education institutions' interchangeably in many of the policy documents (Pabian, 2007).

This tendency is exacerbated by the division between public and private sector: most universities (all except three) are public while most non-university institutions (all except two) are private. The fact that public research policy focuses primarily on public higher education institutions is made most visible in the annual research assessment exercise. This assessment, carried out by the governmental Research and Development Council, includes in the category of 'higher education institutions' only public institutions while private HEIs are found in the same categories as other for-profit and non-profit organisations (Research and Development Council, 2008a).

Even more conspicuous is the complete absence of the professional college sector from public research policy. Not only are they not expected to carry out research but teaching at these colleges is also not expected to be research-based. They are also not expected to incite an interest in research in their students (National Research and Development Policy, 2004, para. 37 and 64). In other words, professional education colleges constitute a blind spot of the Czech public research policy (Pabian, 2007).

In sum, the priorities set by the national research policy are supposed to apply to the entire higher education sector while the professional education sector is left aside.

Policy Objectives for Research

Czech HEIs are not presented with unequivocally formulated and easily accessible public objectives for research, a situation caused by poor coordination of higher education and research policies. This results in a complex web of policy documents, governing bodies and funding mechanisms (Šima, 2008, 2009) The formulation of national objectives is further limited by the fact that Czech higher education institutions exercise institutional autonomy to a degree quite exceptional in the international context (Karran, 2007; Pabian 2009).

In general, research policy in the Czech Republic is framed in economic terms: 'Governmental policy documents view an efficient research and development sector as a premise for economic development' (Melichar & Pabian, 2007, p. 46). The guiding document of higher education policy, the strategic plan of the Ministry of Education, states plainly: 'The main objective ... is to ensure that research and development foster, to a larger degree, economic growth and increase the technological standards of the country and, in this way, enhance its prosperity and competitiveness. This should be done primarily through successful innovations' (Ministry of Education, 2005, p. 9). In more specific terms, however, this document bears witness to strong institutional autonomy as it sets objectives not for higher education institutions but for the ministry to support (1) doctoral studies, (2) inclusion of students in research projects, (3) cooperation between HEIs and companies in innovation and knowledge transfer, and (4) funding of research from third-party sources.

Similarly, the most important research policy document at the governmental level, National Research and Development Policy of the Czech Republic for 2004–2008, formulates priorities for governmental bodies involved in research policy-making and funding, not for institutions carrying out research. The following five priorities are listed in the document: development of human resources in research; international cooperation; contribution to regional development; practical application of research; and research evaluation (National Research and Development Policy, 2004). The document also formulates five priority thematic areas (energy production, information society, quality of life, new materials and social–economic needs of the Czech Republic). These priorities are so broadly defined that their formulation could have very little practical impact and therefore their importance remains uncertain at best.

This was one of the reasons behind the recent attempts to reform both higher education and research policies, initiated by the right-wing government after 2006. Reform of research policy and funding, laying much more emphasis on excellence and concentration of resources as well as on scientometric indicators and innovation, was approved by parliament in 2008 to be fully implemented from 2010 (Research and Development Council, 2008b), but even before that, it caused such an uproar among academics that its future remains uncertain. The parallel (but characteristically uncoordinated) reform of higher education policy and funding (Ministry of Education, 2009b) met the same fate even before entering the parliament. The two aborted reform initiatives aiming at creating new policy environment thus resulted only in more of the old – confusion and uncertainty.

It is thus safe to say, whatever the future may bring, up until now there have been no explicit research objectives prescribed by the public authorities for higher education institutions, including the non-university HEIs. The existing objectives are rather indirect, arising from the increasing general emphasis on the economic potential of research and from the research evaluation system. Within these broad boundaries, higher education institutions have so far been free to set up their own research policies.

Public Funding of Research and the Non-university Sector

Two fundamental rules characterise the position of non-university HEIs in the Czech system of public research funding: on the one hand, there exists no specialised funding programme for research in the non-university sector; on the other hand, they are eligible for the same public research funding as universities. In order to receive funding, however, they have to fulfil the same criteria as universities and in most cases to compete against them. Professional education colleges, however, are effectively excluded from all forms of public research funding.

The Czech research funding policy distinguishes between two broad categories: *institutional* and *targeted* funding. Targeted funding is simply project funding with earmarked expenditures, distributed through competitive selective processes by a variety of intermediaries (various ministries, Czech Science Foundation and, until recently, the Academy of Sciences – to be replaced by Innovation Agency). Institutional funding has for the last decade consisted of two main funding mechanisms: 'specific research', which is a type of core funding for HEIs based on a formula (earmarked to ensure student involvement in research), and 'research plans' that combines characteristics of both core and project funding, such as competitive selection process (Šima, 2007). (The system of institutional funding is set to be completely overhauled by the reform of research funding but in this section I will stick to describing the situation within which Czech non-university HEIs have operated since their emergence in the late 1990s.)

Specific research has been the only funding instrument distributed to HEIs without competition – all institutions fulfilling the required criteria receive the amount calculated according to the formula. However, all the criteria are very difficult for the non-university HEIs to fulfil: number of professors and associate professors, number of doctoral students and master graduates and finally the amount of project funding received from other funding bodies. So far only one non-university institution succeeded in receiving specific research funding (since 2007) but it received by far the lowest amount of all HEIs, 366,000 CZK (cca €14,500 EUR) over the 3-year period out of the total sum of more than 3 billion CZK (€120 million).

In contrast to specific research, research plans funding was awarded on the basis of a highly competitive selection process. 'Research plans' were basically research projects that were long-term (5–7 years) and very inclusive (covering an entire institution or its large part). In the selection process, the project proposals were peer reviewed and evaluated on the basis of their scholarly merit and the institution's previous research performance. No non-university institution succeeded in the selection process, certainly due to the fact that they had to compete with universities.

Project funding has so far been distributed by various intermediaries, the most important among them being the Ministry of Education and the Czech Science Foundation. All providers have organised competition in which project proposals were evaluated by peer review. This is the funding mechanism from which the non-university institutions received practically all of their public research funding – until 2009, they were awarded 60 projects, 27 of them by the Czech Science Foundation, 30 by the various government ministries and 3 by the Academy of Sciences.

However, the total amount of public research funding awarded to non-university HEIs represents only a tiny fraction of the total research expenditures in the higher education sector. Between 2002 and 2006, non-university institutions received 16.8 million CZK (649 000 EUR) of research funding while public universities received more than 20 billion CZK (Research and Development Council, 2008a).

In sum, research in the non-university sector is not greatly supported by public funding: none of the institutions have been awarded research plan funding, only one of them recently received specific research funding, and half of the institutions (25 out of 50) succeeded in competitions for project funding. The total amount of public research funding awarded to non-university HEIs is negligible (less than 0.1%) in comparison to the amount received by public universities. All non-university HEIs therefore have to build research capacities in the absence of core funding and many of them also in the absence of public project funding.

Accreditation of Study Programmes and the Research Requirement

Although public support of funding in the non-university sector is almost non-existent, all institutions and their academic staff are required to carry out research activities. This requirement originates in the obligation to submit all new study programmes to accreditation and to periodic re-accreditation, because one of the principal prerequisites for accreditation relates to research credentials and research output of the academic staff.

The Accreditation Commission, an intermediary body responsible for the assessment of all higher education programmes, sets the standards required for a programme to receive approval, among which staffing plays a crucial role. According to these standards for bachelor programmes, the teaching must be research-based and a large part of courses has to be led by staff holding a doctoral degree or even an associate or full professorship. Furthermore, all of these teachers have to demonstrate active involvement in research, preferably in the form of research publications. The standards for master's programmes are quite similar, only the share of teaching carried out by staff with advanced research credentials is to be still higher and the requirements for their research output even more stringent (Accreditation Commission, 2005).

Conclusion

Czech non-university HEIs find themselves in a paradoxical situation: on the one hand, they have no role in the public research policy and public research funding is almost unattainable for them; on the other hand, the institutions (or at least their staff) are required to achieve advanced research credentials and to carry out considerable research activities in order to receive accreditation of any degree programme. Institutional strategies of the non-university HEIs have to find a way through these contradictory messages.

Non-university Institutions and Their Research Strategies

While research is virtually absent from professional education colleges, because there are neither pressures nor incentives for their leadership and staff to engage in research, non-university HEIs face enormous pressure to develop research activities and to enhance research productivity. This section thus reviews the research strategies and practices of these institutions.

Institutional Strategies and Priorities

In contrast to professional education colleges, virtually all non-university HEIs claim an involvement in research either as institutions or at least on part of their academic staff. They all dedicate a chapter in their institutional strategic plans (required by law) to research activities and develop strategies to attract staff with research credentials. Nevertheless, all institutions focus primarily on the provision of bachelor and master degrees, in most cases distinctly professionally oriented. I would characterise the position of research vis-à-vis teaching in the institutional strategies as *research in the service of teaching*. As one of the institutional strategic plans says, the objective is 'the improvement of the teaching process through research' (Brno International Business School, 2005, p. 11).

In the most straightforward and widespread form, research is understood at the institutions as the practice of developing and improving the existing degree and continuing education programmes as well as textbooks and other teaching materials. Many institutions also accord prominent roles in their research strategies to activities carried out by students as part of their studies, especially to the universal practice of writing bachelor and master theses. Finally, institutions aspiring to the accreditation of degree programmes on the master or even doctoral level intentionally and explicitly focus their research activities on these prospective fields in order to comply with the accreditation standards.

This instrumental conception of research in the service of teaching marks a fundamental difference from the traditional universities, where both the academics and institutional strategies commonly operate within the *research for research* paradigm. However, the division between the university and non-university sectors is far from absolute, since many of the existing public universities are quite young themselves, having been established only in the first half of the 1990s and are therefore still only developing their own research capacities. The instrumental understanding of research at the non-university HEIs also leads them to largely ignore national research priorities. In the absence of public research policy and support for the non-university sector, the institutions have nothing to gain from trying to respect national research objectives. In the end, research activities in the non-university HEIs serve the interests of institutional development, especially the provision and development of degree programmes.

Of course, this does not mean that public policies have no impact on the institutions. As a result of the accreditation policies, all non-university HEIs face two enormous challenges: first, to attract and preserve academic staff equipped with the required research credentials and second, closely related, to develop their own research activities. The staffing pressure from the Accreditation Commission dominates institutional strategies in areas of both research and staff development, and therefore its consequences are discussed in the immediately following section. This is followed by the analysis of the most common strategy that enables the institutions to develop the required research activities – the extension of what is included in the category 'research'. Finally, I turn to the more standard issues of organisational framework, funding and output of research activities in the non-university HEIs.

Human Resources and Careers

Academic staff is the Achilles' heel of the non-university sector of Czech higher education. 'Insufficient staffing provision' is the most common reason given by the Accreditation Commission when rejecting an application for the accreditation of a degree programme and for the establishment of a new non-university institution. Fulfilling the required standards certainly constitutes one of the greatest challenges in creating a new non-university institution and all non-university HEIs struggle to attract and preserve academics with research credentials and/or potential.

In the Czech system, the standards for accreditation require that a certain share of any given programme is taught by academic staff with research credentials – from doctoral degrees to associate and full professorships. These academic categories share three fundamental characteristics. First, they represent an academic qualification, not a position – they are awarded on the basis of a qualification process and then held by the recipient for life. Second, peer evaluation of research output constitutes the principal criterion for awarding the qualification – defence of a dissertation for the doctoral degree and of a *habilitation* thesis for the associate professorship and an assessment of a lifetime work for the professorship. Third, only universities can award doctoral degrees and confer associate and full professorships (Melichar & Pabian, 2007).

For non-university institutions, the combination of the accreditation staffing requirements and of the rigid academic career system poses a number of significant challenges. First, the creation of a new institution and the accreditation of a new study programme necessitates, in effect, attracting academics from the public universities. This headhunt is, however, complicated by the general shortage of qualified academics in the Czech Republic, caused by steeply rising student participation and only slight increase in academic staff numbers. Between 1989 and 2004, the number of teaching staff at public HEIs increased by about 25% while student numbers increased by more than 140%. As a result, the student–teacher ratio has almost doubled from 9.7 in 1989 to 18.8 in 2004 (Melichar & Pabian, 2007, p. 36).

The second challenge arises from the area of staff development. The higher education law and the accreditation requirements imposed the university career structure on the non-university HEIs. However, without the right to confer higher academic qualifications, the institutions cannot ensure career growth for their staff and their academic staff members have to seek doctorates and professorships at public universities. In doing so, they have to balance responsibilities to two institutions because universities commonly require the candidates to fulfil at least some tasks at the qualification-conferring university; at the very least, the candidates have to carry out research and teaching relevant to both institutions. This situation certainly favours public universities that offer lower teaching loads, availability of institutional research funding and more straightforward academic career prospects. As a result, only 3 of the 2,478 associate professors appointed between 1999 and 2007 were primarily affiliated with a non-university HEI (Ministry of Education, 2007) and not even a single one of the 1,554 professors appointed between 1999 and 2009 (Ministry of Education, 2009a).

The combination of these two factors gave rise to the common practice of dual (or even multiple) affiliation: many academics retain their position at a public university in addition to accepting a new post at a non-university institution. This practice is criticised and resented by the Accreditation Commission that has developed and implemented a number of measures to contain and curtail it (Kohoutek,

Sojka, Šebková, & Vinš, 2006). Dual affiliation of many of their active researchers presents the non-university institutions with a further challenge: the 'affiliation' of these academics' research results. This question is vitally important for the assessment both of study programmes submitted to accreditation and of research project proposals.

Finally, the fact that non-university institutions are dependent on universities for their staff development is further complicated by the fact that the universities in question are often their direct competitors for undergraduate students and research funding.

Redefining Research

In the environment that is not exactly friendly to research in the non-university sector, the most important institutional strategy to develop research is to *redefine research*. All the non-university HEIs claiming a research mission engage in this strategy, which takes two principal forms. First, they redefine the boundaries of research to include activities not recognised by other actors as research. Second, they redefine the boundaries of the institution to claim for themselves research carried out by their dually affiliated staff members at the other institution.

Let us start with the latter strategy, which has less far-reaching consequences. The *redefinition of institutional boundaries* in research activities arises as a response to the accreditation research requirements. One of the institutional documents succinctly captures the substance of this practice: 'at the present, academic staff members of [our institution] are engaged in nine research projects; in most cases, the recipient of research funding is not [our institution] but another institution' (Newton, 2005, p. 11). The aim is obviously to demonstrate more research activities than the institution actually carries out. Dubious as it may be, this practice certainly reveals recognition of the value and importance of research for the institutional mission.

The strategy of *redefining research boundaries* has important implications for any analysis of research in the Czech non-university sector. Virtually, all non-university institutions extend the boundaries of research to include activities excluded from the definition of research deployed by both policy-makers and the traditional universities. The non-university institutions thus claim as research projects not only those funded by the Czech Science Foundation, the Academy of Sciences and the research programmes of various ministries. They also include various projects funded from the European Regional Development Fund and the European Social Fund (24 institutions), training and consultancy programmes funded by the regional and municipal authorities (17 institutions), course development within the framework of the EU education programmes, e.g. Socrates and Leonardo (8 institutions), as well as consultancy to various private companies (7 institutions). The redefinition influences the area of research outputs as well: in addition to peer-reviewed journals and patents, the institutions enlist as research output new and updated courses and teaching materials, in-house publications, conferences and student bachelor and master theses.

Organisation and Management of Research

Even though the non-university HEIs find themselves under the same external pressures and even follow largely similar strategies to face these challenges, these pressures do not produce uniformity across the sector. The non-university HEIs differ considerably in size (from more than 5,000 students to less than 100), in institutional histories (while most institutions were established only in the last 10 years, several have histories going back to the first half of the 1990s or even earlier) and consequently also in terms of research engagement. In this respect, it is possible to distinguish two broad groups of institutions. On the one hand, there are institutions that consider research an integral part of their mission and consequently develop the relevant organisational capacities, attract research-competent staff and support their career development and regularly enter competitions for research funding. On the other hand, there are institutions that unabashedly focus on providing professionally oriented bachelor programmes and do not consider research at the institution necessary for the fulfilment of this mission.

Research organisation and management is one of the areas where the differences are clearly visible, especially when compared to Czech public universities who commonly feature four bodies to manage and supervise research – a top management position (typically a vice-rector), administrative research unit, institutional research funding agency and at least one academic department dedicated mostly or exclusively to research. Among the non-university HEIs, more than a quarter of institutions (14) have not established any of these bodies; on the other end of the spectrum, there are two institutions that have already created a full range of bodies comparable to public universities. The organisational structure most commonly found at non-university HEIs is the position of a vice-rector responsible for research, existing at more than a half of institutions. Administrative research unit and academic research centre have been established at about a quarter of institutions, while institutional research funding agency remains a province of a few exceptionally research-minded institutions (Table 7.2).

Table 7.2 Organisation and management of research at non-university HEIs

Number of institutions that have established								
Vice-rector for research	Administrative unit	Research centre	Funding agency	None of the bodies	One of the bodies	Two of the bodies	Three of the bodies	All four bodies
31	14	12	4	14	18	13	3	2

Total number of institutions: 50.
Source: Institutional annual reports and web sites, current as of September 2009.

Funding Sources and Collaboration with External Partners

As discussed in the section Public Policies and Research in the Non-University Sector above, non-university HEIs are virtually excluded from the system of public core research funding and experience significant difficulties in competing for public project funding with the established universities. So far, only a half (25) of the non-university HEIs have succeeded in obtaining public project funding; furthermore, only 13 of them won public funding for more than one research project and just 4 have won five or more projects. In total, non-university HEIs were awarded funding for 60 research projects, of which 30 were funded by the research programmes of the various government ministries, 27 by the Czech Science Foundation and 3 by the Academy of Sciences Foundation.

While most of the awarded projects are carried out by the non-university HEIs alone, public universities dominate as research partners, taking part in 17 projects, followed by private companies (11) and public research institutes (7). The majority (34) of the publicly funded projects are classified as 'basic research' while 21 projects are classified as 'applied research' and mere 4 as 'experimental development'.

Besides public research funding, the most widespread sources of project funding are the EU structural funds, especially the European Social Fund and the European Regional Development Funds. More than a half of the non-university institutions reported these projects among their research activities. More than a third of the institutions included among their research activities publicly funded projects that do not fall into the officially defined category of research funding, most often training and consultancy programmes for municipal or regional authorities. Quite a few institutions included projects funded by the EU education programmes, i.e. Erasmus, Leonardo da Vinci and Grundtvig.

Czech non-university HEIs are not involved in extensive research collaboration with private enterprises: only eight institutions collaborated with private companies on publicly funded research projects and the same seven institutions reported privately funded research projects (of these, only three institutions were involved in more than one project). This may seem surprising given the fact that more than a half of programmes in this sector are in the field of business, but it corresponds with the pattern found at public universities, which obtain only about 1% of their research funding from private sources (Šima, 2009).

The Extent and Output of Research

On the national scale, the extent of research carried out in the non-university HEIs is negligible. The institutions receive less than 0.1% of the total public research funding spent in higher education and produce even less research output as measured by the governmental Research and Development Council (Research and Development Council, 2008a). Research carried out at the non-university HEIs is also largely irrelevant from the regional perspective, because in all regions they stand in the shadow of public universities with significantly higher research capacities and output. Consequently, non-university HEIs play no role in either the national research policies or the regional innovation policies that have been developed in the last few years (Blažek & Uhlíř, 2007). While the vast majority of non-university HEIs align themselves closely to the region where they operate, they focus on areas of cooperation and outreach other than research (e.g. provision of training courses).

While the research output of the non-university HEIs may be largely insignificant when viewed from the outside, it still can play an important role within the institutions themselves. This role of research is, however, based on different types of output than those valued in the national system of research assessment. While the national assessment prefers scholarly publications and patents/new technologies, the most common types of output mentioned in the non-university HEIs' documents are closely related to teaching: the development and improvement of degree programmes, training courses and textbooks (most of them published in-house). Other types of research output recorded in the institutional documents also reflect a conception of research differing from the 'official': publications in professional rather than academic journals; organisation of conferences, again in-house and professional rather than academic; and student theses on the bachelor and master level.

Dilemmas and Challenges

The three types of institutions currently existing in the Czech tertiary education system, i.e. universities, non-university HEIs and professional education colleges, have clearly differentiated positions in the national research policy. On the one end of the spectrum, all universities are expected to be 'research universities': research constitutes an integral part of their mission and is correspondingly supported by public research funding. On the other end, professional education colleges are expected to be teaching-only institutions: research is not part of their mission and they are excluded from public research support. Non-university HEIs find themselves sitting uncomfortably in the middle, expected to carry out research but not adequately supported to do so.

This situation is currently challenged from two different directions. First, the recent emphasis on 'excellence' in both higher education policy (Ministry of Education, 2009b) and research policy (Research and Development Council, 2008b) may bring about a differentiation within the dominant university sector, distinguishing research-intensive universities from those with a mostly teaching focus. The so far predominant egalitarian ethos is clearly losing ground to the drive towards differentiation. In the words of the recent government proposal of research policy reform, it is time to end 'the support of mediocrity at the expense of excellence' (Research and Development Council, 2008b, p. 6). This development may disrupt the prevalent assumption that all HEIs and their academic staff are involved in research and subsequently lighten the pressure on non-university HEIs to employ research-active staff and to demonstrate research productivity in order to receive accreditation.

These changes at the top levels of the institutional hierarchy, driven by the push towards excellence, are accompanied by reform initiatives at the other end of the institutional spectrum, i.e. in the professional college sector. The reform initiatives come from two directions and suggest two different institutional solutions; what they both agree upon is that the current situation is unsustainable any longer. The main reason for reform is in both cases the fact that the colleges cannot confer bachelor degrees even though they provide programmes of the same duration as bachelor programmes at HEIs and in some fields (e.g. social work) even follow the same standards. The first reform initiative came from the largest association of professional education colleges that demanded the right to award professional bachelor degrees for the existing colleges (Janyš et al., 2007). The recent OECD review of Czech tertiary education proposed a different model: some of the professional colleges would be demoted to post-secondary education while the rest would be integrated into the existing universities as self-standing 'university colleges of professional studies' (File et al., 2006). Despite the differences in the proposed institutional configurations, both proposals reject the current accreditation requirements on academic staff. According to the association of professional colleges, the only staffing requirement at the professional bachelor level should be that 20% of academic staff are doctorate holders; the OECD review recommended the creation of an alternative career model in which status would be based on a tenure system, not on *habilitation*. Both proposals would therefore lead to the creation of a new higher education sector that would not be expected to carry out research, at least not to the same extent as the current non-university HEIs.

Both policy initiatives mentioned above thus point to the most problematic aspect of the Czech situation: the precarious position of the non-university HEIs. These institutions find themselves under pressure to demonstrate research credentials and outcomes without corresponding support for developing research capacities. This paradox stems from the fact that Czech higher education and research policies are centred on the dominant university sector. The Czech national research policy and funding are virtually blind to non-university HEIs, forcing them to fulfil the same criteria as public universities to receive formula-based institutional funding and to compete with public universities (and other research organisations) for other forms of institutional and project funding. In the area of higher education policy, non-university HEIs are subject to the same academically based accreditation requirements as public universities, of which the staffing requirement consistently proves the most significant. I have argued that Czech non-university HEIs employ two fundamental strategies to manage the pressure: in their institutional staffing strategy, they rely to a large extent on academics simultaneously affiliated to public universities; in their research strategy, they redefine the content and the boundaries of what constitutes research. While the causes and consequences of the first strategy have already been extensively commented upon both in the Czech context (e.g. Machálková, 2006; Možný, 2006) and internationally (e.g. Kwiek, 2003), I would like to focus on the latter issue.

As I have argued above, Czech non-university HEIs use considerably more inclusive definition of research than is that employed by the state authorities. The research assessment supervised by the governmental Research and Development Council lays emphasis on traditional bibliometric criteria (impact factor, peer-reviewed journals and monographs) and on indicators of innovation (patents, technology transfer), while the standards employed by the Accreditation Commission emphasise research qualifications and peer-reviewed journal publications (Research and Development Council, 2007; Accreditation Commission, 2005). In contrast, non-university HEIs include much broader range of activities and outputs (most often closely related to teaching) into their definition of research. This redefinition of research is implicit rather than explicit in the institutional documents and has not yet been discussed publicly in the Czech context. Nonetheless, it obviously resonates with the US and international debates about the expansion of the category of 'scholarship' beyond the traditional category of 'research' (Boyer, 1990; Harman, 2006). Viewed in the context of these debates, Czech non-university HEIs and their academic staff suffer from the fact that Czech higher education and research policies systematically prefer the 'scholarship of discovery' to other dimensions of scholarship that are clearly discernible in the activities of these institutions, especially the scholarship of teaching and scholarship of application.

The redefinition and expansion of the 'official' categories is visible also in the external outreach of the Czech non-university HEIs. In contrast to the focus on research collaboration with industry and on technology transfer, which dominates the public debates and policies (e.g. Klusáček, Kučera, & Pazour, 2008), Czech non-university HEIs collaborate more frequently with institutions in the public sector and definitely prefer the area of teaching and training. Again, their activities correspond to broader definition of 'knowledge transfer' between higher education and their environment. Marilyn Wedgwood (2006) has recently argued that the focus on the collaboration with business, which revolves around research in the sciences and is driven by the economic growth agenda, should be expanded to include knowledge transfer in other academic disciplines, carried out in collaboration with non-profit and public actors and driven by social and cultural policy agendas. Using Wedgwood's analytical categories, the external outreach of the Czech non-university HEIs may be conceptualised as teaching-led, engaged with the 'community' rather than 'business' and frequently transcending the economic growth perspective to include the 'quality of life agenda'. As in the case of the category of 'research', this extension of the external mission of the non-university HEIs is implicit in their activities rather than explicitly developed in the institutional strategies. In fact, there has been so far no strategic or policy debate on this topic in the Czech Republic, which also means that there are no policy and funding instruments to support these forms of external engagement. Recognising the diversity of institutional and academic activities thus presents one of the most important challenges for the future development of the Czech non-university sector.

Acknowledgements I would like to thank Dominika Šrajerová for her assistance in researching this topic, and Michael Voříšek and Karel Šima for their comments on earlier versions of this chapter.

References

Accreditation Commission. (2005). *Standardy Akreditační komise pro posuzování žádostí o akreditaci, rozšíření akreditace a prodloužení doby platnosti akreditace studijních programů a jejich oborů.* Praha: Akreditační komise.
Association of Professional Education Colleges. (2006). *Výzvy na závěr konference konané u příležitosti 10.výročí vzniku vyšších odborných škol* (2006). Praha: Asociace vyšších odborných škol.

Blažek, J., & Uhlíř, D. (2007). Regional innovation policies in the Czech Republic and the case of Prague: An emerging role of a regional level? *European Planning Studies, 15*, 871–888.

Boyer, E. L. (1990). *Scholarship reconsidered: Priorities of the professoriate*. Princeton, NJ: Carnegie Foundation.

Brno International Business School. (2005). *Dlouhodobý záměr vzdělávací, vědecké, výzkumné, a další tvůrčí činnosti Brno International Business School – B.I.B.S., a.s. na období let 2006–2010*. Brno: Brno International Business School.

Čerych, L., Anweiler, O., Blume, S., Jerschina, J., & Wagner, A. (1992). *Review of higher education in the Czech and Slovak Federal Republic: Examiners' report and questions*. Paris: OECD.

File, J., Weko, T., Hauptman, A., Kristensen, B., & Herlitschka, S. (2006). *Czech Republic country note: OECD thematic review of tertiary education*. Prague: Centre for Higher Education Studies.

Government of the Czech Republic. (2004). *National Research and Development Policy of the Czech Republic for 2004–2008*. Praha: Vláda České republiky.

Harman, G. (2006). Research and scholarship. In J. F. Forest & P. G. Altbach (Eds.), *International handbook of higher education* (pp. 309–328). Dordrecht: Springer.

Hartman, J., & Drnka, P. (1987). *Vysoké školy*. Praha: SPN.

Janyš, B., Homolka, J., Macura, J., Pražmová, M., Riedl, M., & Sekot, J. (2007). *Návrh řešení transformace vyšších odborných škol ČR do terciárního sektoru vzdělávání a jeho legislativní zabezpečení* (2007). Praha: Asociace vyšších odborných škol.

Karran, T. (2007). Academic freedom in Europe: A preliminary comparative analysis. *Higher Education Policy, 20*, 289–313.

Klusáček, K., Kučera, Z., & Pazour, M. (2008). *Zelená kniha výzkumu, vývoje a inovací v České republice*. Praha: Technologické centrum AV ČR.

Kohoutek, J., Sojka, M., Šebková, H., & Vinš, V. (2006). Assuring the quality of tertiary education. In H. Šebková (Ed.), *Tertiary education in the Czech Republic: Country background report for OECD thematic review of tertiary education* (pp. 82–90). Prague: Centre for Higher Education Studies.

Kwiek, M. (2003). Academe in transition: Transformations in the Polish academic profession. *Higher Education, 45*, 455–476.

Machálková, J. (2006, July 8). Létající profesoři. *Lidové noviny*, 2006.

Melichar, M., & Pabian, P. (2007). Shifting peripheries: A state of the art report on the Czech academic profession. In W. Locke & U. Teichler (Eds.), *The changing conditions for academic work and careers in select countries* (pp. 39–56). Kassel: INCHER.

Ministry of Education. (2005). *Long-term plan for educational, scientific, research, development, artistic, and other creative activities of higher education institutions for 2006–2010*. Prague: Ministry of Education, Youth and Sports.

Ministry of Education. (2007). *Docenti jmenovaní od roku 1999*. Praha: Ministerstvo školství, mládeže a tělovýchovy.

Ministry of Education. (2009a). *Profesoři jmenovaní od roku 1999*. Praha: Ministerstvo školství, mládeže a tělovýchovy.

Ministry of Education. (2009b). *White paper on tertiary education*. Praha: Ministerstvo školství, mládeže a tělovýchovy.

Možný, I. (2006, July 22). Proč létající profesoři daleko nedoletí. *Lidové noviny*, 2006.

Newton, C. (2005). *Dlouhodobý záměr vzdělávací, výzkumné, vývojové a další tvůrčí činnosti NEWTON College pro období 2006–2010* (2005). Brno: Newton College.

Pabian, P. (2007). Role výzkumu a vývoje v neuniverzitním sektoru terciárního vzdělávání: Česká republika v evropském kontextu. In Littera scripta: Sborník z II. konference "Problematika terciárního vzdělávání" (pp. 60–68). České Budějovice: VŠTE.

Pabian, P. (2009). Europeanisation of higher education governance in the post-communist context: The case of the Czech Republic. In A. Amaral, G. Neave, C. Musselin, & P. Maassen (Eds.), *European integration and the governance of higher education and research* (257–278). Dordrecht: Springer.

Research and Development Council. (2007). *Metodika hodnocení výzkumu a vývoje a jejich výsledků v roce 2007*. Praha: Rada pro vědu a výzkum.

Research and Development Council. (2008a). *Hodnocení výzkumu a vývoje a jejich výsledkuů v roce 2007*. Praha: Rada pro vědu a výzkum.

Research and Development Council. (2008b). *Reform of the system of research, development and innovation in the Czech Republic*. Praha: Rada pro vědu a výzkum.

Šima, K. (2007). Institucionální financování výzkumu a vývoje v ČR. *Aula, 15*, 60–74.

Šima, K. (2008). *Public funding of research in Central and Eastern European countries: Czech Republic country report*. Lugano: European Network of Indicators Designers.

Šima, K. (2009). Výzkum v terciárním vzdělávání. In L. Prudký, P. Pabian, & K. Šima (Eds.), *Vysoké školství v ČR: jen pro elitu, nebo pro všechny?* Praha: Grada.

Wedgwood, M. (2006). Mainstreaming the third stream. In I. McNay (Ed.), *Beyond mass higher education: Building on experience* (pp. 134–157). Maidenhead: SRHE & Open University Press.

Chapter 8
'We Are a Training and Development Organisation' – Research and Development in Finnish Polytechnics

Jussi Välimaa and Marja-Liisa Neuvonen-Rauhala

Introduction

Finnish higher education became a mass higher education system in the 1970s. The expansion of the higher education system from the 1960s to the 1990s was closely linked with a strong welfare-state agenda (Välimaa, 2001). The Finnish tradition of higher education is rooted in the Nordic ideology of a welfare state in which citizens and permanent residents may pursue a place in the tuition-free higher education system. In 2006, there were about 307,000 students in Finnish higher education. About 177,000 of them studied in universities and 130,000 in polytechnics.

Finnish polytechnics and universities are understood as 'equal but different'. This means that the mission of universities is to conduct research and provide undergraduate and postgraduate education based on it, whereas the polytechnics aim to train professionals in response to labour market needs and conduct R&D which supports instruction and promotes regional development in particular. This dividing line is, however, challenged both by higher education policies which have introduced research and development functions and master's degrees to polytechnics and by polytechnics themselves which have started to call themselves as 'universities of applied sciences'. In this chapter we will refer to them as polytechnics for simplicity. The aim of this study is to analyse how the research and development (R&D) function influences the internal dynamics of polytechnics.

There were 28 polytechnics and 20 universities in Finland in 2008. According to the Ministry of Education, there will be only 15 universities and 18 polytechnics by the year 2020. Polytechnics are located all over the country, and most of them (26) are multidisciplinary institutions operating under the Ministry of Education. In addition to the 26 polytechnics funded by the Ministry of Education, the category of polytechnics also includes the Police College (funded and steered by the Ministry of Interior) and Åland University of Applied Sciences, subordinated to the self-governing Åland Islands.

J. Välimaa (✉)
Finnish Institute for Educational Research, University of Jyväskylä, Jyväskylä, Finland
e-mail: jussi.p.valimaa@jyu.fi

S. Kyvik, B. Lepori (eds.), *The Research Mission of Higher Education Institutions Outside the University Sector*, Higher Education Dynamics 31, DOI 10.1007/978-1-4020-9244-2_8, © Springer Science+Business Media B.V. 2010

The establishment of polytechnics was initiated at the beginning of the 1990s, when the Finnish state was hit by a severe and sudden economic recession after a decade of national economic boom. Within this context, the social crisis made new initiatives both politically and practically desirable. The Finnish government launched the polytechnic reform as an experiment – which is a typical Finnish reform strategy (Välimaa, 2005) – also because the decision-makers were quite unprepared for such a grand move to accept the rapid establishment of a new sector of higher education. The establishment of polytechnics was the major reform of the Finnish higher education in the 1990s. By 2000 all of the experimental polytechnics had developed into polytechnics operating on a permanent basis (Välimaa & Neuvonen-Rauhala, 2008).

All of the 19 regions of Finland have at least one polytechnic, while the more densely populated regions have several. The 26 polytechnics steered by the Ministry of Education have about 200 units in their regions – from single small units in small towns to several units in larger towns (OECD, 2003). The education provided by the polytechnics falls into seven main sectors. These are: (1) business and administration, (2) culture, (3) health care and social services, (4) humanities and education, (5) natural resources, (6) technology and communication, and (7) tourism, catering and institutional management (OECD, 2003).

Finnish polytechnics are most often local and regional establishments operated either by a federation of municipalities (10 polytechnics), a limited company of which most are operated by municipalities and/or federations of municipalities (11 polytechnics) or an urban municipality (5 polytechnics). Polytechnics can be divided into three categories on the basis of their student numbers, which is perhaps the best way to describe their regional influence (see Table 8.1). The category of small polytechnics consists of ten institutions, including two polytechnics not steered by the Ministry of Education. This category contains also one Swedish-speaking polytechnic, two nation-wide polytechnics and three polytechnics located in the more remote regions of Finland. The category of medium-sized polytechnics consists of 11 higher education institutions based all over the country, whereas the largest polytechnics (8 institutions) are located mainly in the Southern parts of Finland. The number of study fields offered by a polytechnic depends mainly on its traditions and region without any connection to its size. The smallest polytechnics may have 3–7 study fields, medium-sized and large polytechnics 4–8.

Table 8.1 Finnish polytechnics by student numbers in 2004–2005

Categories of polytechnics	Number of students	Number of polytechnics
Small polytechnics	<3,000	10
Medium-sized polytechnics	3,000–5,500	11
Large polytechnics	5,500–10,000	8

Source: OPM (2005, 2006).

The smallest polytechnic among those subordinated to the Ministry of Education has about 1,300 students (Humanistic Polytechnic), whereas the largest polytechnic by student number is Haaga-Helia University of Applied Sciences with about 10,000 students. The largest polytechnic is a new polytechnic, called Metropolia, with its 13,000 students in 2008. For the purpose of providing a comparative perspective it should be mentioned that there were 4,300 students in the smallest multidisciplinary university (University of Lapland) and 35,300 students in the largest one (University of Helsinki) in 2005.

National Policies for Research in Non-university Institutions

The Finnish higher education system is steered by the Ministry of Education. However, in line with the Nordic traditions of higher education, Finnish tertiary education institutions enjoy a high degree of institutional autonomy, which is both secured in the Finnish Constitution and guaranteed by laws governing universities (Universities Act 715/2004) and polytechnics (Polytechnic Act 351/2003). In this social context, it is natural that the institutions themselves take full responsibility for the standard and quality of the education and research they provide. According to the Polytechnic Act (351/2003, 4§), the tasks of the polytechnics are *to provide teaching which is based on scientific or artistic foundations aiming to produce high expertise in the related fields, to support the students' professional development, to conduct applied research and development which supports both the development of teaching and regional development and working life with the aim of advancing regional economic structures* (Free translation, J.V.).

This Polytechnic Act changed the traditional tasks of polytechnics quite radically, because it states that polytechnics are supposed to take care of applied research and development projects in cooperation with the enterprises in their regions. This is a radical change in Finland, because originally polytechnics were established as higher vocational teaching institutions. In the first Polytechnic Act (255/1995) research was connected to the polytechnic's teaching task. The definition was rather imprecise and led to different interpretations in practice.

The aims of the national legislation are translated into action through the Development Plan for Education and Research, written by the Ministry of Education for each new government (for a 5-year period). The present Development Plan for Education and Research covered the years 2003–2008, whereas the new one will cover the 5 years between 2007 and 2012. It is quite normal that Development Plans have a thematic continuity, even though every government normally wishes to emphasise the policy goals somewhat differently. This document is an important policy-making paper, because together with the Programme of the Government it sets the frames and objectives for national policy-making for the government. The Development Plan focuses on an abstract national level, but it is taken seriously by all the actors in the field of higher education policy-making, because it can be utilised as a point of reference in policy-implementation debates.

In the Development Plan (2007–2012) the primary mission of polytechnics is to provide and develop professional higher education closely connected with working life and to conduct R&D which serves working life and regional development as well as teaching (OPM, 2007). The Development Plan defines polytechnics as active partners in innovation networks, both through education in the workplaces and through R&D activities, especially with the service sector's business enterprises. The development plan also emphasises the quality of higher education and the need to continue 'structural development' of Finnish higher education.

The steering of the national higher education system is based on performance agreements. This means that each year every higher education institution signs a performance agreement with the Ministry of Education. In the social context of trust, performance agreements define the funding of higher education institutions and set the targets for their outputs (in terms of degrees) and development activities to be carried out. In the Finnish cultural context it is, again, natural for the institutions and academics to take the agreements seriously.

Strategic points emphasised in governmental documents and strategies are normally included in the strategies of polytechnics (see, e.g. OPM, 2004, p. 7). Consequently, it is commonly mentioned in the performance agreements that students with their teachers are seen as key actors in regional activities. Furthermore, practical working-life issues in need of development activities are seen as one of the most important starting points for R&D in polytechnics. Entrepreneurial objectives are also commonly mentioned in performance agreements.

Strategic Goals and Guidelines for Research

According to the Ministry of Education, polytechnics have already become essential actors in the regional innovation system, but they should enhance their regional impact with measures taken to develop the structure of education provision, to combine polytechnics' regional development projects into larger entities linking different sectors and to boost networking with different stakeholders, higher education institutions and schools (OPM, 2004, p. 8). Polytechnics' contacts with the world of work have also improved significantly with the aim of evolving into development processes, which benefit all the partners involved. Supporting small and medium-sized enterprises and developing welfare services is a special responsibility for polytechnics in the light of regional development. The networked regional higher education institutions composed of polytechnics and universities are also developed in response to regional needs. According to the Ministry of Education, the aim is to strengthen the role of polytechnics in the promotion of business incubators and to undertake projects to facilitate business successions and women's entrepreneurship.

'Structural development' is often used as euphemism to hide the fact that the number of Finnish higher education institutions (both polytechnics and universities) needs to be reduced. In this higher education policy context, Finnish polytechnics have been 'encouraged' to merge into larger units. This has lead to merger operations between smaller units, or to the discontinuation of those units that were not seen as viable by the Ministry of Education in 2007. The aim of the 'structural development' is to create more efficient and viable higher education institutions and/or their combinations. One of the consequences of this policy objective is the fact that polytechnics have been active in starting merger operations by themselves. The first merger of two polytechnics took place at the beginning of year 2007.

One of the most important policy goals of the 'structural development' of Finnish higher education is to develop the polytechnic network and education. The goal is to achieve a balanced provision both as to the regions and the linguistic groups, to target provision according to the needs of working life and to build efficient units. The aim is to create a network in which each unit offering degree education is large enough to be able to provide education of a sufficiently high standard and to conduct R&D which serves the region. The restructuring aims at enabling each polytechnic unit to develop into an entity that provides degree education and conducts regionally relevant R&D, which also reaches high European and international standards. The aim is to develop the structure and education of polytechnics in order to enable them, as key players in the innovation system, to provide adult education and services which cater to the development aspirations of the local authorities in the region, local businesses and work communities, and local residents (OPM, 2004, p. 8).

The basis for this development and cooperation is created by higher education institutions' joint regional strategies and plans for the development of international research cooperation and the utilisation of research findings. Universities and polytechnics are encouraged to strengthen their relations with working life by developing their business know-how and innovation services and by developing the commercialisation of research findings. The aim is also to promote the social and cultural utilisation of their research and knowledge production. Furthermore, the Ministry of Education states that 'Prerequisites for university research and polytechnic R&D will be strengthened. Research development will stress internationally competitive and ethically sustainable high-quality research. The procedures for the commercialisation of research findings will be clarified' (OPM, 2004, p. 8).

As can be seen from these citations, the Ministry of Education does not make an essential difference between the aims of polytechnics and universities regarding R&D tasks. The only and primary difference is defined by the kind of research polytechnics and universities are expected to conduct. The focus of university research is on basic research, whereas polytechnics are expected to conduct research and development projects which promote regional innovations in particular.

Priority Setting Between Teaching and Research

The National Audit Office (NAO) audited R&D performance in polytechnics in 2006. The NAO report (2006, pp. 162–163) share the views of the Ministry of Education, when they state that the majority of the research and development activities in polytechnics can be characterised as adaptive projects, which are linked to industry or which support teaching in their regions. These objectives are also those defined by the Ministry of Education, because it is expected that R&D in polytechnics both support teaching and take students into the research and development projects. These aims have also been emphasised in the postgraduate polytechnic degrees (or, polytechnic master's degrees). For the year 2007 the Ministry of Education emphasised the development of R&D in teaching and the connections between R&D and developing activities in polytechnics. The Ministry of Education expects that teachers and students should have better possibilities to take part in R&D activities and researchers and project staff should be connected to teaching more closely.

According to their report (NAO, 2006, pp. 163–165), the polytechnics and their stakeholders were asked to assess how R&D and teaching are connected to each other in polytechnics. One of the main outcomes is that there are many connections. Theses are generally seen as a key way for organising local R&D activities in polytechnics. Postgraduate polytechnic degrees emphasise theses in this context, because the function of a thesis is determined based on the development of the working life. Ideally, theses should be done in close connection with working life and with the R&D in polytechnics. A crucial question is: what kind of R&D should polytechnics conduct and how should it be organised? This question is significant, because the answer to it is strongly related to the ways in which R&D will be developed in polytechnics by their staff (Kainulainen, 2004).

Funding of Research

The exact estimation of R&D conducted in Finnish higher education institutions is rather difficult, because of the variation and mixture between basic and applied research. However, it can be estimated that R&D conducted in polytechnics formed about 10% of the R&D conducted in universities in 2004. Funding based non-governmental resources in polytechnics is only 15% of such funding in universities (NAO, 2006). According to the National Audit Office's report, the proportions of the polytechnics' own R&D funding have not changed substantially the funding of teaching in polytechnics, because polytechnics have other funding resources than governmental funding. However, polytechnics evaluate that their incomes from business activities do not cover the polytechnics' own share demanded for R&D funding. This means that there are pressures to transfer resources from teaching to R&D, especially when other funding instruments are not yet available for funding polytechnics and the EU funding period is ending.

Funding is defined as the main problem in R&D activities. There are many reasons for that. First, many funding decisions are directed to small projects and to many kinds of projects, instead of focusing funding on strategically important larger projects. Second, and traditionally, the Academy of Finland – the most important academic funding agency – does not allocate funding to polytechnics. The second most relevant funding body is Tekes, which supports cooperation projects between researchers and business enterprises. However, Tekes allocates only partial funding to polytechnics, whereas universities receive total funding as long as they are civil service offices. Universities can not use governmental funding to co-fund Tekes projects but polytechnics are treated in a different way because of their different maintaining organisations. Third, the European Social Fund (ESF) is the most important funding body for R&D in polytechnics. However, one of problems for polytechnics is the fact that ESF funding will be reduced during the funding period of 2008–2012 (NAO, 2006, pp. 159–162).

The European Union is a very important funding body for funding R&D staff resources in polytechnics as can be seen in Table 8.2, because the staff funded by the EU funding instruments make up almost half of the total number of R&D staff. Staff in R&D means researchers, but it also includes teachers' working hours used for R&D (see also Table 8.4 for more details). Staff for business activities refers to continuing education funded by participants and enterprises, which often includes development activities. However, it may also means services that are for sale, for instance, restaurant and congress services, laboratory services for different purposes, etc.

Performance agreements between polytechnics and the Ministry of Education for the years 2007–2009 state that the quantitative objective for R&D resources is to collect 10% of the funding from other sources than the government.

Table 8.2 Characteristics of research and development in polytechnics

	2000	2001	2002	2003	2004	2005	2006
R&D costs (€ million)	32	44	56	49.6	88.7	99.6	
Staff (excluding. teachers) for projects funded by public institutions (incl. EU)	411	455	422	421	446	455	492
Staff for R&D	*	*	296	482	484	579	614
Staff for business activities	341	327	288	278	274	270	276

R&D was not a staff category until 2002.
Source: OPM (2004, p. 7, 2006, p. 42), AMKOTA Database.

Research Strategy in Non-university Institutions

All polytechnics have agreed with the Ministry of Education – in their performance agreements – that they will contribute to the regional higher education strategies and regional strategies with partners and working life. The Ministry of Education and polytechnics have investigated possibilities of advancing R&D. There are opportunities to develop the role of the polytechnics in the regional innovation systems. This means cooperation with other polytechnics and universities, intensification of working-life connections of teachers and other staff with possibilities to take part in R&D activities, and the aim to motivate students to participate in R&D while studying for their postgraduate polytechnic degrees (NAO, 2006, p. 152).

Almost every polytechnic has an R&D strategy, and even those polytechnics which do not have it have included R&D into the general development strategy for the whole polytechnic. Most of the polytechnics emphasise that they are responsible for applied R&D (see, e.g. OPM, 2004, p. 7).

The Organisation and Management of Research

In 2004, the variation in the allocation of manpower for R&D in different polytechnics ranged from one person to as many as 100 persons allocated for R&D (OPM, 2004). Due to this variation, there are many different organisational solutions for meeting the needs of R&D in polytechnics. Most of the polytechnics emphasise that their R&D is connected to teaching, or at least they will strengthen this connection. Many polytechnics emphasise that their R&D is a part of teaching and for that reason R&D is tied to all educational activities. Some polytechnics have established an R&D unit to support R&D activities and projects, whereas other polytechnics have positioned research coordination into their service centres. Practically, all polytechnics have persons responsible for coordinating research projects, whether they are called project managers (or coordinators) or directors of research.

For example, Lahti University of Applied Sciences has established an Innovation Centre in order to promote and coordinate R&D projects. This polytechnic has also established the position of the Director of Research with the aim to better coordinate R&D in the institution. In HAMK University of Applied Sciences the organisational decision is to organise research and development into 'Centres of Know How', with the idea of combining R&D with teaching and student theses. Some polytechnics (like Jyväskylä University of Applied Sciences) have allocated, in turn, the responsibility for developing R&D to the Director of Development, while the actual R&D is carried out in R&D projects.

Again, the Ministry of Education is supporting organisational and developmental issues of R&D in polytechnics by funding the cooperational network of polytechnics called AMKtutka (R&D as a part of tasks of polytechnics) during years 2007–2009. The network is coordinated by one of the polytechnics – Mikkeli University of Applied Sciences. The aim of the AMKtutka is to develop connections between teaching and R&D. The network aims at developing new pedagogical innovations, strategic and structural solutions for connecting all the tasks of polytechnics. The goal is also to develop and share common concepts and views concerning R&D in polytechnics. It may be argued that the 'equal but different' higher education policy principle guiding the cooperation with universities will also guide R&D to be developed in the forthcoming years (see also Vesterinen, 2006; Kainulainen, 2004).

Collaboration with Universities and Industry

According to a study by Marttila, Kautonen, Niemonen, and von Bell (2004, pp. 60–65), polytechnics collaborate extensively with industry. In some cases most of the studied companies had connections with polytechnics in Central parts of Finland and in the Tampere Region. The most common cooperation took place through student theses, but contract research and development projects were also usual ways of organising cooperation. According to Marttila et al. (2004, p. 61), companies that collaborated with polytechnics did it also with universities and research companies or with other consultation organisations. This cooperation was supported by the funding of public finance organisations.

The most common method of collaboration between industry and polytechnics is an R&D activity and working-life connection through teaching. This involves student theses, practicing periods in companies and different kinds of projects. The second most common method is through service activities offered by polytechnics to companies. These activities include continuing education and renting buildings and facilities. The third method of collaboration includes organising recruitment, presentations or meetings with the boards of education in the fields where polytechnics offer teaching (Marttila et al., 2004).

Marttila et al. (2004, pp. 103–104) conclude that locality is the most important factor when companies choose whom they collaborate with, even though the activity of polytechnic teachers is crucial when the collaboration starts. However, the intensity of collaboration also depends on the general economic situation.

Human Resources and Careers

In 2004, Finnish polytechnics employed 955 senior teachers, 3,431 lecturers and 1,493 full-time teachers and 5,921 other staff (AMKOTA, 2004). The composition and structure of the polytechnic teaching staff differs significantly from that of the universities, because there are neither professorships nor assistantships. This is due to polytechnics' tradition and mission to provide vocational education. The most prestigious category of polytechnic teachers is the senior lecturer (yliopettaja), who is responsible for developing the professional fields. Required by the Ministry of Education, polytechnics aim at recruiting PhDs or holders of licentiate degrees to these positions also because they are defined as equal further education degrees by the Ministry of Education. Polytechnics have also succeeded rather well in achieving this objective, as can be seen in Table 8.3.

Polytechnic lecturers' job profiles resemble those of traditional university lecturers, because neither of them is expected to do research. Most lecturers and full-time teachers in polytechnics hold either an MA or a professional degree. Senior lecturers, lecturers and full-time teachers have a permanent position, unlike part-time teachers. The high proportion of women teachers may be explained by the polytechnics' orientation. In social work, health care, culture and tourism women are

Table 8.3 Staff in Finnish polytechnics funded by the Ministry of Education by gender and degree in 2004

	Proportion of female staff (in 2005)	PhD	Lic.Phil	M.A.	B.A.	Polytechnic degree or other	Total (N)
Senior lecturer	40.2%	30.5% (291)	39.2% (375)	26.8% (256)	1.1% (11)	2.3% (23)	(955)
Lecturer	62%	2.1% (72)	5.7% (195)	84.2% (2,888)	1.8% (62)	6.4% (219)	(3,431)
Full-time teacher	53.4%	1.7% (26)	3.1% (47)	55.6% (830)	8.9% (133)	30.7% (458)	(1,493)
Project staff	49.5%	4.6% (43)	2.4% (22)	32.5% (302)	1.6% (15)	51.4% (478)	(860)
Total (N)	58.3%	6.4% (432)	9.5% (639)	63.5% (4,276)	3.3% (221)	17.5% (1,178)	(6,739)

Source: AMKOTA database.

the majority. These are also strong fields in most polytechnics (OECD, 2003). Increasing numbers of staff members are engaged in research and development activities. In 2004, polytechnics had 484 people with duties of this kind in addition to 446 project workers. These expanding staff groups – called here the 'project staff' – are an interesting group also from the point of view of policy, because they indicate a growth in research and development activities.

The Extent and Output of Research

In order to see more precisely what the activities carried out in Finnish polytechnics are, we will rely on two different sources. The National Audit Office (NAO) audited R&D performance in polytechnics in 2006, whereas Statistics Finland has analysed the use of working hours in Finnish higher education between various tasks (Statistics Finland, 2006). The category of research consists of several different activities carried out in universities and polytechnics. These are as follows: (1) completing one's doctoral dissertation (or licentiate thesis), (2) other research tasks (including management of research), (3) artistic work, (4) participation in scientific and professional meetings, and (5) participation in other training.

The statistical analysis is based on the survey sent to a sample of Finnish higher education staff members (teachers and researchers), who were funded by the Ministry of Education in 2004. The response rate was 53.8% for polytechnics and 58% in universities. However, the statistical analysis excludes the staff not funded through direct budget funding from the Ministry of Education. This also explains why the number of posts differs from the data provided by the AMKOTA database (Table 8.4).

Teaching is the most important activity in all groups of polytechnic teachers. Lecturers and full-time teachers use most of their working hours for teaching (75–81%), whereas senior lecturers use two thirds of their working hours for teaching activities. Also, the group of researchers is rather active in teaching, using almost one third of their working hours for teaching. The category of teaching consists of many kinds of different activities and tasks. It includes both preparatory hours for basic level (bachelor) teaching and contact teaching hours. It also includes other basic level teaching and tutoring. Furthermore, literary and other examinations belong to teaching activities, as well as teaching of professional teacher

Table 8.4 Weekly working hours of polytechnic teachers and researchers, and proportion of time spent on different activities (funded through direct budget funding/Ministry of Education), in 2004

Staff category	Teaching (%)	Research (%)	Other	Total h/week	(N)
Senior lecturer	64	16	20	42	(747)
Lecturer	75	8	17	42	(2,740)
FT teacher	81	7	12	40	(1,098)
Researcher	30	47	24	35	(49)
Total	74	10	16	41	(4,635)

Source: Statistics Finland (2006).

training. Teaching also consists of open higher education tutoring and preparatory hours, and higher level (master's level) contact teaching and its preparatory
hours.

It is quite natural that researchers are the most active group carrying out research.
They used almost half of their working time for research activities. The total amount
of research done by researchers is, however, rather small due to their small number in polytechnics: 49 persons is only about 1% of the whole population funded
through direct budget funding. However, when we take into account also the staff
for R&D funded through other sources – 484 persons in 2004 (see Table 8.2) – it is
evident that the research mission is becoming rather extensive also in polytechnics
(Statistics Finland, 2006).

Crucially important for the research function in polytechnics is the fact that
senior lecturers use as much as 16% of their weekly working hours for some kind of
research activities. This indicates that it is socially accepted and expected of them to
conduct research projects and to take care of the research development in polytechnics. This is also quite natural, because as many as 64% of them have an academic
research training (see Table 8.3). The most research-active group of senior lecturers
consists of people aged 30–50 years. They use as much as 19% of their working
time for research, whereas the senior lecturers older than 50 years of age use only
14% of their working time for research (Statistics Finland, 2006).

Lecturers and full-time teachers do very little research, only 7–8% of their
weekly working hours. According to the survey, this research work consists of doing
their doctoral dissertations or licentiate theses (1 h/week). This university research
category is, however, quite problematic in polytechnics, where the common rule is
not to allow lecturers to write a dissertation during office hours. It consists of other
research (1.3 weekly working hours) and participating in scientific conferences and
meetings (1.8 weekly working hours), which makes about 4 h a week, whereas
senior lecturers use almost 7 working hours per week for these activities (Statistics
Finland, 2006).

The most 'research-intensive' fields of research in polytechnics are culture (14%
of working hours allocated for research) and social work, health and physical education (11% of working hours allocated for research), whereas the fields of natural
resources (with 6% of working hours allocated for research) and humanities (with
7% of working hours allocated for research) are the least 'research-intensive' fields
in polytechnics.

We can also see remarkable differences in the time allocated to research between
different polytechnics. There is a group of polytechnics (four polytechnics) which
allocate 14–18% of their working hours to research. The most 'research-intensive'
polytechnics are the Swedish-speaking polytechnics. Also, some Finnish-speaking
polytechnics belong to this group. The second group allocates 9–13% of their working time funded by the Ministry of Education to research. This is the largest group
consisting of 13 polytechnics. The third group consists of polytechnics, which allocate 5–8% of their working time to research. This group consists of 12 polytechnics
(Statistics Finland, 2006).

As to the time allocated to research, no simple causal relationship exists between the study fields and polytechnics, because all polytechnics consist of a combination of 3–8 study fields. It is evident, however, that institutional traditions play a role. In addition, the local situation (close to universities) and conditions may play a role in this kind of statistical information gathering. For example, full-time concentration on doing one's dissertation or licentiate thesis may have a significant impact on the average hours calculated in one's institutions, especially in small polytechnics (Statistics Finland, 2006).

When comparing these figures with those of universities, it can be seen that universities allocate 43% of their working hours to teaching, which is almost half of that allocated in polytechnics (74%). Working time allocated to research is 39% in universities, which is almost four times more than the time allocated to research in polytechnics (Statistics Finland, 2006).

R&D in Two Non-university Institutions

In order to understand the relevance of research for regional community better, we will analyse the cases of Lahti University of Applied Sciences and that of the Jyväskylä University of Applied Sciences. Lahti represents a polytechnic where the aim is to organise research and development through a special 'Innovation Centre', whereas Jyväskylä represents a polytechnic where R&D is more integrated into the normal teaching activities. Both of these polytechnics received extra funding from the Ministry of Education on the basis of their performance in R&D in 2006. These case studies are based on the web pages of the polytechnics, interviews and literary sources (Karppanen et al., 2007; Käyhkö et al., 2006).

The Case of Lahti University of Applied Sciences

Lahti University of Applied Sciences (LUAS) is a multidisciplinary higher education institution located in the city of Lahti in the southern part of Finland, with 5,000 students and 450 staff members. LUAS aims at creating innovations which promote welfare, economic and cultural life in the region and internal development in the higher education institution itself. Research and development is defined in LUAS as a systematic action to increase the amount of information and to apply the gained information to finding new applications and solving practical problems. The criterion for R&D is to pursue, find or produce something that is not only new, but also consequential.

The majority of the R&D projects are led and run by project staff working in the Innovation Centre, which is a specific unit within LUAS. It was established in 2004 with the aim to lead, coordinate and develop research and development in LUAS. The volume of R&D has developed rapidly from €1.1 million in 2003 to

€3.8 million in 2005. The organisational role of the Innovation Centre has been evaluated as central for LUAS (Karppanen et al., 2007.)

There were approximately 30 on-going projects in LUAS in the autumn of 2007. They were partly funded by The European Social Fund (ESF) or by the European Commission, together with funding from companies and using the funding of the LUAS. Most of the projects aimed (1) to develop the know-how and the skills of the staff in companies, or (2) to develop education. The other project categories include: (3) developing business, competitiveness and internationalisation and establishment into new market areas; (4) entrepreneurship and business succession; (5) tourism development; (6) anticipating future needs of the labour force and education, and (7) promoting R&D activities and education in disciplinary fields. The projects include, for example, staff training projects for business enterprises to teach new ICT technologies and visual design, or leadership training. Educational development projects aim at developing cooperation between higher education units and training development in a specific educational fields or target groups. Some of the projects are conducted in cooperation with partners from different countries.

The promotion of entrepreneurship takes place in degree education and it is supported by the FINPIN Network (Finnish Polytechnics Entrepreneurship Network), which is run by LUAS for all the Finnish polytechnics. All these activities are professionally administrated and run by the Innovation Centre. However, and in addition to these projects, there are many activities which are connected to teaching and learning, and taken care of by teachers and senior lecturers. These activities include students' project works and theses done in companies and other organisations as part of their degree studies. The director of research at LUAS also emphasised that the R&D activities connected to teaching will be crucial in the near future in polytechnics. When defining the purpose of LUAS, he said that 'we are a training and development organisation'.

The Case of Jyväskylä University of Applied Sciences

Jyväskylä University of Applied Sciences (JUAS) is a multidisciplinary institution with several units located around the city of Jyväskylä – also in two rural communities. This higher education institution includes the following eight schools: Cultural Studies, Business, Engineering and Technology, Information Technology, Health and Social Care, Tourism and Services Management, Institute of Natural Resources and Teacher Education College, which is responsible for training vocational education teachers. The number of students is about 8,000 and that of the staff 780 in 2007. There were 32 bachelor-level study programmes and two master's-level study programmes.

According to their web pages JUAS 'assumes responsibility for the development of Central Finland and reacts quickly to the region's educational needs. Our responsibilities include research and development activity concerned with enterprise and working life. Our activities emphasise, in particular, the promotion of small and medium-sized enterprises as well as development within the public sector.' In 2004,

JUAS allocated about 100 working years for R&D projects, and currently they have about 50 on-going R&D projects, which can be categorised according to their focus as follows:

- Agricultural training and development projects
- Business skills development projects
- Education
- Energy/Bio-energy development projects
- Internationalisation
- IT development and training projects
- Regional business development projects
- Social infrastructure development projects
- Tourism
- Wellness technologies.

These projects aim at the development of the region with the help of training and information gathering and analysis. In this sense, they differ from traditional university research projects, which primarily focus on research and only secondarily think about the possible implementation into practice. The aim of these projects is to develop a variety of regional activities through training and network building. These development projects focus on the region of Central Finland. According to the rector of the JUAS, the mission and objectives of R&D are to promote internationally oriented training and the development of the community, which enhances competences, competitiveness, entrepreneurship and well-being for the population in the Central Finland. This means that the JUAS is a practically oriented organisation aiming to solve the problems raised by working-life organisations (Halttunen, 2006). According to Kainulainen (2004, p. 73), useful research means results which are quickly transferred and implemented into practice.

There are a number of critical factors when analysing the nature of these R&D projects. First, teachers normally act as the project researchers in the R&D projects. This means that the JUAS do not have a special category of a 'project researcher', who would be responsible for running projects. There are only a couple of exceptions to this rule. This institutional policy also means that teaching and the development of projects are integrated activities that aim at developing both teaching and the region. Second, students practicing in local labour market are seen as a very important source (and channel) of new ideas. This means that students often produce new ideas, which are further developed by their teachers. Third, there is a systematic way to strengthen the weak signals from the region in order to establish development projects which the region benefits from.

The crucial elements in this systematic way to strengthen the weak signals include the following practices: (1) it is recognised that the best ideas are born over a cup of coffee. In other words: there are informal social structures, which favour the brainstorming of new ideas and exchange of ideas in the study fields, (2) every study field has a project manager, who is responsible for developing new ideas into new projects, (3) there is also institutional support for developing ideas into projects.

The staff responsible for developing ideas into projects (three people) are located in the central administration. They choose the best projects and help to find funding for them. (4) The strategy of the JUAS guides the activities in these R&D projects.

A good example of the nature of an R&D project is provided by the Wellness Dream Lab, which is a project based on cooperation between regional business, JUAS and the University of Jyväskylä. The project employs four people (and a project manager), and it consists of 40–50 projects initiated by business enterprises. Normally, the students of the JUAS are employed by and in business enterprises. The project aims at and has succeeded in integrating the research capacity of the university with the interests of regional business and the development of teaching in the JUAS. The project has been funded mainly by public sources (Marttila et al., 2004).

The performance of the JUAS has been evaluated as one at an excellent level and it was rewarded by the Ministry of Education as one of the four centres of excellence for the regional development impact in Finland (Käyhkö et al., 2006). It was evaluated as being especially efficient in creating and implementing its strategy, with the main aim of the development of the Central Finland region. The strategy also guides the functioning of the polytechnic in all its activities, thus creating no need for a special strategy for regional development. In order to develop the functioning of the regional development further, the evaluators also suggested that JUAS should focus its activities on selected fields. In addition, they recommended that the polytechnic should increase cooperation with the University of Jyväskylä (which is located in the same city) (Käyhkö et al., 2006, pp. 46–48).

It has been argued that successes with R&D in the JUAS is made possible, at least partly, by the fact that practically all full-time teachers were transferred into total working-time in 2000, because of a new collective bargaining agreement. This, together with the new Polytechnic Act, is seen as the key to expanding the R&D work in polytechnics (Halttunen, 2006). However, in some polytechnics old staff members may be in a different agreement, which is based on the idea of counting teaching hours as the only basis for salary. In practice, this means that all work (except for teaching) has to be negotiated separately and teachers do not attend polytechnics full time.

Dilemmas and Challenges

Research and development in general did not originally belong to the objectives of polytechnics, but they were introduced to the polytechnics about 10 years after their establishment. This new task has raised a number of dilemmas and challenges. The basic question is always, which should come first: teaching or research? What is the nature of R&D in polytechnics, and who should do it and how? These issues have also been debated by the staff members of polytechnics over recent years. In this context, it is therefore understandable that the Ministry of Education supports activities like AMKtutka for building up common principles and practices. This indicates that there are emerging issues in polytechnics regarding the need to clarify what R&D polytechnics should be involved in, and how R&D should be implemented. In order to contribute to this discussion, we have conceptualised two different solutions for organising and managing R&D in polytechnics.

The Organisation and Management of Research

There are two major strategies for promoting research (in the sense of Weberian ideal types) to illuminate the main ways of organising R&D in Finnish polytechnics. These can be called *the strategy of centralisation* and *the strategy of integration*.

The strategy of centralisation describes an organisational solution for concentrating all R&D activities into one separate R&D unit. The aim is to make R&D as efficient as possible through central steering of the development projects. The establishment of a central unit helps to recognise the importance of R&D. It also makes the use of resources more efficient, because of the qualified project management personnel. The emergence of a specialised staff, taking care of the development projects, enables the accumulation of project development and management expertise in the higher education institution. However, there can also be some problems with this strategy, because the emergence of a group of research specialists may lead to a situation in which people are more interested in finding new funding for paying their salaries than in thinking about the needs of the region. Another problem is the question of strengthening weak signals from the region.

The strategy of integration describes, in turn, the other end of the same continuum. According to this ideal type, the objective is to create institutional support structures for promoting the execution of R&D projects in the polytechnic and to integrate teaching development with R&D. This way of organising the R&D aims at strengthening weak signals from the region systematically and developing them into R&D projects. This activity is steered by the institutional strategy. This strategy also more easily integrates teachers with the R&D projects, which helps to maintain institutional curriculum development and regional development projects. However, the main problem with this strategy is the accumulation of expertise to run R&D projects. How to secure the accumulation of project management expertise, when there is no specialised group of staff members specialised in R&D projects?

Teaching and Research

Teaching higher vocational skills is the main objective of Finnish polytechnics. There are, however, three different traditions defining the purpose of teaching and training. According to Kotila (2004), the first of these may be called *apprenticeship ideal* with the social structure of novice (apprentice), journeyman and master. Basically, this is the continuation of traditional craft-guild model (Välimaa, 2007), which is based on the transfer of tacit knowledge from the master to the apprentice. Pedagogically, it takes support from the constructionist perspectives to learning and from the idea of learning by doing. The second tradition may be called the *tradition of vocational training.* It is strongly influenced by the traditions of (for-mer) secondary level vocational schools. Historically, it is important to remember that the present 28 polytechnics have been formed by merging some 215 vocational education institutions. Pedagogically, this tradition emphasises a strong teaching profession and hierarchical social structures between students and teachers. The *university tradition* is the most recent one. It exists in study fields that are clos-est to the disciplinary traditions in universities. Pedagogically, it repeats teaching methods used in universities in their respective disciplines. Basically, the main idea is to implement theoretical knowledge into practice.

These different traditions may be seen interacting with each other in Finnish polytechnics. Theoretically, we can see tensions between the aims to develop (tacit) skills through conceptualising the processes of making, producing and working in work places, as opposed to a traditional academic way which is based on the imple-mentation of theoretical knowledge into practice (Pohjola, 2007). These tensions are related to the dichotomy between theoretical knowledge and praxis, or practical knowledge (see Dewey, 1929). There are also tensions between the expectations of students, who value learning by doing as opposed to the expectations of teachers, who belong to the tradition of vocational training with its emphasis on teaching the right skills to the students in the context of strong teaching profession.

These questions are connected back to the organisation of R&D in polytechnics. Namely, if one assumes that the university tradition should be followed, then one should organise R&D by following the model provided by the universities, where research outcomes are implemented into practice. The nature of the process would then be that of an implementation of research. However, if one assumes that appren-ticeship ideal should be followed, the challenge is to conceptualise the practices in work places in order to reveal their tacit knowledge. These two extremes thus aim at pointing out that the organisation of R&D and teaching are closely related to each other in polytechnics. Therefore, it is quite important to decide which of the R&D implementation strategies will be followed.

Discussion: R&D or T&D Projects?

The two cases presented help to raise a fundamental question on the applicability of the concept of research and development, when trying to describe what is done in the name of R&D. Namely, the nature of the projects described above resembles that of 'training and development' more than that of 'research and development' projects. The idea of R&D may even be misleading, since it focuses attention on the traditional academic process of knowledge production with the aim to imple-ment research findings into action. However, the training and development (T&D) projects are developed in the context of application – thus reminding us about the nature of Mode 2 knowledge production (Gibbons et al., 1994) – aiming at chang-ing practices in cooperation with practical actors. This is not to say that these T&D projects would not utilise research. What we intend to say is that research activities are applied in the course of the T&D project, if and when needed. For this reason, the traditional academic research is not necessarily the starting point for a development project. A case study conducted by Hyrkkänen (2007) also supports this argumentation. She noted that when R&D was started systematically in polytechnics, there were different views not only about the role of the students' theses in these projects, but also about the targets, contents, actors and the ways of organising training and development activities. In her research Hyrkkänen (2007) studied how teachers redefined the thesis process and its connections to R&D. She concludes that the concept of research and development is new to polytechnics, and when implemented, it requires the adoption of developmental research methods with different actors building the activities in polytechnics through discussions, analyses and arguments. This means that R&D as an idea needs to transport certain intellectual devices and techniques (from academic research) in order to be an efficient instrument for polytechnics.

Our concern for a proper concept has also a practical dimension, if and when we assume that concepts influence practices. We should investigate more closely the extent to which the category of R&D (as introduced by OECD) is a relevant concept for describing the T&D processes taking place in Finnish polytechnics. This is not to say that we should cancel the category of R&D, but the aim is to say that we should understand what it means in the context of polytechnics, which have both apprenticeship ideals and vocational and academic traditions influencing their organisation of teaching and development processes.

References

AMKOTA Database. (2004). Official statistics of polytechnic education in Finland. www.amkota2csc.fi
AMKtutka. The updated project plan 16.4.2007 (in Finnish), available at www.amktutka.fi
Ammattikorkeakoulujen tutkimus- ja kehitystyö. Nykytila ja tavoitteet. Arene ry. 2007.
Davies, J., Weko, T., Kim, L., & Thulstrup, E. (2006). Thematic review of tertiary education. Finland. Country note. Paris: OECD.
Dewey, J. (1929). The quest for certainty. A study on the relation of knowledge and action. Vol. 4. The collected works of John Dewey, later works. Carbondale: Southern Illinois University Press.
Gibbons, M., Limogenes, C., Nowotny, H., Schwartzman, S., Scott, P., & Trow, M. (1994). The new production of knowledge: The dynamics of science and research in contemporary societies. London: Sage.
Halttunen, J. (2006). Ammattikorkeakoulun t&k-toiminta yliopistovetoisessa toimintaympäristössä. In Korkeakoulutieto, 2006 (3–4), 28–30.
Hyrkkänen, U. (2007). Käsityksistä ajatuksen poluille: Ammattikorkeakoulun tutkimus- ja kehitystoiminnan kehittäminen. Helsingin yliopisto, käyttäytymistieteellinen tiedekunta, kasvatustieteen laitos.
Kainulainen, S. (2004). Oikein, totta ja hyödyllistä. In H. Kotila & A. Mutanen (Eds.), Tutkiva ja kehittävä ammattikorkeakoulu (pp. 68–77). Helsinki: Edita.
Karppanen, E., Tornikoski, E., Töytäri, R., Urponen, H., Uusitalo, T., & Holm, K. (2007). Lahden ammattikorkeakoulun laadunvarmistusjärjestelmän auditointi. Helsinki: The Finnish Higher Education Evaluation Council (FINHEEC).
Käyhkö, R., Hakamäki, S., Kananen, M., Kavonius, V., Pirhonen, J., Puusaari, P., et al. (2006). Uudenlaista sankaruutta. Ammattikorkeakoulujen aluekehitysvaikutuksen

huippuyksiköt 2006–2007. Helsinki: Korkeakoulujen arviointineuvosto. Korkeakoulujen arviointineuvoston julkaisuja 13:2006.

Kotila, H. (2004). Tutkimus- ja kehitystoiminnan haasteet ammattikorkeakoulussa. In H. Kotila & A. Mutanen (Eds.), *Tutkiva ja kehittävä ammattikorkeakoulu* (pp. 11–23). Helsinki: Edita.

Marttila, L., Kautonen, M., Niemonen, H., & von Bell, K. (2004). *Yritysten ja ammattikorkeakoulujen T&K-yhteistyö. Ammattikorkeakoulut alueellisessa innovaatiojärjestelmässä: koulutuksen ja työelämän verkottumisen mallit, osaprojekti III.* Tampereen yliopisto, Yhteiskuntatieteiden tutkimuslaitos, Työelämän tutkimuskeskus. Työryhmäraportteja 69/2004.

NAO (National Audit Office of Finland). (2006). Valtiontilintarkastajien kertomus K 16/2006 vp.

OECD. (2003). *Polytechnic education in Finland. Reviews of national policies for education.* Paris: OECD.

OPM. (2004). *Development plan. Education and research 2003–2008.* Helsinki: Ministry of Education.

OPM. (2005). Ammattikorkeakoulut. Taulukoita AMKOTA-tietokannasta. *Opetusministeriön julkaisuja, 23.*

OPM. (2006). Ammattikorkeakoulut. Taulukoita AMKOTA-tietokannasta. *Opetusministeriön julkaisuja, 42.*

OPM. (2007). *Draft for development plan. Education and research.* Helsinki: Ministry of Education.

Pohjola, P. (2007). Taito, toiminta ja taustatieto. In H. Kotila, A. Mutanen, & M.-V. Volanen (Eds.), *Taidon tieto* (pp. 164–179). Helsinki: Edita.

Statistics Finland. (2006). *Yliopistojen ja ammattikorkeakoulujen ajankäyttötutkimus.* Helsinki: Edita.

Tutkimus- ja kehitystyö suomalaisissa ammattikorkeakouluissa. Opetusministeriön työryhmämuistioita ja selvityksiä 2004:7.

Välimaa, J. (2001). The changing nature of academic employment in Finnish higher education. In J. Enders (Ed.), *Academic staff in Europe: Changing contexts and conditions* (pp. 67–91). London: Greenwood Publishing Group.

Välimaa, J. (2005). Social dynamics of higher education reforms: The case of Finland. In A. Amaral, Å. Gornitzka, & M. Kogan (Eds.), *Reform and change in higher education* (pp. 245–268). Dordrecht: Springer.

Välimaa, J. (2007). Two training models in the continuum of Finnish doctoral training. In B. M. Kehm (Ed.), *Looking back to look forward* (pp. 73–92). Kassel: INCHER-KASSEL.

Välimaa, J., & Neuvonen-Rauhala, M. L. (2008). Polytechnics in Finnish higher education. In J. S. Taylor, J. B. Ferreira, M. L. Machado, & R. Santiago (Eds.), *Non-university higher education in Europe* (pp. 77–98). Dordrecht: Springer.

Valtiontilintarkastajien kertomus 2006. K 16/2006 vp.

Vesterinen, M. L. (2006). Tutkimus- ja kehitystyön kokonaisuus. In H. Kotila & A. Mutanen (Eds.), *Tutkiva ja kehittävä ammattikorkeakoulu* (pp. 40–67). Helsinki: Edita.

Chapter 9
The Role of Research in German Universities of Applied Sciences

Marianne Kulicke and Thomas Stahlecker

Introduction

For the past 40 years, the German higher education system has been enriched by the practice-oriented teaching as well as applied research at the universities of applied sciences (UASs) or *Fachhochschulen*. The current set-up as institutions of higher education (universities) came about by the agreements between the states of the Federal Republic of Germany to standardise in the field of UASs on 31 October 1968. About one third of the UASs have their origin in institutions (i.e. higher technical educational establishments, higher technical colleges), which were founded before 1969. The other third were established in the 1970s, mainly in 1971 and 1972. A renewed wave of establishing UASs took place in the 1990s, mainly in the new *Länder*, but also in the old states. The objective of establishing the UAS was to create institutions that would offer the students, on a scientific basis, a practice and career-oriented education and enable them for self-determined activities in the professions. At the end of 2007, the number of students attending UASs was 545,000 according to the Federal Office of Statistics, which corresponds to 28% of all students in Germany.

Unlike universities, UASs do not have the right to award doctorate or *habilitation* degrees. The typical mix between education and research differs considerably between universities and UASs: lecturers from UASs have a teaching load of 18 h/week and longer lecturing time within the semester. In contrast, lecturers at universities have a 60% time budget for research with comparatively low teaching schedules. In comparison to universities, UASs frequently have, with respect to the offered fields of study, a limited number of courses and lower number of students. In the early stages, research was not considered a profile feature at UASs. However, with the amendment of HRG 1985 (University Act), applied R&D now belongs to the tasks of UASs.

M. Kulicke (✉)
Fraunhofer ISI, Karlsruhe, Germany
e-mail: Marianne.Kulicke@isi.fraunhofer.de

S. Kyvik, B. Lepori (eds.), *The Research Mission of Higher Education Institutions Outside the University Sector*, Higher Education Dynamics 31, DOI 10.1007/978-1-4020-9244-2_9, © Springer Science+Business Media B.V. 2010

In the course of the Bologna Process, the UASs have relative quickly modi-
fied their academic programmes and introduced a variety of bachelor and master
programmes in recent years. This shift was faster than in universities. From the current 3,763 courses at UASs 55.0% lead to a bachelor's degree, 33.8% to a master
degree and 11.2% to a diploma. In contrast the data for universities are the following: bachelor's degree: 33.5%, master's degree: 30.6% and diploma: 35.9% (source:
www.akkreditierungsrat.de, 2008).

The German higher education system currently comprises some 350 higher education institutions (HEIs), state and state-approved, including the following different
types of institutions: (1) universities, (2) universities of applied sciences, (3) colleges of education, and (4) academies of fine arts. The largest groups according
to the number are the UASs (184) and the universities (109). Of these 350 HEIs,
however, 79 can be excluded as their specialisation is not relevant for the issue we
are addressing here, e.g. art and music academies, colleges of theology or social
education.

On the whole, the 164 state or private UASs do not have a standardised profile.
They vary considerably in terms of enrolments, the study courses they offer (with
a broad range of subjects in the engineering sciences, the social sciences and economics) and their R&D capacities. This variation results from the differences in the
regional environments of UASs and the areas from which the institutions draw their
students. UASs focus strongly on the needs of regional industry and commerce in
their areas. These institutions have enlarged their spectrum of tasks since the early
1980s. Among the new tasks and activities, efforts in the areas of technology and
knowledge transfer are especially important. Most state UASs have 2,000–8,000
students. They are considerably smaller than universities. There are also a number
of UASs, which have – according to the number of students (10,000–15,000) – a
size similar to medium-sized universities. Seventy-two per cent of students (1.32
million) attend state universities; private, state-approved universities are attended
by only 3% (59,400), whereas 25% (470,000) are at state UASs and less than 1%
(8,600) at private, state-approved UASs.

According to the shares of single subject groups, two main focuses can be
discerned for UASs (see Fig. 9.1); half of the students (49%) belong to the non-
technical areas 'legal, economic and social sciences', 'art, art history' and 'linguistic
and cultural sciences', the other half (51%) can be allotted to the technical/natural
science disciplines 'engineering sciences', 'mathematics, natural sciences', 'agriculture, forestry and nutrition sciences' and 'human medicine and health care'.
The UAS group is very heterogeneous here too, as there are UASs which offer
almost exclusively technical/natural science courses of study and others in which
economics and social sciences dominate.

In the year 2007, 88,000 students completed a course of study at a UAS, with
approximately 42,300 of them specialising in a technical/natural science course of
study. In contrast, the number of graduates from universities amounted to 170,100
(79,000 of whom specialised in a technical/natural science subject). Around 13,300
professors work in UASs, in universities about 21,000 (see Statistisches Bundesamt,
2008b). Basic running costs per student amounted to €3,990 in the UASs, whereas

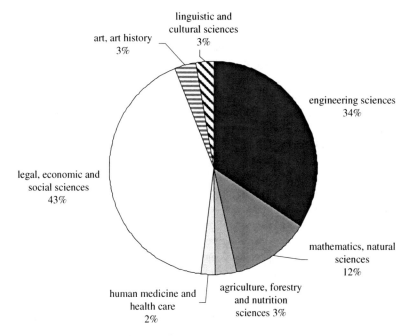

Fig. 9.1   Subject groups in UASs by number of students in 2007. Source: Statistisches Bundesamt (2008b)

in the universities the amount is more than double, at €8,390 (2006, see Statistisches Bundesamt, 2008a). This means that education at UASs costs considerably less than an education at universities. This is not caused by a fundamentally different curriculum structure, although universities have a large number of students of human medicine/healthcare sciences, which are characterised by high basic running costs per student (€26,560). In the last 10 years, the basic costs remained essentially unchanged with a simultaneously increasing number of students, which clearly restricted the financial leeway of the UASs and universities, given the simultaneously growing demands on the quality of education.

The R&D Potential of Universities of Applied Sciences

Within the national innovation system of large enterprises active in R&D, universities and non-university research institutions play a central role along the entire value-added chain, from basic research up to market-oriented R&D; the profile and the sphere of activity the UASs have expanded increasingly in the past years. Besides their contribution through a practice-oriented education – above all in engineering, but also in the natural sciences and economics – their significance as regional knowledge and research anchors or supports in the area of applied R&D is increasing. Many UASs are usually well connected in regional networks and also possess (profound) knowledge about the regional industrial structures. This does not apply for all UASs ubiquitously, rather, great differences still exist in the experience, professional and personnel potentials and leeway time-wise for application-oriented R&D. This has various reasons: first of all, the unfavourable structural framework conditions must be mentioned. Other than in universities, the UASs, due to their strong focus on teaching, only have a limited number of scientific staff at their disposal who assist the professors in conducting lectures or in research projects.

The degree to which a change in culture and mentality has taken place plays a role in the status of R&D in the UAS. The attractiveness of conducting R&D projects depends for the professors on the extent to which application-oriented research projects attract attention, recognition and support in the institution in question and how the projects are promoted/supported financially by the HEI administration and the governing bodies. Thus the success does not depend only on the personal involvement and interests of individual professors.

According to the calculations of the Federal Office of Statistics, the expenditures of the UASs on R&D in the year 2005, however, still amounted to €673.9 million. This clearly lies below the outlay of the universities (€8.13 billion). The lion's share of the R&D expenditures (see Fig. 9.2) fell to 'engineering sciences' (€360.2 million), followed after a large gap by 'mathematics, natural sciences' (€106.5 million) and 'human medicine and health care' (€83.6 million). The structure in universities differs completely: 18% is allotted to 'engineering sciences', 32% to 'mathematics, natural sciences', 27% to 'human medicine and health care', 8% to 'legal, economic and social sciences', 12% to 'linguistic and cultural sciences', and 3% to

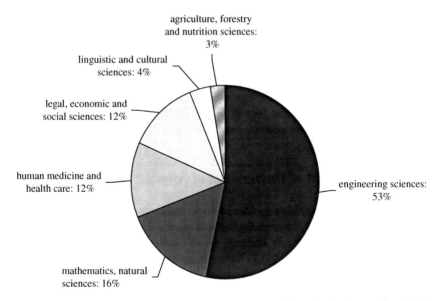

Fig. 9.2 Structure of R&D expenditures by subject groups in 2005 at UASs. Source: Statistisches Bundesamt (2008c)

'agriculture, forestry and nutrition sciences'. The considerably higher status of the 'engineering sciences' expresses the stronger application orientation of the R&D activities in the UASs.

National Policies for Research in Non-university Institutions

Strategic Goals and Guidelines for Research

The development of UASs is shaped to a high degree by the higher education policy objectives of the *Länder*; the financial support by the sponsoring ministry determines the performance of educational and research tasks. In view of the disastrous household situation in all *Länder*, funding has been cut considerably in the last 5 years, especially in 2003/2004. In the last 5 years, amendments were made to the universities acts of the *Länder*, giving applied R&D in UASs greater importance. In the meantime, R&D has become an official mission at UASs in all *Länder*, although with varying degrees of importance: in 11 *Länder* it is regarded as an official mission independent of the educational mandate and in five states it is a mission within the context of their educational mandate.

The view of the UASs as primarily teaching institutions coloured the policy of the *Länder* for many decades. Since the beginning of the 1970s, the UAS landscape has altered in many and varied ways. The various recommendations on the part of the Science Council (*Wissenschaftsrat*) on the role of the UAS contributed decisively in this context (Wissenschaftsrat, 1981, 1991, 1993, 2000, 2002). The tasks of application-oriented R&D and technology transfer gained considerably in importance in the UASs. In connection with application-oriented R&D its function for teaching is repeatedly emphasised: it is a structural requirement because research establishes the relation to work practice among the teaching staff via cooperation with industry and supervision of the students' bachelor or master theses in firms. Without this constant feedback with professional practice and the changes therein, successful courses of study providing professional qualifications would not be possible.

Priority-Setting Between Teaching and Research

The typical ratio of teaching to research differs clearly between the UASs und universities: UAS lecturers complain frequently about their teaching commitments of 18 h/week during the semester (semester hours), in addition the lecture period in a semester at the UASs is longer than at universities. Lecturers at universities have a 60% research share in their time budget with comparatively few teaching hours. In contrast to universities, UASs – measured by the number of courses – frequently have a limited teaching load and fewer students. There are, however, possibilities to reduce the extent of the teaching commitments if R&D work is conducted instead.

This is regulated differently from one federal state to another. In the most favourable case, a reduction to 9 h/week is possible if R&D projects are being carried out on a large scale. However, only a small number of professors in UASs can profit from this regulation. In a study on research in UASs (Kulicke & Stahlecker, 2004), Fraunhofer ISI came to the conclusion that in most of the 69 UASs investigated only a small number of professors conducted any R&D projects at all: in almost half the share of these professors out of all UAS professors lay between 11 and 30%, for a further 37% the share varied between 31 and 60%.

Personnel limitations result not only from the high-teaching commitments at UASs, but also the almost totally missing middle level of academic and administrative staff and the restricted possibilities to hire qualified graduates as staff (only possible in the framework of cooperative doctoral theses, i.e. in cooperation with an university with the right to award doctorate degrees). In addition, the self-conception of the professors also plays a role to a certain extent, if they concentrate on tuition in view of the high-teaching commitment. The incentive and motivational instruments available to HEI management were mostly not so strong in the past to effect short-term, tangible changes in behaviour of this group. The room to manoeuvre on the part of the HEI management to reward professors' R&D activities by reducing teaching hours varies from one federal state to the other, but is on the whole limited. A number of indications in the recent past signal that, on the whole, the interest of UAS professors in application-oriented R&D has greatly increased. The public promotional programmes encouraged this trend, also the fact that technology transfer and the acquisition of third-party funds play a heavier role in the allocation of basic funds to the UASs by the *Länder*.

Funding of Research

R&D was defined some years ago in the state university law as one of several tasks of the UAS, but no commensurate increase in UAS budgets for such activities took place, nor have any concrete guidelines been introduced to specify the extent of research to be undertaken. Thus the scope for R&D in UASs is determined primarily by public promotional programmes, which are run either by the *Länder* or the federal government. Not all *Länder* implement such programmes. This applies above all to the larger states such as North Rhine-Westphalia, Baden-Württemberg and Lower Saxony. They mainly promoted the development of human resources and infrastructure. Programmes which finance individual R&D projects can offer more funding.

Three types of programmes should be differentiated:

(1) Programmes which target a stronger collaboration of firms with universities, UASs and research institutions (e.g. PRO INNO II or ZIM – *Zentrales Innovationsprogramm Mittelstand*); the focus is on small and medium enterprises (SMEs) whose innovativeness should be strengthened. The research partners in universities, UASs or non-university research institutions can also be promoted. In this programme HEIs are important research partners of SMEs.

Besides universities (share 41.0%), UASs also have a strong position (12.7%) (see Kulicke, Bührer, & Ruhland, 2006).

(2) Programmes which promote joint projects between industry and science in selected technology fields and make high demands of the technological project goals and the innovation potentials of the participating research partners. UASs only seldom participate in such technologically demanding projects, at most as junior partners of large firms, universities and non-university research institutions.

(3) Programmes which are tailor-made to suit the UAS capabilities. They aim to strengthen the R&D potentials of UASs, so that they can primarily carry out application-oriented R&D projects for and with SMEs.

Since 1992, the category (3) programmes of the Federal Ministry of Education and Research (BMBF) in chronological order are: 'Application oriented research and development at Universities of Applied Sciences' (aFuE), 'Applied Research at Universities of Applied Sciences in cooperation with Business' (FH³, since 2004) and 'R&D at Universities of Applied Sciences in Cooperation with Business' (FhprofUnd, since 2007). These three programmes had different strategic goals for the development of UASs, aimed to develop the area of R&D step-by-step into a profile-enhancing characteristic.

The first programme, aFuE, was aimed at enhancing external funding at UASs, i.e. the success of such institutions in obtaining third-party funding for application-oriented R&D projects. From 1992 through 2003, the BMBF received a total of some 5,800 applications (see BMBF, 2003 and Kulicke & Stahlecker, 2004). Of these, 951 received support, with total project funding of €83 million. In 2004, the BMBF implemented a shift in focus towards supporting regional research consortia at UASs which are relevant for business and industry. This re-orientation of funding policy objectives was set for stronger interdisciplinary and inter-institutional cooperation, through which UASs should cooperate with partners from business (preferably SMEs), science (research facilities, universities) and partners from other fields. This was also reflected in the new programme name: Applied Research at Universities of Applied Sciences in cooperation with Business – FH³. The focal point was to strengthen the capability of UASs to work in consortia (see Kulicke, Zimmermann, Kroll, & Bührer, 2008). Hence industry-relevant cooperative projects of UASs were promoted, whereby special attention was given to the cooperation with SMEs in this region. Through the support of interdisciplinary and inter-institutional cooperation, these UASs should be put in the position to have stronger involvement in research consortia. It was thereby intended that structural deficits of staffing at UASs (the absence of professional 'academic middle level', i.e. academic staff below professor/lecturer status, such as junior or assistant lecturers, and research fellows and assistants) are compensated and their R&D potential in regard to participation in research consortia is strengthened. By means of the FH³ Programme's requirement that science partners must be integrated in the single R&D projects, a greater cooperation of UASs with other elements of the innovation system should be achieved, above all with universities and non-university research institutions. The promotional programme FH[3] received a total of over 1,500 applications in the period 2004 until 2006, of which 255 were promoted. With a subsidy amount totalling €52.9 million, this corresponds to an average of €207,000 per approved application.

The programme FhprofUnd continued to promote UASs with similar instruments to FH[3]. In 2007, €23.2 million were granted for 106 projects (mean: €219,000). It

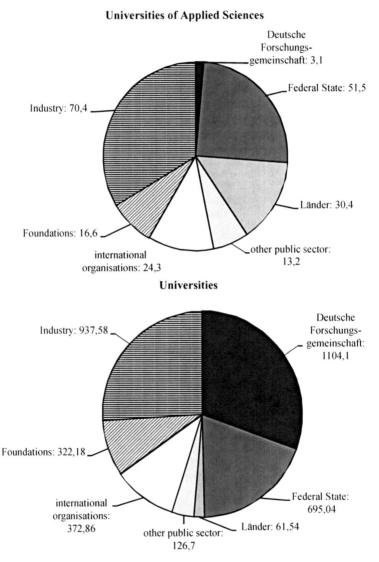

Fig. 9.3 Source of third-party funding (€ million) in 2006. Source: Statistisches Bundesamt (2008a)

presented a line of funding in the programme *Forschung an Fachhochschulen*. In addition, the BMBF has been promoting the study of engineering at UASs since 2006 by means of the new funding line *IngenieurNachwuchs*. Moreover, a higher participation of UASs in the specialist programmes, such as microsystems technology or optical technologies in the funding line 'Profil-NT' is supported. This is aimed to attract to UASs more well-funded specialist programmes which promote ambitious R&D projects.

Länder have also been running several promotional programmes for many years, promoting application-oriented R&D at UASs. Up to now, however, all the promotional programmes for UASs had too small subsidy amounts measured against the number of applications, i.e. many good applications could not be supported. The BMBF funds have been greatly increased since 2007. The promotional measures of the BMBF and the *Länder* have undoubtedly contributed to the fact that applied R&D for knowledge and technology transfer to the firms could be developed into a second characteristic profile for the majority of UASs in the past 15 years, besides their practice-oriented teaching profile. The *Länder* are utilising the financial scope afforded them by the higher status accorded to the promotion of innovations within the European Fund for Regional Development (EFRE). For the period 2007 until 2013 they are planning to expand R&D in universities and UASs. The measures of the federal government in its High-tech Strategy (see BMBF, 2007) are also heading in this direction, the main concern here being to build up research capacity in science, which the UASs will also profit from even if they are not the main addressee of the measure.

As the UASs can utilise basic funding for R&D only to a limited extent, third-party funds remain the crucial source for R&D for UASs. Public financiers play a large role in these third-party projects. Particularly striking, however, is the great significance of industry compared to universities. Whereas the German Research Association (DFG) provides the universities with considerable funds for research purposes, this does not apply to the UASs, as their R&D projects are not directed towards basic research. Figure 9.3 also points out the very large differences between UASs and universities as regards the amounts of third-party funds.

Research Strategy in Non-university Institutions

Institutional Strategy and Priority Setting

The extent to which R&D is performed in UASs depends on a number of factors: some of the UASs evolved out of engineering schools and they understood themselves as purely teaching institutions. Only gradually, in the course of the last decades, have some of the professors increasingly devoted their attention to conducting application-oriented R&D. UASs of this type are to be mainly found in southern Germany. On the other hand, UASs in the new *Länder* evolved out of HEIs with an R&D tradition of many years, in which the majority of the professors regularly carried out R&D projects. A further group is formed by UASs in *Länder* which promoted the R&D capacities and competences of their UASs in the last decades by the targeted use of promotional programmes. Size also plays a considerable role. In the many small UASs, their role as teaching establishments dominates, with R&D projects only conducted by individual professors. One cannot speak of an R&D strategy of the UASs as a whole here.

The study of Kulicke and Stahlecker (2004) shows the following results, based on interviews with 69 rectors or pro-rectors of 69 UASs: The status of R&D has increased over the years at all UASs and further efforts are being made to expand this. The representatives of UASs classify the framework conditions totally differently. The reasons given were the succession of generations presently taking place (young R&D-oriented professors increasingly replacing older colleagues with stronger affinity to teaching). But these efforts are limited through funding available and an almost non-existent professional academic middle-level staff. Essential instruments to intensify research at UASs are: support for the establishment of focal research areas, allocation of internal research budgets, further financial incentives (e.g. performance-oriented budgets), reduction of teaching load, establishment of competence centres across departments, consideration of R&D orientation with new appointments, intensification of cooperative PhD procedures, expansion of At-institutes, etc. Thereby the group of professors involved in research should be expanded and applied R&D put on a broader base.

There are great differences at UASs if one compares the number of professors conducting research with all other professors. The average of this quota lies at approximately 33%, the median value at 28%. The band width ranges from 4 to 100%. The regional distribution of UASs with professors doing research shows that there are considerable differences among the *Länder*: the UASs in the new *Länder* show a considerably higher proportion of research active professors compared to those of western German institutions. The higher proportions in the new *Länder* originate from a different research culture; a number of UASs emerged at the beginning of the 1990s from facilities which had university status. Conspicuous is the predominantly small share of professors involved in research in most of the southern German UASs, where less than a quarter of the professors pursue research.

As the proportion of professors doing research at most UASs is low, the indicator 'third stream funding per research professor' yields totally different values, i.e. clearly higher results than the Statistical Federal Office is giving for the indicator for 'third stream funding per professor'. There is also a considerable spread between the UASs. The average value lies at €48,300, the median value at €41,300 and the highest results at €100,000 or more. A high share of professors doing research does not necessarily mean a high level of third-party funding.

The interviews of Fraunhofer ISI with the representatives of 69 UASs already revealed a trend which has clearly grown stronger in the recent past (see Kulicke & Stahlecker, 2004). The *Länder*, as governing bodies of the state-run UASs, are increasingly pushing to build a stronger profile based on teaching and research. In a number of UASs, which had not previously possessed an explicit R&D strategy, this set off a strategy discovery process in which an appropriate strategy was developed. The switch to bachelor's and master's study courses also made considerable impacts on the status of R&D in the UASs: in order to compete with universities, research-oriented master's degree courses were established on a larger scale. Research-based teaching modules are a pre-requisite for the accreditation of these courses. As a result, work in R&D will become a stable component in many UAS departments so that they are attractive for students in the future.

The Organisation and Management of Research

The Fraunhofer ISI study (Kulicke & Stahlecker, 2004) also revealed the organisational weaknesses and frequently low capacities in the UASs for R&D. In the majority (85.5%) of the 69 interviewed UASs, R&D projects are either implemented within the normal business operation of the department as a key activity or – equally important – with other organisational entities, such as central facilities of the institution (24.6%), in special facilities of the department (24.6%) or – organisationally independent from the UASs – in At-institutes (30.4%). Two thirds of the 69 UASs maintain At-institutes, which are often run by a lecturer, but mainly have their own staff. In about one third of them, employees below the professor level are working for the At-institute. These institutes are judged by the interviewed persons mainly positively under the given basic framework conditions at the UAS (no academic middle-level staff, low flexibility in employing/retaining qualified employees, intensive teaching load, inflexible financial management system and others). Advantages are: support of research climate at the UAS, improvement of the quality of the teaching, representation of the UASs as regional competence centres for R&D, and fund-raising for research areas that are normally not accessible for UASs. It was stressed that At-institutes make the administrative process for implementing contracts with industry considerably easier.

Collaboration with Universities and Industry

As already mentioned, in its programme FH[3] and the successor programme FhprofUnd, the BMBF has promoted cooperation between UASs and enterprises and with science partners, above all with universities, since 2004. The Fraunhofer ISI appraisal study (Kulicke et al., 2008) on the impacts of FH[3] depicts a broad spectrum of R&D cooperation partners for the promoted UAS, i.e. cooperation with quite different institutions takes place on a regular basis or from time to time (see Fig. 9.4). One hundred sixty-two professors from all large- and medium-sized UASs as well as a large number from smaller institutions in Germany participated in this study. In first place in the category 'several times' are SMEs (72.1%), followed by large enterprises (61.7%) and universities (52.7%). Only one single interviewee stated that projects are typically carried out without external partners.

No information is, however, available to what extent UASs have entered into strategic alliances with enterprises, universities or non-university research facilities. The enterprises which were partners of UASs in the promoted R&D projects were

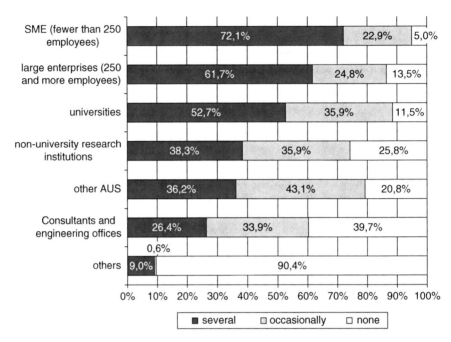

Fig. 9.4 R&D Partners of the UASs. Source: Kulicke et al. (2008)

also questioned. A total of 95 firms participated in this survey. They also have a dense network of cooperation partners. As far as entering into strategic alliances was concerned, UASs were scarcely mentioned. This type of function is most frequently the preserve of other companies (named by 29.8% of the 95 enterprises) or – already with a distinctly lower status – domestic and foreign universities (13.6 and 13.8%).

Most federal government programmes promoting R&D in firms have for many years required cooperation with other enterprises or with universities, UASs or non-university research institutions as a pre-requisite. This has led in the last 10–15 years to a much closer coalescence of industry and science. The UASs also profit from this. However, this applies almost exclusively to the area of application-oriented R&D. Basic research or pre-competitive research does not take place in UASs, not even in cooperation with universities. The latter collaborate in R&D projects of this type with other universities, non-university research facilities and large enterprises.

Human Resources and Careers

In 2007, UASs in Germany had a total of 12,900 professors, 7,900 positions for academic staff and 15,400 positions for non-academic staff (Statistisches Bundesamt, 2008b). Personnel structures at UASs differ from those at other types of HEIs (see BMBF, 2003). With few exceptions, professors do the teaching at UASs. The job profile is initially homogeneous, which means there is no division in teaching or R&D-focused activities. In their teaching duties, they are supported and complemented by additional instructors (some of whom have temporary appointments). The number of such instructors (title: *'Lehrbeauftragte'*) varies depending on the type of department and UAS. There are, however, far fewer of these positions than professors. In order to be able to work at a UAS, professors require specific qualification profiles. These qualifications include completed higher education studies, along with proof of special competence in scientific/academic work or of special artistic abilities. This special group of required qualifications, which is set forth in the Framework Act for Higher Education and implemented by the higher education acts of the *Länder*, reflects the special requirements pertaining to teaching at UASs. The close links between career experience and scientific qualification requirements are considered to be especially conducive to the fulfilment of the educational mission of UASs. In some *Länder*, UASs also have research assistants. In some *Länder*, professors at UASs also have the option of taking 6-month leaves of absence from teaching and research, at regular intervals (usually, every 4 years), to carry out work aimed at bringing their knowledge up to the latest standards in their field. In 2001, laws pertaining to employment of higher education teaching staff were amended in order to reform salary scales for professors. As a result, the salary scale for UAS professors is now basically the same as that for university professors.

The problems of UASs conducting R&D projects due to their lack of personnel resources have already been addressed. The following data shows the human resources for R&D: most R&D personnel are employed at universities. The Federal Statistical Office estimates for universities in 2006 a total of about 70,600 persons in the R&D area, which corresponds to a share of 71% of the entire R&D personnel in HEIs. This figure admittedly also contains the personnel for comprehensive universities, as well as colleges of education and theology, but their share is very small. The second largest group with about 25,000 is found in the medical institutions of the universities, which corresponds to a share of 25%. UASs only account for 3,400 (3.4%) and art colleges 877 (0.9%) of personnel for R&D. This data underlines that the human resources in UASs are extremely limited for performing R&D, but they can be greatly extended via the successful acquisition of research projects (from public bodies or industry). In the past years the scale on which application-oriented R&D is conducted in UASs has clearly risen. Public promotional programmes have primarily contributed to this, but also measures within the individual UASs, in which the professors were offered incentives to conduct R&D along with their extensive teaching load.

A central problem for UASs is the short-term of many R&D projects and, with that, the problem of employing and keeping staff active. In the study by Fraunhofer ISI of 2004, the 69 UASs interviewed referred to the following issues: the project employees usually (92.8%) have short-term contracts corresponding to the time span of the R&D projects. Regular non-fixed term employees play a complementary role (40.6%). Many qualified graduates find more attractive job opportunities outside the UAS – in particular, in the private sector. Cooperative PhD procedures are a possibility to attract qualified graduates for R&D projects: the candidates do their doctorate at a university, but are still employed at the UAS. Especially, universities from eastern Germany are open to such methods, but this does not seem to be popular in western Germany.

The Allocation of Resources for Research

As the room to manoeuvre of the UASs for teaching and application-oriented R&D are determined to a great extent by the regulations in each federal state and by their promotional programmes, there is no standardised pattern Germany-wide for how the institutions allocate money and working time to research for individual staff members. There are no uniform rules on how much time could be used for research, for example, a fixed percentage of working time. Until a few years ago, it was entirely up to individuals in the UASs to determine how they spent their time, as long as they fulfilled their teaching obligations. In most UASs only limited incentives to research existed, as the teaching commitments clearly dominated and the HEI management often only had little leeway to provide professors with a breathing space to conduct application-oriented R&D projects by reducing their teaching workload. This does not apply to all UASs, however, as already mentioned above. In the past years changes have taken place in many UASs, triggered not least by the pressure among the UASs themselves to create stronger profiles and in their bid for demarcation from the universities. This resulted in not only the heads of the UASs, but also individual faculties or departments defining their strategic orientation more clearly than before, fixed on teaching and research focuses and giving R&D activities a higher status. It is now regulated when and under which circumstances a reduction of tuition obligations is possible in order to support research activities, which persons can profit from this, and how the teaching workload will be fulfilled. However, it is not to be expected that in the years to come a great majority of the professors in UASs will perform R&D regularly, but the group of professors performing R&D should grow considerably, compared with the situation today.

Research Performance in Non-university Institutions

The Extent and Output of Research

If one utilises common indicators to measure the outputs of R&D, as are customarily used, for example, for universities or non-university research institutions (patents, number of publications in peer review journals or the like), then UASs perform relatively badly. A study by Fraunhofer ISI of the spin-off potential in universities, UASs and non-university research institutions in Germany (Kulicke & Schleinkofer, 2008), also contains an estimate of the number of patent applications filed by UASs and universities (see Table 9.1). Only 37% of the HEI patents are applied for by UASs, the majority of patents are filed (63%) by individuals, enterprises or other organisations. The composition underlines the importance of the (technical) universities in the patenting area: 89.7% of all HEI patents originate from universities.

Table 9.1 Patent applications in 2005 by patentees and type of universities

	Technical universities ($n = 17$)	Universities ($n = 65$)	UASs ($n = 96$)	Total
Patent applications by university or UAS	282 (12.1%)	516 (22.1%)	62 (2.7%)	860 (36.8%)
Patent applications by individuals or enterprises	443 (19.0%)	854 (36.6%)	179 (7.7%)	1,476 (63.2%)
Total	725 (31.0%)	1,370 (58.6%)	241 (10.3%)	2,336 (100.0%)

Source: Own calculation acc. to Fraunhofer ISI surveys.

In particular, the 17 technical universities are responsible for 31% of such patents. Only 10.3% stem from UASs. However, in view of the low personnel R&D capacities in UASs and their strong application orientation, this is still quite a high share.

Application activity is concentrated within a few universities: over 50% of all patents stem from 20 universities. The number of patents from the universities correlates above all with the number of professors, the number of scientific staff in the engineering sciences, in mathematics and natural sciences and with the amount of third-party funds acquired from industry.

Seventy-seven out of 96 UASs applied for a total of 241 patents in 2005. This corresponds to an average of 3.1. The other 19 UASs did not file for patents in this year. Compared with the average values for technical universities (42.6) and the other universities (21.1), this indicator is naturally very low. Mechanical engineering and instruments are the most significant technology fields with 123 and 74 patents respectively in the UASs, no applications were made in the area medicine/health care science. As for the university patents (from technical and other universities), most patent applications originate from the technology fields of chemistry (819 patents), instruments (547 patents) and mechanical engineering (472 patents). In 2005 no UAS published more than 10 patents. The UAS patent numbers were determined by the number of scientific personnel as a whole and in engineering.

The Fraunhofer ISI study of 2004 on research activity in UASs (Kulicke & Stahlecker, 2004) was able to identify, for the years 2000–2003, a total of 6,005 R&D projects which were conducted in the 97 UASs examined. The technology and thematic areas of R&D projects correspond with the teaching focuses of the UAS: The area of information technology occupies the first place (incl. multimedia and production engineering; share: 23%); many projects (523) fall into the multimedia field. Another big share (17%) is taken by the technology area, 'material research, physical and chemical technologies', which accounts for a variety of current projects in the areas of metrology and analytical techniques, as well as measurement and control engineering. Of great importance is mechanical engineering, which was to be expected due to the traditional strength of UASs in this field. Similar importance applies to economics (share 10%). The other topics or fields of technology are of minor importance even though the number of projects is not that small.

The financial volume of the 6,003 projects also shows a wide range, without the small projects dominating. UASs implemented a number of projects with a financial volume of €500,000 or more, which is considerable when taking into account their capacities. The founder is of importance here: projects financed by the EU (average approx. €270,000), public foundations (€150,000) and *Länder* (€144,000) or state departments (€133,000; including the respective subordinate offices) show, on average, substantially higher project funding than those of other donors (e.g. business: €37,000). This shows clearly why public support programmes are very attractive for UASs.

The Relevance of Research for the Regional Community

In the analysis of the 6,005 R&D projects which the investigated UASs carried out in the years 2000 until 2003 (Kulicke & Stahlecker, 2004), we also inquired about the commissioning clients. With respect to the number of projects, enterprises are in top position as sponsors for R&D projects at UASs: 27% of all projects where information is available on founders were financed by business, compared to federal government (25%) and states (23%). Projects financed by business are mostly small in volume, very practice-led and with a short time frame. Most of the interviewed UASs from the old *Länder* consider regional location of client enterprises as highly important. The structure of the regional economy, as well as the compatibility of subject area coverage of the UAS with the sectoral structure of regional business, plays an important role. In the new *Länder*, the orders from business clearly are on a lower scale than in many West German UASs. The reasons for this are primarily the fewer R&D activities in the regional businesses, as well as the lower density of enterprises. Representatives of those West German UASs attaching less importance to the regional economy gave the following reasons: supra-regional networks of professors, high degree of specialisation of the UAS in combination with a few similarly specialised enterprises in the region, supra-regional reputation of the UAS, and the strengthening of R&D activities within the UAS still being in an early stage.

Publicly financed projects differ from business financed ones in the following ways: 'holistic character' (thematically comprehensive), handling of partial projects within research consortia, possibility of interdisciplinary cooperation across faculties, long-term (with the possibility of employment of qualified staff) as well as higher project volumes. In contrast, contracts from businesses normally have the following features: dominance of applied research as an input into the internal pre-development or pre-competitive product development, addressing partial aspects of product or process development, solution of detail problems by the UAS, broad spectrum of product and process-oriented service delivery, and short-term projects with relatively low volumes.

Half of the interviewees pointed out that the annual R&D potential for orders from regional business have little relevance, as the university-specific conditions in research are the decisive factors limiting more research contracts from business and not their potential. Where quantitative data on the annual R&D potential for contracts from business was available, it varied between a couple of hundred thousand and €2.5 million. For most of the UASs which were examined (almost 57%) the number of potential regional customers (at least 50) could be considered relatively large.

Typical competitors for R&D contracts are other regional universities (UASs and universities). Non-university research facilities on the other hand hardly play a role: however, partnership relations between UASs and the mentioned institutions frequently weigh more than the pressure of competition. Problems with the implementation of R&D projects are usually observed not on the part of enterprises, but rather on the side of the UAS. The reason for this is, according to reports of UASs, the problematic situation in the areas of research and teaching: A high teaching load and a limited number of non-teaching academic middle-level staff lead to problems with personnel deployment and a lack of flexibility in HR management.

Also in the latest study of the Fraunhofer ISI (Kulicke et al., 2008) on research in UASs (Evaluation of the Promotional Programme FH[3]), the question was examined what relevance the regional economy has for UASs. The interviewed professors stated that the UAS departments in which the promoted R&D projects were conducted were mainly integrated in a comparatively dense network with other institutions for which they had carried out R&D projects in the past 5 years. A good half had thereafter realised similar projects several times on behalf of SMEs from the region (54.2%) or of SMEs outside the region (52.2%). The corresponding statistics for large enterprises from the region are 29.8% as well as 52.2% for large enterprises outside the region in which the UASs are located. Public promotional programmes dominate as the main financers (78.1%).

The Relevance of Research for the Development of Professional Expertise

A precondition of qualitatively demanding master's programmes at UASs are application- and research-oriented courses. The latter aim is to put students in a position to work independently, following scientific principles and to apply scientific methods and findings. Besides research-oriented master's programmes, corresponding bachelor courses are also being offered (target: Bachelor of Science or Bachelor of Arts), which aim to qualify graduates to actively participate in research tasks. Research-oriented master's programmes aim to enable the graduates to take part in more highly qualified professional activities with a comprehensive theoretical–analytical orientation, as a rule for active participation in research tasks.

The share of research-oriented teaching events in the curriculum of the department or institute lies, according to the 159 professors who were interviewed, in the framework of the evaluation of FH[3] (Kulicke et al., 2008), at present on average at 16.9% (median value: 15.0%). However, the spectrum is large and ranges from 0 to 60%. The majority (59.4%) of the professors interviewed assumed that this share will rise slightly, as a result of the FH[3] project. However, only 14.5% expected a noticeable increase.

Table 9.2 Number of research-oriented qualifications as an output of the FH³ project (already realised or expected)

	Share of UASs with such theses (%)	Average number per project
Diploma theses	77.5	3.7
Bachelor theses	48.4	4.1
Master's theses	61.9	2.4
Cooperative doctoral theses	51.0	1.3

Source: Kulicke et al. (2008).

In the evaluation of the promotional programme FH³, we also examined to what extent the promoted R&D projects led to research-oriented qualifications. We understand hereby diploma, bachelor's and master's theses, as well as cooperative doctoral theses. The answers of the 159 professors who managed a promoted project and participated in the survey show that in many UASs such theses were already made possible by the FH³ project or are expected to be made possible (see Table 9.2). About half expected bachelor theses and cooperative doctoral theses (i.e. in cooperation with a university with the right to award doctorate degrees). It must be taken into consideration that the three first named categories in the course of the transformation of study courses to bachelor/master degrees are not free of overlapping. The largest output consists of research-based diploma theses.

Dilemmas and Challenges

The entire German higher education landscape is presently in a phase of upheaval, characterised by many and varied developments, by numerous demands for a structural re-organisation, and at the same time, limited basic funds. Examples include:

1. The Bologna Process to create a common European HEI area, which opens up the possibility for the UASs, among others, to make their curricula internationally compatible by developing bachelor and master's study courses;
2. The develop of research capacities at HEIs, primarily at the universities and strengthening cutting-edge research;
3. Reductions in the general state funding (above all limit budgetary funds by the governing bodies);
4. Introductions of performance-related remuneration systems for professors and the allocation of funds to HEIs and faculties or departments according to performance criteria;
5. Extending the freedom of HEIs, in particular to strengthen their own profiles;
6. Abolishing university professors' privileges in the law governing employees' inventions and improving the political will to utilise the innovation potential in universities.

The present promotion of excellence in the HEI area is practically bypassing the UASs. The federal government, above all in its High-tech Strategy (see BMBF, 2007), has been supporting the building up of research capacities at universities and non-university research institutions considerably since 2006. The goal of building up internationally recognised research focuses is hereby emphasised. The allocation of the extensive promotional funds is based on the principle of 'Strengthen the strong'. Focuses lie not only on the performance of research, but also on their utilisation via commercial applications. UASs profit only to a very small extent from this programme. The UASs, however, in the conversion of the study courses to bachelor and master's degrees, are under political pressure to sharpen their profiles and develop competitive competence fields. In contrast to the universities, the UASs have a structural problem, then as now, to conduct nationally and internationally visible R&D. An academic middle-level engaging in research is missing, as well as a corresponding basic funding which would compensate for the higher teaching workload of the UAS professors, and allow them more leeway for creative R&D work and commercialisable activities. In addition, both options would give UASs the possibility to offer graduates a perspective to work in the area of application-oriented R&D, which is not subject to the pressures of project financing which only provides short-term security. The UASs are generally confronted with the problem that they are not in a position to build up a stable, permanent basis of personnel resources outside longer term publicly funded R&D projects.

But the status of R&D has increased over the years at nearly all UASs and further efforts are being made to expand this. There are very different constellations in terms of the driving forces for a stronger role of R&D in UASs. First, the *Länder* as the governing bodies of the UASs have an important impact. But there are major differences in the extent to which individual countries extend the scope of the UAS for R&D through the allocation of resources or special government programmes. Another important factor is the extent to which the UAS presidents support activities in R&D by a generous allocation of available funds. In recent years there were very large differences between the various UAS administrations, with the consequence of large differences in their R&D orientation. The third group under the driving forces are the professors themselves. Their interests in R&D, experiences and contact networks ultimately determine how they exploit their low margin from the high teaching load. Other important driving forces are the support programmes of the BMBF for R&D projects. In recent years, however, on all these different levels the value of R&D has increased. In particular, there were no differences in the political objectives of the *Länder* and the BMBF.

Representatives of UASs classify the framework conditions totally differently. The reasons given were the succession of generations presently taking place (young R&D-oriented professors increasingly replacing older colleagues with stronger affinity to teaching). Essential instruments to intensify research at UASs are as follows: support the establishment focal research areas, allocation of internal research budgets, further financial incentives (e.g. performance-oriented budgets), reduction of teaching load, establishment of competence centres across departments, consideration of R&D orientation with new appointments, intensification of cooperative

PhD procedures, expansion of At-institutes, etc. Thereby the group of professors involved in research should be expanded and applied R&D put on a broader base. Within a background of considerably fewer finances and personnel, when compared to universities the applied research and development has expanded rapidly within UASs over the last decade – thematically as well as content-wise. Contributing factors were the improvements in the structural environment of R&D within UASs, as well as the supply of support programmes either tailor-made for UASs or open to such facilities.

References

Federal Ministry of Education and Research (BMBF) (Ed.). (2003). *Universities of applied sciences in Germany* (4th Rev. ed.). Bonn.

Federal Ministry of Education and Research (BMBF) (Ed.). (2007). *The high-tech strategy for Germany.* Download: http://www.hightech-strategie.de/_media/faktenpapier_hts_englisch.pdf

Kulicke, M., Bührer, S., & Ruhland, S. (2008). *PRO INNO II – PROgramm zur Förderung der Erhöhung der INNOvationskompetenz mittelständischer Unternehmen. Entwicklung des Programmanlaufs von August 2004 bis Ende 2005.* Stuttgart.

Kulicke, M., & Schleinkofer, M. (2008). *Rahmenbedingungen und Potenziale für Ausgründungen aus der Wissenschaft. Aktueller Stand im Kontext von EXIST – Existenzgründungen aus der Wissenschaft.* Karlsruhe.

Kulicke, M., & Stahlecker, T. (2004). *Forschungslandkarte Fachhochschulen. Potenzialstudie.* Federal Ministry of Education and Research (BMBF) (Ed.), Bonn.

Kulicke, M., Zimmermann, A., Kroll, H., & Bührer, S. (2008). *Evaluation des BMBF-Förderprogramms FH³ "angewandte Forschung an Fachhochschulen im Verbund mit der Wirtschaft" – Bewilligungszeitraum 2004 bis 2006.* Federal Ministry of Education and Research (BMBF) (Ed.), Bonn-Berlin.

Statistisches Bundesamt. (2008a). *Bildung und Kultur. Monetäre hochschulstatistische Kennzahlen 2006.* Fachserie 11 Reihe 4.3.2. Wiesbaden.

Statistisches Bundesamt. (2008b). *Bildung und Kultur. Nichtmonetäre hochschulstatistische Kennzahlen. 1980 – 2006.* Fachserie 11 Reihe 4.3.1. Wiesbaden.

Statistisches Bundesamt. (2008c). *FuE-Ausgaben an Hochschulen 2005 nach Hochschulen. Sonderauswertung.* Wiesbaden.

Wissenschaftsrat. (1981). *Empfehlungen zu Aufgaben und Stellung der Fachhochschulen.* Köln.

Wissenschaftsrat. (1991). *Empfehlungen zur Entwicklung der Fachhochschulen in den 90er Jahren.* Köln.

Wissenschaftsrat. (1993). *10 Thesen zur Hochschulpolitik.* Drs. 1001/93. Berlin.

Wissenschaftsrat. (2000). *Thesen zur künftigen Entwicklung des Wissenschaftssystems in Deutschland.* Köln.

Wissenschaftsrat. (2002). *Empfehlungen zur Entwicklung der Fachhochschulen.* Drs. 5102/02. Berlin.

Chapter 10
Ireland: The Challenges of Building Research in a Binary Higher Education Culture

Ellen Hazelkorn and Amanda Moynihan

Introduction

The Irish higher education environment has changed dramatically and rapidly over the last few decades. Not only was Ireland transformed from a predominantly agricultural economy, with an ethnically and religiously homogeneous population, but it also effectively skipped the industrial age. The country was catapulted into the twenty-first century, with over half the population employed either in public or private services, e.g. retail, tourism, finance/business, administration, health and education, which accounted for 64% GDP in 2007. This was complemented by strong export growth led by foreign owned multi-nationals, especially in pharmaceuticals, medical devices and software. During the 'Celtic tiger' days, society was transformed from being labour-exporting to one heavily dependent upon immigration with new training needs.

Ireland's growth was strongly predicated upon policy attention and financial support to education and the formation of 'human capital' since the late 1950s. A critical element had been the synergy between the introduction of free secondary education in the mid-1960s and economic growth, which, in turn drove demand for higher education. The desire to widen participation led to the abolition of tuition fees in 1997; today, over 55% of second-level students go on to higher education, up from 44% a decade ago, and the government has set a target of 72% by 2020. This growth helped transform public sentiment in favour of significant expansion in national funding for research and S&T-related matters, and greater focus on enterprise–academy collaboration. Between 1997 and 2008, approximately €3 billion was invested, albeit Ireland still lagged behind EU and OECD neighbours as a percentage of GDP.

By 2009, all had changed utterly. The global recession, acerbated by domestic problems, brutally ended Ireland's 'Celtic tiger' status. Higher education – a

E. Hazelkorn (✉)
Higher Education Policy Research Unit (HEPRU), Dublin Institute of Technology,
Dublin, Ireland
e-mail: Ellen.Hazelkorn@dit.ie

S. Kyvik, B. Lepori (eds.), *The Research Mission of Higher Education Institutions Outside the University Sector*, Higher Education Dynamics 31,
DOI 10.1007/978-1-4020-9244-2_10, © Springer Science+Business Media B.V. 2010

beneficiary of the boom – became a casualty of the politically charged and financially challenging environment. Higher education policy reflects this volte-face. Until recently it was dominated by questions of massification and access, getting more people well-educated; today, the emphasis is on quality and world-class excellence – but within the context of achieving greater coherence, collaboration and efficiency across the system. These objectives are reflected in three major and concurrent policy initiatives: the *Strategic Review of Irish Higher Education* (2009–2010), the government's strategy for *Building Ireland's Smart Economy* (2008), and the Ministry of Finance's *Special Group on Public Service Numbers and Expenditure Programmes*.

Overview

Prior to the 1970s, higher education was dominated by five universities, whose lineage stretched back to the nineteenth century with the exception of Trinity College Dublin, established in 1592. To meet these new challenges, the government established two national institutes of higher education, in Limerick (1972) and Dublin (1975), to provide technologically focused programmes. After some controversy, both institutions effectively declared themselves universities forcing the government to pass legislation in 1989. At this stage, it is fair to say that they bear little relationship to the alternative mission the government had envisaged (White, 2001).

Given that experience, it is perhaps not surprising the government has been more steadfast in maintaining a de jure binary system. In response to publication of *Technician Training in Ireland* (OECD, 1964) and *Investment in Education* (OECD, 1965), the *Steering Committee on Technical Education* concluded there was an urgent need to produce technically qualified people in order to plan for industrial development. Regional Technical Colleges (RTCs) should educate 'for trade and industry over a broad spectrum of occupations ranging from craft to professional level, notably in engineering and science, but also in commercial, linguistic and other specialities' (Government of Ireland, 1967). Under the RTC and Dublin Institute of Technology (DIT) Acts, 1992, their functions were further identified as

> To provide vocational and technical education and training for the economic, technological, scientific, commercial, industrial, social and cultural development of the State with particular reference to the region served by the Colleges, as well as to:
>
> - Engage in research, development and consultancy work,
> - Exploit any research, consultancy or development work,
> - Enter into arrangements with other institutions in or outside the State for the purpose of joint programmes in both teaching and research.

There were 11 colleges when the Acts were introduced, and 13 in 2000. In 2007, all institutes of technology, including Dublin Institute of Technology, were brought under the remit of the Higher Education Authority (HEA).

By 2000, all RTCs had been renamed 'institutes of technology' (IoTs) in somewhat controversial circumstances, officially in recognition of their university-level teaching and research but unofficially because the nomenclature of 'institute of technology' was perceived as having higher status; similarly, permission was given in 2007 to rename the 'Director' as 'President'. Both actions sought to build on the singular experience of the older and larger Dublin Institute of Technology (DIT). Its establishment in 1992 brought together six former science, engineering, business and music colleges, with lineage dating to the late nineteenth century. DIT has its own legislation and authority to make academic awards from apprenticeship to PhD, including Honourary Doctorates, under the Qualifications (Education and Training Act) 1999, while other IoTs have delegated authority from the Higher Education and Training Awards Council (HETAC). In recent years, it has sought re-designation as a university in order to remove any and all confusion about its dual sector position.

All IoTs, with the exception of DIT, work through the Institutes of Technology Ireland (IOTI) formerly Council of Directors (CoD). It acts as a representative and lobby group for the sector, through which negotiations with the government and trade unions are conducted. Given growing disparity in ambitions and size of the various IoTs, the larger ones, e.g. Waterford and Cork, have tended to operate in a semi-detached manner. WIT and CIT have also made submissions for University designation. DIT has an ambiguous relationship with the other IoTs, arguing that its awarding powers make it a university-in-all-but-name (Norton, 2008).

Irish higher education is generally described as a binary system. It is, however, more complex and varied than the term usually suggests (Skilbeck, 2003). There are 7 universities, 14 IoTs, 9 Colleges of Education, the National College of Art and Design, 2 non-state-aided private colleges and other national institutions. The universities and IoTs have been treated differently in policy, funding and recognition. Until March 2006, the HEA, the statutory planning and development body for higher education and research, was only concerned with the university sector, while the IoTs were governed by the Department of Education and Science.

Distinctions between programme type, qualification and students further emphasise the differences between the two sectors. The university sector is now significantly larger and expanding rapidly. In 2007/2008 of the total 159,978 students, 58% were enrolled in universities and 42% in IoTs, of which DIT had 8% and the other IoTs 33%, representing a significant turn-about since 2000 (HEA, 2009a). Seven IoTs have fewer than 3,000 full-time students. While postgraduate enrolment is increasing in the IoTs, that have only 17% of all postgraduates while universities have 83% (HEA, 2009a) IoTs account for 46% of first admissions (HEA, 2009b), and in 2007/2008 approximately 53.7% of its students were at diploma, certificate and BA(Ordinary) level (HEA, 2009a).

Another distinction has been the role of research. The 1967 steering committee did not specify research as a fundamental function, although both the 1992 RTC and DIT Acts acknowledged this role 'subject to such conditions as the Minister may determine'. In contrast, the 1997 University Act reconfirmed research as an unqualified function of universities stating that a 'university shall promote and facilitate research'. This delayed development of research in the IoTs.

As competition for students, finance and reputation accelerates, the gap between universities and IoTs is widening. During the 'Celtic Tiger' days, some IoTs struggled to recruit students; with high unemployment, student applications to all HEIs has risen. Evidence continues to show students are choosing universities over IoTs, all things being equal (Fitzgerald, 2006; Walshe, 2007; Flynn, 2007), which is increasing socio-economic stratification. This gap is most apparent in postgraduate education, primarily the PhD cohort. Universities, on the back of EU and Irish Government declarations to considerably increase the number of PhD students, have promoted the concept of fourth level or postgraduate education. By using this term, they are trying to distinguish between themselves as the postgraduate provider and IoTs as the undergraduate or third level provider (IUA, 2007).

Table 10.1 below provides an overview of all the IoTs, which are named in accordance with the county or town/city. Throughout, DIT, given its size and the way data is collected, is indicated separately in some tables, omitted in others or subsumed under the generic IoT label. Unfortunately, there is no comprehensive regularly updated published and verifiable information; while academic staff numbers are likely to be constant, research performance across the other categories will have changed in some cases quite significantly since the dates given albeit the relativities would be fairly accurate.

Table 10.1 The relative size and performance of the IoTs and DIT

	Total student 2007/2008	Total MPhil and PhD 2007/2008	WTE academic staff 2008	Research awards € millions 2006	Refereed publications 2005
Dublin Institute of Technology (DIT)	13,555	331	954	6.7	143[a]
Athlone (AIT)	4,178	61	272	1.7	4
Cork (CIT)	8,592	119	656	4.7	49[a]
Dundalk (DKIT)	4,041	19	300	3.4	98[a]
Institute of Art, Design and Technology (DLIADT)	1,687	9	128	–	7
Galway-Mayo (GMIT)	5,888	84	394	2.6	11[a]
Blanchardstown (ITB)	1,665	12	120	–	24
Carlow (ITC)	4,107	34	222	0.3	11
Sligo (ITS)	4,484	31	301	1	13
Tallaght (ITT)	3,321	71	212	1.9	n/a
Tralee (ITTR)	2,222	17	226	0.2	28
Limerick (LIT)	3,444	10	308	0.2	n/a
Letterkenny (LYIT)	2,107	5	198	0.4	4
Waterford (WIT)	7,463	175	579	9.2	123
Total	66,754	978	4,869	32.3	515

[a]Includes refereed and non-refereed publications.
Source: Adopted HEA/Forfás (2007), Forfás (2007a) and IOTI (2008).

In 2003, the Department of Education and Science invited the OECD to evaluate the performance of higher education and recommend how it could better meet Ireland's strategic objectives. The OECD (2004) reaffirmed the binary as the best mechanism to maintain diversity. It also recommended that HETAC's decision to devolve authority to award doctorates to four IoTs should be rescinded. Given the intensity of local politics in Ireland, the government has been slow to take action. Recent government and HEA initiatives to encourage and promote critical mass and synergies between all HEIs, and especially between universities and IoTs, have also contributed to a realignment within higher education, under the guise of collaboration. The provision of advanced qualifications and growth of research activity within the IoT sector has helped blur the boundaries between universities and IoTs, with all the accompanying demands for funding and support. This has revealed significant gaps in capacity and capability, calls to concentrate activity in only a few institutions and counter-calls for the end of 'restrictive practices'. These issues will be explored in the last section of this chapter.

National Policies for Research

There is no official research policy that relates specifically to the IoTs although there are references in the underpinning legislation and other documents that IoTs should focus on applied research with a regional focus. In reality, differences in core and capital funding, and curriculum and qualifications level, between IoTs and universities have played a greater role defining respective research mission.

Since intensification of globalisation and the dynamics of the knowledge society, policy has focused on the link between research and international competitiveness (DETE, 2006, p. 8; DETE, 2004):

> Ireland by 2013 will be internationally renowned for the excellence of its research, and will be to the forefront in generating and using new knowledge for economic and social progress, within an innovation driven culture.

To meet this goal, all competitions, with a few exceptions, are open to all HEIs. In recent years, the HEA, which funds Programme for Research in Third Level Institutions (PRTLI) and the various research councils, has actively encouraged collaboration across sectoral lines in all its programmes. As a result, many large research projects, Centres-of-Excellence and Graduate Schools involve both universities and IoTs, some of which are led by the latter. Science Foundation Ireland (SFI), principally because it supports basic research in biotechnology, ICT and now energy, has been closer to the universities but the IoTs have also been successful.

While there are nuanced differences in opinion between national agencies, the prevailing view, heretofore, is that research excellence should be supported wherever it occurs, because Ireland is at too early a stage to concentrate all its resources in a few universities. There is also a very strong local political dimension which would oppose efforts to centralise and/or undermine regional capacity. It could be argued that in the absence of a formal statement competition is defining policy.

Priority Setting Between Teaching and Research

Institutional differentiation is embedded in the fabric of how the university and IoT sectors are organised and managed, and how academic work is determined. Practical, vocationally oriented teaching has been a defining characteristic of the IoTs, exemplified by low student/staff ratios compared to the universities: 14:1 versus 20:1, respectively, in 2007/2008.

IoT academics are contractually obliged to teach 560 h/year or 16 h/week, which is often reinterpreted by some academics and their trade unions as only doing 16 h work per week. The academic year concludes on the 21 June and academic staff are not required to return to work until 1 September; any changes outside these times are to be compensated. In addition, there are the normal national holidays. The emphasis is on teaching, and only recently on research and service, provoking additional claims for reduction in teaching in order to undertake research or participate on committees, etc. In contrast, academic work in the universities is widely accepted as comprising the three components of teaching, research and service.

A 2004 study revealed significant differences between time spent on research in each sector (see Fig. 10.1). Estimates suggest that between 9 and 11% of IoT

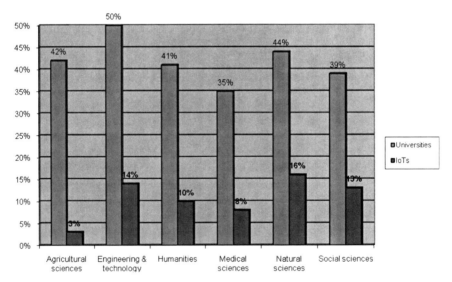

Fig. 10.1 Average percentage of time spent on research by academic staff across universities and IoTs by field of science, 2004
Source: Adapted from (Forfás 2005)

staff are involved in research but this figure is highly variable across the different institutions (IOTI, 2008, pp. 22, 17).

While national bargaining, under social partnership, sets salary and broad socio-economic determinates, the definition of academic work differs between sectors. In addition, for the IoTs, detailed employment and contractual issues are negotiated with the academic trade union and the Department of Education and Science in tripartite talks. This makes individual institutional requirements difficult to agree and implement.

Funding Research

Beginning 2008, all HEA-funded HEIs (universities and IoTs) are funded according to the recurrent grant allocation model (RGAM), based on input (student numbers) and output metrics with a percentage tied to research performance. This is a significant change from when approximately 30% of university budgets were attributed to R&D using estimates of academic time spent on research, and IoTs were funded by the Department of Education and Science on the basis of hours taught in the classroom with little flexibility to move between pay and non-pay accounts.

Because of infrastructural inequities that have developed over time, the universities have been significantly more successful. Despite new money, this historical gap plus differences in bid capacity and capability exist, with a few notable exceptions. IoTs accounted for only 5.5% of total R&D spending in the higher education sector in 2006 despite the fact that R&D funding for IoTs grew by 77.7% from 1998 to 2000 (Forfas, 2007b). Since 1998, R&D spending performed in the IoTs has risen from €13.5 million in 1998 to €33.3 million in 2006 (Forfás, 2008). Table 10.2 – which covers 80% of research expenditure for the period listed – breaks down the sources of direct funding (from government departments, state agencies and research councils) most of which are competitive. Different agencies use different formats for different periods. Only Enterprise Ireland (EI) and the Department of Education and Science provide targeted funding for IoTs. In addition, DIT and WIT receive significant EU Framework funding.

Table 10.2   R&D funding sources of IoTs (€ millions), 2000–2007

Source	Science Foundation Ireland	Enterprise Ireland	EU Framework 6	Technology Sector Research	Programme for Research in Third-Level Institutions	Misc.	Total
Period covered	2000–2007	2001–2007	2001–2007	2000–2007	2000–2007	2000–2007[a]	
R&D funds	13.1	32.5	9.4	5.1	51.5	9.8	167.3
Percent	8%	19%	6.5%	30%	30%	6.5%	100%

[a]Approximately 15 additional national and international funds.
Source: IOTI (2008, p. 19).

IoTs success is all the more 'significant when measured against high teaching loads and a relative deficit of research infrastructure' (CoD, 2003, p. 41). Targeted initiatives are being considered but this may be hard to justify when quality is emphasised. There is the additional problem of attempting to develop sustainable applied or industrial-relevant research without research excellence in the underpinning sciences (Conlon, 2007).

IoT Research Strategy

HEI strategic plans and, in particular, research plans are new developments in Ireland, but they are now a legislative requirement and prerequisite for some funding initiatives. All institutions must provide evidence of a published and publicly available institutional strategy against which research priorities are closely mapped. This should be a rolling 3-year strategy, with action plans and targets aligned to national strategic priorities, and not change annually to fit different funding criteria. In this way, the HEA is steering change and mission differentiation across the HE system, and closer alignment between research activity and institutional and national priorities. Other funding initiatives, such as SFI or the research councils, have not adopted this position but by requiring all proposals to be signed by an institution's vice-president for research there is an assumption of institutional alignment. In other instances, agencies require matching funds, another way of ensuring a proposal meets institutional priorities.

While each IoT has gone about strategic planning in its own way, there is broad consensus that drafting a plan should involve consultation with key internal and external stakeholders. Governing bodies, which usually include industry, students and other public stakeholders, should be involved. Both DIT and WIT have established a dedicated Office of Strategic Planning to lead and oversee this annual process.

Institutional Strategy and Priority Setting

When compared internationally, Ireland has a young research system. As already stated, there is no specific research policy for the IoTs but there is a distinctive approach to their research which reflects their history, particular competences and emphasis on social applicability and innovation (Table 10.3). In addition to strengths in science and technology disciplines, there is burgeoning humanities and social science research, especially in business, the environment, and creative arts and media.

The IOTI plus DIT came together to produce a *Framework for the Development of Research in the Institutes of Technology* (IOTI, 2008). Its aim was to provide a strategic voice for research which has often existed below the public and policy radar. Nevertheless, the final document, in addition to identifying broad targets, was controversial among the institutions because it sought to provide a common

Table 10.3 R&D Priorities in IoTs and DIT

	Life sciences	Physics and engineering	Other
DIT	Food, nutrition and health	New materials and technology	Business and social development
		Sustainable energy	Creative arts and media
		ICT	
AIT	Toxicology, Biomed	Nanotechnology	Social care
CIT	BioPharma/chemical	Wireless systems photonics	
DKIT	Smooth muscle		Entrepreneurship
DLIADT			Creative arts
			Entrepreneurship
			Learning science
GMIT	Marine, forestry and energy	Biomedical device design	Tourism and hospitality
ITB		Graphics/gaming e-learning, speech, etc. Processing occupational road safety	Occupational road safety
ITC	Environment and BioRemediation	Networks	Design
ITS	Environment	Mechanical and manufacturing engineering	Socio-economic research
ITT	BioPharma	Sensors and medical devices	
ITTR	Biological sciences	Geometric optics	Social science
LIT	Neutraceuticals	Renewable energy controls	Internationally traded services
LYIT	Marine biotech	Computing/animation Wireless technology Sustainable and renewable energy	Creative industries
WIT	Bio/pharma science Health sciences	Telecommunications	Business management

Source: Adapted IOTI (2008).

strategic objective for institutions of various capacity and capability. In addition to aiming to double the amount of research funding earned, number of researchers and PhDs completions, the Framework also focused on achieving an integrated research continuum of 30% basic, 55% applied and strategic, and 15% industry-focused research (IOTI, 2008, p. 7).

Each IoT is developing a strategy and defining a priority domain. Strategies also identify structural challenges, e.g. high teaching workloads, weak research management infrastructure, development of IP management, provision of seed funding, research overheads, and training. The need for collaboration, within the academy and particularly with other public or private partners, is seen as vital. Table 10.4 identifies other issues, including assessment metrics, albeit as Lillis (2007) suggests there may not always be alignment between objectives and performance.

Organisation and Management of Research

Research management is a big challenge for IoTs who wish to engage to a significant extent in research (Hazelkorn, 2004, 2005). Only half have appointed a designated head of research (DIT has the equivalent of a VP of Research and Enterprise) or established the equivalent of a Research Support Unit to identify funding opportunities, advise on proposal preparation, assist with research project administration, coordinate institutional funding applications and provide research performance statistics. To compensate, the IOTI has established a research office funded by a government initiative to provide services and advocate on behalf of the IoTs.

Research centres are an institutional issue; larger IoTs, e.g. DIT and WIT, have a significant and growing number of centres some of which work in close collaboration with the universities, and the public or private sector. Competitive large-scale funding for Enterprise Ireland designated Centres-of-Excellence are an important development but are dependent upon close collaboration with indigenous industry and future funding being available.

Within the parameters described above, each IoT allocates research time according to its own priorities and budgets. The larger institutions are flexible, supporting research interests regardless of position or status, and reducing teaching on the basis of research output or earned income. This view would stem from the realisation that new appointments are more likely to be research active. In contrast, other IoTs, would be much more rigid, and allow only senior academic staff additional time for research.

Collaboration with Universities and Industry

Ireland places a high priority on collaboration within and across sectors, and with private industry in order to maximise critical mass in key priority domain. Both PRTLI and SIF have made collaboration a requirement (Government of Ireland, 2007, p. 206). There have been growing number of research partnerships and strategic institutional alliances, across the binary. There are clear advantages to all HEIs, including strengthening research capacity and broadening programme provision. Cork Institute of Technology and University College Cork have jointly developed a maritime research campus. The Dublin Regional Higher Education Alliance involves four universities, DIT, and three IoTs, while the universities and DIT are involved in a Graduate Education Network. These initiatives follow a successful collaboration between HEIs along the western seaboard, the Shannon Consortium.

Table 10.4 Institutional research strategies and performance measurements

	Research strategy	Research metrics	Encourage basic research	Develop/recruit research-active staff	Encourage research activity
DIT	Research strategy	• PhD-track students and completions • Refereed publications • Books/monographs • Conference/policy papers • Major works in production, performances and exhibitions • International collaboration • Patents, licenses, invention Disclosures • Company start-ups	Yes	Yes	Yes
AIT	Included in strategic plan	• Refereed and non-refereed publications • Conference/policy papers • Licenses	Not specified	Yes	Yes
CIT	Included in strategic plan	• Refereed and non-refereed publications • Conference/policy papers • Patents	Yes	Not specified	Yes
DKIT	Research strategy	• Publications • Conference/policy papers • Other published Research	Not specified	Yes	Yes
DLIADT	Research strategy	• Refereed and non-refereed publications • Conference/policy papers • Research papers • Training courses	Not specified	Yes	Yes

Table 10.4 (continued)

	Research strategy	Research metrics	Encourage basic research	Develop/recruit research-active staff	Encourage research activity
GMIT	Internal Research Development programme (IRDP)	• Refereed and non-refereed publications • Conference/policy papers • Patents	Not specified	Yes	Yes
ITB	Included in strategic plan	• Refereed and non-refereed publications • Conference/policy papers	Applied Focus	Yes	Yes
ITC	Strategy statement for R&D	• Refereed and non-refereed publications • Conference/policy papers • Patents	Not specified	Not specified	Yes
ITS	Included in strategic plan	• Refereed and non-refereed Publications • Conference/policy papers	Not specified	Not specified	Yes
ITT	Included in strategic plan	• Publications • Paper/presentations • Prizes	Not specified	Yes	Yes
ITTR	Included in strategic plan	• Refereed and non-refereed Publications • Conference/policy papers	Not specified	Not specified	Not specified
LIT	Included in strategic plan	• No	Not specified	Not specified	Not specified
LYIT	Included in strategic plan	• Refereed and non-refereed Publications • Conference/Policy papers	Not specified	Not specified	Yes
WIT	Included in strategic plan	• Refereed publications • Conference/Policy Papers	Not specified	Yes	Yes

Source: Adapted from HEA/Forfás (2007).

However, there is little interaction between industry and higher education. A recent report shows that in 2005–2006 only 17% of research-active companies in Ireland collaborate with the higher education sector. Despite policy emphasis on increasing collaboration with industry, this was a decrease from 19% in 2001 (Forfás, 2007c).

IoTs, supported by Enterprise Ireland, are boosting enterprise-related research and company creation; €24 million was allocated in 2002 for nine new on-campus business incubation centres and the expansion of three centres, opened in the late 1980s, in IoTs which border Northern Ireland. Incubator centres provide start-up facilities, mentoring and office support for new business concepts and small inward-investing companies; clients are recent graduates or new 'entrepreneurs'. Usually, a company takes up a tenancy for 3 years on the basis that if they are unable to survive at that stage, their chances of longer term viability are slim.

IoTs are also embedding 'entrepreneurship' in education and training modules. The latter has received targeted competitive funding via the Enterprise Platform Programme (EPP). Emphasis is on spin-ins, e.g. participants from newly establish SMEs or multinationals, in contrast to the universities where the emphasis is on spin-outs, e.g. from the university's own research. The extent to which EPP participants and/or incubator tenants translate into sustainable and growing companies is variable across the regions. Technology transfer activity is also limited. Several companies highlighted the lack of technology transfer competence in HEIs as an obstacle (cf. Jordan & O'Leary, 2007).

IoTs were established to provide vocational and technical education and training. While the majority focuses on higher certificate and BA (Ord.) level, only the larger IoTs concentrate on advanced professional competence, at doctorate level. DIT, for example, has adopted the concept of 'professional doctorates' as developed in the UK and Australia; thus far, it has validated one for architecture. It has also validated structured PhD programmes with a work-based research component. Continuing professional development has often been viewed as a distinctive mission for the IoTs, although initial restrictions on operating at advanced levels and growth in the universities has meant that in some disciplines, e.g. business, architecture and nursing, the IoTs face stiff competition from the universities.

Human Resources and Careers

Until recently, academic staff appointed to IoTs were recruited primarily on the basis of their ability to teach, and depending upon the institution, to teach at undergraduate level only. The growth of postgraduate programmes coupled with emphasis on research has required a sea-change in human resource strategy and implementation. Today, new academic appointments are likely to have a PhD, research-performance skills and a publication profile. This focus clashes with appointment criteria determined by the Department of Education and Science, which has specified that candidates have industrial/professional experience. While research-focused appointments may not have the same experience or commitment to industry as their predecessors, it has proved difficult to recruit established professionals with appropriate research experience or capability, at the appropriate level and salary. These developments may ironically undermine a core IoT attribute.

With few exceptions, all appointments must be made at assistant lecturer level, although there are few contractual differences between assistant lecturer, lecturer or senior lecturer grades.

> The policy of recruiting staff at Assistant Lecturer level, i.e., the start-point on the promotional scale, allows little flexibility in recruitment and makes the IoT less competitive in attracting more experienced staff (IOTI, 2008, p. 21).

The number of teaching hours per week is specified as 18 h/week for assistant lecturers and 16 h/week for others. All academic staff are expected to be involved in research and service but in reality the emphasis is on teaching – and academics respond accordingly. Movement between assistant and lecturer grade – which requires a master's degree and evidence of research/scholarly activity – is termed 'progression' not promotion – a subtle distinction suggesting the process is largely a paper exercise and certainly that is the trade union's perception. The number of senior lecturer posts is a fixed-proportion of all academic staff, and there are few such opportunities. Those who do wish to progress on the salary scale have little option but to move into management positions, e.g. Head of Department or School, or in the case of DIT as Dean of Faculty. Upon appointment, all staff are tenured, with public service entitlements; neither dismissal nor redundancy is acceptable, legislatively or politically.

Not all IoTs share a common vision as to what is required in the future. This is not surprising given their different sizes, strengths and ambitions. Yet, the Department of Education and Science negotiates on human resource matters with the IoTs as a single group, and academic staff are represented by a trade union whose membership is drawn primarily from the secondary sector. Due to collective bargaining, individual IoTs are prohibited from developing their own career structure, and until recently, required Department of Education and Science approval for all new positions, even replacement of resignations or retirements. Flexibility in entry salary or grade, to attract particular candidates, has been strictly monitored.

Management and academic staff in the IoTs share few characteristics with their counterparts in the universities; indeed, as stated above, the understanding of academic work also differs. While this has created a very complex environment, with little flexibility, there has been a gradual change in the profile and ambitions of academic staff and correspondingly institutional profile (see Table 10.1). However, it is likely to be several decades before the full effect of new recruitment and staff development policies take effect. Because high calibre research-active individuals are attracted to institutions which can best meet their ambitions, it will take considerable time before IoTs can build the appropriate infrastructure to recruit and retain such staff.

Research Performance

The pattern of research activity varies considerably across the IoT sector. Estimates show only five institutions claim over 20% research-active staff, while several conduct almost no research. This uneven pattern is reflected in tensions across the sector, between the larger and more active institutions and the universities, and with the government and HEA.

Extent and Output of Research

The most significant sources of funding to the IoT sector are the Technology Sector Research programme (30% of the funding), Enterprise Ireland (19%) and PRTLI Cycles 1–4 (30%). These three sources represent approximately 80% of the total R&D funding to the sector (see Table 10.2 above, IOTI, 2008, p. 20). Concentration in the first two programmes is not surprising given their specific orientation; indeed the former is only open to IoTs to compete.

The pattern of research income varies significantly and unevenly across IoTs, with the most active, e.g. DIT and WIT, earning almost 50% of total IoT research income – and others reporting little or no research. This pattern is reflected in the Programme for Research in Third-Level Institutions (PRTLIT). In 2007, while the IoT sector increased its funding share from 4.1% (in cycles 1–3) to 19.8% in cycle 4, i.e. from €25 million to €42 million, only three IoTs (ITT, CIT, WIT) were project leaders of major PRTLI projects in cycle 4. In the 2009 competition, all but four IoTs (DIT, WIT, CIT and LYIT) were successful in the first round. In the absence of up-to-date, comprehensive and verifiable information, the data below reflects this differentiation.

- Publications: Of 515 publications during 2005, over 50% came from two institutions, DIT and WIT (see Table 10.1).
- Research Income: IoT research income ranged from €191,000 to €9.1 million, with an average of €2.7 million. In comparison, university funding ranged from €14.3 million to €60.5 million (Forfás, 2007a).
- Patents: According to the HEA/Forfas report (2007) only eight patents were registered by IoTs in 2005 (ITC 2, CIT 3, GMIT 1, DIT 2) albeit it is unclear whether these numbers represent patents granted or only submissions. This unevenness is reflected in more recent data from the European Patent Office (November 2009) which showed only three patents granted to IoTs, all of which were granted to DIT.

A recent study of research strengths in Ireland has grouped DIT with the National University of Ireland at Maynooth and the University of Limerick in terms of comparitive research performance. No other IoT is mentioned (Forfas, HEA, 2009).

Relevance of Research for the Region

IoTs were established with the specific mission of contributing to the technological, scientific, commercial, industrial, social and cultural development of Ireland, with particular reference to technical skills, applied research and knowledge/technology transfer appropriate to their region. The location of the IoTs reflects this orientation. Four are located in Dublin alongside four universities, three are located outside Dublin close to universities, while the remaining seven are the main higher education providers in their respective area.

The National Spatial Strategy (NSS) (Government of Ireland, 2002) identified 'gateways' and 'hubs' around the country through which Irish social and economic development should be developed – a key motivation being to spread people, employment and resources more evenly around the country rather than the current concentration in Dublin. All IoTs, with the exception of Carlow, are located in 'gateways'. Proposals to tie individual IoTs and universities to specific regional foci and partnerships have, however, proved controversial, and the NSS has for various reasons been largely ignored.

At an official level, enterprise development agencies are specifically required to meet regularly with IoTs but this often tends to be 'on an ad-hoc basis, while others are more strategic' (HEA/Forfás, 2007, p. 176). Enterprise Ireland has responsibility to 'work closely with the Institutes of Technology . . . to strengthen their ability to support industry at regional level' while IDA Ireland tends to work with its existing and potential client base in the region. Overall, there would be general agreement that despite their remit, there is no over-riding evidence of specific regionally relevant research. Indeed, it is not clear the extent to which the universities have done more in this area.

Dilemmas and Challenges

The Irish higher education system is at a crossroad. The binary system is constrained by historical circumstances and unresponsive to changing national and global requirements, there are low levels of internationalisation, and weak governance and strategic leadership. Despite significant investment in recent years, it remains below that of appropriate peers nations and institutions, and the possible emergence of a super-league of universities at the European level could be unfavourable to Ireland's small research community. Even if the economy had not experienced the current deep recession, Irish higher education required structural and policy attention. Indeed, it is arguable that Ireland has been late tackling many issues.

The *Strategic Review of Irish Higher Education* was conceived prior to the current recession, but the latter is now framing both the context and likely recommendations. Announced in February 2009, the Review has been tasked with assessing higher education's fitness-for-purpose, developing a vision and national policy objectives, and identifying 'focused targets' for the next 5 years. It has been asked to consider the number and roles of institutions, governance and accountability, level of resources and potential for greater efficiency 'having particular regard to the difficult budgetary and economic climate that is in prospect in the medium term'. Two other government initiatives, despite being oppositional to each other in objectives and strategic vision, share the view that Irish higher education requires reform and restructuring, including mergers. *Building Ireland's Smart Economy* endorses investment in R&D while the *Special Group on Public Service Numbers and Expenditure Programmes* has, inter alia, recommended significant reductions in funding for higher education, suggested rationalisation of provision and institutional mergers, questioned research spending and the number of PhDs, and criticised academic contracts in both the universities and IoTs.

There are probably five key challenges for the IoT sector.

Higher Education System

Ireland has operated a binary system since the 1970s, but like experience elsewhere, statutory instruments as a means for regulating diversity are becoming recognisably too restrictive and inflexible. Moreover, in the Irish case, the number and range of institutions is more complex than the traditional binary implies. Many IoTs, especially DIT, provide education and research to PhD. In so doing, they challenge traditional assumptions about the academic and geographic boundaries of their mission. Professions serviced by the IoTs require advanced qualifications and the research to underpin the quality of those qualifications. This has driven a sea-change within the institutions, many of which have developed research portfolios similar to the universities. In addition, while studies suggest proximity matters when it comes to innovation, new technology and the importance of status and reputation are undermining what may have originally been seen as their unique selling point.

Unfortunately, IoTs struggle with their brand and identity, with internal and external stakeholders. Evidence suggests that industry, philanthropists and students (domestic and international) tend to choose partnerships with universities rather than IoTs. SMEs, and their larger colleagues, desire to work with leaders in the field, not just the local HEI. In addition, the decline in the number of secondary school leavers has been matched by students choosing to study at universities rather than IoTs because of the social and cultural capital attached to those qualifications. Not surprisingly, the two larger IoTs, DIT and WIT, have recently applied for university designation, although DIT's position in the *Times QS Ranking of World Universities* (2009) could ironically undermine its bid. DIT is the sixth highest ranked Irish HEI, significantly higher than two universities, and the highest ranked UAS-type institution excluding Ecole Polytechnique.

The big policy debate concerns how to retain diversity without encouraging 'mission drift', and how to reconcile institutional ambition with tightening resources and the pursuit of excellence. Don Thornhill (2003) former chairman of the HEA, acknowledged 'concern with nomenclature and titles and a perception that there is not parity of esteem between the two sectors of higher education'. The OECD

(2004, pp. 37, 39) was supportive of the need to retain a 'differentiated tertiary education system' and said 'steps [should be taken] to integrate the components better than . . . at present'. However, 'for the foreseeable future there [should] be no further institutional transfers into the university sector'.

Taking an opposing stance, Skilbeck (2003, p. 12) questioned whether providing more advanced programmes to increase the proportion of enrolments in higher level qualifications did represent 'mission drift in a negative sense' as distinct from responding to 'individual demands for advanced qualifications' and societal 'demands for higher levels of competence and knowledge'. Coolahan foresaw that such developments were likely to 'see more pressure from the extra-university sector for greater status within the higher education system . . . confirming the desire to move towards a more open, even-structured higher education system' (CoD, 2003, p. 18). His view was echoed by the IoTI, which anticipated that if the OECD's recommendation was implemented, 'the impact would be to initiate a drift towards convergence and to incentivize perversely that which the report least desires' (Coy, 2005).

These examples illustrate the voracity of the debate leading up to the Strategic Review, albeit at the time they were conducted in the context of the larger IoTs seeking university designation and whether that was a positive or negative development. Today's discussion is still concerned with 'mission drift' but this is matched by the need to enhance national capability and capacity, and ensure efficiency and value-for-money. In this context, strategic clusters, collaborative networks and/or mergers are being openly (and secretly) discussed, including those between universities and IoTs within the same city/region. An alternative view is shaped by concern that mergers between universities and IoTs could encourage de-differentiation. A National Technological University (NTU), including all or most IoTs, is promoted by the IOTI albeit without endorsement from all member IoTs. The NTU would be enabled by a common governance structure. Yet, while this proposal would reduce the number of autonomous institutions, it would not readily resolve many of the other challenges identified. Another concept, based on the 'California' or 'Wisconsin' system models, would formalise the division between undergraduate and postgraduate activity, whereby some IoTs would be 'feeder' institutions – either to the universities or larger IoTs. A further proposal, which is gaining prominence, favours adapting international practice with respect to planning agreements or compacts. Rather than using legislative controls or regulatory frameworks to maintain mission and institutional strategy, core funding could be provided in exchange for specific objectives and targets. In turn, this approach would be used to shape and maintain differentiation.

All three government initiatives have identified the need to reform and restructure higher education. It is unclear how far this will actually go because any change is likely to unfurl political and local objections. Thus, the Strategic Review group may opt to define a policy vision and framework, and actively encourage HEIs towards that end. No matter which approach is adopted, the IoTs are probably most likely to experience the greatest change. However, unless there is recognition of differences in capacity and capability among the IoTs, it will not succeed in stemming individual submissions for re-designation.

Research

Dynamics of Ireland's knowledge-economy strategy is eroding the binary, and widening the gap between the de jure and de facto research role for the IoTs, and especially for DIT and WIT (Hazelkorn, 2004; Jerrams & Donovan, 2005). Government strategy aims to 'allow each of our existing Universities and Institutes of Technology to be supported in developing and enhancing their roles according to their existing strengths' (Government of Ireland, 2007, p. 204) but IoTs should develop 'into an effective technology resource, focused on collaboration with local industry on the basis of applied research and technology development' (DETE, 2006). The OECD was especially forthright stating 'the role of the institutes of technology should be much more targeted towards particular areas of applied research so that they can act as technology development partners to industry, especially SMEs, particularly on a regional or even a national basis' (OECD, 2004, p. 35). That recommendation was tied to another, that IoT funding should come from Enterprise Ireland (applied) and not SFI (fundamental).

Despite these statements, there is a growing realisation that national capacity and capability is unlikely to be met by reliance on the universities alone. Yet, there is also concern over the lack of critical mass in key fields of science and yawning investment/funding gap vis-a-vis peer nations. This political and economic reality has underpinned a consistent requirement by the Higher Education Authority that HEIs show evidence of research concentration, consolidation and collaboration in order to be successful in competitive processes. Today, both DIT and WIT have a research and income mix nearing that of the smaller universities, as noted throughout this chapter.

Funding Deficit

Historic differentials in funding between the universities and IoT sector are aggravated by the current economic recession in Ireland. There has been an infrastructure deficit because the university and IoT sectors have been funded according to different criteria and standards. Moreover, because Irish higher education has been dependent upon the exchequer for almost 90% of its funding, there is little history of diversified earnings, due to a combination of philosophical, economic and taxation issues. IoTs were, until recently, unable to seek loans or establish campus companies without permission, a restriction which did not apply to the universities. Moreover, given their status and reputation, the universities have been able to attract philanthropy to support massive capital building programmes across their campuses.

The new recurrent grant allocation model (RGAM) aims to shift the burden of funding away from the public exchequer and towards institutions, via a combination of performance, output and competitive metrics. However, the unit cost model is likely to be less beneficial to IoTs which have traditionally had a low student/staff ratio. It will also challenge the traditional small-class model of teaching, with its emphasis on practice-based learning, which has been one of the sector's defining characteristics. Finally, the core funding given per PhD student – which has enabled the universities to underpin research growth – is likely to be replaced by a competitive and proportionate element, which is likely to further disadvantage the IoTs. The recession is likely to impact disproportionately on the sector.

These difficulties are compounded by the overall investment gap. Ireland abolished tuition fees for all full-time undergraduate students in 1997. Today's public deficit had paved the way for their re-introduction, and an income contingent loan scheme based on the Australian Higher Education Contribution Scheme (HECS) was being considered. However, a *New Programme for Government* (October 2009) ruled that out. While the new revenue generated would only have replaced existing core funding, the decision not to proceed will pose financial difficulty for the entire higher education sector. The government has introduced budget and employment restrictions to cope with the public sector deficit, and several IoTs are struggling. For a sector already coming from behind, this new environment will widen the gap between institutions, leading to greater differentiation, reform and restructuring.

Academic Work and the Human Resources/Industrial Relations Environment

The majority of existing academic staff within the IoT sector have been employed to teach. This is reflected in the contracts and the way IoTs are funded. As demand rises for postgraduate qualifications and research, these traditional concepts of academic work are being challenged. Is research part of the job or additional? What about academic staff who do not possess the requisite skills or who, heretofore, have shown a lack of commitment to undertaking research?

The social partnership/national bargaining model which underpins Ireland's approach to industrial relations has precluded easy or fast changes in contracts or alterations to reflect individual institutional requirements or ambitions. This has made it extremely difficult to offer contracts which may attract and retain highly skilled and experienced academic researchers. In addition, there is no effective career structure; promotion is often on the basis of seniority, and appointment criteria and salary levels cannot be competitively adjusted. The academic trade union is primarily a secondary teachers union, with an 'industrial' rather than 'professional' conception of academic work and approach to its affairs. The universities, in contrast, have few of these difficulties despite the fact that their academic staff are represented by a variety of different trade unions. The key difference would appear to be a shared and embedded understanding of what constitutes academic work, even if there may be disagreement around the edges.

In reality, there has been no easy solution to the industrial relations environment facing the IoTs. Ironically, the current economic environment may be the catalyst because issues concerning academic contracts and performance are now the subject of wider political discussion following the report of the Department of Finance's *Special Group on Public Service Numbers and Expenditure Programmes.* The latter openly challenged the basis of academic and administration contracts across the entire higher education sector, stating that there was scope for greater productivity.

There is little doubt but that academic reform will emerge as a recommendation from the *Strategic Review of Irish Higher Education*, including review of work-loads, performance-related pay and promotion, and the introduction of a research assessment-type exercise and teaching and learning surveys. As a comprehensive approach to higher education develops, there may also be greater convergence between types of academic contracts and expectations.

Poor Infrastructure and Organisation

The IoTs were built, in the main, in the 1970s and 1980s, at a time when they performed a traditional vocational function and Ireland was experiencing eco-nomic difficulties. Building specifications were more typical of a secondary rather than a higher education environment. While there was an injection of investment into the IoTs in recent years, it remains far below that which has gone into the university sector, much of which was funded through a combination of private philanthropy, competitive government funding and their own resources, including borrowings. Many IoTs have facilities which are not-fit-for-purpose and do not have the resources to independently fund development. Earlier estimates had suggested that an additional investment of €154 million was required up to 2013 to meet the needs for adequate and appropriate research infrastructure. This included equipment and approximately 20,000 m^2 of space inclusive of refurbished/converted space (IOTI, 2008, p. 44). In the current economic environment – in which economists are warning that the 'golden years' of Irish higher education is unlikely to return – it is difficult to see how these disparities will be rectified.

Organisationally, the difficulties described about the lack of academic career structures spills over into management. Because IoTs were closely managed by the Department of Education and Science until their recent relocation to the Higher Education Authority, the establishment of appropriate positions, salary, career struc-ture, etc. was never contemplated. Across the sector as a whole there is a need for more strategic leadership and management, especially for the difficult times ahead.

In order to move forward, both of these issues will need to be resolved not least if the IoTs are to remain attractive to staff and students who, given the competi-tive environment, make choices, inter alia, based on the quality of the facilities and working environment/conditions.

Conclusion

The rise and growth of the IoT sector was a success story of massification, laying the foundation for Ireland's 'Celtic tiger'. Today, deteriorating public finances present a massive challenge. Ireland's binary system – lauded as a model of differentia-tion – has become a straightjacket; there is an insufficient critical mass to ensure Ireland's participation in world science and underpin the government's drive for a smart economy. The Bologna Process and the new Irish Qualifications Framework have harmonised qualifications, thus removing a traditional distinction. Many IoTs are struggling against public preference for university-based qualifications. Recent initiatives had sent out mixed-messages by fostering cross-sectoral collaboration and rewarding research performance/excellence wherever it occurs. These developments have induced new thinking and realignment across the system, challenging the semi-protected position of both universities and IoTs. How can Ireland best promote a diversified HE system while paying homage to regionality, critical mass and excellence? If funding simply rewards existing strengths and experience, it is likely to promote steep vertical differentiation, widening the gap between elite and mass institutions – maintaining the IoTs in a competitive race they can never win and promoting social selectivity by sector. A National Technological University, although promulgated as a means of boosting the status and reputation of the IoTs, is likely without additional investment to concretise differences. On the other hand, if clustering of HEIs – along regional or strategic lines – is encouraged, then the system as a whole might be able to mobilise its capacity beyond individual capability. This could be accomplished by linking funding to policy objectives and institutional mission – recognising a spectrum of strengths across teaching, research and community engagement – thereby encouraging greater horizontal differentiation and opportunities (Sörlin, 2007, pp. 434–435). A nation-wide governance structure might help to ensure greater coordination and cohesion across the sector as a whole. While the latter ideas are gaining growth/support, it is uncertain which direction policy will go.

References

Building Ireland's Smart Economy: A Framework for Sustainable Economic Renewal. (2008). Department of the Taoiseach, Ireland. Retrieved October 18, 2009, from http://www.taoiseach.gov.ie/eng/Building_Ireland's_Smart_Economy/

CoD – Council of Directors of the Institutes of Technology. (2003). *Institutes of technology and the knowledge society: Their future position and roles.* Report of the Expert Working Group. Dublin: Council of Directors of the Institutes of Technology.

Conlon, T. (2007). Email correspondence with author.

Coy, M. (2005). *The OECD review of higher education in Ireland: The implications for the institutes of technology sector.* Paper presented to Institutes of Technology Colloquium.

DETE – Department of Enterprise, Trade and Employment. (2004). *Building Ireland's knowledge economy. The Irish action plan for promoting investment in R&D to 2010.* Dublin: The Stationery Office.

DETE – Department of Enterprise, Trade and Employment. (2006). *Strategy for science, technology and innovation 2006–2013.* Dublin: The Stationery Office.

European Patent Office. (2009). Retrieved November 4, 2009, from https://register.epoline.org/espacenet/regviewer.

Fitzgerald, G. (2006, March 11). ITs suffer from change in student social base. *Irish Times.*

Flynn, S. (2007, December 13). Record entry to higher education as interest in computing slides. *The Irish Times.*

Forfás. (2005). *Survey of research and development in the higher education sector 2004.* Dublin: The Stationary Office.

Forfás. (2007a). *The higher education R&D survey 2006 HERD first findings.* Dublin: The Stationery Office.

Forfás. (2007b). *State expenditure on science & technology and research & development 2005 and 2006.* Dublin: Forfás.

Forfás. (2007c). *Research and development performance in the business sector Ireland 2005/2006.* Dublin: The Stationery Office.

Forfás. (2008). *The higher education R&D survey 2006 HERD detailed findings.* Dublin: The Stationery Office.

Forfás/HHEA (2009). Research strengths in Ireland: A bibliometric study of the public research base. Retrieved April 17, 2010, from http://www.forfas.ie/publications/2009/title,5126,en.php.

Government of Ireland. (1967). *Steering Committee on Technical Education (1967).* Report to the Minister for Education on regional technical colleges. Dublin: The Stationery Office.

Government of Ireland. (2002). *National spatial strategy for Ireland, 2002–2020. People, places and potential.* Dublin: The Stationery Office.

Government of Ireland. (2007). *National development plan 2007–2013. Transforming Ireland. A better quality of life for all.* Dublin: The Stationery Office.

HEA. (2009a). Statistics summary reports 2007/2008. Retrieved October 22, 2009, from http://www.hea.ie/en/statistics

HEA. (2009b). Statistics new entrants 2007/2008. Retrieved October 22, 2009, from http://www.hea.ie/en/statistics

HEA/Forfás. (2007). *Role of the institutes of technology in enterprise development. Profiles and emerging findings.* Dublin: The Stationary Office.

Hazelkorn, E. (2004). Developing research in a new HEI. Dublin institute of technology, Ireland. In H. Connell (Ed.), *University research management. Meeting the institutional challenge* (pp. 231–250). Paris: OECD.

Hazelkorn, E. (2005). *Developing research in new institutions.* Paris: OECD.

IOTI – Institutes of Technology Ireland. (2008). *Framework for the development of research in the institutes of technology, 2008–2013.* Ireland: IOTI.

Irish University Association. (2007). *Fourth level Ireland. Your future graduate and postdoctoral experience in Irish universities.* Dublin.

Jerrams, S., & Donovan, J. (2005). Contradictions in Irish academic research. *Research Management Review, 14*(2), 29–37.

Jordan, D., & O'Leary, E. (2007). *Is Irish innovation policy working? Evidence from Irish high technology businesses.* Paper to Statistical and Social Inquiry Society of Ireland. See also *Innovation, The Irish Times,* 14 January 2008, p. 10.

Lillis, D. (2007). *Reconciling organizational realities with the research mission of the Irish institutes of technology.* Paper presented to CHER conference, Dublin.

Norton, B. (2008, January 15). University is the only accurate word for what DIT is now. *The Irish Times.*

OECD (1964). *The Training of Technicians in Ireland,* Paris: OECD.

OECD (1965). *Investment in Education,* Paris: OECD.

OECD (2006). *Review of national policies for education: Review of higher education in Ireland.* Paris: OECD.

Skilbeck, M. (2003). *Towards an integrated system of tertiary education – A discussion paper.* Unpublished.

Sörlin, S. (2007). Funding diversity: Performance-based funding regimes as drivers of differentiation in higher education systems. *Higher Education Policy, 20,* 413–440.

Special Group on Public Service Numbers and Expenditure Programmes. (2009). Department of Finance, Ireland. Retrieved October 18, 2009, from http://www.finance.gov.ie/viewdoc.asp?DocID=5906&CatID=45&StartDate=1+January+2009&m=p

Thornhill, D. (2003). Education and the economy: What can business do? Paper presented to Irish Business and Employers Confederation. Cork.

Times QS World Universities. (2009). Retrieved August 12, 2009, from http://www.topuniversities.com/worlduniversityrankings/%20methodology/simple%20overview/

Walshe, J. (2007, December 10). Class gap exposed in our two-tier schools. *Irish Independent.*

White, T. (2001). *Investing in people. Higher education in Ireland from 1960 to 2000.* Dublin: Institute of Public Administration.

Chapter 11
Practice-Oriented Research: The Extended Function of Dutch Universities of Applied Sciences

Egbert de Weert and Frans Leijnse

The Dutch Binary System

A main feature of Dutch higher education is its binary structure, which distinguishes universities from institutions for higher professional education – *Hogescholen voor Hoger Beroepsonderwijs* or HBO. Universities and HBOs are developed under very different historical conditions and are based on different rationales.

There are 13 Dutch universities, 9 of which provide teaching and conduct research in a wide range of academic disciplines, 3 with predominantly a technological focus and 1 agricultural university. In addition there is the Open University and a number of small institutes with university status.

Many *hogescholen* have a long-standing tradition, but the HBO sector as part of tertiary education dates back to the 1960s, when colleges for higher professional training were upgraded. Formally, *hogescholen* belonged to secondary education until, in 1986, they were legally acknowledged as a subsector of the higher education system. Because of the sector's fragmented character, the government initiated major reforms in the 1980s. These resulted in the merging of more than 400 smaller colleges into large institutions, currently providing a wide range of professional courses with a standard period of study of 4 years leading to the bachelors degree. Today there are some 45 publicly funded *hogescholen*. Their main task is to provide theoretical and practical training with an explicit professional orientation. Since 2001, they also have the task of transferring and developing knowledge for the benefit of the professions in both the industrial and service sectors. Their primary focus is on regional and local needs – although, increasingly, they tend to operate nationally and internationally too.

In the international context *hogescholen* have adopted the name 'universities of applied sciences' (UASs). After having stuck for some time to 'universities for professional education', the Minister of Education in 2008 recognised the new name of UAS formally for all multi-sectoral *hogescholen*. Institutions focusing on

E. de Weert (✉)
Centre for Higher Education Policy Studies (CHEPS), University of Twente, Enschede,
The Netherlands
e-mail: e.deweert@utwente.nl

S. Kyvik, B. Lepori (eds.), *The Research Mission of Higher Education Institutions*   199
Outside the University Sector, Higher Education Dynamics 31,
DOI 10.1007/978-1-4020-9244-2_11, © Springer Science+Business Media B.V. 2010

specialised areas may suggest their own names. The Minister motivated his decision by referring to the need for a univocal name of *hogescholen* in the international context. Moreover, the name expresses both the extended task and the applied character of teaching and research. In his view, the name UAS fits into the bachelor's–master's structure, in which academic and professionally oriented education can be distinguished. Such a name contributes to the international transparency of UASs as providers of practice-oriented higher education and research. Because of this recognition, the term UAS will be used alongside *hogescholen* in this chapter referring to all HBO institutions.

The relationship between universities and UASs has been the subject of continuous debate. Although there are growing areas of overlap between these institutions, the government maintains a basic distinction between the two as a guarantee of institutional differentiation. Despite the binary policy, both sectors are incorporated in a single Higher Education and Research Act of 1993, encompassing a range of regulations that apply identically to both sectors. This law also describes as an explicit aim of universities to ensure that knowledge is transmitted for the benefit of society, an aim which over the years has been strengthened by emphasising societal relevance in teaching and research. Universities are also engaged in higher professional education in the sense that a fair majority of their graduates will enter professional life rather than the academic world.

However, a major difference is the status of research and the provision of postgraduate studies. For universities, research seems to have become their main task but for UASs it still is an auxiliary function in the context of professional development and education. Although this task was already acknowledged in the 1993 law, only the last few years witnessed a strong trend towards the extension of the research function of UASs and the provision of postgraduate studies (master's and professional doctorates). Traditional universities consider these claims as a threat to their privileged status and fear a closer parity in terms of research resources. Nevertheless, from 2001 onwards the Government has supplied the UASs with a modest but distinct budget for the development of their research.

This chapter seeks to analyse the legitimate research claims of Dutch UASs. It subsequently analyses how the research function has been conceived in national policies, the emerging funding schemes for research, strategies developed by *hogescholen* regarding organisational structures, human resources and research reward systems.

Before turning to these issues, three structural features of the Dutch higher education system will be highlighted which have to be taken into account in an international comparative analysis of UASs.

First, the comparatively large share of UASs in the Dutch higher education system. In 2007, out of a total of about 586,500 higher education students, 65% were enrolled in UASs (374,500), against 35% (212,000) in universities. This nearly 2:1 balance in favour of the UASs is much higher than the OECD averages and higher than in most other countries with a binary structure. Mass higher education in The Netherlands is mainly in the UASs. The traditional university sector serves only about 15% of the youth generation and the UAS sector roughly 30%, resulting in a total participation rate in higher education of about 45% presently.

The comparatively large share of the student body in Dutch UASs is partly due to the fact that the *hogescholen* cover a very broad range of subject areas and provide an enormous variety of study programmes. Subjects like teacher training, nursing, paramedics and fine arts are provided by UASs, whereas in other countries these are provided by universities. Since there is no general rule that courses in these subjects are of a lower level in The Netherlands than in countries where they belong to the university sector (in some instances on the contrary), the binary divide gets in the international perspective a somewhat arbitrary character. The following figure presents the student enrolment in the major fields of study.

The UASs have a total of 27,175 full-time equivalent staff (FTE) in 2007, divided between a teaching faculty of 14,886 (FTE) and a non-academic auxiliary staff of 12,289 (FTE). The faculty to student ratio is thus roughly 1:26, whereas the faculty to auxiliary staff ratio seems unduly low.

Second, *hogescholen* differ considerably in scale. Some 15 out of the 45 UASs are multi-sectoral institutions, encompassing a broad range of fields of study; their student enrolment ranges from 12,000 to 35,000. Another 15 focus mainly on one or two areas such as teacher training, fine arts, agriculture or hotel management; their enrolment will range from several hundreds to a few thousand students. The middle category of some 15 UASs will cover more than one subject area, but have student numbers that do not exceed 10,000. Some UASs have recently expanded their role in shorter programmes (2-year Associate Degree, similar to the Foundation Degree in the UK), in dual programmes (work-based learning) and part-time education.

In addition to the bachelor phase, programmes at master level are gaining in importance. There is a growing demand, especially by graduates from UASs, who after a period of working experience are confronted with the need for advanced levels of training. When in 2000 in The Netherlands the bachelor–master system was introduced, the right to provide accredited 'professional masters' was unequivocally granted to the UASs as well, but they were not eligible for public funding.

However, in 2007 the Minister of Education decided to make a limited number of these so-called 'professional masters' eligible for public funding. These concern labour market relevant UAS master's in some priority areas, mainly in health, teacher training and arts. The funding is on a temporary basis for a maximum of 4 years and thereafter these programmes have to be financed privately. This public funding of UAS master's occurs on a structural basis which means that there will be a reserved budget for new master's to be eligible for public funding (a budget of €5 million available in 2008, growing to €20 million by 2011; Ministry of Education, 2007).

As Table 11.1 shows, in 2007 about 3% (12,500) of the total UAS student population enrolled in master's and advanced professional diploma courses. Many of the latter courses have been converted into master's programmes under the formal national accreditation scheme. However, the number of privately funded professional master courses in Dutch UASs is also steadily increasing, particularly in

Table 11.1 Enrolment in Dutch UASs in 2007

Main fields of study	Bachelor's	Master's	Advanced professional diploma
Economics, management, law	135,000		
Agriculture	9,000		
Engineering	60,000		
Health	29,800	700	
Social studies	54,900		100
Teacher training/pedagogy	57,200	3,200	6,600
Arts	16,100	600	1,300
Total	362,000	4,500	8,000

Source: Ministry of Education, Culture and Science (2008) (data round off).

engineering and economics/management. As part of their human resources strategy some *hogescholen* now also develop an active policy to attract students and faculty who are prepared to do a doctoral programme leading to a PhD in collaboration with universities.

Third, access requirements to higher education differ between universities and UASs. The 6-year university preparatory education (VWO) qualifies for admittance to both university and UAS (first year) courses. The UAS has two additional entry qualifications: a 5-year general secondary education (HAVO) and a senior 4-year, level 4 vocational education. For obvious reasons university freshmen are thus better qualified when they enter higher education than the average UAS freshmen; the difference is generally estimated to be a year of secondary education. UAS bachelor courses for this reason have a standard length of 4 years (240 ECTS) as compared to 3 years for a university bachelor (180 ECTS), resulting in a roughly equal graduation level. Additionally, other entry qualifications are increasingly applied, such as work-related qualifications and other acquired competencies.

These structural features make UASs, as a whole, an extremely diversified sector of higher education. Clearly, the UAS 4-year bachelor degree is the formally recognised professional qualification, and its quality level is assured by the national accreditation system, but the route to that degree can vary substantially. The UASs have to deal with the demands of a very heterogeneous student population, and they see it increasingly as their mission to deliver education that is tailored to the individual needs and capabilities of their students.

National Policies for Research in UASs

National Goals and Conceptions of Research

Although the word 'research' in relation to the *hogescholen* already appeared in the 1993 Higher Education Law, the term was not defined in a clear way: *Hogescholen have as a task to provide higher professional education. They can carry out research to the extent that this is connected with the education at the institution.* The law does not contain further regulations regarding research and in subsequent years no budget was available for this education-related research.

This changed against the background of the public debate on the growing importance of knowledge utilisation and innovation in the context of the Lisbon 2000 Agenda and the need to increase investments in research and education. The national Innovation Platform, chaired by the Prime Minister, was established to foster ways of enhancing the innovative capacity of the knowledge-based economy. Given the professional orientation of the UASs it seemed natural to assign to them a specific role in the innovation process by intensifying collaboration with industry and particularly with SMEs. Various national policy agencies stressed the particular role of UASs to develop new ways of knowledge transfer, knowledge circulation, and attempted to define a distinctive research function for UASs. The major views on such a function will be highlighted here.

In their joint report, the Advisory Council on Science and Technology (AWT) and the Education Policy Council (*Onderwijsraad*) advocated a strengthening of knowledge circulation by establishing more systematic partnerships between higher education institutions and their external stakeholders. Central in their view is the concept of knowledge exchange between UASs and professional practice – also indicated as 'knowledge circulation' (AWT, 2001). In other reports by a working group of the national employer's association (VNO-NCW) and the HBO-council, and by the national association for SMEs (*MKB-Nederland*) the view was expressed to transform UASs from a mere education centre into a 'knowledge gateway'. Knowledge circulation is not merely a matter of education, but also of innovation-oriented collaborative research and development. Business would, through exchange of personnel such as guest lectureships, internships for teaching faculty in industry, as well as through applied and design-oriented research, support UASs in taking up new trends and build up new knowledge (MKB-Nederland, 2006; Werkgroep, 1999). All these reports laid the foundation for a further conceptualisation of research by UASs.

Several attempts have been made to distinguish the type of research envisaged for the UAS from university research. In various documents reference has been made to distinction of Mode 1 and Mode 2 type of knowledge production (Gibbons et al., 1994), arguing that various components of Mode 2 research would be the domain of the UAS. However, since also traditional universities do a substantial part of their research in the broad Mode 2 category it is difficult to make this into a clear cut demarcation between universities and UASs. The AWT (2001, 2005) considers 'design and development' as an appropriate term. Whereas the universities contribute to the development of basic scientific knowledge as well as to the utilisation of this knowledge in society, research in UASs should contribute to the maintenance and development of professional practice in society. As this practice is increasingly evidence-based and thus knowledge-intensive, innovative research and knowledge transfer play an ever-growing part in it. Referring to types of research, the AWT provides a schematic overview of the different research activities which distinguish research by universities and UASs. The council typified research by the UASs as 'Edison research' compared to the 'Bohr research' of the universities, thereby referring to Donald Stokes' classification of four types of research known as 'Pasteurs' quadrant' (Stokes, 1996). According to the AWT this typology should not to be understood as if research at universities and UASs would be mutually exclusive, and in research practice there will be much room for variation and overlap in individual research projects. But generally, this conceptualisation gives an initial rough distinction between the research activities of universities and UASs.

Another reason for assigning a research function to UASs stems from the changing conditions of professionalism. There is a growing awareness that in many contemporary work settings professionals are in a permanent process of learning and innovation. Although there is still a certain amount of routine involved, UAS graduates will, as professionals, have to be adaptive and actively involved in continuous change rather than applying a fixed set of knowledge and skills. Competencies to analyse problems, to synthesise, to propose solutions and to communicate about various challenges also in a multidisciplinary environment, are becoming increasingly important (de Weert, 2006). An international commission argued that these abilities are not only important in research environments but also in industry and society at large: 'Practical and professional experience of students, by preference from the start of their study and in combination with applied research, will allow these competences to develop' (Committee Review Degrees, 2005).

The role of applied research in professional practice implies a growing need of professional curricula to pay attention to research-related subjects and to enhance the abilities to translate knowledge to application. Basic research competencies of graduates are felt to be necessary to support evidence-based practice.

The distinctive research function of UASs has been broadly supported by virtually all major stakeholders on the national level. The outcome of this debate is that from 2001 onwards the Government supplied the UASs with a modest but distinct budget for the appointment of a new faculty position of *lector* and the creation of *lectorates*. In addition, programme subsidies have been made available in the context of national innovation projects (see for further details below).

Overall two main objectives of research at Dutch UASs stand out. First, the improvement of education through the interface between education and professional practice. Second, the contribution to innovation through knowledge exchange with industry and regional collaboration, especially with SMEs. Terms most widely used are 'design and development' and particularly 'practice-oriented research' or 'design research' rather than 'applied research'. The term 'practice-oriented research' is believed to do more justice to the professionally oriented character of research as it encompasses a diversity of research practices to be carried out by UASs (Borgdorff, van Staa, & van der Vos, 2007).

Priority Setting Between Teaching and Research

There is no explicit reference made in government or other papers to the weight of research compared to teaching. As *hogescholen* are predominantly 'teaching institutions', it was clear that research should be placed in the context of teaching.

A separate development of teaching and research is seen as against the general philosophy of the role of practice-oriented research being an integral aspect of the educational process. Politically, this has been a strong argument to find a majority to assign the UAS a distinctive research role.

Given the other objective of research – knowledge exchange with industry – it is clear that the demand for problem-solving knowledge from professional practice dominates the agenda, making research programming and the construction of a sustainable research infrastructure of prime importance. It is seen as a challenge for UASs to combine effectively the development of their research agenda with curriculum development and innovation, and the active involvement of teaching faculty and students in research projects.

Funding of Research

University research is, parallel to but apart from the funding of education, directly funded by the Ministry of Education (first flow), by the national research council (second flow) and by third party contract (third flow). Allocation of funds by the research council is based on evaluation of research excellence. Recent years show an increase of the second flow to about 20% of the total budget at the expense of the first flow which is presently still 50%, whereas some 30% of funding comes from third party contracts. Research is increasingly assessed in terms of utility, relevance and 'valorisation' of results.

Figure 11.1 presents the different income sources of UASs. The block grant is with 67% the largest part, predominantly meant for education. The grant is indirectly based on the number of enrolments, being an estimate of the teaching load ('student demand'). This teaching load is a multiplication of enrolment and a

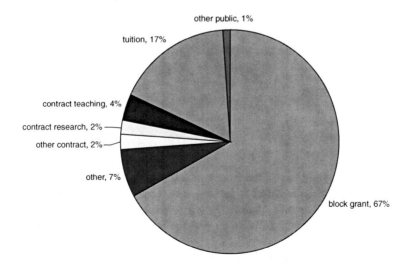

Fig. 11.1 Budget of UASs, by source of income (2005/2006). Source: Dutch Bureau for Statistics

so-called dynamic demand factor. This dynamic demand factor can be interpreted as the ratio of the normative funding period and the actual registration period for graduates and drop-outs. Funding is therefore also dependent on graduation rates.

The block grant includes as a targeted element the government funding of the *lector* as leader of a *lectorate*, to be understood as an organisational setting consisting of a number of faculty members around a *lector* that aims to give UASs an impulse to develop their research activities. For the allocation of this funding, initially a special foundation has been established (*SKO – Stichting Kennisontwikkeling HBO*), which under the authority of the HBO council plays a key role in awarding applications by UASs to install a *lectorate*. The funds allow the recruitment of a *lector* plus the funding of activities of faculty and some external members of a 'knowledge circle'. For this purpose the Ministry and the HBO council signed a covenant on the basis of which SKO developed the following indicators which are used to assess applications for *lectorates* (SKO, 2005):

1. Sustainable effects on the adaptation of the curricula, professionalisation of teaching faculty or change in curricular structures.
2. Relationship as far as content is concerned with similar networks of teaching faculty internationally.
3. Relationship as far as content is concerned with companies or non-profit institutions (in the region and beyond).
4. Significant increase of knowledge transfer towards the private sector or professional domain.
5. Substantial increase of revenues from contract activities and applied research.

The system of *lectorates* started in 2001, with a government budget of around €12 million which over the years increased to €50 million in 2007. The number of *lector* positions has grown rapidly, from 18 in 2002 to 290 in 2006 and over 350 in 2008. The aim is that in a few years time about half of all teaching staff will belong to some knowledge circle, which obviously presupposes a substantial further growth of the number of *lectorates*.

The SKO-regulation came to an end in 2008. Thereafter the funding of *lectorates* became part of the block funding of UASs as targeted funding of €50 million for R&D in 2008.

There are three streams to fund the *lectorate*:

- Government funds
- Funds made available by the UASs themselves
- Revenues from contract activities.

Over the years the share of the latter two streams has increased, which indicates that the position of the *lectorate* is increasingly recognised by both the UASs and their external constituencies. On average a *lectorate* will presently be funded from these three sources by a 50:25:25 ratio, with the latter source growing and the first diminishing.

In addition to the funding of *lectorates*, there are two other resources for research, namely, the so-called RAAK-programme and the 'knowledge vouchers'.

The RAAK-programme (*The Regional Action and Action for Knowledge Circulation*) aims to stimulate regional collaboration between UASs and business, especially SMEs and public institutions with a view to develop joint innovation activities and stimulate knowledge exchange and circulation. With government funding, the RAAK-programme is on the national level managed by a foundation, the *Stichting Innovation Alliance* (*SIA*), in which various partners are participating such as SME-Netherlands (National federation of SMEs), the Confederation of Netherlands Industry and Employers (VNO-NCW), the HBO, as well as some (applied) research institutions. Joint projects can be submitted to SIA.

Altogether overall funding of over €30 million annually is attracted by an initial contribution from RAAK of about €20 million. The other part of the total project costs are financed by the cooperating small and medium enterprises (SMEs) and public institutions. Although there are no formal conditions for parties to co-finance, they contribute about a third of the costs (SIA, 2009).

The so-called *knowledge vouchers*, issued by the Minister of Economic Affairs, are in essence a subsidy for companies (SMEs) to buy research services from knowledge institutions in order to improve knowledge utilisation and the innovation of processes, products and services. The value of a 'knowledge voucher' is €7,500 of which SMEs should contribute one third themselves. Since 2006, there are also smaller vouchers available representing a value of €2,500 aiming to get SMEs acquainted with research institutions. The use of these vouchers has increased from 100 initially to over 6,000 vouchers. UASs in general take about a one third share in the spending of these vouchers, thereby attracting another €10–15 million, albeit in small portions.

If all these resources are taken together, the total research (non-education) government grant to UASs amounts to nearly €80 million in 2008 out of a total public UAS funding of around €2.05 billion in 2007 (thus roughly 4%).

Research Strategy in Dutch UASs

Institutional Strategy and Priority Setting

Inspired by the national debate and policy, most *hogescholen* have in the last few years incorporated the research function in their strategic plans. Despite some institutional variance, UASs display a remarkably consistent and uncontested frame of reference on the nature and place of research in the organisation. From an analysis of the institutional annual reports the following common components can be discerned (CFI, 2006):

- Initiatives for research emanate from the needs of professional practice
- Research should be relevant for the quality and innovation of education and the professionalisation of the teaching faculty
- Research should be practice-driven in that it is oriented to solve practical problems and to intensify collaboration with external constituencies.

These three elements in combination mark the specific character of the research by UASs.

It would be misleading to assume that the practice-driven research at UASs is restricted to short-term and small-scale research and that the focus is solely on providing direct solutions to day-to-day practical problems. Although UASs would not exclude such activities, practice-oriented research – the term also preferred by UASs themselves – encompasses more than a collection of more or less separate short-term advices and problem-solving. Practice-oriented research focuses mainly on the more strategic issues deriving from professional practice and from problem-solving demands of SMEs. The ambition of UASs is to employ the larger part of their research capacity on these strategic issues in long-term research programmes, rather than in short-term consultancy.

Research is understood as knowledge production which contributes to the development of an 'evidence based professional practice' (Leijnse, 2005). The research questions emanate from the cooperation with professionals in the world of work and their relevance for sustainable network structures. Such a view has important consequences for the way UASs organise their research and how the quality of research is assessed by both peers and external stakeholders.

The Lectorate *as the Organisational Setting of Research*

The initiative of the *lectorate* as a system for the development of research in UASs has found a warm reception in the institutions. This was all the more surprising as this did not fit in with their standing tradition nor with the composition and qualification of their faculty. Since its existence in 2001 the number of *lectores* has increased rapidly and given the budget available the number of lectores increased by the end of 2008 to over 400.

The creation of the highly qualified position of *lector* (at professorial level[1]) was seen as a means to enhance the quality of professional education and the qualities of the teaching faculty. The leading idea is that *lectores* are to respond to the knowledge needs of SMEs and professional organisations among others and to enhance research skills and capabilities in UASs by conducting research projects to which faculty members are recruited on a part-time basis. For this purpose, *lectores* are expected to create 'knowledge circles', each consisting of a group of 10–15 staff members. A knowledge circle aims to enhance contacts and knowledge exchange with industry in the field of applied and developmental research. Through such a circle the *lector* plays a crucial role in strengthening the links between UASs and industry and other organisations. *Lectores* are expected to acquire contracts from third parties and to develop professional networks in their domain.

---

[1] The *lector* should not be confused with the traditional positions of lecturer or reader in the Anglo-Saxon tradition; Dutch UASs tend to use internationally the term 'professor' for their lectores.

One of the conditions for funding is that the *lectorates* should be evaluated on a continuous basis. In the meantime two evaluation studies were carried out and a final assessment is foreseen in 2008. The evaluation studies (SKO, 2005, 2006) indicated that the various tasks assigned to *lectores* cover a broad range of activities. There is a tendency to emphasise one or a few of the tasks. It seems that choices are made according to the individual preferences of the *lector* and depends on the actual position within a UAS, as well as a particular relationship with the professional field. Since the nature of the *lectorate* also differs between *lectores* within the same UAS, this indicates that priority setting is up to the decision of an individual *lector* and that a clear institutional strategy by most UASs is lacking.

This observation has led to the concern – also expressed by the OECD thematic review on the Netherlands (OECD, 2007) – that the process by which *lectores* are allocated broadly disperses the available resources. This limits the capacity to build a critical mass of sufficient depth and expertise for UASs to function more effectively as innovation partners for enterprises. One of the reasons for this is the fact that the average *lector* has no more than a 0.6–0.7 job, has no tenure but rather is appointed for a 4-year period, and as a rule has a 'knowledge circle' the total capacity of which does not exceed two FTEs. This relatively small scale of the *lectorate* is enforced by the fact that in the first round of assignments the UAS executives tended to disperse the number of *lector* places equally across the different departments as a form of distributive justice, which has led to a fragmentation of resources.

This picture, however, is changing rapidly as after the first 4-year period most UASs have moved to create more focus and critical mass. Several institutions are in the process of giving their research more profile and cluster their research activities around one principal or some well-defined knowledge domains or thematic areas. Some UASs have clustered their research in a number of research centres each with their own research programme. Other UASs have organised all their research in one central research centre in which all *lectores* and members of the *lectorate* participate. Such a clustering of the *lectorate* in larger centres strengthens the research profile of the institutions. It is expected that this will increase the visibility of research on (regionally) relevant thematic areas and create more opportunities for multidisciplinary research.

Collaboration with Industry and Universities

One of the objectives of the *lectorate* is to strengthen the external orientation of UASs and to contribute to the process of knowledge circulation. Employers have shown considerable interest in the *lectorate* which fits into the idea of the 'knowledge gateway'. Leading idea is that the UASs are not merely teaching institutions, but also gateways incorporating knowledge from outside and in their turn disseminate knowledge to professional organisations and SMEs. The *lectorate* is seen as a 'knowledge bridge' (Renique, 2003) which functions to reinforce the interface between education and enterprise. Examples are the creation of dynamic course trajectories whereby students alternate periods of study and work, and the monitoring of innovations in the professional field which can be translated in education, design and development.

The position of the *lectorate* in the knowledge infrastructure shows a positive development. It appears that compared to some years ago there is more intensive collaboration through individual contacts, guest lectureships and collaboration in research projects. It turns out that about 80% of all *lectores* are in their fourth year involved in research projects in collaboration with industry or public institutions with a mean of five projects per *lector* (SKO, 2006).

There is also a growing rapprochement between UASs and universities both on the administrative and managerial levels and increasingly on education and research. An important development is the perceived necessity to upgrade the faculty of UASs and equip them with research skills. Since UASs have no right to grant doctoral degrees and neither do *lectores* have the *ius promovendi*, several UASs collaborate with universities to enable faculty members to pursue a doctoral degree. In most of these doctorate trajectories the *lector* functions as a daily supervisor and co-promoter, whereas a university professor takes the formal supervisor's role.

The collaboration between universities, UASs and other (applied) research institutions is also growing, mainly in the context of regional consortia in which (usually smaller) companies take part as well. These consortia aim to strengthen the research function of UASs and to disseminate research results in the context of application. While universities take care of the fundamental aspects of the research, the UASs are keen to convey practical results to the companies involved.

Human Resources and Careers

Until recently the *hogescholen* restricted their activities to undergraduate professional education, the sector mostly refrained from serious endeavours to raise the qualification levels of their faculty. Whereas the Dutch universities have since the 1980s put much effort in upgrading their faculties by increasing the number of PhD courses and setting the PhD level as a minimum requirement to enter the academic faculty, *hogescholen* have soldiered on with a teaching faculty which for 47% has a bachelor degree only (most of them at the UAS level) and (thus) no research qualifications whatsoever (Table 11.2).

Table 11.2 Educational level of academic staff in UASs and mobility in 2006 (%)

Educational level of UAS staff	Sitting	Inflow	Outflow
UAS bachelor	39.3	31.0	39.3
University-bachelor	7.4	7.3	11.4
University-master	45.8	55.8	45.0
University PhD	3.7	4.6	0.8
Other qualification	3.9	1.3	3.6
Sum	100	100	100

Source: Stichting Mobiliteitsfonds hbo (2007).

As the UASs were not supposed to build any research capacity, this has led – in conjuncture with a steady growing teaching load and increasing faculty to student ratios – to a lack of consistent investments in qualifications of academic staff.

The first experience with higher qualified and research-oriented professionals in the *lector* positions increased awareness among UAS executives about serious flaws in their human resources. Many *lectores* signalled that their attempts to set up research programmes, and their relations with the external professional networks, were in jeopardy should they have to work with sitting teaching faculty alone. Many 'knowledge circles' changed profoundly in composition over the first 2 years, with *lectores* insisting that they should be allowed to hire qualified researchers alongside sitting faculty. As a rule this was conceded to a certain degree, and most knowledge circles around the *lector* nowadays will encumber one or two researchers.

The percentages in Table 11.2 reflect the current debate on faculty quality as a prime policy issue for the UAS sector. It appears that there is a relatively lower proportion of the new faculty with a bachelor degree compared to those with a master's degree. Since the inflow of master's degree holders exceeds the outflow, and for the bachelor degrees the shift is the reverse, the proportion of master's will increase.

Nowadays UASs have considerable autonomy in defining academic staff positions. The most common term adopted by *hogescholen* is *hogeschooldocent*. Functional differentiation takes place according to four major salary scales (total teaching staff is about 15,000 in FTE). No exact figures of the distribution across the scales are available. The percentages are estimated on the basis of information from the HBO council:

- Scale 10 (the lowest) involves basic teaching and instruction (comprises about 15% of all academic staff)
- Scale 11 includes curriculum development (40%)
- Scale 12 adds the faculty roles of scale 11 plus coordinating and management roles regarding education (40%)
- Scale 13 and higher includes a research component (about 5%). This category includes the *lectores* which predominantly are in scale 16 and occasionally in scale 17.

The traditional universities have a ranking system, broadly equivalent to the three positions of assistant, associate and full professor. The corresponding figures are as follows (out of a total of 15,000 academic staff):

- Assistant professor: scale 11/12 (31% of all academic staff)
- Associate professor: scale 13/14 (15%)
- Full professor: scale 17/18 (16%)
- Other academic staff (38%), distributed across various salary ranks.

This comparison explains that the structure of positions at universities is more differentiated than at UASs, which on average, are substantially lower on the scale. Also the balance of faculty grades is rather distorted. While *lectores* in the UASs should be seen as having the same academically leading position as university professors, they are not numerous enough to exert this leadership effectively. To every full-time *lector* Dutch UASs have roughly 56 teaching faculty and 1,400 students, while the universities have on average 10 faculty members and 100 students to every full-time professor (Ministry of OCW, 2007).

Many *hogescholen* are aware of this difference and are developing policies to differentiate mainly in the higher salary scales. Because of their extended research function, the larger UASs strive to increase the share of PhD's in the faculty from 3.7% now to 25% in 2020 (on average) and to make a master's degree the minimum requirement for access to junior staff positions. Programmes have been developed to create PhD trajectories for sitting and new academic staff, as well as personal development possibilities up to the master's level. New positions are defined to encompass teaching as well as research and require a minimum of research experience. These programmes receive a modest but conscious government support, also financially through 'promotion vouchers' to enable at least 80 faculty members to pursue a PhD trajectory. Most *hogescholen* now add part of their own budget to these government vouchers in order to raise the number of PhD trajectories. Starting point is that such trajectories result in a PhD degree that meets both the standard scientific qualifications and practice-oriented research. Several UASs have made agreements with universities as 'preferred partner' whereby the university professor is responsible for the quality of the doctoral programme and the research of the candidates is supervised by their own *lectores*. Such a construction combines the methodological expertise provided by universities and the practice-oriented research attitude in UASs. It is expected that this upgrading of the teachers in combination with their participation in the *lectorate* will contribute to a further professionalisation of the academic staff.

The Allocation of Resources for Research

The allocation of resources for research to UASs occurs mainly through the government budget for *lectorates*. Parallel to this SKO-funding the phenomenon of a *special lectorate* exists, funded by external partners from industry and public organisations. In addition, UASs may extend the number of lectores by funding them at least partly from their block grant. This happens increasingly, possibly anticipating the end of SKO-funding and the government budget will be allocated to the UASs directly as targeted part of the block grant. Thus, the allocation of resources for research is not solely dependent on external funding, but also part of the internal (strategic) decision-making.

The evaluation of the *lectorate* indicates that *lectores* are to a considerable extent able to attract members of the teaching staff into their research groups, mainly on a part-time and temporary basis. Their research time is determined mainly on the basis of individual agreements and their teaching load will be reduced correspondingly. It turns out that a substantial number of teaching staff (over 25%) have been involved in research projects, in curriculum innovation, professional development and knowledge transfer (SKO, 2006). The gradual extension of the number of *lectores* entails that an increased number of academic staff will become member of a knowledge circle. Furthermore, many *lectorates* have experienced that the initial 0.2 appointments of faculty members to the research group is too weak to develop a real commitment to research given the day-to-day pressure from teaching obligations. Gradually, this has been stretched to on average 0.5 appointments for at least 2 or 3 years in order to build more sustainable research groups making 50–50 teaching-research appointment the preferred pattern for new UAS staff members.

As said before, there is a clear trend to concentrate research into research centres. These centres in their turn can propose to establish a new *lectorate* and to determine the number of faculty members in their centre and other organisational arrangements. This will lead to more streamlining between teaching and research, but this requires at the same time commitment to research programmes and an actual effort by the staff. This effort is financially compensated because the research programmes increasingly control their own budgets.

Research Performance in UASs

The Assessment and Output of Research

The question how research performance has to be assessed and how the output measured, has been subject of much thought and discussion. From the beginning, *hogescholen* took the view that the measurement of research output solely in terms of publications in refereed journals – as is common but not uncontested in university research – would do no justice to the specific character of UAS research. Since this research is practice-oriented, and aims to contribute to the innovative capacity of professionals, the views of stakeholders as to its relevance and applicability should constitute an essential part of the research assessment.

Regarding the research output, several indicators have been considered, such as number of institutes with which intensive exchange takes place, number of research projects, number of publications (scientific and/or professional) and the contribution to the education process and professional training.

Representatives from business, in particular, emphasise indicators that express the relevance for enterprises. These stakeholders feel that the number of publications in periodicals of sectors of industry or professions should be valued higher than publications in scientific journals (Renique, 2003). However, it is interesting to see that these two ways of knowledge dissemination do not necessarily contradict and that many *lectores* publish in both scientific and professional journals. A more clear-cut distinction seems to be between *lectores* who publish very little anyhow because their focus is on consultancy and *lectores* who concentrate on (long-term) practice-oriented research and publish their results in both scientific and professional journals. Figure 11.2 shows the various types of publications by *lectores* in the third year of their *lectorate*.

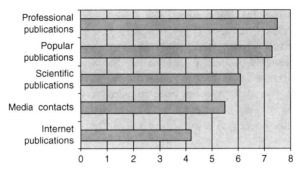

Fig. 11.2 Mean number of publications per lector (third year) by publication type
Source: SKO (2006).

Considering the variety of tasks assigned to the *lector*, it would be too limited to measure the success of *lectorates* on the basis of the number of publications alone. An overemphasis on publication behaviour would lose sight of the practice-oriented character of research and of the task of *lectores* to develop partnerships with industry in a practical sense, a point also mentioned in one of the first evaluations of the *lectorate* (SKO, 2005). However, although research at UASs encompasses a broader area of activities than university research, this does not imply that normal scientific criteria can be relinquished. On the contrary, the quality of practice-oriented research and its value to business and professional practice can only be assured if the method of knowledge acquisition complies with scientific quality requirements. If research does not meet current standards of scientific rigour, it is useful neither as practice-oriented nor as 'design research' since it produces no valid and reliable knowledge (Leijnse, Hulst, & Vroomans, 2007).

Also the requirement of generating new knowledge that is transferable to other contexts as well as the public character of research in order to utilise the outcomes in education and in professional practice is frequently mentioned as reasons for methodological rigour in research at UASs (Van Weert & Andriessen, 2005).

The Dutch UASs have agreed with a protocol for the entire sector that regulates quality assessment of research for the next 6 years. Basic idea is that research will be evaluated and validated by a special committee to be appointed by the HBO council in cooperation with the Dutch Ministry of Education. This committee will be formed by experts in research, education, business and the public sector. The assessment procedure starts from the quality assurance systems of the institutions and encompasses both the societal relevance and the scientific soundness of the research. Some UASs have already developed audit systems to assess their *lectorates* as a pilot for the coming national system. The (planned) national committee will mainly assess and certify (accredit) the audit systems of the UASs.

The Relevance of Research for the Regional Community

As mentioned before, the RAAK-programme (*Regional Action and Action for Knowledge Circulation*) aims to stimulate regional collaboration between UASs and business. The leading idea of RAAK is that there is not a one-sided direction of knowledge utilisation, but that in regional networks various partners collaborate with a view on knowledge circulation and innovative outcomes. The programme aims to enhance the knowledge exchange between knowledge institutions and SMEs and their role in the regional knowledge infrastructure. Since 2006 RAAK has also a parallel public sector scheme.

Started in 2005 with nine projects, the RAAK-programme supported 81 regional innovation programmes in 2006, 66 of them with SMEs and 15 with public institutions. These programmes have to be submitted to consortia consisting of parties that agreed to collaborate for a longer period to stimulate knowledge exchange in the region. RAAK requires that in a consortium at least one UAS participates.

Furthermore, an intermediary body called *Syntens* has been established by the Ministry of Economic Affairs which aims to assist SMEs in their innovation capacity, to advise them on innovation projects and to facilitate the link between UASs and other applied research institutions.

From the start of the scheme it was decided to monitor the innovation projects regarding the functioning of the network, the sustainability, how SMEs articulate their demands and how the parties contribute to the stated objectives. It appears that the RAAK-programme is an effective way of bringing together different parties in the region. It positions the UAS as an important knowledge centre in the triangle of education, research and innovation.

The Future of Research in Dutch UASs

The development of Dutch UASs from mere teaching institutions to centres of expertise in the professions has made a modest start. The evaluation of the scant research endeavours of the *lectorate* so far (SKO, 2008) shows a rather positive outcome, both with regard to the quality of the research and its relevance for stakeholders as well as for professional education. On the other hand, the evaluation confirms the OECD's earlier observation that the *lectorate* is at present 'scarcely more than a drop in the ocean' (OECD, 2007). With proven and growing demand for applicable knowledge and innovation, the government will be under obvious pressure to increase the budget for *lectorates*, enabling the UASs to increase the number of *lectores* up to 800, roughly one *lector* to 20 teaching staff and 500 students.

At the same time a further extension of the budget for the 'second flow' of research funding, presently mainly in the RAAK-programme is to be expected. This aims to keep pace with the increase of the number of *lectorates* in order to facilitate long-term research projects and the building of a sustainable research infrastructure. This will in their turn enable UASs to attract more third party-funded research. The demand from professional communities and society at large for applicable knowledge and innovation is high and growing, and Dutch UASs may be praised for having positioned themselves as a prime object for this demand. They are also increasingly becoming an attractive partner for research groups from universities to cooperate with given the current emphasis on relevance and valorisation of university research. This will bring *hogescholen* in a position to gradually increase the size of their research activities from a mere 4% at present to 10–15% of their total turnover in 2015 on average, although the differences between *hogescholen* may be substantial.

As practice-oriented research becomes more common within UASs, the construction of a sustainable long-term research infrastructure (programmes, dedicated human resources, funding) is on the agenda. The *hogescholen* will have to realise that to meet the needs of the profession and stakeholder expectations in the long run, an extended programme of short-term advisory and consultancy projects will not suffice. More thorough analyses and reflection are necessary and therefore research must become more 'scientific' in nature to produce more high-quality applicable knowledge (however, paradoxical this may sound in the tradition of the binary divide). The envisaged national quality assurance system for practice-oriented research may be a necessary instrument to set and sustain high standards. Nevertheless, a fair number of Dutch UASs will likely be unable to define and attain proper standards for their research infrastructure and activities and, therefore, may become stuck in the middle: their expertise will not exceed that of an average consultancy.

For Dutch UASs the main challenge will be to balance this imminent growth of research with their present culture and with their human resources. Traditionally, the Dutch UASs have a succinct teachers' culture. In this kind of culture, all activities have been valued in relation to their contribution to education. It is therefore understandable that from the beginning, the introduction of the *lectorate* was argued on the basis of its expected contribution to the quality of teachers and their teaching. Politically, this argument was all the more necessary to find a majority for this policy change. However, the idea that practice-oriented research in itself is a worthwhile activity of UASs has gained some ground, particularly among the professional stakeholders. The *hogescholen* themselves nevertheless still struggle to overcome the old teachers' culture and to view knowledge production as part of their core competence.

This is not to say that UASs must develop their research activities in a separate and independent institutional setting to 'insulate' them from the dominant teaching culture. In their endeavours to develop practice-oriented research, Dutch UASs maintain the relation of their growing research programmes with teaching. A *sine qua non* for this is the rise of a scholarly culture in which excellence in (practice-oriented) research and excellence in teaching are seen as intertwined. The metaphor of the classical *scholar* as being a great thinker and researcher and a great teacher at the same time – a 'master' in both senses of the word – could be closer to modern reflective professional practice than the metaphor of the modern scientist.

The other challenge regards the balance between the growth of research and the need to upgrade the qualifications of the academic staff. Although the executives seem to be fully aware of this challenge, and an aging faculty provides opportunities for renewal, effective HRM strategies and instruments are still lacking. Likewise, UASs should overcome the government policy to deny UASs some of the rights that are crucial for recognition as a serious institution for higher education, such as the right to grant doctorates, to appoint professors and to grant these leading faculty members the *ius promovendi*. The persistence to deny these rights can be questioned in the light of the substantial graduate programmes and the extended research function of Dutch *hogescholen*.

References

Adviesraad voor het Wetenschaps- en Technologiebeleid & Onderwijsraad. (2001). *Hogeschool van Kennis, Kennisuitwisseling tussen Beroepspraktijk en Hogescholen*. Den Haag: AWT & Onderwijsraad.
Adviesraad voor het Wetenschaps- en Technologiebeleid AWT. (2005). *Ontwerp en Ontwikkeling. De functie en plaats van onderzoeksactiviteiten in hogescholen*. Den Haag: AWT.
Borgdorff, H., van Staa, A., & van der Vos, J. (2007). Kennis in context. Onderzoek aan hogescholen. *TH&MA, 5*, 10–17.
Centrale Financiën Instelligen. (2006). *Analyse Jaarverslagen Hogescholen*. Agentschap Ministry of Education, Culture and Science.
Committee Review Degrees. (2005). *Bridging the gap between theory and practice. Possible degrees from binary system*. Den Haag: NVAO.
de Weert, E. (2006). *Professional competence and research in the non-university sector: Systems convergence after Bologna?* Conference paper. CHER 19th Conference Kassel, 7–9 September 2006.
Gibbons, M., Limoges, C., Nowotny, H., Scott, P., Schwartzman, S., & Trow, M. (1994). *The new production of knowledge: The dynamics of science and research in contemporary societies*. London: Sage.
Leijnse, F. (2005). *Hooggeleerde domheid en andere gebreken. Over kennisproductie in de polder*. Utrecht: Hogeschool Utrecht.
Leijnse, F., Hulst, J., & Vroomans, L. (2007). *Passie en precisie. Over de veranderende functie van de hogescholen*. Hogeschool Utrecht: 01 Kennis voor Kennis.
Ministry of Education, Culture and Science (OCW). (2007). *Het Hoogste Goed. Strategische agenda voor het hoger onderwijs-, onderzoek- en wetenschapsbeleid*, The Hague.
Ministry of Education, Culture and Science (OCW). (2008). Kennis in Kaart 2008, The Hague.
MKB-Nederland & VNO NCW. (2006). *Hogescholen en Branches: Partners in Professie*, Den Haag.
OECD. (2007). *Thematic review of tertiary education: The Netherlands*. Paris: OECD.
Renique, C. (2003). Het Lectoraat als Kennisbrug. *TH&MA, 2*, 4–9.
SKO (Stichting Kennisontwikkeling HBO). (2005). *Succesfactoren voor Lectoraten in het HBO*. Den Haag: SKO.
SKO. (2006). *Lectoraten in het Hoger Beroepsonderwijs*. Meting 2006.
SKO. (2008) *Lectoraten in het Hoger Beroepsonderwijs 2001–2008*. Eindevaluatie van de Stichting Kennisontwikkeling HBO.
Stichting Innovatie Alliantie (SIA). (2009). *RAAK! Beleidsevaluatie 2005–2008*. The Hague: SIA.
Stichting Mobiliteitsfonds hbo. (2007). *Zwaar weer op Komst. Arbeidsmarktmonitor voor personeel in het HBO 2007*, Den Haag.
Stokes, D. (1996). *Pasteurs quadrant. Basic science and technological innovation*. Washington, DC: Brookings Press.
van Weert, T., & Andriessen, D. (2005). *Onderzoeken door te verbeteren. Overbruggen van de kloof tussen theorie en praktijk in HBO-onderzoek*. Hogeschool Utrecht/ InHolland. (www.Creative Commons.org/licenses).
Werkgroep VNO-NCW & HBO-raad. (1999). *De Hogeschool als Kennispoort*, Den Haag.

Chapter 12
Norway: Strong State Support of Research in University Colleges

Svein Kyvik and Ingvild Marheim Larsen

Introduction

Since the mid-1990s, the research mission of university colleges in Norway has been increasingly emphasised. This development has several reasons: a wish by colleges and their staff to conduct research, an expectation by state authorities that colleges should engage in such activity and pressure from regional stakeholders that the colleges should contribute in innovation and development processes at the local level. Even though the extent of research in these institutions is relatively modest in comparison to the universities, the colleges have progressively developed organisational structures to support and fund this activity, and the research function will definitely become more important in the years to come. An important reason is that, since 2004, these colleges have had the opportunity to apply for accreditation to university status by fulfilling given criteria related to research and doctoral education.

In this chapter, after giving some background information about the Norwegian higher education system, we will first present national policies and guidelines for research in these colleges and state measures to implement this policy. Thereafter, we focus on research strategy within the colleges, before giving an overview of the research performance of these institutions. Finally, we will discuss some dilemmas and tensions related to the development of research in the college sector.

In 1994, Norway established 26 state colleges based on regional mergers of colleges for teacher training, engineering, nursing, social work and a number of specialist colleges for other vocations. In addition, 14 district colleges with programmes in economics and business administration, many other types of vocational courses, and some university courses, were encompassed by this reform (Kyvik, 2002). Most of the formerly independent colleges (98 in total) were not, however, relocated to a joint regional centre, but were retained as geographically separate faculties or departments within the new regional institutions.

S. Kyvik (✉)
Norwegian Institute for Studies in Innovation, Research and Education (NIFU STEP),
Oslo, Norway
e-mail: svein.kyvik@nifustep.no

S. Kyvik, B. Lepori (eds.), *The Research Mission of Higher Education Institutions Outside the University Sector*, Higher Education Dynamics 31,
DOI 10.1007/978-1-4020-9244-2_12, © Springer Science+Business Media B.V. 2010

The merger process resulted in the creation of a formal binary system with a clear division between a university sector (four comprehensive universities and six specialised university institutions) and a college sector encompassing 26 state colleges and some private colleges. The universities should be responsible for basic research, graduate education and research training, while the colleges should be responsible for a wide variety of short-cycle professional and vocational study programmes and, in addition, take on some of the university programmes for basic and undergraduate education. Within certain fields, where the universities did not offer similar programmes, the new colleges could offer graduate education.

However, over the next decade differences between the two sectors in many ways decreased (Kyvik, 2009a). In 1995, the university academic rank system was introduced in the colleges, and in 1996, all public higher education institutions were regulated by a common act which specifically asserted that the colleges should engage in research and that teaching should be research based. Since 1999, the colleges have had the possibility to establish PhD programmes if some specific criteria are fulfilled. Even though relatively few programmes have been established, the binary system has come under pressure from colleges with university ambitions, and at the turn of the millennium it was discussed whether the binary divide should be abolished. In 2004, the government decided that colleges which fulfil certain minimum standards could apply for accreditation to university status, and two of the colleges attained this status in 2005 and 2007. Many of the other colleges are discussing how they can obtain university status, either by themselves, by merging with other university colleges to create larger entities or by merging with a university (which one college did in 2009).

The official English name of these colleges has shifted over time. From 1971 on, the name was 'regional colleges'. In 1994, it was changed to 'state colleges' and in 2000 to 'university colleges' after active lobbying by the Norwegian Council of State Colleges among members of the Education Committee in Parliament. These colleges are, however, not entitled to use the university label in Norwegian contexts.

In 2009, the colleges and the universities each had roughly 5,000 academic staff in permanent positions. Non-tenured staff amounted to another 5,000 in the university sector and to less than 1,000 in the colleges. The largest college programmes are bachelor studies in teacher training, nursing, engineering and economics and business administration. In addition, there are bachelor programmes in fields like social work, journalism, library education, tourism, hotel management, various health educations, art and music, as well as many different university courses.

The colleges differ greatly in size and the selection of study programmes. The size of these colleges varies considerably from less than 1,000 students to more than 10,000 students (which is more than the smallest universities) and from less than 100 to more than 600 academic staff. The colleges offer bachelor's programmes in professional and vocational fields as well as some lower level university courses. Virtually, all colleges also offer master's degree programmes, some of them in collaboration with a university. In addition, several colleges offer doctoral training in specific subjects. Half of the colleges have programmes in professional fields only, while the other half offers programmes in both professional and academic fields.

There are also differences in staff competence and research activities. When the individual institutions were incorporated into the state college system in 1994, they had very different presumptions for conducting research. These differences were mirrored in the proportion of working time used for R&D. While most staff members in the district colleges were involved in research, very few of the teachers in the colleges of engineering and health education were qualified for and actively engaged in R&D. Staff members regarded themselves predominantly as teachers. It was mainly through the recruitment of new staff who had an interest in and the ability to carry out research that this activity became established (Kyvik & Skodvin, 2003).

For a variety of reasons, there has been considerable resistance to the development of research in the college sector. First, the universities were concerned that they would lose out in the competition for research resources, particularly on account of the strong position of the colleges in Parliament. Second, many were genuinely concerned that the quality of research in these colleges would be below standard. In addition to the lack of associate professors – not to mention full professors – the small and isolated professional communities were frequently used as an argument against allocating research resources to institutions which would hardly be able to develop research of any significance. Third, many were critical towards the development of research that could draw attention away from practice-oriented vocational training. However, such arguments were gradually losing momentum, and research should eventually come to play a larger role in these institutions. Attempts by the Ministry of Education and Research to slow the pace of change on several occasions were opposed by Parliament, mainly because the colleges had more local support and were also considerably more effective in lobbying than the universities.

National Policies for Research in the Colleges

Over the last two decades, Parliament, the Government and the Ministry of Education and Research have repeatedly discussed the research mission of the colleges. We may distinguish between (1) principal objectives for research in the colleges, (2) other specific guidelines related to the research mission of colleges, and (3) general guidelines related to the research mission of all higher education institutions.

State authorities have formulated three principal objectives for the research mission of the colleges: (1) research shall contribute to regional development, (2) research shall contribute to improved professional practice, and (3) research shall aim at improving teaching and education of students.

The role of the colleges in regional innovation and development is an objective that increasingly has been underlined and is a task that is specified in the Act on Universities and Colleges. In 2005, a white paper on research policy stated that in order to contribute to the creation of a culture of entrepreneurship in the region, the institutions have to develop study programmes that fulfil the competence needs of the same region (Larsen & Kyvik, 2006). A recent OECD review of tertiary education in Norway characterised the strong commitment to regional needs as a virtue of the Norwegian system. In line with this, the regional aspect 'has been reinforced through an emphasis on the need for the institutions to meet the training and research need of regional economic development' (OECD, 2006, p. 17).

Another aspect of the research mission is that the different programmes have an obligation to undertake R&D that strengthens and improves professional practice. Furthermore, the importance of contact and cooperation between the colleges and different actors in professional practice is accentuated.

Finally, the principle of research-based teaching is specified in the joint Act on Universities and Colleges. There are, however, different interpretations of what research-based teaching actually means. Should all staff do research, or is it sufficient to disseminate advanced knowledge produced by other researchers? The OECD review on tertiary education in Norway stated that the meaning of the term 'research-based teaching' needs to be clarified (OECD, 2006, p. 29).

In addition to the main objectives listed above, state authorities have given a number of other guidelines on the research mission of the colleges: (a) the extent of research, (b) allocation of time for research, and (c) enhancement of research competence.

The colleges are not supposed to have the same role in the national R&D-system as the universities. In 1991, the Ministry stated that the share of R&D activities should generally be around 25% versus 75% for teaching (in comparison to 50% for each task in the universities), but the colleges should consider this distribution according to the requirements of the different study programmes. However, the Education Committee in Parliament, after having been exposed to lobbyists from the colleges, opposed a limit of 25% of the working year for academic staff to devote to R&D and stated that there should be considerable flexibility. As a general rule, the present level of research should be upheld as a minimum with possibilities for extending this.

Furthermore, the government has made it clear that in the colleges, undertaking research is neither an individual duty nor right, but an institutional responsibility. It is the college that shall determine the distribution of time resources among the staff according to certain constraints laid down by the Ministry of Education and Research when determining the annual work programme for each individual. In general, research competent staff shall have the opportunity to undertake research, while others should concentrate on keeping themselves abreast of recent research relevant to the skills students are to be taught. In 1995, these general guidelines were challenged with the introduction of a common career structure in universities and colleges. Parliament then stated that 'it is reasonable that academic staff who work within the same field and at the same level, over time shall have the same working conditions independent of institutional type'. The formulation by Parliament has been used by the researcher unions for what it is worth, while the Ministry has maintained that the actual distribution of working time for R&D is up to the colleges to decide upon.

Finally, as pointed out above, the idea that teaching should be based on research has found its way into the legislation for all higher education institutions. Even though the meaning of 'based on research' is unclear, this statutory provision has strengthened the need to improve the formal research competence of academic staff in the colleges. This is also a precondition if the colleges shall be able to meet demands for contributing to regional development and to improved professional practice.

While we above have focused on principle objectives and specific guidelines for research in the college sector, we also have to mention some important policy objectives for all higher education institutions. Among these is *concentration of research resources*. Both universities and colleges are challenged by public authorities to concentrate and profile their scholarly activities. In addition, state authorities have consistently emphasised that all higher education institutions, including the state colleges, should aim at *improving the quality of research*. Furthermore, to sustain and develop Norway as a knowledge society, the necessity of *increased contact and collaboration between research establishments* has been emphasised. The government has also stressed the importance of close contact with the international research community, and increased *internationalisation* is a recurrent theme in research policy documents. Internationalisation is regarded as a necessity both to strengthen the quality of research and to strengthen innovation in the public and private sectors. *Promoting a better gender balance* in academic positions is another state goal encompassing both universities and colleges. It is a well-known fact that relatively fewer women than men in academia have made it to the top of the career pyramid. Finally, the government has stated that the individual researcher must have *academic freedom* in the choice of research problems, methodology and approach within the frames of the research strategy of the institution for the programme or field in which the researcher is employed.

Strategic Measures by State Authorities

We can distinguish between four important strategic measures by the Ministry of Education and Research to implement its policy objectives on research in the colleges; (a) the introduction of a university-like career structure, (b) the instruction of colleges to formulate strategic plans, (c) the establishment of specific research programmes for this sector, and (d) the introduction of an incentive-based funding system.

The Introduction of a University-Like Career System

Since 1995, universities and colleges have essentially practiced a common career structure. The permanent academic positions are professor and associate professor, which are combined teaching and research positions, while senior lecturer and lecturer are predominantly teaching positions, but with the possibility of doing some research. A doctorate is not a requirement for obtaining tenure in the latter positions. The position as college teacher is used in practice-related programmes, mainly in teacher training and health education, and the holders of this position do not have a master's degree.

Since 1993, associate professors in both universities and colleges can apply for promotion to full professor on the basis of their research competence (Olsen, Kyvik, & Hovdhaugen, 2005). This reform made it possible to become a full professor in three different ways: (a) by applying for a vacant professorship in open competition and becoming appointed as the best qualified applicant, (b) by applying for a vacant professorship in open competition, being found competent but not the best qualified by the evaluation committee and then being promoted to full professor at his or her department, and (c) by applying for promotion to full professor on the basis of their research competence and being found competent by a unanimous national peer-review committee. The latter strategy has now become the most important way of becoming a full professor, while few are appointed to an ordinary professorship due to few vacant positions.

Establishment of Strategic Plans

The Ministry of Education and Research has instructed higher education institutions to formulate strategic plans (Larsen & Langfeldt, 2005). These plans should include strategies for the further development of research and strategies for how the colleges can fulfil policy objectives given by state authorities: contribution to regional development and improved professional practice, concentration of research resources, development of research competence, improved quality of research, increased contact and collaboration with domestic and foreign research establishments, etc. (Kyvik, 2008).

Establishment of Research Programmes

Over the last decade, the Ministry of Education and Research in cooperation with the Research Council of Norway has established several research programmes to strengthen research and research competence in the university colleges. While some programmes aim at strengthening the relationship between the private business sector and the colleges, others emphasise the need to improve research in specific educational programmes and professions. The Research Council of Norway funds a programme targeted towards a closer interplay and mutual competence development between SMEs and the university colleges, with the aim to improving the regional innovative capabilities in both the SMEs and the university colleges. In addition, the Research Council has funded a strategic research programme for the university colleges meant to stimulate high-quality research, particularly related to their regional responsibility for innovation and knowledge transfer. However, in its strategic plan for research in the university colleges (2008–2012), the Research Council announced that it will no longer support special programmes targeted towards the university colleges and that they in the future will have to compete with universities and research institutes for funding. Nevertheless, the Research Council has continued to fund a strategic research programme for the colleges.

Introduction of an Incentive-Based Funding System

Higher education is for the most part funded by public sources and above all by the Ministry of Education and Research, but changes have taken place in the mechanisms by which general government grants are transferred to universities and colleges. The funding of these institutions has changed from a system where the total budget was broadly based on the number of students and specified in great detail on expense categories, to a system where the institutions are relatively free to decide for themselves on how to allocate their block grant between different types of costs. The relative size of the block grant in relation to the total budget has, however, decreased gradually and the share of research funding from external sources has increased.

In 2002, the Ministry introduced a new funding model for higher education. The reform means a shift to an incentive-based funding system. The new funding model is set up to advantage those institutions that do well in producing student credit points and are active in research. As a general rule, 40% of the total funding from the government is incentive based, of which 25% of the budget is based on the production of credits and graduates and 15% on research production. These are average percentages which will vary between institutions and from year to year. The research grant is based on four performance indicators: (a) the number of PhD candidates (0.3 points), (b) the extent of funding from European Union research programmes (0.2 points), (c) the extent of national research council funding (0.2 points), and (d) the number of publications according to type of publication, quality of journal and book publisher and the number of co-authors (0.3 points).

Research Strategy in the Colleges

Institutional Strategy and Priority Setting

All colleges have developed a research strategy either as part of a general plan for all institutional activities or as separate research plans (Kyvik, 2008). An examination of these strategies reveals that there are significant differences between the colleges in the extent and degree of specificity of these documents. This is due to different traditions for research, differences in administrative competence and resources and different priorities given to strategy work. Furthermore, there are differences between the colleges when it comes to the degree of centralisation of research policy. While some colleges have developed rather detailed guidelines for their research activity, others have delegated the main responsibility for the research strategy to the individual faculties.

In their strategy documents, all colleges largely refer to, or have similar formulations, as those objectives and guidelines set by state authorities. This coalescence of aims can be interpreted in different ways. On the one hand, those responsible for the preparation and approval of strategy documents in the colleges can be regarded as extremely loyal to the Ministry of Education and Research. On the other hand, administrative and professional leaders in these institutions may, in fact, share the same objectives for research as state authorities, and the strategy documents accordingly may be regarded as an important platform for action. A third interpretation of the reasons why research strategy documents comply with objectives set by the state might be that such plans can be regarded as symbolic response to external expectations (Larsen, 2000). The colleges formally state that they are loyal to state policy for research, but in reality they do little to implement these objectives. The latter interpretation, though not irrelevant, probably is the least important. It is difficult to imagine that the leaders of the colleges do not take their strategy seriously, in the sense that they disagree or do not care about those aims or visions they have formulated. It can hardly be controversial that the colleges should contribute to regional development, improve professional practice and the teaching and education of students, improve the quality of the research, engage in international research cooperation, enhance the research competence of staff members and so forth.

The recommendation by state authorities that the colleges to a larger extent should concentrate their research efforts, with the internal redistribution of resources this necessitates, conflicts however with the wish in individual colleges for a more equal distribution between the different fields and programmes to maintain academic breadth and to serve the diverse needs of the region, the professions and the students. Even though some of the colleges have established one or more PhD programmes, they still have a responsibility in maintaining the professional programmes they offer. However, steps are now taken by some colleges to profile and concentrate their research activity in such a way that a redistribution of resources is a likely outcome of the strategy process.

The Organisation and Management of Research

Most of the university colleges have established research committees which are responsible for developing plans for research activity, for giving advice to the board and for being a consultative body for faculties, departments and individuals. Even though the advisory function of the research committees is underlined in most institutions, these committees often play a key role in the formulation and implementation of the research strategy. In some colleges, the research committee is also given decision-making authority in some matters. The size and composition of these committees vary, but usually the rector or pro-rector is the chairman, and in most colleges each faculty is represented in the committee, either by the dean or by a professor. At some colleges, research committees have been set up also at the faculty level.

The majority of the colleges have separate research administrative units or staff to take care of the organisation and coordination of internal and external research affairs. Due to the different sizes of the colleges, the number of such administrative positions differs from a part-time position to ten staff members.

About half of the colleges have set up research centres and/or established research programmes to strengthen and profile research activities. Research centres often have a more permanent and formal organisational status than programmes which are established for a given period. In some colleges, academic staff are affiliated to a centre as well as to a department, and this double organisational membership sometimes causes conflict. The establishment of formal research groups within individual departments is another measure initiated by some of the colleges.

In general, the organisation and management of research are decentralised to the faculty and department level, and academic staff have great influence on decisions made on these levels.

Enhancement of Research Qualifications and Distribution of Resources for Research

Formal research qualifications of academic staff in the colleges are generally low compared to those of university staff. In 2008, 20% of the permanent teaching staff in the colleges had a doctorate, an increase from 9% in 1997. Only 6% were full professors, while more than 70% had the status as lecturer or teacher (Table 12.1). In contrast, more than 40% of the permanent academic staff in the universities were full professors.

The colleges have introduced several measures to enhance the research qualifications of staff members. First, the colleges have established various types of research grants (funding of research projects, PhD scholarships, sabbaticals). Second, they allocate time for research as a percentage of regular work hours. Third, most colleges have established senior lecturer programmes to encourage lecturers to qualify for a higher position. Fourth, many colleges fund PhD scholarships, and some colleges have established PhD programmes. Academic staff in the colleges can also enrol in doctoral programmes in the universities with funding from their institution.

All colleges have set aside resources for research grants which are distributed at an institutional level, but decisions are made on the basis of recommendations from research committees and faculty boards where academic staff are in

Table 12.1 Academic staff in permanent positions in the university colleges and the universities in 2008, by position

	University colleges		Universities	
	Number	Percent	Number	Percent
Professor	322	6	2,301	43
Associate professor	948	19	1,706	32
Assistant professor	75	1	168	3
Senior lecturer	570	11	174	3
Lecturer	2,488	50	723	14
Other tenured staff	135	3	240	4
College teacher	487	10	38	1
Total	5,025	100	5,350	100

Source: NIFU STEP. Research Personnel Register.

majority. These resources represent, however, only a small share of the colleges' total resources for such activities. The most important resource for undertaking research is the proportion of regular working hours that may be used for such activity, and which is regulated by individual work plans and agreed upon annually at faculty or department level.

The different research traditions and unequal research competence in the various programmes have been important challenges for most colleges. Thus, the institutions practice a variety of rules, partly based on different traditions in the various programmes, partly on differentiation according to academic rank and partly on specific needs of individual staff members and the institutions themselves.

College teachers have no formal research competence and have therefore generally not been allocated time for research. On average they may, however, use about 15% of their working time for scholarly activities and competence development. In general, college teachers are encouraged to raise their academic qualifications and to obtain a master's degree. Thus, over the last decade, the share of college teachers of the total staff has decreased substantially.

The considerable differences in formal research competence among staff members reveal the need for priority making in the distribution of research resources. In this respect the colleges face a fundamental dilemma: How many resources should be used to develop research skills among the staff and how many should be allocated to individuals who have the qualifications necessary to undertake research of a reasonable quality? Both needs are important and legitimate as distribution criteria in relation to overall policy goals for the enhancement of research in the state colleges (Kyvik 2009b).

State guidelines with respect to the internal distribution of working time for research are very general, to some extent unclear, and sometimes also in conflict with each other. This means that there is considerable leeway in the colleges for the interpretation of guidelines and actual allocation policy. In addition, the relationship between institutional research strategy and individual autonomy in the choice of research problems is unclear. Academic staff are supposed to follow the strategy of their institution, but the question remains as to the extent to which it is possible to direct research activities of individual staff members.

Research Performance in the Colleges

Several indicators will be used to illuminate research performance in the colleges: funding, research profile, time used for research and related activities, scientific and scholarly publishing, internationalisation and collaboration with other research establishments. The data is drawn from several extensive empirical enquiries of research and development in the college sector. The data was compiled in 1998 and 2006 by mail surveys to all academic staff (except college teachers who do not hold a degree on a master's level). The first survey includes a total of 2,272 staff of the rank of college lecturer and higher (response rate 71%) (Kyvik & Skodvin, 1998), the second one 2,672 staff (response rate 61%) (Larsen & Kyvik, 2006).

A corresponding mail survey in 2001 to all academic staff of the rank of assistant professor and higher in the four comprehensive universities (response rate 60%) has enabled comparisons of research output across the two sectors. In addition, national R&D-statistical data has been used to compare R&D expenditures in colleges and universities.

Funding

Most research in the colleges is undertaken within the frame of the annual budget appropriations by the Ministry of Education and Research, but the institutions have to an increasing extent had to compete for external research grants in order to maintain their level of operations. Still, the percentage of extra-budgetary funding of total R&D expenditures did not increase much from 1997 to 2007. The latter year, R&D expenditures in the colleges amounted to approximately €150 million, as compared to about €1,150 million in the university sector. Slightly less than 20% of these expenditures were drawn from extra-budgetary sources (about €31 million), of which the Research Council of Norway accounted for almost half of them (Table 12.2). In 2007, less than 5% of the external research funding came from the EU (about €1.4 million), about the same percentage as in 1997.

As mentioned above, to stimulate higher education institutions to improve quality and efficiency in teaching and research, a new model for basic funding was introduced in 2002, partly based on performance as measured by a diverse set of indicators. So far, it is difficult to assess the implications of this reform, although the funding model will obviously have some effect on the internal distribution of resources in universities and colleges. The institutions now have become much more concerned about the recruitment of students, drop-out rates and time to degree, as well as quality of research and published output.

Table 12.2 Extra-budgetary funding for R&D in the university colleges in 1997 and 2005

	1997		2007	
	€ million	%	€ million	%
Central government	3.0	29.1	5.5	17.9
Local government	1.9	18.5	2.5	8.3
Research council of Norway	2.6	24.9	14.1	45.3
Industry	1.4	13.6	3.6	11.8
Other national sources	0.5	4.7	2.9	9.3
International sources	1.0	9.3	2.3	7.4
(European commission)	(0.5)	(4.4)	(1.4)	(4.7)
Total	10.5	100	31.1	100
External funding in % of total R&D expenditures	19.7%		21.0%	

Source: NIFU STEP R&D statistics.

R&D Profile

In the mail survey to all academic staff in the colleges in 2006, individuals were requested to classify which percentage of their research fell within each of five categories. We distinguished between *basic research*, *applied research* and *experimental development* according to the OECD statistical definitions (OECD, 2002), and between *educational development* and *artistic development* in order to present a diverse picture of R&D and related activities in the colleges.

Figure 12.1 shows the R&D profile of the colleges, indicating that applied research is the most common activity, followed by development according to the OECD definition and educational development. Less than 20% of these activities were used for basic research, in contrast to close to 60% in the universities. In addition, more than 20% of the R&D activity was classified as educational development. The majority of staff distributed their activities across several categories. Thus, 38% reported that all or parts of their work could be classified as basic research, 65% reported applied research, 61% development, 53% educational development and 8% artistic development (Larsen & Kyvik, 2006).

There were large differences in R&D profile according to academic rank. Full professors classified on average 40% of their activities as basic research, while the corresponding figure for associate professors was 30%, for senior lecturers 15% and for lecturers 10%. There were also large differences in R&D profile between colleges. Thus, the amount of basic research varied between 10 and 30%.

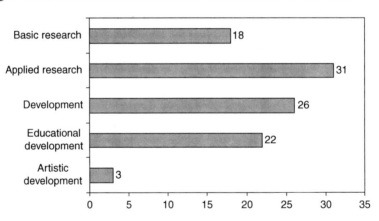

Fig. 12.1 Classification of R&D in the university colleges in 2005. Percentages

Time Used for Research and Related Activities

The mail survey to college staff in 2006 showed that on average 20% of their total working time was used for research and development (Larsen & Kyvik, 2006), the same percentage as in 1998 (Kyvik & Skodvin, 1998). In comparison, university staff spent about 30% of their time on R&D (Kyvik & Smeby, 2004). Unlike in the universities, there are significant differences in average time used for R&D among staff members according to academic rank. Full professors and associate professors used on average about the same proportion of their time for R&D as their counterparts in universities, while college lecturers used half as much time.

There were large differences in time used for R&D between programmes, varying between less than 15% in engineering, about 20% in teacher training and health education and close to 30% in some of the smaller programmes like social work and journalism.

There were also large differences between individual colleges, varying from 15% to more than 30%. Institutions offering many vocational and professional programmes, particularly in engineering and health education, spent relatively little time for R&D, while those institutions which are based primarily on the former district colleges used substantially more time on these activities.

Scientific and Scholarly Publishing

Although research and scholarly work have been increasingly emphasised, a relatively large share of the academic staff are poorly qualified to undertake such activity. The extent of publishing must therefore be considered with this in mind. Nevertheless, the publication pattern is an important indicator of what comes out of the time at the disposition for research and related work. In the mail surveys, staff members were requested to report the total number of scientific and scholarly publications in the 3-year periods 1995–1997 and 2003–2005, respectively. In the first survey, 51% of the academic staff had at least one publication and on average, each staff member published 2.3 articles, books or reports during the 3-year period. In the second survey, 57% reported at least one publication, and each staff member had on average 2.7 publications. In contrast, university staff reported on average 9.0 such publications in the years 1998–2000 (Kyvik, 2003). Full professors and associate professors in the colleges reported fewer publications than their counterparts in the universities, but differences were relatively small. There were, however, large differences in published output between the various domains. In the 3-year period 2003–2005, average number of publications per academic staff member in the major professional bachelor programmes varied between 1.6 in health education and 3.1 in social work. There were also large individual differences in publishing activity; approximately 10% of the staff accounted for half of all scientific and scholarly publications.

Internationalisation

State policies for increased internationalisation of research include also the colleges. The survey shows that the share of English-language publications increased from 35% in the period 1995–1997 to 40% in the years 2003–2005. In contrast,

70% of the publications in the universities were published in English or another non-Scandinavian language. Furthermore, 45% of the college staff attended a conference or seminar abroad and two thirds of them presented a paper. Thus, there is some evidence that a relatively large share of the college staff is internationally oriented in their research. In fact, professors in university colleges are almost as international in their research practice as are university professors (Larsen & Kyvik, 2006). However, in total, less than 20% of the college staff collaborated with colleagues in other countries (in contrast to 65% in the universities), and in 2005, only 5% of the staff reported research funding from sources abroad (3% from the EU and 2% from other sources).

Collaboration with Other Research Establishments

The 2006 survey shows that in the period 2003–2005, 24% of the college staff collaborated in research with colleagues in Norwegian universities, 18% with colleagues in other countries, 10% with research institutes and only 6% with industry. The corresponding survey among university staff in 2000 demonstrates that a far larger share of university faculty reported research collaboration. This difference can be explained partly by the fact that a large proportion of the staff in the colleges undertakes relatively little R&D. Furthermore, the survey shows that staff in the highest positions have more research collaboration. When comparing professors and associate professors across the two sectors, their cooperation pattern is almost at the same level (Larsen & Kyvik, 2006).

Half of the university colleges have close relationships to a regional research institute. These institutes were established partly on the initiative of the colleges themselves, partly on the initiative of the county council, local industry and the governmental ministry responsible for regional affairs. The rationale for these establishments was to promote regional development and innovation, and the institutes were meant to play an important role in regional knowledge networks. Some of these institutes are co-localised with a university college, and in these cases there is an intimate relationship between the institute and the college in terms of collaboration on projects and exchange of personnel. The institutes receive a small basic appropriation from the government, thus being totally dependent on external funding from a variety of regional and national sources. Some of these regional institutes have evolved into competitors with national research institutions. The government has encouraged the regional institutes and the university colleges to merge in order to create larger and stronger research environments, and the policy of the Research Council is to stimulate collaboration between the two types of institutions through funding measures.

The Future of Research in the University Colleges

The reasons for the development of research in the university colleges can be regarded as the outcome of mutually reinforcing academisation processes taking place in the college sector, in the state apparatus, and in the regions, as well as through the interaction between important actors across these sectors (Kyvik, 2009). In the colleges, research-oriented staff have tended to copy the research and publication practice of their colleagues in the universities, programme leaders have developed professionalisation strategies, characterised by the scientification of the knowledge core and the curriculum through the establishment of a research capability, and college leaders have been eager to raise the status of their institutions by establishing master's degree and PhD programmes, a strategy which presupposes a strong research base. The state has implemented far-reaching reforms like the introduction of a joint Act on Universities and Colleges which states that teaching shall be based on research, the introduction of a common academic career system in universities and colleges, and the possibility for colleges to advance to university status provided the accreditation of at least four PhD programmes. Finally, regional stakeholders demand that the colleges shall contribute in local innovation processes and that these institutions need more resources from the state to develop a stronger research capacity.

Although the colleges only account for 13% of the total R&D expenditures in higher education, in 2005, academic staff at these institutions spent about 1,000 man-years for R&D. In comparison to the universities, this amount is rather high. However, despite the fact that the percentage of professors and the share of staff with a doctoral degree have doubled over the last decade, the formal qualifications of staff in the college sector are still low. This is reflected in low publication rates compared to the time used for research and demonstrates that it takes time to develop research competence and research activity in programmes where there is no or little tradition for such work. However, changes can be expected in the coming years due to the increasing number of staff enrolled in PhD programmes, and with the gradual replacement of staff recruited to teach with staff holding a PhD.

We will end this chapter by focusing on the three principal objectives for research in the college sector. The main question is whether the results of the R&D activities in the colleges fulfil the main goals set for research in this sector.

The Relevance of Research for the Regional Community

To be a driving force for regional development has been part of the public policy for colleges for many years, and increasingly also the colleges' role in regional innovation processes have been emphasised. To assess the importance of the colleges for regional development and innovation is not an easy task, but there is undoubtedly great distance between public goals and the actual role of the colleges. Only 6% of academic staff in the colleges collaborated with industry during a 3-year period (Larsen & Kyvik, 2006). Several factors might explain this gap. First, many of the programmes in the college sector have a limited potential for conducting research towards regional needs. Second, engineering, which is the programme with most potential for regional development and innovation, has relatively low R&D competence and activity. Third, the incentive structure for higher education institutions does not encourage this kind of activity. Consequently, it will be a great challenge to both public authorities and the institutions to meet this goal.

The above-mentioned OECD expert committee emphasised that the many geographically separate entities in one and the same college do not lead to strong academic institutions. In the opinion of the committee, small entities are not in the interest of regional development even though strong regional forces want to maintain the decentralised structure (OECD, 2006, p. 17). Consequently, the committee found that there is a need to review the role and location of colleges. In line with the view of the OECD report, a governmental committee set up to consider the future organisation of Norwegian higher education recently recommended a stronger regional concentration of this part of the educational system, and that a possible solution might be to abolish the binary system and to merge the colleges with the nearby universities (NOU, 2008). However, the Ministry of Education and Research has declared that it wants to sustain a diversified higher education system, and that such mergers eventually have to be the outcome of mutual and voluntary agreements between universities and colleges.

The Relevance of Research for the Development of Professional Practice

To build up competence of high standard in professional education and professional practice is an important objective in the public policy for the colleges. Due to this, the orientation towards practice in the different programmes should be noticeable. To strengthen research on professional practice is another part of this objective. The mail survey undertaken in 2006 shows that the majority of staff in teacher education, engineering, nursing and health education have carried out research related to professional practice over the last 3 years (Larsen & Kyvik, 2006). However, there are still many staff members in professional programmes who do not report that their research activity can be characterised as research for professional practice, and a pertinent question is what kind of research or scholarly activity they actually undertake. On the other hand, the main objective of the state colleges is to train students for various professions. Thus it might be more important that staff have some practical experience from professional work than that they possess formal research qualifications.

The Relevance of Research for Teaching and Education

The Act on Universities and Colleges specifies that teaching and learning should be research based. As discussed above, it is not clear what is meant by this statement. Nevertheless, there is some scattered evidence that this objective is being met. Educational development takes place not only in teacher training, but in all study programmes. The mail survey indicates that this type of R&D is connected to teaching and learning in teacher training, engineering, nursing and health and social education, and that students to a certain extent participate in these kinds of R&D projects (Larsen & Kyvik, 2006).

Concluding Remarks

As we have seen, state authorities have emphasised that the colleges shall undertake research preferably linked to education for and practice in the respective professions and to problems particularly relevant to the region. Not least does this apply to professional programmes where there is a potential for research that may strengthen the skills necessary for specific services in the public sector. However, as in the universities, the funding model for research and the individual reward system gives particular credit to traditional academic merits. There is no specific incentive structure aimed at fulfilling the three principal objectives. The new funding formula introduced in 2003 is aimed at rewarding publishing of articles in refereed journals and books with academic publishers. As such the funding system is not an incentive for the colleges to contribute to regional development, improve professional practice or improve teaching and education of students. A logical consequence of such a funding model and career system is that institutional leaders and staff members might give priority to research related to the discipline instead of concentrating on research and development related to the improvement of teaching and professional practice, or to the solving of practical problems in local industry or public services. Such a development might be accentuated with the increasing numbers of qualified researchers with a PhD in the colleges. However, it has been claimed that training in the professions scarcely benefits from staff who do research within the frames of the academic discipline, while research associated with the main objectives of the colleges remains the responsibility of staff with close links to the professions but with weak research traditions.

References

Kyvik, S. (2002). The merger of non-university colleges in Norway. *Higher Education, 44*, 53–72.
Kyvik, S. (2003). Changing trends in publishing behaviour among university faculty, 1980–2000. *Scientometrics, 58*, 35–48.
Kyvik, S. (2008). *FoU-strategi ved statlige høgskoler*. Oslo: NIFU STEP.
Kyvik, S. (2009a). *The dynamics of change in higher education. Expansion and contraction in an organisational field*. Dordrecht: Springer.
Kyvik, S. (2009b). Allocating time resources for research between academic staff: The case of Norwegian university colleges. *Higher Education Management and Policy, 21*, 109–122.
Kyvik, S., & Skodvin, O.J. (2003). Research in the non-university higher education sector – tensions and dilemmas. *Higher Education, 45*, 203–222.
Kyvik, S., & Smeby, J.C. (2004). The academic workplace. Country report Norway. In J. Enders, & E. de Weert (Eds.), The international attractiveness of the academic workplace in Europe (pp. 310–331). Frankfurt/Main: Gewerkschaft Erziehung und Wissenschaft.
Larsen, I. M. (2000). Research policy at Norwegian universities – Walking the tightrope between internal and external interests. *European Journal of Education, 35*, 385–402.
Larsen, I. M., & Kyvik, S. (2006). *12 år etter høgskolereformen. En statusrapport om FOU ved statlige høgskoler*. Oslo: NIFU STEP.
Larsen, I. M., & Langfeldt, L. (2005). Profiling comprehensiveness? Strategy formulation and effects of strategic programmes at traditional universities. In Å. Gornitzka, M. Kogan, & A. Amaral (Eds.), *Reform and change in higher education* (pp. 343–361). Dordrecht: Springer.

NOU. (2008). *Sett under ett: Ny struktur i høyere utdanning.* Norges Offentlige Utredninger 2008:3. Oslo: Statens forvaltningstjeneste.

OECD. (2002). *The measurement of scientific and technological activities. Frascati manual 2002: Proposed standard practice for surveys on research and experimental development.* Paris: OECD.

OECD. (2006). *Thematic review of tertiary education – Norway – country note.* Paris: OECD.

Olsen, T. B., Kyvik, S., & Hovdhaugen, E. (2005). The promotion to full professor – through competition or by individual competence? *Tertiary Education and Management, 11*, 299–316.

Chapter 13
Striving for Differentiation: Ambiguities of the Applied Research Mandate in Swiss Universities of Applied Sciences

Benedetto Lepori

Introduction

In the European non-university higher education landscape, the Swiss Universities of Applied Sciences (UASs) represent a very specific case, since their creation in 1997 these institutions received a research mandate, and the development of research was considered as one of the key objectives in the transformation of vocational schools in higher education institutions. Moreover, the research mandate of UASs was clearly distinct from universities, being focused on applied research and transfer of knowledge to private companies. Hence, it was an integral component of the binary divide and helped to distinguish the two sectors rather than to promote their convergence like in other countries (Lepori, 2008).

Moreover, in the second half of the 1990s, the Swiss state launched a number of initiatives and support measures to promote research in UASs, since these institutions started with a very low level of research activities. As we shall see, this policy was quite successful and after a few years Swiss UASs grew into significant research actors, at least in technology.

The aim of this chapter is twofold. First, I will explain the rationales and the forces behind these choices, as well as the reasons of the success of this policy. Second, I will discuss a number of open issues and ambiguities which emerged in the recent years, concerning the function of research in UASs and the delimitation of the applied research mandate, the relative priority of research and education and, finally, the extreme differences between subject domains in the extent and level of research activities. Thus, I will argue that both of these issues and a number of developments in the Swiss higher education system – including the introduction of the Bologna model and the foreseen reforms of the governance of higher education – are likely to lead to major changes in the UAS organisation in the next years and, to some

B. Lepori (✉)
Faculty of Economics, Centre for Organizational Research, University of Lugano,
Lugano, Switzerland
e-mail: blepori@unisi.ch

S. Kyvik, B. Lepori (eds.), *The Research Mission of Higher Education Institutions Outside the University Sector*, Higher Education Dynamics 31,
DOI 10.1007/978-1-4020-9244-2_13, © Springer Science+Business Media B.V. 2010

extent, might lead to a weakening of a binary divide which has proved until now to be quite stable.

This chapter is organised in five sections. First, I introduce the overall organisation of the Swiss higher education system and some specificities which are relevant also for analysing UASs. Second, I deal with the definition of the applied research mandate, with the public policies used to implement it and the nation-wide discussions on its future. Third, I look at the institutions themselves, analysing their research strategies, profile and support measures, and provide information on the extent and distribution of research activities and their development in the recent years. The fourth section discusses some tensions and issues which emerged concerning the development of research activities in UASs, while the last section frames them in the overall future evolution of Swiss higher education and of the binary system.

The chapter is based on an extensive body of research conducted on research in Swiss UASs, including a large study commissioned by the Swiss Innovation Agency and based on an on-line questionnaire and face-to-face interviews with research seniors (Lepori & Attar, 2006), as well as two studies on the funding of research, financed by the Federal Office of Professional Education and Technology and by the Rectors' Conference of Swiss UASs (Lepori, 2007a). Moreover, I will draw largely on documents concerning research strategies of the institutions and of some of their departments, for example, research reports and strategic documents, as well as the systematic analysis of institutional websites, looking for descriptions of the research mission and of research units and their competences. This also includes official documents, like the UAS law, the UAS strategic plan for each 4-year period (*Masterplan*, BBT, 2007) and a number of documents published by the Federal Office of Professional Education and Technology, the Swiss Innovation Agency and the Rectors' Conference of Swiss UASs.

The Policy Context: Swiss Higher Education and the Binary Divide

It is hardly possible to understand the development of research in the Swiss UASs without some background information on the organisation of the Swiss higher education system and of its specificities.

A Fragmented Governance Landscape

Switzerland is a federal state where competences are shared between the Confederation and the Cantons. In general, education is a strict competence domain of the Cantons and, thus, until the secondary level, federal competences are extremely limited. However, concerning higher education, the historical development has led to a complex division of competences, which largely impairs the coordination of the system (Perellon, 2001).

Historically, some Cantons have had their own university since the middle ages (University of Basel was created in 1460): nowadays, there are ten cantonal universities, directly ruled by their host canton through cantonal laws. With the creation of the federal state in 1848, the Confederation received the right to create and manage polytechnic schools: thus, two Federal Institutes of Technology (FITs) were created in Zurich (ETHZ) in 1854 and in Lausanne (EPFL) in 1968. FITs have the same degree structure as universities, but are specialised in natural sciences and technology.

Since the Second World War, the separated system has evolved towards a more integrated setting, however, without the clarification of jurisdiction. Thus, the Confederation has progressively developed a set of instruments financing project research also in higher education, the two most important being the Swiss National Science Foundation (SNF) and the Swiss Innovation Agency (CTI). Moreover, since 1967 the Confederation has financed cantonal universities and, accordingly, a framework law has been introduced; a joint body between the Confederation and the Cantons named the Swiss University Conference (SUC) progressively emerged as the *locus* for construction of consensus in higher education, while a large part of the coordination has been delegated to the Rectors' Conference of Swiss Universities.

What should be retained is that there is no common system of rules for Swiss higher education institutions (Lepori, 2007). Thus, individual universities and FIT are funded according to different channels and rules, there are no uniform organisational structures, or personnel statutes, career organisation and wage level. The unity of the system has been largely kept by academic rules and norms, even with quite different interpretations according to the regions. Concerning curricula, the introduction of the Bologna model brought uniformity in the length of the curricula, but there are no basic curricular plans at national level. Moreover, the coordination has been essentially based on mutual consensus, with a number of actors having a de facto blocking power on reforms: this strongly limits the ability of redesigning the system and led repeatedly in the past to partial reforms, which increased the complexity of the system.

The Vocational Education Sector and the Creation of a Binary System

Historically, Switzerland has been characterised by a very large vocational education sector both at the secondary and at the tertiary level. Namely, the separation between general curricula and vocational curricula began already at the secondary level, with the widespread practice of the apprenticeship (OECD, 2003). Progressively, vocational tertiary-level schools began to emerge, mostly offering rather short curricula. This model and the early selection between general and vocational curricula explain why Switzerland has been characterised by very low levels of access to higher education when compared to the other European countries (OECD, 2003; Perellon, 2003).

Like other European countries (Kyvik, 2004), the non-university higher education sector emerged through the upgrade of vocational institutions. This process was pushed from the early 1990s from concerns on the quality of vocational education; thus, in 1994, the Confederation introduced a professional maturity as the main diploma for access into the professional tertiary level, while in 1995 the new UAS act was approved (Conseil fédéral, 1994), which provided the framework for the merging of existing tertiary-level schools in technology, economics and management and applied arts (Lepori & Attar, 2006; Perellon, 2003). Seven public UASs were then created, each covering different regions of Switzerland followed, in 2005 and 2007, by two private UASs which were accredited, but without the right to public subsidies.

A fundamental difference with universities is that for vocational education the Confederation has the right to edict common rules and thus has a more direct power of intervention. A second difference is that, historically, vocational education has been considered as a part of economic policy and thus it is managed at the federal level by the Ministry of Economic Affairs (while general education and research are the resort of the Ministry of Internal Affairs).

The second stream leading to the creation of UASs was the perceived need to reinforce Swiss technology policy and to promote cooperation between higher education and private companies. While Swiss research policy had (and still largely has) a tradition of separation of functions between public and private research, from the 1970s it was perceived that some economic sectors and SMEs needed more support (Conseil fédéral, 1992; OECD, 1989). The chosen solution was not to directly finance industrial R&D, but to create a research actor situated downstream from basic research performed in universities towards applied research and development in cooperation with private companies. At the end of the 1990s, the two streams converged also organisationally with the merging of the offices in the Ministry of Economic Affairs responsible of technological policy and vocational education, into the new Federal Office of Professional Education and Technology (BBT), which became the main body supervising UASs.

Thus, the creation of UASs was accompanied by the creation in the Ministry of Economy of a parallel structure to the Ministry of Internal Affairs oriented towards vocational education and applied research, including a specific Swiss Innovation Agency funding applied research in cooperation with private companies. Thus, the binary divide was built from the beginning on two different institutional structures and this largely explains its stability (Lepori, 2006).

Merging and Expansion

While at the beginning UASs included only a few sectors with a strong focus on technology, in the last 10 years they have progressively integrated tertiary vocational schools in domains like social work, health, arts, teacher education. As a consequence, student numbers have grown from about 24,000 students in 2000 to 63,000 in 2008, against 121,000 in universities and in FITs. According to the forecasts of the Swiss Federal Statistical Office, the number of bachelor diplomas awarded by UASs will exceed those awarded by universities in the next years. Moreover, they evolved from institutions focused on engineering and technology (which comprised about half of the students in 1998) to generalist institutions covering most of the fields and with three quarters of students in non-technical domains.

The creation of UASs has been decisive to promote the expansion of higher education in a country historically characterised by a very low participation rate in higher education and by a very large tertiary professional sector (ISCED 5B level, OECD, 2003). The entry rate into higher education increased from 16.1% in 1995 to 34.5% in 2008 (source: Swiss Federal Statistical Office). This led also to a strong increase of expenditures since upgrading vocational education entailed also an increase of the costs per student. Public expenditures in tertiary education were stable around 1% of GDP from 1981 to 1995/6 and then increased to 1.5% in 2006 (source: OECD. Education at glance). Overall, the total expenditures of UASs have almost doubled between 2000 and 2007 from 678 to 1,922 million CHF (against about 6 billion CHF spent for universities and FITs).

Nowadays, UASs offer essentially a 3-year curricula which has been adapted to fit into the Bologna model and lead to the title of UAS bachelor; from 2008 they will be allowed to offer professionally oriented master degrees in a limited number of domains. While in the beginning the university and UAS curricula were considered as completely separated, the introduction of the Bologna model has led to some reconsideration and, at least in the same subject domains, UAS bachelor holders will, in the future, be allowed to enrol into university master's, subject to some conditions. As in other countries, the introduction of the bachelor–master is thus profoundly influencing the binary divide (De Weert, 2006).

Complexities in the Governance Structure

The creation of UASs was essentially based on geographical criteria, with each of the seven UASs covering a part of the Swiss territory. This implied that not only UASs started as a conglomerate of more than 60 pre-existing schools, but also five of seven UASs happened to cover more than one canton and this complicated the merger process and the set-up of central structures. Namely, intercantonal UASs are based on intercantonal agreements, which are difficult to modify and are subject to internal tensions, with each Canton supporting the schools located in its territory. Moreover, UASs are subject to federal (framework) regulations while the institutions themselves are subject to cantonal rules, for example, concerning accounting practices, employment rules, etc., being the transformation of former cantonal professional schools. As a consequence, the responsibility for the steering of the system is fragmented among different bodies and jurisdictions (Lepori, 2007; Perellon, 2003).

Both the UAS peer review (Commission fédérale des HES, 2002) and our work have showed a great deal of variation in the strength of the central UAS directions and in the progress of their transformation from groupings of individual schools to more unitary structures. Key elements of this process are the creation of a governing board and the nomination of a director with strong power; the centralisation of the allocation of financial resources; the reorganisation in subject departments and the concentration of subject domains in a single location. While some UASs have now well-defined central structures and rules and are organised in subject departments like universities, others have to be largely considered as holding organisations of largely autonomous individual institutions, with practically no central structures and power and, in many cases, with the same subject domains present in different locations. As a consequence, for some UASs, the level of the individual schools is more relevant for the development of research strategies than the whole UAS.

The Applied Research Mandate and Its Implementation

The research mandate of the UAS was already defined in the act of 1995. Namely, UASs should concentrate on applied research and development, focusing on the support to small and medium enterprises (SMEs; Conseil fédéral, 1994, 1997). The official documents position UASs as the link between the basic research performed in the universities and the private economy, thus with the function of transferring existing knowledge into application useful for the companies in direct cooperation with them (BBT, 2002; Conseil fédéral, 1997). Even if it is not any more accepted as a relevant description of the innovation process (Nightingale & Martin, 2000), the linear model of innovation still was the conceptual basis of the Swiss innovation policy in the 1990s.

The background of this discourse was the perception that the Swiss research system was very good in the production of basic knowledge, but weak in its transfer towards innovation and concerns about the diminishing innovation performance of the Swiss economy and the lack of an explicit technology policy (Conseil fédéral, 1992; OECD, 1989).

Thus, the attribution of a research mandate was one of the main policy goals behind the creation of the UAS and helped to clearly differentiate them from universities; this is critical since in the Swiss context the existence of a research mandate and of sizeable research activity is considered as necessary for belonging to higher education (and distinguishing UASs from other tertiary education schools). We also notice the strong reference of these formulations to technology, which constituted the core of the UAS at their creation.

In the last 10 years, the applied research mandate has been quite stable. Some shifts have occurred in two directions, as stated by the most recent document of the Rector's Conference of Swiss UASs (KFH, 2005): first, emphasising the reference to the application of knowledge and cooperation with practice, without an explicit reference to technology (thus including, for example, action-research in social sciences); second, accepting that UASs can and should develop basic knowledge in emerging fields where this is critically needed for application (use-inspired basic research; Stokes, 1997).

An Active Policy to Develop Research

The schools that merged into UASs in 1997 had quite limited research competencies, were concentrated in informatics, mechanical engineering and production processes and were largely the outcome of a national programme launched in the 1990s to support the introduction of Computer Integrated Manufacturing in the Swiss manufacturing industry. Activities were mostly concerned with the development of applications and performed by individual teachers or very small teams. For UASs to be able to fulfil their mandate, support measures were clearly needed.

An action plan was launched in 1997 by the Confederation, which attributed to the Swiss Innovation Agency additional funds to coach UASs in the development of their research strategies, to train their personnel and to finance exploratory projects and competence networks among Swiss UASs in specific research areas (Conseil fédéral, 1997). In the period 1997–2007 more than 120 million euros has been invested, a substantial amount given that in the year 2000 total R&D expenditures of UASs were just 50 million euros. To provide a comparison, the German programme for research in *Fachhochschulen* had in 2006 a volume of €16 million, while Dutch *Hogescholen* received €35 million for their *lectorates*.

The second measure was the reinforcement of the Swiss Innovation Agency (CTI) and its reorientation as an instrument to finance applied research in UASs. The CTI had a difficult life since its creation in 1944, but regained progressively a role in the Swiss research policy from the 1970s (Lepori, 2006). At the end of the 1990s, it was explicitly designed as the agency for supporting applied research, thus mirroring the role of SNF for academic research. Moreover, its main funding instrument – collaborative projects between HEIs and private companies – was very well adapted to research in UASs. Not only has the CTI budget strongly increased in the last 10 years, but UASs have also become the main beneficiary surpassing the FITs. Thus, the second ingredient for the development of research was the availability of a specific funding agency for the type of research done in UASs.

Finally, additional support to research activities was provided by the Confederation and by the Cantons through the general budget of UASs. Thus, the Confederation has, since 2004, a specific budgetary line for research in their general subsidy to UASs, while Cantons granted support either in the general budget or as strategic funds for research.

If we compare the funding volume provided through these measures with the starting level – even if there is no precise data, total R&D expenditures in 1997 probably did not exceed 30 million euros – we can conclude that research in UASs was promoted and supported by the state to an extent where financial means were probably a less important issue than building the necessary research competences.

A Funding System Oriented Towards Education

A closer look to the funding system of UASs allows a better understanding of the role of research and emerging tensions with education. Namely, most of the UASs' budgets are attributed for education and calculated on the basis of standard costs per student, fixed in their 4-year development plan agreed between Cantons and the Confederation (*Masterplan*). Of these costs, about three quarters are borne by the Cantons and one quarter by the Confederation (Lepori, 2007a).

Research is funded through three main sources (Fig. 13.1): direct contributions of the Cantons, a small contribution of the Confederation allocated on the basis of the third-party funds and of the personnel engaged both in research and in education and, finally, third-party funds, especially CTI projects and contracts from private companies. There are, however, large differences between UASs in the amount of research funds attributed by their Cantons, since, unlike education, there are no standard national rules.

While it was originally assumed that research, being of direct interest to customers, should be essentially financed by third-party funds, today general funds cover about 60% of the total R&D expenditures. A specific feature of UASs is their bookkeeping system, which requires a strict separation between educational and research activities (with daily time sheets); at least in principle, it is assumed that the educational and the research budget are clearly separated and there are no transfers between the two.

The drawback of this funding system is that, with the today's mechanism, an increase in the number of students automatically increases the educational budget, since the standard costs per student are almost fixed, while at the same time resources for research have to be additionally set aside by the state; in the today's situation where the Cantons push for integrating most of tertiary vocational education into UASs – to get also the right to the federal subsidies – and the number of

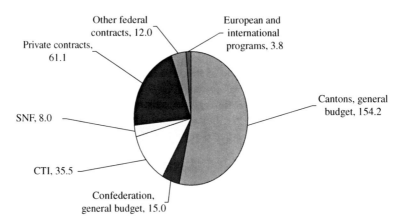

Fig. 13.1 Funding (million CHF) of R&D in Swiss UASs (2007)
Source: Swiss Federal Statistical Office

UAS students is strongly increasing, educational funding has the priority and R&D funding is limited to the remaining resources for UASs.

A Weakly – Regulated Environment

If we go beyond the general definition of the research mandate and the funding system, general norms and rules concerning the organisation of research are quite limited in the Swiss context. Namely, the Confederation has decided detailed rules concerning the organisation of curricula and their accreditation, but much less concerning research. How research should be organised, its repartition by domains, the organisation of researcher's careers and their qualification are essentially the responsibilities of the UASs themselves.

To some extent, the Rectors' Conference of Swiss UASs tried to promote common practices between UASs through internal discussion and the publication of guidelines, for example, on the nature of applied R&D, on careers, etc.; but as the quite different application of the title of UAS professors clearly shows, practices in the individual UASs can differ strongly.

However, it is relevant that research activities are considered as a necessary component of UASs and thus examined in the overall assessment of these schools (as in the peer review exercise performed in 2002; Commission fédérale des HES, 2002). Moreover, the Swiss Innovation Agency has financed a number of studies on the development of research in UASs, including a study on UAS research strategies (Lepori & Attar, 2006), an analysis of the development of research competences (Mayer, Sturn, & Zellweger, 2006) and an evaluation of the UAS research networks. Thus, strong normative pressure has been put on UASs to develop research and to demonstrate its quality.

Research Development and Institutional Strategies

In the last 10 years research in UASs has developed strongly. Total R&D expenditures have increased from 79 million CHF in 2000 to 194 million CHF in 2005 and to 289 million CHF in 2007 (Fig. 13.2). UASs also have been successful in getting funds from the CTI for collaborative projects with private companies, as well as direct contracts from the companies themselves (26 million CHF in 2004 from the CTI and 34 million CHF from private contracts). Moreover, in a recent survey the number of companies mentioning UASs as a partner in technology transfer was very close to those mentioning the two FITs and much higher than the cantonal universities (Arvanitis, Kubli, Sydow, & Wörter, 2005). Research is also now clearly identifiable in the website of all UASs and of most departments, and in most cases, indications are given about research domains and units.

If compared to the starting situation these developments are impressive, but in quantitative terms UASs account for only about 8% of the total R&D expenditures of the Swiss higher education sector. On the average, UASs spend only about 15% of

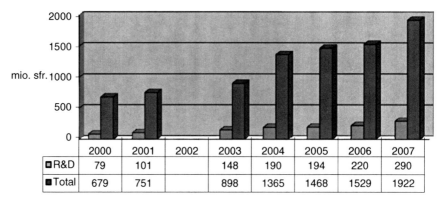

Fig. 13.2 Expenditures of UASs (million CHF)
Source: Swiss Federal Statistical Office. Data for 2002 have not been released due to insufficient quality

their budget for R&D against more than 50% in universities. Moreover, the increase of research was largely offset by the strong expansion of educational activities and by the integration of new domains with practically no research activities. According to the UAS planning for 2008–2011, the growth of R&D expenditures will slow down in the next years due to the lack of financial means; at the same time, expenditures devoted to R&D will stay at about 15% of total expenditures, the same level as in 2001, while the long-term objective is to reach 20%.

Active Institutional Policies and Instruments

The national policy has been actively backed up by strategies and actions at the level of the UASs themselves and their departments. Thus, five out of the seven UASs have produced a strategic document concerning research. Earlier documents of the period 2000–2003 have been mostly concerned with the establishment of general principles, the set-up of structures and internal funding mechanisms, while recently at least four of the seven UASs have developed a list of competence or priority domains. At the management level, five out of seven UASs created a research commission in charge of developing strategies and of managing central research funds; the exceptions are the two UASs where overall central structures do not exist. Four out of seven UASs dispose of internal project funds allocated by competitive procedures. The allocation of additional resources to external contracts has also become a widespread practice.

The most important actions have been taken at the level of the departments and subject units, especially in technology, informatics and, to some extent, economy and social work. Namely, departments tried to structure their research activity in a number of identifiable units, like research institutes, centres and research groups, with defined research domains. Our investigation shows that in almost all domains with a significant research activity, UASs have undergone the transition from largely individual and sporadic research to more structured organisation with identifiable units. A related aspect has been the emergence of research managers as a distinct function, who actively promote research and look for external funding.

Thus, the successful development of research in UASs can be interpreted as a case of convergence between the objectives of the different actors involved: the state, which defined the normative framework and provided the needed financial means; the UAS directions, which endorsed this mission as one of the core tasks of their institutions, and, finally, the researchers themselves, which have seen the development of research not only as an institutional mission, but also as an opportunity to develop their interests and competences.

However, there is still a considerable fragmentation of research units, which limits their ability of getting external funding and of competing with universities. A rough estimate based on the number of teams identified in their websites leads to an average size of about five full-time equivalents in R&D per team. Also, most respondents to our on-line questionnaire affirmed that their team was too small to compete with other players and to ensure a regular flow of funds. In fact, the main issue in this phase was not shortage of funds, but dependence on a small number of contracts, meaning uncertainty and difficulty in developing human resources (since researcher positions are in many cases financed through external contracts).

This situation has been explained in our interviews as the outcome of a soft consolidation process, where UASs tried to group people with similar research interests, but without defining precise priorities. This leads to a rather large number of research priorities if compared with the limited research volume of these institutions.

Most of the respondents agreed that further consolidation and focalisation on priority domains is needed. However, this conflicts with two framework conditions: first, the increasing diversity of the subject domains in UASs and, second, the diversity of the needs of the customers in the regional market, which require a large palette of competences (for example, in technology). Thus, for institutions oriented towards the regional market and SMEs, to focus on research niches might be more difficult than in basic research.

A Strong Concentration in Technology

This helicopter view oversees a major issue, namely the extreme differences between subject domains. Namely, the development of research has taken place essentially in technology (including construction and chemistry), which accounted in 2007 for 55% of the research volume. In these domains the share of research in the overall activities exceeds 20%; while significantly lower than universities (where the share of R&D reaches 50%), research is a major activity at the department level (see Table 13.1). In domains with an R&D share lower than 10% research can be a relevant activity of some subunits, but these are in largely teaching-only departments. Moreover, since this data covers seven UASs and, in some of them, subject

Table 13.1 Research resources (full-time equivalent staff; FTE) and students in UASs by domain (2007)

	Personnel			Students
	FTE	FTE R&D	% R&D	
Architecture and construction	650	184	28	2,992
Technology and informatics	2,124	788	37	9,005
Chemistry and life sciences	466	134	29	1,706
Agriculture and forestry	91	27	30	337
Economics	1,553	239	15	18,457
Design	413	58	14	2,356
Sport	17	5	30	131
Music and theatre	957	61	6	5,014
Linguistics	78	16	21	524
Social work	640	96	15	6,435
Psychology	93	17	18	731
Health	638	50	8	3,968
Teacher training	2,681	229	9	12,069
Undivided	1,635	77	5	22
Total	12,036	1,982	16	63,347

Source: The Swiss Federal Statistical Office.

domains are not concentrated in a single location, the volume of research outside technology is insufficient to maintain sizeable research units everywhere.

Our interviews confirmed this view. Most technology departments in UASs are recognised regional poles of applied R&D and transfer, with a considerable portfolio of projects and of competences. Unsurprisingly, all of them are in medium-size towns outside the cities hosting the two FITs and the large cantonal universities. These departments made the largest progress in the consolidation of research in institutes, in developing management capacities and specialised personnel.

In other domains, like economics, social work and design, we identified a number of research units of smaller size (typically five to ten people) scattered in basically teaching departments. Competences are a major problem, since practical experience (for example, in the private economy) is no substitute for methodological competences requiring a university degree and most of the teachers have no research experience. Finally, in some of the newly integrated domains, like music, theatre, health and, to some extent, teacher training, there is practically no research tradition in Switzerland.

A number of factors make these differences difficult to overcome. First, some domains with low research intensity like economics, social work and teacher training account for large and increasing numbers of students; second, as we shall see, the interpretation and application in practice of the applied research mandate has proved to be more difficult than in technology; finally, in these domains UASs are more directly confronted with the competition with cantonal universities, which in reality perform much of the applied work and consultancy in domains like economics.

Human Resources Policies

From the beginning, the development of human resources appeared a central issue as UASs inherited a large part of their personnel from previous professional schools with practically no research experience. The existing data shows that this problem has been essentially solved by the creation of a category of research assistants performing about two thirds of the whole research effort. These include young research assistants with a UAS bachelor who work for 3–4 years in applied research projects and then leave to private companies, but also a number of senior research assistants with a more permanent status (see Table 13.2). On the contrary, professors and teachers devote only a small part of their time to R&D activities, even if one has to take into account the extreme differences between individuals and domains.

In this respect, clear differences emerge between domains in the profile of the recruited people: while in technology most junior researchers come directly from the UASs themselves and senior researchers from private companies (some years after a university degree and in many cases a PhD), in the soft domains UASs hire for their research mostly university graduates with no prior professional experience.

At the upper level, the introduction of the UAS professor title (which is not equivalent to the university professor) was meant to select the best people in UASs having also research competences. In practice, in many UASs this title has been attributed to most full-time teachers and thus largely lost its specific value. According to the interviews, research competences and activities are concentrated in just a fraction of the UAS professors. However, for the recruitment of new professors, at least in domains with existing research activities, most UASs have introduced selection procedures which better take into account research competences.

This overview raises two major issues for the future. The first one is how to handle the discrepancy between the official definition of UAS professors as teachers-researchers and a reality where most of them are just teachers. Realistically, both the lack of research competences and the sheer number of UAS professors make it impossible to attribute some research time to all of them, in a context where most of research activities are performed by specialised people (an option which

Table 13.2 Personnel structure of UASs (2007)

	Persons	FTE	FTE in R&D activities	% of R&D in total activities
Professors	6,369	4,167	533	13%
Other teachers	19,373	1,945	129	7%
Assistants and researchers	4,970	2,268	1,106	49%
Technical and administrative staff	6,524	3,656	215	6%
Total	37,236	12,036	1,982	16%

Source: Swiss Federal Statistical Office.

certainly is better suited to the customer-orientation of today's UAS research) and where research resources are limited.

The second issue concerns recruitment and career perspectives of UAS researchers. Namely, most of these positions are temporary – except at the upper researcher's level, where there is an opportunity to get the permanent professor status. Moreover, since UASs cannot attribute the PhD title, junior researchers lack the incentive to work in UASs and, as a result, UASs have to pay salaries similar to private companies to attract good graduates (unlike universities which employ large numbers of PhD students as a comparatively cheap workforce). The introduction of master studies will probably address some of these issues for junior staff, who could work part time and in parallel get a master diploma, but for senior research staff this issue is largely unsolved.

Which Role for Research in Swiss UASs?

UASs have successfully established themselves in the recent years as actors in the Swiss research and higher education system and the fact that they perform research and are part of the same system as universities (albeit with a different mandate and rules) is not any more in discussion. However, the central issues for the next years pertain to the precise role of research in these institutions and, more precisely, the nature and applicability of the applied research mandate, the choice between concentration and diffusion of research and, finally, the relationship between research and education.

Success and Limitations of the Applied Research Mandate

As already discussed, the original research mandate the UASs aimed at responding to the technological needs of SMEs. This choice has proved to be largely successful in technology: UASs succeeded in building a specific profile distinguished from universities and found a market niche in cooperation with SMEs (both through contract funding and thanks to the CTI subsidies). At the same time, the level of development of research, but also the features of technical training, made the integration between research and education easier, especially in the practical work for the diploma and in the practice of engaging for some years bachelor recipients as research staff, before they leave to private industry. The introduction of the professional master studies from 2008 is likely to reinforce this model. Thus, the applied research mandate was crucial to the establishment of UASs as research actors and to justify their funding.

Outside technology the situation is more complex and research managers are not very comfortable with the applied research mandate or, even, deny that it is a useful guidance. This is the result of different factors: the lack of a workable distinction between basic and applied research and of accepted concepts of what is applied research, for example, in social sciences or in economics; a stronger competition with cantonal universities, which are more present in the regions and in some fields perform essentially applied research; the weakness of the funding instruments for applied and practice-oriented research, and finally, the lack of clearly identifiable customers like companies (the amount of public administration mandates being much smaller). A final factor is that, unlike in technology, in most of these domains there is no distinct competence profile for a UAS researcher, since the required methodological competences are largely the same as in a university and practical experience plays a more limited role.

In this respect, Swiss UASs are confronted with a difficult choice: broadening the research mandate would help to find suitable approaches outside technology, but at the price of weakening their identity and the risk of losing political support. Taking the opposite way entails the risk of reinforcing the divide between technological departments, active both in professional education and in applied research and teaching-only departments in other domains.

Specialisation or Diffusion of Research Activities?

A second issue concerns the distribution of research activities between domains and the UAS personnel. Even if it is not officially stated, it is more or less assumed that research should be present in all UAS subject domains equally because research is considered to be a constitutive element of these institutions (distinguishing them from other tertiary schools). However, to some extent this idea is in contradiction with the model of applied research oriented towards specific customers, which implies that research should be developed where there is an external demand for it. This debate reflects itself also in the funding model of research: in a customer-oriented model general research funds should be used primarily to develop the domains where there is an external demand and, thus, linked to the funds received from external contracts, while if research should be present almost everywhere, it would be better to distribute more evenly these resources.

The relevance of this issue is given by the merger in UASs of domains which have practically no research competences and activities, like arts, teacher training and, to a less extent, social work, and by the concentration of existing research activities in a few domains only. Given the available resources, there is a risk that a catching-up strategy in all domains would fail to develop research to a sufficient level and would weaken the domains where UASs have successfully positioned themselves at the national level, namely technology. However, a concentration strategy, supporting only a limited number of sectors (either already established or with favourable perspectives), would require a profound revision of the concept of the UAS and their research model, accepting that some departments are teaching-only (with all the relevant implications for the status of education, but also of teachers).

Research and Education: Conflicting Priorities

The third issue concerns conflicting priorities between education and research for public resources. As explained, the professional education and the applied research mandate of UASs came from two quite different rationales and thus it is not surprising that their funding and budgeting systems provide for a clear separation between the two activities, which should also be financed differently.

What makes this discussion relevant is the increase in student numbers and the high costs per student in social sciences. Namely, even if data should be treated with care since accounting systems are different, in technical sciences educational costs per student in UASs are similar to universities, while in social and human sciences they are significantly higher.

This is not surprising since UASs have maintained the model of small classes in most of their activity domains, with small ratios of students to teachers, while universities have a strongly differentiated model, with high students to teacher ratios in social sciences and much smaller ratios in natural sciences, technology and medicine; costs per student differ accordingly (Filippini & Lepori, 2007). Since in the last two decades the increase in student numbers was concentrated in social sciences, educational costs did not rise to the same extent as enrolments and this reduced conflicts for resources between education and research.

Since UASs profile themselves as providers of quality professional education, it is not easy for UASs to reduce the costs per student to compensate the increasing numbers. Moreover, while in technology the level of research activities makes integration with education feasible (for example, in diploma work) and thus benefits of the joint mandate are apparent, in other domains the development of research is a cost subtracted from education (at least in the short run).

This issue was overseen at the beginning because of the assumption that UAS research, being market-oriented, could be funded by external sources. However, in 2004 R&D expenditures were covered only by 40% with external sources and thus even in technology the development of research has been possible only thanks to a substantial investment from the general budget and this will be even more the case in soft sciences.

In my view UASs are caught in a dilemma: developing research outside technology will be possible only by subtracting resources available to education, in a context where educational costs are already under pressure. Not only this is not acceptable politically, but it would also impair the main marketing argument in education, namely specific professional education in small classes. However, today's level of research outside technology is too low to justify its existence in a long-term perspective and would lead to pressures to limit the research mandate for technology (as already advocated by Economiesuisse).

Research and Future of the Binary Divide

After a long preparation phase, in spring 2009, the Swiss government has published the proposal for a new higher education act, which shall replace from the year 2012 the university act and the UAS act, providing a common framework for the whole Swiss higher education sector (Conseil fédéral, 2007; Département fédéral de l'intérieur, 2004). The new act will create a joint political body between the Confederation and the Cantons to steer the whole higher education system and the administrations responsible for universities and UASs will probably be merged into a single ministry. Even if the two types of institutions will keep largely distinct missions, organisation and funding models, and even if, to some extent, the binary divide will be kept also at the institutional level – for example, the future rectors' conference will have two chambers for universities and UASs respectively – it is clear that this reform makes a decisive step towards considering universities and UASs as a part a unique system and thus destabilising the binary divide by removing some institutional barriers (even if this is not wished by all actors).

The introduction of the Bologna model and the start of UAS (professional) master's from 2008/2009 are also very likely to promote some convergence between the two domains (De Weert, 2006). First, the bachelor–master organisation of studies includes a provision for mutual access to universities and UAS master's: thus, UAS bachelor recipients will have access to university master's in the same fields by recuperating a number of credits; even if the maximum is 1 year, it is likely that in some domains the number of credits will be lower and they can be recuperated during the same year. Second, at least in some domains, UASs are pushing for a standard curriculum of 5 years and this will weaken the basic distinction between the two sectors based on the today's different length of the curricula.

The implications for research in the non-university sector are largely open and will depend on the strategic choices of the different actors, especially of the UASs themselves. From one side, at the system level, the rationale for a distinct research profile of these institutions will be probably weakened. Moreover, most specific research support measures for UASs in technology have been terminated, while the SNF plans to integrate its programme to support practice-oriented research in social sciences (the DO-RE programme) within its normal funding from 2012; thus, UASs will have to compete with universities for research funding according to the same rules.

These evolutions are likely to support voices inside the UASs themselves pushing for a more generic research mandate and convergence with universities, including the right of delivering a doctorate, especially in the sectors which are less comfortable with the today's applied research mandate.

To the other side, the experience of technology shows that a specific research mandate concentrated in a niche not well-covered by other research actors was crucial for allowing the successful development of research, precisely because competition with universities from institutions with lower research intensity and institutional priorities proves to be difficult. In reality, convergence with university could even reinforce the today's differences between domains in UASs, since the new sectors will be faced to much more difficult conditions for the development of research than in technology.

Thus, the key issue for UAS research in the next years will be to find a balance between the convergence tendencies and the need of developing a specific profile inside Swiss higher education in order to compete with stronger institutions; while in the past this differentiation was successfully promoted by regulatory intervention of the state, in the future it will be more and more left to the strategic decision of the actors themselves. Stronger differentiation between the UASs themselves is likely to occur in this respect.

References

Arvanitis, S., Kubli, U., Sydow, N., & Wörter, M. (2005). *Knowledge and technology transfer (KTT) activities between universities and firms in Switzerland: The main facts.* Zurich: KOF-ETHZ.

BBT. (2002). *Die Schweiz im weltweiten innovationswettbewerb.* Bern: Innovationsbericht.

BBT. (2007). Masterplan Fachhochschulen 2008–2011, Bern.

Commission fédérale des HES. (2002). *HES 2002.* Rapport sur la création des Hautes écoles spécialisées suisses, Berne.

Conseil fédéral. (1992). *Technologiepolitik des Bundes.* Bern 1992.

Conseil fédéral. (1994). *Message du Conseil fédéral relatif à la loi sur les HES du 30 mai 1994.* Berne.

Conseil fédéral. (1997). *Message sur le financement de mesures de la Commission pour la technologie et l'innovation visant à créer, dans les hautes écoles spécialisées, les compétences nécessaires en matière de recherche appliquée et de développement durant les années 1998 et 1999 du 6 octobre 1997.* Berne.

Conseil fédéral. (2007). *Loi fédérale sur l'aide aux hautes écoles et la coordination dans le domaine suisse des hautes écoles LAHE projet.* Berne, September 2007.

Département fédéral de l'intérieur. (2004). Rapport sur la refondation du paysage suisse des hautes écoles, Berne.

de Weert, E. (2006). *Professional competencies and research in the non-university sector: Systems convergence after Bologna?* Paper presented at the CHER annual conference, Kassel, 7–9 September 2006.

Filippini, M., & Lepori, B. (2007). Cost structure, economies of capacity utilization and scope in Swiss higher education institutions. In A. Bonaccorsi & C. Daraio (Eds.), *Universities and strategic knowledge creation* (pp. 272–305). Cheltenam: Edward Elgar.

KFH. (2005). *Forschung und Entwicklung an Fachhochschulen.* Bern: Grundsatzpapier.

Kyvik, S. (2004). Structural changes in higher education systems in Western Europe. *Higher Education in Europe,* 29, 393–409.

Lepori, B. (2006). *La politique de la recherche en Suisse. Institutions, Acteurs et Dynamique Historique.* Bern: Haupt.

Lepori, B. (2007a). Patterns of diversity in the Swiss higher education system. In A. Bonaccorsi & C. Daraio (Eds.), *Universities and strategic knowledge creation* (pp. 209–240). Cheltenam: Edward Elgar.

Lepori, B. (2007b). *Funding models of universities of applied sciences.* Report on behalf of the Rector's conference of Swiss universities of applied sciences, Lugano.

Lepori, B. (2008). Research in non-university higher education institutions. The case of the Swiss universities of applied sciences. *Higher Education.*

Lepori, B., & Attar, L. (2006). *Research strategies and framework conditions for research in Swiss universities of applied sciences.* Report to the Federal Office of Professional Education and Technology, Lugano.

Mayer, S., Sturn, D., & Zellweger, E. (2006). *Evaluierung des Kompetenzaufbaus für angewandte FuE an Fachhochschulen durch die KTI/CTI 1998–2004,* Wien-Bern.

Nightingale, P., & Martin, B. (2000). Introduction. In P. Nightingale & B. Martin (Eds.), *The political economy of science, technology and innovation* (pp. XIIIss). Cheltenam: Edward Elgar.

OCDE. (1989). *Politiques nationales de la science et de la technologie. Suisse.* Paris: OECD.

OECD. (2003). *Tertiary education in Switzerland*. Paris: OECD.
Perellon, J. F. (2001). The governance of higher education in a federal country. The case of Switzerland. *Tertiary Education and Management, 7*, 211–224.
Perellon, J. F. (2003). The creation of a vocational sector in Swiss higher education: Balancing trends of system differentiation and integration. *European Journal of Education, 38*, 357–370.
Stokes, D. (1997). *Pasteur's quadrant. Basic science and technological innovation*. Washington, DC: Brookings Institutions Press.

Part IV
Conclusion

Chapter 14
Sitting in the Middle: Tensions and Dynamics of Research in UASs

Benedetto Lepori and Svein Kyvik

Introduction

As shown in Chapter 1, most European countries now have a binary higher education system consisting of a university sector and a sector constituted predominantly by multi-faculty institutions offering primarily professional and vocational study programmes at a bachelor's level. While the universities have a very long tradition for undertaking research and research training, and the knowledge about the organisation and outcome of these tasks in these institutions is fairly good, the role of research within polytechnic institutions has largely been bypassed in the international literature on higher education. The purpose of this book accordingly has been to provide information on the research mission of higher education institutions outside the universities in a selection of European countries, to examine why and how research has become a task for these institutions and to discuss the challenges facing governments and polytechnics in their aim to enhance research activity in this part of the educational system.

A first observation is that this issue is high on the political agenda in all considered countries; thus, in all of them national policies state that universities of applied sciences (UASs) should have the right to perform research and that, without some research, these are not rightly part of higher education. Although most vocationally oriented institutions were created without a research mission, this is now an integral part of their being. In countries like Finland and Switzerland, which established a higher education sector outside the university sector more recently, the UASs received from the onset an explicit research mandate.

A second observation is that there are large differences between European countries and between institutions within countries to the extent that the UASs have developed research as an important part of their tasks alongside teaching. Norway, Finland and Switzerland have a much stronger developed research base in the UAS sector than Belgium and The Netherlands, not to mention the Czech Republic.

B. Lepori (✉)
Faculty of Economics, Centre for Organizational Research, University of Lugano,
Lugano, Switzerland
e-mail: blepori@unisi.ch

S. Kyvik, B. Lepori (eds.), *The Research Mission of Higher Education Institutions*
Outside the University Sector, Higher Education Dynamics 31,
DOI 10.1007/978-1-4020-9244-2_14, © Springer Science+Business Media B.V. 2010

A third observation is that there are differences between programmes or domains in research emphasis. In most of the countries, engineering and technology programmes have a much stronger research orientation than programmes in nursing, teacher training, social work, art and design, etc. This pattern, however, does not apply to all countries; Norway is probably the country which differs most from the overall picture, with a much more even distribution of research resources across the various programmes.

A fourth observation is that relatively few UAS staff members are active in research. Even in Norway, where the majority of staff members undertake some kind of research, approximately 10% of the staff account for half of all scientific and scholarly publications.

Both the national case studies and the thematic chapters demonstrate that it is one thing to develop (or to get acknowledged) a generic status as a research institution, but another thing to truly develop research in a context where universities and public research organisations have long-established research traditions. Thus, reports from polytechnic institutions are full of complaints about lack of financial resources, shortage of human resources and discriminating behaviour by research allocation bodies which impede UASs from taking on their full role as research institutions. Beyond the political nature of such complaints, they express largely the tensions to which UASs themselves are exposed from the recognition of a research mandate.

These include questions related to the balance between education and research, qualifications of staff and the internal organisation of research activities. The basic underlying issue concerns, however, the positioning of the UAS in the whole higher education system, once the simple divide between teaching-only and research institutions has been removed. As we shall come back to, this issue is closely related to the structuring of the higher education system and to the balance between functional specialisation and vertical stratification as organising principles of the system (Bleiklie, 2008). Thus, the different approaches in the examined countries concerning the development of research in UASs largely reflect the relative emphasis of these principles in each national political and cultural context.

This concluding chapter is organised in three main sections. First, we will present an overview of the main findings of the book, focusing especially on the differences between countries, but also between programmes and individual institutions. Second, we will analyse the driving forces in the development of research by looking back and discussing the model presented in the introduction. Finally, we will frame research in the overall evolution of the higher education system in a comparative perspective and, on this basis, discuss the main open issues and critical choices which are likely to shape the future of research in these institutions.

Where Do We Stand Now? A Status of Research in UASs

When looking at the data provided in some of the chapters, as well as at some qualitative judgements, it seems that the euphoria about research in UASs should be somewhat dampened. In the considered countries, UASs are at best a minor actor

Table 14.1   UAS R&D expenditures and public R&D expenditures

	Belgium	Germany	Ireland	The Netherlands	Finland	Norway	Switzerland
Year	2005	2005	2006	2005	2004	2007	2007
R&D exp. € million	57.7	674	33	82	100	150	217
% of R&D exp. in the public sector[a]	3%	4.1%	4.8%	2.3%	6.5%	7.2%	9.5%
% funding from core budget	20%	45%	0%	19%	25%	79%	62%

[a]Sum of the expenditures in the State, Higher Education and non-profit sector.
Source: Eurostat and country chapters for UAS data. No data available on Czech Republic, but R&D expenditures are probably very low.

in the public research system and in many of them a marginal one. Thus, UASs account at best for 12% of R&D expenditures in higher education (Norway) and for less than 10% of total research expenditures in the public sector (including Public Research Organisations) in all the considered countries (see Table 14.1). These figures should be compared with a share of first-year enrolment in higher education ranging between 70% in The Netherlands and 30% in Germany (see Chapter 1). A look at the share of R&D of total expenditures in higher education provides a similar picture: the little data available on UASs provides figures slightly above 10% for the most developed countries and even lower in the other countries, compared to typical figures of between 40 and 50% in universities. Clearly, despite the research mandate, the share and the priority-setting between research and education differ widely between the two sectors and, as we shall discuss later, this has profound implications both for the development of research in UASs and for the relationship between the two sectors.

Moreover, all indicators show that, with a few exceptions, UASs are weak competitors with universities for all types of funding, including those which should be of a better fit for them, like funding from innovation agencies and private contracts (see Chapter 4). In these respects, there are only a few exceptions like Swiss UASs, which are now the main recipients of funding from the Swiss innovation agency.

The same holds true for research outputs: information presented in national chapters shows that UAS staff have relatively few publications compared to university staff, and the number of technological products like patents is also much lower. Of course, one has to acknowledge the methodological difficulties of measuring the output of applied research and that most existing measurement schemes focus on scholarly publications (Deen & Vossensteyn, 2006), but it is unlikely that the picture would change significantly using other indicators.

These remarks are not to deny the symbolic and cultural value of the recognition of a research mandate, but to explain the amount of tensions implicated by it in the face of a largely different reality and to recognise the different types of strategies actors can mobilise to cope with it. Those shown by the national chapters include the forced development of research capacity (Switzerland), attempts at upgrading their status by the accreditation as universities (Ireland, Norway), the building of partnerships with universities (Belgium), or more mimetic behaviours like broadening the perimeter of the institution (Czech Republic), or of what is considered as research (a pattern emerging in most countries).

Moreover, the national cases indicate that research activities in UASs have undergone a significant growth over the last decade. This development can, however, be interpreted in different ways. Thus, some might argue that the continuation of this process is likely to transform some units of UASs into strong research actors in a few years (see, for example, Verhoeven, Chapter 6). Others could interpret it as developing something from almost no research and that the real issues and limitations – for example, in terms of funding and human resources, but also of competition with universities – are likely to emerge once some threshold has been reached.

Yet, this helicopter picture hides in reality profound differences in the extent and function of research between countries, institutions, programmes and individuals, which are much larger than those we find in universities (at least outside strongly stratified systems like in the United States or in the UK). In the following section, we therefore will look more in-depth into the internal diversity in the UAS sector, because this issue is closely linked to the discussion on specialisation and integration that we will develop in the last part of this chapter.

National Differences in Models and Functions of Research in UASs

In this survey, we can broadly distinguish between three groups of countries, those where research activities are already well-established and considered as an important part of UAS activities (Finland, Norway, Switzerland), those which are still largely in an experimental phase (Belgium, the Czech Republic, the Netherlands) and those which come in a middle position (Ireland, Germany).

In the first group, which includes Finland, Norway and Switzerland, not only the relative size of research expenditures is higher than in the rest of the countries considered, but research has become institutionalised as part of institutional strategies, and UASs are explicitly recognised as research actors at a national level (Norway and Switzerland being the clearest examples). Moreover, some basic features of research in these institutions and of their positioning in respect to universities can be identified (see the discussion below). Official recognition of research functions implies also that rather detailed data on R&D activities of UASs and their funding sources are routinely produced in the higher education statistics, like in Finland (data compiled by Statistics Finland), in Switzerland (data from the Swiss Federal Statistical Office) and in Norway (data from NIFU STEP). This partly applies to Ireland and Germany, while in Belgium, the Netherlands and the Czech Republic, the data is much more incomplete.

In the latter group of countries, the research function of UASs is on the political agenda, and there is no longer a formal exclusion of these institutions from research activities, but the extent of research is much lower and confined to a relatively small segment of the staff.

It is important to recognise that UASs in the three groups of countries are faced with rather different issues. Thus, while in the latter group, the main issue is to build from scratch some research capacity, institutions in the first group of countries increasingly face issues of consolidation and of priority-setting, once the volume of research has exceeded a certain threshold. These include the balance between regional commitments and participation in national and international research networks (see Chapter 2), the relationship between education and research (see Chapter 3), the development of research profiles and finding resources in the core budget for research (see Chapter 4), and, finally, the systematic build-up of research competence (see Chapter 5).

However, differences between countries cannot just be reduced to evolutionary stages, depending on when UASs started to develop research and on the level of support they got from the state. In addition, structural differences concerning the extent and the function of research in UASs are emerging. At least two basic models seem to emerge, which can be represented by the extreme cases of Norway on the one side and of Switzerland and Finland on the other side.

In the first model, the rationale for developing research is mostly sought in the improvement of the quality of professional education through enhanced research qualifications of teachers. Thus, research and research resources should be spread evenly among the programmes in the institutions, either as a part of the core budget (Norway) or as specific allotment for curricula improvement (Belgium). Actually, the official policy goals for UAS research in these countries also include regional relevance and knowledge transfer, but the purpose of improving the quality of professional education seems to get more attention.

In the second model, the main policy rationale for developing research in UASs has to be sought in the support to the regional economy and the improvement of knowledge transfer, especially towards small and medium enterprises. Being more customer-driven, research should be essentially funded through external contracts or incentive programmes for cooperation with private companies, a distinguishing feature of the Finnish and Swiss system. Accordingly, some concentration of research is required to achieve critical mass; the Dutch *lectorate* programme being a good example of this approach. Of course, there is some idea that, once research units have been established, research will spread throughout the whole institution and benefit also education, but this is largely considered a second step in the process.

These two models have different implications for the positioning of UASs in the whole higher education system, and this might lead to largely different configurations of the whole system (see the concluding section of this chapter).

A Very Differentiated Internal Landscape

A discussion in terms of national models can be somewhat incorrect since most national case studies show a strong internal differentiation in the non-university sector itself concerning the development of research. Moreover, the prevailing line of differentiation differs across countries – respectively between institutions, between programmes and between individuals – and this is likely to have wide-ranging implications for the future structure of the system.

Thus, in some countries we witness strong distinctions between individual UASs, with some of them not only having a much higher share of research activities (strong concentration in a few UASs is shown, for example, in Belgium and Ireland), but some UASs also strive to achieve a status nearer to universities and distinct from the rest of the UAS sector. Typical cases are the Dublin Institute of Technology, as well as the two Norwegian university colleges that got the accreditation to universities. In countries like Finland, Netherlands and Switzerland there is a strong sense of collective development of UAS specific research activities according to the notion 'equal but different' to universities. In these countries, UAS rectors conferences took an active role in developing joint objectives and strategies for research, or even took a role in allocating research funding (like the HBO-Raad in the Netherlands for the *lectorate* programme). Of course, the extent of research is likely to be different among individual UASs, but what matters here is this collective understanding of their research mission, which is likely to have profound influences on the resulting system configuration.

A second, much less investigated distinction is between programme sectors. The little available data displays, for some of the countries, a strong concentration of the research volume in engineering and technology; this is the case in Belgium and Germany, where engineering accounts for half of the research volume, and for Switzerland, where the available data shows a very strong concentration in technological sectors and extreme differences in the share of R&D expenditures by sectors, from 25% in technology to less than 5% in some domains of social sciences. On the contrary, in Norway half of the R&D expenditures are in the social sciences domain, which account for a large share of students, an expected outcome given the stronger link between education and research. The prevalence of engineering and technology in the former countries likely reflects the orientation towards application and transfer to SMEs of research in UASs (see Chapter 2). This internal differentiation raises the question to what extent UASs might be able to develop a single concept and strategy of research when faced with selective requests from their environment. For instance, the main Swiss economic association (*Economiesuisse*) clearly stated that research in Swiss UASs should be developed only in technical sectors, leaving social sciences and humanities as teaching-only domains. Since mergers and reorganizations have been more common in the non-university sector than in the university sector, one cannot exclude that these differences will lead to new institutional configurations, for example, splitting research-strong departments from the rest of these institutions.

The third differentiation concerns organisational integration of research activities and their distribution between individual staff members. All the available information shows that research activities are strongly concentrated in a few people receiving most of the third-party funding. This pattern is expected since research competences are also concentrated in the few people with past research experience, as witnessed by the overall low share of teachers with a PhD degree, while in all countries UASs inherit a large stock of teachers with little or no research competence. This concentration policy has been explicitly reinforced through public policies, like in the case of the Dutch *lectorates*. The central issue concerns, however, the future development path from this starting situation; will this lead to a dual career structure, with research professors and senior research staff concentrated in research units alongside a large number of lecturers (with no research competence)? Or will research activities progressively diffuse throughout the whole personnel and organisational structure?

At the organisational level, UASs seem to have taken different routes in the integration of research: the extreme case is in UASs where most research activities are concentrated in a single centre (see the example of Lahti UAS in Finland). In many countries the approach of creating distinct research units inside institutions or departments prevails (Switzerland being a typical case), while in other countries this varies greatly between individual UASs.

Of course, one can find good arguments for both strategies. Cumulative effects in research are likely to push in the first direction, since the units with research traditions will be able to attract more qualified personnel and third-party funding; at the same time, normative pressures are more likely to push towards diffusion of research, as well as to avoid dual internal careers and to limit internal differences among staff. It is likely that the balance will critically depend not only on national environments, for example, the degree of competitiveness for research funding where customer-driven models will generate stronger internal differentiation, but also on the strength of the UASs themselves as strategic actors able to promote a relatively unitary research culture throughout the institution.

Driving Forces and Important Actors

In the introduction of this book, we put forward a simple model to explain the development of research in UASs as the interaction between the internal dynamics of the institutions themselves and four types of external actors: state authorities, supranational organisations, societal stakeholders and the university sector. Now, it is relevant to look more in-depth at the role of these actors, as well as to differences between countries.

Integration Through International Standards: Bologna and Beyond

International organisations seem to have played a rather limited role in the development of research in the UAS sector. However, in most of the countries analysed in this book, the OECD undertook in the recent years reviews of the whole tertiary education sector, or specific reviews of the non-university sector (like in Finland; OECD, 2003). According to most national chapters, in most cases OECD experts clearly supported the binary policy and the need of keeping a distinction between the two sectors, but at the same time indicated the importance of research in UASs for the development of a knowledge society and pointed to the gap between official declarations and ambitions and the actual state of research (see the cases of Finland and Ireland).

A much stronger driving force has been the harmonisation of degrees through the introduction of the so-called Bologna model (de Weert, 2006; Witte, van der Wende, & Huisman, 2008). In most of the countries considered in this book, UASs have switched to a 3-year bachelor diploma and have obtained the right to offer master studies; although to a limited extent.

The Bologna Process is impacting research in UASs in two directions: First, the harmonisation of degrees is pushing towards integration of the two sectors and, thus, to some extent, reinforces the rights of UASs to develop their own research. Second, offering master degrees puts higher requirements on the competences of the teachers and, in many cases, requires some research capacity, either because of the needed competences to teach some subjects or because of official regulations and accreditation requirements (like in Belgium, the Czech Republic, Norway and Switzerland).

Moreover, diffusion of practices between countries seems to have played an important role in the development of research. Visits to other countries to look at their strategies in the development of research seem to have taken place rather frequently, while recently the European Commission in the Lifelong Learning Programme has funded a network on professional education and research at the UASs coordinated by the Dutch HBO-Raad (de Weert & Soo, 2009). Beyond their practical value, it seems that these exchanges are meant to reinforce the identity and collective sense-making of the UAS sector when faced at a national level with a much stronger university sector in terms of research.

The State as a Driving Force for Research in UASs

The national chapters provide an unequivocal result in this respect; in many countries, the state has been a major actor in promoting research in UASs and defining its directions. The analysis of funding models offers some interesting clues to look at national variations in this respect; thus, two categories of countries emerge (see Chapter 4).

The first category is constituted by countries where the state took a strong proactive role, not only providing most of resources of research through specific schemes, but also used these measures to orient research activities in a specific direction. We include in this category the Netherlands with the *lector* programme; Switzerland, where the research mandate has been attributed to UASs by their founding law, and active organisational and funding measures have been introduced from the beginning; and Finland with the strong focus on the regional functions of UASs. Belgium could be considered as sitting in an intermediate position between this group and the second one.

In terms of the policy rationale and cultural norms, it seems that in these countries a coherent rationale for a specific role of UASs in research has been elaborated jointly by the state, by the UAS sector itself and by societal stakeholders (especially representatives of the private sector), which are able to promote a coherent action between these actors, especially between ministries, funding agencies, UAS associations and the UASs themselves. This coalition of values and interests seems to be sufficiently strong to build an alternative to the academic values and support a specific representation of research in UASs, as is evident from the case of the Netherlands and, especially, Switzerland.

The second category is constituted by countries where the development of research was promoted internally to the UASs themselves through the reallocation of parts of the core budget and, then, official policy followed by recognising explicitly the research mission and the right of using the core budget for research (Norway), but without developing a specific policy and active measure to develop research in UASs (the Czech Republic, Germany and Ireland).

In these countries, the rationale for developing research in UASs is weaker and exposes much more these institutions to the normative pressure of the academic sector. As a result, most policy measures also resulted in granting to UASs some of the rights and conditions of universities, for example, the same personnel status, the right to use core funding for research and the right to award doctorates and/or to become accredited as universities when fulfilling some conditions (this is the case in Norway and the Czech Republic, while also in Ireland some UASs have been granted the right to award doctorates). Significantly, the national chapters explicitly signal that in some of these countries the lack of tailored policies addressing the specific conditions of UASs is a major issue (see the Irish and Czech case), a remark which emerged also for the UK polytechnics where some observers argued that promoting a specific research profile would have been a better strategy than just integrating them in the university sector (Pratt, 1997).

Unfortunately, the national case studies provide little information on the forces behind these different policies. At least in the Swiss case, a decisive factor was the perceived shortcomings of the Swiss technological and innovation policy, which was traditionally built on a clear functional separation between public and private research, meeting the requirements of the research-intensive sectors like the pharmaceutical industry, but not at the same level those of small and medium enterprises and machine industry. This suggests that societal stakeholders can be decisive actors in promoting the development of a specific rationale for research in UASs and their role largely depends on the (perceived) ability of the university sector to meet their needs. However, this issue would clearly deserve more careful comparative analysis.

Coping with the Big Brother: The Relationships with Universities

It is more than obvious that to develop their research activities UASs need also to define their position and relationship with the university sector. The issue has both practical aspects – for example, competing on research funding, organising research careers, etc. – and institutional aspects, thus defining the specific profile and role of UASs and legitimating the emergence of a new research actor and the request for public resources for it. Moreover, it involves directly the two sectors, but also norms and actions of other actors like the state or private enterprises which might legitimate and support different strategies.

Many of these issues have been already discussed in the previous sections. Summarising, we can distinguish between three different models; (a) distinction and complementary roles, (b) integration, and (c) partnership.

Distinction and Complementary Roles

A specific rationale and model for research in UASs is elaborated and accepted by the institutions themselves and by the social actors. This includes a definition of research in UASs as distinct from universities – based on notions like applied research and knowledge transfer, and on policy rationales like Mode 2 research and 'triple helix', as well as on an explicit or implicit criticism of universities as an 'ivory tower' disconnected from economic and social reality. This political discourse largely underpins the development of research in UASs, but it makes a strong difference to which extent social actors in each country endorse their criticism to their own universities.

This model has also relevant strategic and practical implications. First, to become like universities is not an explicit goal and even the right to award doctorates is a rather secondary goal. Also, UASs strive to occupy specific niches and functions in the research system not well covered by universities, like cooperation with SMEs. The availability of these niches depends strongly on contextual factors. Thus, Swiss UASs were strongly favoured by the fact that in this country technological research is concentrated in the two Federal Institutes of Technology which have a much stronger international focus. Finally, there is an effort to develop their own organisational form and career structures, as displayed by the case of Netherlands with the *lectorate* programme and Switzerland – where UASs employ UAS professors with distinct qualifications different from university professors. Since the functions are different, there are no strong reasons to harmonise legal requirements and funding systems, even though there might be a single higher education act, like in the Netherlands.

The strength of this model is to allow UASs to build a specific profile which protects them also from competition from the big brother; Finland and Switzerland are clear success cases in this respect. The weakness is that when the whole higher education system becomes more integrated, different rules might make collaboration more difficult and distort competition (for example, for research funding).

Integration

In this model, university status and research build the reference also for UASs. This is clearly expressed by the request to get the right to award doctorates, the creation of accreditation mechanisms where UASs can legally become universities upon fulfilling certain requirements (Norway, the Czech Republic) and the set-up of similar career structures and funding mechanisms as universities. Thus the difference between universities and UASs concerning research is a matter of degree – having less trained research personnel, less resources – and not of type. The attraction of the university status is strong enough to compromise the collective identity of UASs, with some of them changing status individually.

In normative terms, while the first model builds on a stylised representation of university research as being directed towards fundamental research and separated from practice, this model is based on a broader vision where the diversity and complexities of the university world are acknowledged – including large areas of professional education and applied research and the impossibility of drawing a clear separation between basic and applied research. While integrated into the university world, this plurality still leaves UASs the opportunity to stress their specific role as focused on regions and professions, however as an alternative to the traditional academic value system rather than in opposition to it.

The national case studies display that in all countries conforming to this model – Norway, Ireland and the Czech Republic – UASs tend to become the little brother of universities, with little chance of achieving a similar share of research (see the Czech case). However, their fate depends largely on the overall governance of higher education. Where public policies strongly support stratification among universities, UASs tend to end in the lower tail with limited possibilities of improvement; like for the UK polytechnics (Stiles, 2000). In countries with more equalitarian approaches, where some competition is introduced but there is still a logic of giving all institutions a chance to become a research university, more mixing between the two groups might occur in the long run.

Partnership

Finally, the Belgian case is very specific in this context since the research strategy of UASs is largely based on the creation of formal partnerships with universities, especially in Flanders through the establishment of associations between UASs and universities. This has been motivated by the government as a policy to help UASs to meet the accreditation criteria for their academic educational stream, but can have wider implications given the imbalance of forces between the partners. Thus, transferring academic curricula and research from UASs to universities and merging parts of UASs into universities could be an outcome (as explicitly stated by the university rectors in the Flemish community).

This approach displays also some implications of a different configuration of public policies. In conditions of strong imbalance, for example, concerning staff competences, if accreditation criteria are applied to activities (programmes or research activities) instead of to institutions, the activities that meet these criteria might be moved to other institutions, thus reinforcing the binary divide.

Conclusion: Between Functional Specialisation and Integration

The analysis in this chapter displays the limitations of the academic drift model in interpreting the development of research in the non-university sector and the need to substitute it with a more refined approach. Academic drift certainly is an adequate description of the aggregate phenomenon, where UASs have strived to acquire some of the basic features of the university sector, especially the right to perform research activities. The two sectors also have become increasingly integrated in what is now considered in most countries a single higher education system, subject in many cases to a single act and to some common rules. Besides the development of research, the harmonisation of curricula promoted by the Bologna Reform has been a decisive factor promoting this evolution. These processes do not, however, necessarily imply that UASs will develop into traditional universities by expanding their research function (Lepori & Kyvik, 2010).

Furthermore, providing UASs with a research mandate and integrating them into the higher education system does not mean that necessarily all distinctions disappear in favour of a pure hierarchical ordering. Depending on national constellations, the research mandate can be mobilised to promote functional specialisation towards some specific niches – like cooperation with SMEs – or convergence towards the academic model thus strengthening vertical differentiation also in systems where universities have been considered largely equal in the past.

In fact, this process was largely enabled by the blurring of the borders between the two sectors, which opened all kinds of intermediate options between the two extremes of being completely different and of complete integration, like focusing on a specific type of research, or on a set of customers or redefining to some extent what is considered as research. The reader should appreciate the subtlety and ambiguity of the distinction between UAS research and university research, where, despite all attempts to characterise the specific UAS role in research, some level of overlap is functional to the recognition of UASs as research institutions.

Finally, these distinctions assume normative force which can structure the system when they are recognised by sufficiently powerful coalitions of actors, which see also their interests well served by them. The Swiss case, where some branches of the private economy assumed a key role in establishing the UAS research mission, with a strong coalition between the economics ministry (in opposition to the internal affairs ministry, ruling universities) and regional authorities, is an excellent example of this. This is also a major difference between the new emerging organisation of higher education and the old binary systems; the latter have been essentially based on state authority, while today's functional specialisation is, to a large extent, sustained by actors' coalitions and stable relationships, for example, those emerging between UASs and some specific customers like SMEs. The latter was static, with the only possible choice between binary and unitary systems, while the former is more dynamic and open to new developments.

In conclusion, it seems unlikely from the national cases presented in this book that research in UASs will converge to some common model between European countries, or that it will become not distinguishable from universities everywhere. We would rather expect different evolutionary paths largely related to specific national factors, but also to history; where the formal distinction between universities and UASs could become less relevant, but functional distinctions could be nonetheless well-present. It might be that progressively a few models emerge, as we attempted to point out in this concluding chapter, but the process is still in most countries in a too early stage to identify them unambiguously.

These remarks lead to some relevant implications both for research in the field and for policy-making. Research on higher education clearly needs to take fully into account their embeddedness in national systems and to go from simple national descriptions towards the development of a framework allowing a more systematic classification and comparison of national systems. A more systematic use of concepts and tools from organisational and institutional theory would be extremely helpful in this respect. For policymaking, our results imply that there is no unique recipe for developing research in UASs nor is transfer of the models of other countries necessarily a viable solution. Rather what is required is a careful analysis of its own system, of its strength and weaknesses, but also of the kind of solutions which are culturally acceptable in each national context. What comparative research can do is to analyse compatibilities and interdependencies between the different choices and to display the palette of available solutions. We hope that this book provides some progress in this direction.

References

Bleiklie, I. (2008). *Excellence and the diversity of higher education systems*. Paper presented ad the 21st CHER annual conference, Pavia.
Deen, J., & Vossensteyn, H. (2006). Measuring performance of applied R&D: A study into performance measurement of applied R&D in the Netherlands and some other countries, CHEPS, University of Twente.
Lepori, B., & Kyvik, S. (2010). The research mission of Universities of Applied Sciences and the future configuration of higher education systems in Europe. *Higher Education Policy, forthcoming*.
de Weert, E. (2006). *Professional competencies and research in the non-university sector: Systems convergence after Bologna?* Paper presented at the CHER annual conference, Kassel, 7–9 September 2006.
de Weert, E., & Soo, M. (2009). *Research at universities of applied sciences in Europe. Conditions, achievements and perspectives*. Enschede: CHEPS, University of Twente.
OECD. (2003). *Polytechnic education in Finland. 2003. Reviews of national policies for education*. Paris: OECD.
Pratt, J. (1997). *The polytechnic experiment 1965–1992*. Buckingham: Society for Research into Higher Education & Open University Press.
Stiles, D. (2000, October–December). Higher education funding patterns since 1990: A new perspective. *Public Money and Management*, pp. 51–57.
Witte, J., van der Wende, M., & Huisman, J. (2008). Blurring boundaries: How the Bologna process changes the relationship between university and non-university higher education in Germany, the Netherlands and France. *Studies in Higher Education, 33*, 217–231.

Author Index

A
Aasland, T., 47
Altbach, P. G., 78
Amaral, A., 17, 64
Andresani, G., 64
Andriessen, D., 214
Arbo, P., 25–26, 39
Arvanitis, S., 245
Attar, L., 17, 78, 238, 240, 245
Augusti, G., 52

B
Barnett, R., 49
Barro, R., 29
Bartelse, J., 77
Becher, T., 12, 49
Benneworth, P., 25–26, 29, 39
Benninghoff, M., 62
Berrell, M., 83
Beuselinck, I., 80
Blackman, T., 51
Bland, C., 78, 88
Blažek, J., 129
Bleiklie, I., 260
Boezerooy, P., 67
Bonaccorsi, A., 17
Boon, A., 99
Borgdorff, H., 204
Boyer, E. L., 132
Bradbeer, J., 51
Bradley, D., 31
Brew, A., 49
Bricall, J. M., 4
Brint, S., 45
Bührer, S., 161
Bulterman-Bos, J. A., 55
Burgess, T., 9
Buursink, J., 25

C
Čerych, L., 117
Carlsten, T. C., 52
Charles, D., 31
Clark, B. R., 12, 65
Collins, R., 10
Conlon, T., 182
Cooke, P., 26, 29
Cools, W., 97
Cousin, G., 51–52
Coy, D., 78
Coy, M., 192

D
Daraio, C., 17
Davies, P., 55
Davis, K., 30
de Lourdes Machado, M., 80
de Weert, E., 3, 77, 81–83, 199–217, 241,
    253, 266
De Wit, K., 105
Debackere, K., 102, 110
Deen, J., 261
Dekelver, N., 102
Devos, G., 97
Dewey, J., 152
Dick, B., 54
DiMaggio, P. J., 10
Donovan, J., 193

E
Elen, J., 53
Elzinga, A., 10, 56
Enders, J., 81–83
Eskelinen, H., 30

F
Farnham, D., 78
Ferlie, E., 64

S. Kyvik, B. Lepori (eds.), *The Research Mission of Higher Education Institutions Outside the University Sector,* Higher Education Dynamics 31,
DOI 10.1007/978-1-4020-9244-2, © Springer Science+Business Media B.V. 2010

Ferreira, J. B., 4, 77
File, J., 118, 131
Filippini, M., 252
Fitzgerald, G., 178
Florax, R., 25
Flynn, S., 178
Frans Leijnse, 199–209
Fukuyama, F., 30

G
Garlick, S., 30
Gellert, C., 79, 83
Geuna, A., 64
Gibbons, J. F., 30
Gibbons, M., 9, 13, 54, 56, 90, 152, 203
Goddard, J. B., 30, 31
Graca, M., 80
Graitson, D., 101
Gysen, M., 102, 107, 109, 111

H
Halttunen, J., 149–150
Hammersley, M., 56
Hannibalsson, I., 30
Hargreaves, D. H., 55
Harman, G., 132
Harvie, C., 26
Hattie, J., 49
Hazelkorn, E., 13–14, 17, 77–83, 90, 167–188,
    184
Healey, M., 51
Heggen, K., 45–58
Heitor, M., 9
Hollebosch, B., 105, 109
Hollingsworth, S., 54
Holm, C., 56
Horta, H., 9, 126, 247, 260
Hospers, G. J., 29
Hovdhaugen, E., 81, 224
Huisman, J., 9, 77, 266
Hulst, J., 214
Humes, W., 53
Hyrkkänen, U. 153

J
Janyš, B., 131
Jensen, K., 53
Jerrams, S., 193
Johnstone, D. B., 63
Jónasson, J. T., 4
Jones, G., 79
Jongbloed, B., 25–42, 64
Jordan, D., 187

K
Kahn-Freund, O., 89
Kainulainen, S., 140, 142, 149
Kaiser, F., 62
Karppanen, E., 147–148
Karran, T., 121
Karseth, B., 45–58
Kautonen, M., 143
Käyhkö, R., 147, 150
Kehm, B., 7
Kessl, F., 56
King, H., 51
Koelman, J., 62
Kohoutek, J., 126
Kotila, H., 151
Kroll, H., 161
Kruse, S., 56
Kubli, U., 245
Kulicke, M., 155–174
Kvale, S., 54
Kwiek, M., 131
Kyvik, S., 3–20, 45–58, 67, 81, 89, 219–128,
    230–234, 240, 259–271

L
Labaree, D. F., 55
Langfeldt, L., 224
Laredo, P., 31
Larsen, I. M., 16, 50, 52, 57, 64, 219–227, 230,
    232–234
Lascoumes, P., 64
Lave, J., 54
Le Gales, P., 7
Leijnse, F., 199–209, 214
Lengkeek, N., 79
Lepori, B., 3–20, 61–75, 78, 237–254,
    259–263, 270
Leresche, J. P., 62
Leslie, D. W., 16
Leslie, L., 78
Leszczensky, M., 69–70
Leuven, K. U., 54, 110
Leydesdorff, L., 26
Libotton, A., 52
Lillis, D., 87, 184
Lindsay, R., 51
Lucas, L., 51

M
Maassen, P., 16
Machado, M. L., 4, 77, 80
Machálková, J., 131
Maffioli, F., 52
Margaritis, D., 78

Marginson, S., 78
Marsh, H. W., 49
Martin, B., 242
Martinsen, K., 56
Marttila, L., 143, 150
Maskell, P., 30
Mayer, S., 145
McHenry, P., 26
Meek, V. L., 17, 64
Meeus, W., 52
Melichar, M., 121, 126
Merton, R. K., 10
Moore, G. E., 30
Morgan, K., 26
Mowery, D. C., 33
Moynihan, A., 77–91, 175–196
Možný, I., 131
Musselin, C., 64

N
Naidoo, R., 64
Neave, G., 11
Nelson, R. R., 33
Nerland, M., 56
Neumann, R., 49, 51
Neuvonen-Rauhala, M.-L., 77, 135–153
Newton, C., 127
Nielsen, K., 54
Niemonen, H., 143
Nightingale, P., 242
Norton, B., 177

O
O'Leary, E., 187
Olsen, J. P., 16, 81
Olsen, T. B., 224
Orr, D., 69–70
Otto, H. U., 56

P
Pabian, P., 115–132
Parellada, M., 4
Parry, S., 49
Paton-Saltzberg, R., 51
Pazour, M., 132
Perellon, J. F., 62, 238–241
Peters, M. A., 53
Pike, A., 31
Plummer, P., 30
Pohjola, P., 152
Potts, G., 31
Powell, W. W., 10
Pratt, J., 4, 46, 267
Pratt, M., 78, 87–88

Presley, J. B., 16
Putnam, R., 30

R
Rasmussen, J., 56, 58
Renique, C., 209, 213
Rhoades, G., 78
Rhoades, G. A., 35
Rosa, M. J., 63
Ruffin, M., 78, 88
Ruhland, S., 161

S
Sala-i-Martin, X., 29
Sampat, B. N., 33
Sanderson, A. R., 26
Santiago, R., 4, 77
Saxenian, A., 30
Schimank, U., 65
Schleinkofer, M., 168
Schön, D., 54
Scott, P., 4, 53, 77
Šebková, H., 127
Siegfried, J. J., 26
Šima, K., 68, 121–122, 129
Simons, M., 53
Skilbeck, M., 177, 192
Skodvin, O. J., 221, 228, 230
Skoie, H., 46
Slaughter, S., 78
Slipersaeter, S., 66
Smolders, C., 97, 109
Sojka, M., 127
Soo, M., 3, 266
Sörlin, S., 196
Sousa, S., 80
Spruyt, E., 102
Stahlecker, T., 155–174
Stiles, D., 64, 68, 75, 269
Stjernø, S., 16, 47
Stokes, D., 55, 204, 243
Strehl, F., 63, 66
Sturn, D., 245
Sydow, N., 245

T
Tan, B., 102
Taylor, J. S., 30, 77, 81–82
Taylor, M., 4, 80
Teichler, U., 4, 7, 83
Teixeira, P. N., 63
Thornhill, D., 191
Trow, M., 35
Trowler, P. R., 12

Trowler, P., 48
Turner, N., 51

U
Uhlíř, D., 129

V
Välimaa, J., 77, 82, 135–145
van der Sijde, P., 31–32
van der Vos, J., 204
Van Dyck, D., 102
Van Looy, B., 101
Van Looy, L., 52
Van Pelt, S., 102
Van Ryssen, S., 102, 105, 109, 111
van Staa, A., 204
van Weert, T., 214
Vandenbroucke, F., 100
Velghe, J., 98, 109
Verhoeven, J. C., 77, 80, 97–113
Verstraete, A., 109
Vesterinen, M. L., 142
Veugelers, R., 102, 110
Vickerman, R. W., 29

Vinš, V., 127
von Bell, K., 143
Vossensteyn, H., 62–63, 261
Vroomans, L., 214

W
Walshe, J., 178
Wareham, T., 48
Wedgwood, M., 132
Wenger, E., 54
White, T., 176
Winnes, M., 65
Wissenschaftsrat, 159
Witte, J., 266
Wörter, M., 245
Wuetherick, B., 51
Wuyts, A., 102

Z
Zamorski, B., 51
Zellweger, E., 245
Ziedonis, A. A., 33
Zimmermann, A., 161
Zwerts, E., 105, 109

Subject Index

A

Academic
achievements, 12
ambitions, 86–87, 89, 119, 177, 188, 191, 194, 208, 220, 266
authority, 12
career, 81, 126, 195, 233
community, 8–9, 12
courses, 99
degree, 112
direction, 130
discipline, 56, 132, 199, 235
drift, 9, 105, 270
environment, 31
fields, 220
identities, 27–28, 191
institutions, 234
d, 10, 56, 83, 107, 121, 125, 160, 173, 184, 247,
knowledge, 12
level, 5, 16–19, 46, 49–53, 77–78, 80–81, 102–103, 118–119, 160–161, 164, 171, 173, 210, 212, 265–267, 270
norms, 239
power, 53
practice, 77–91
profession, 78
profile, 57, 78, 80, 163–164, 226, 230, 256, 263
programmes, 112, 156
quality, 33, 46–47, 157, 165, 252, 263
reputation, 81
research, 72, 87, 128, 146, 152–153, 194, 243
staff, 11, 15–16, 18–19, 35, 42, 48, 50–52, 56–58, 78–84, 87–89, 91, 119, 123–127, 130–132, 161, 166, 178, 180, 184, 187–188, 194, 210–213, 216, 220, 222–223, 227–231, 233

stakeholders, 8–9, 12, 49
standards, 12, 102
status, 3, 5, 11, 81, 88, 117–118, 131, 220, 226–227, 233, 251, 260–261, 264, 268–269
studies, 10, 18, 25, 33, 40, 49, 52, 58, 66, 79, 87, 167, 191, 200, 220, 267, 269
system, 41, 47, 81, 90, 98–99, 135, 138, 191
tradition, 152–153
values, 267, 269
work, 52, 78–80, 83, 87, 89, 167, 180–181, 188, 194–195
Academisation, 28, 68, 70, 74, 78, 80, 85, 99–106, 109, 111–113, 232
Australia, 91, 187, 194
Austria, 5
Authority, 17, 176–177, 179, 193, 206, 270

B

Belgium, 3–8, 28–29, 46, 67–70, 72–74, 77–85, 87–89, 97–113, 259, 261–264, 266
Binary, 3–5, 8, 19, 62–63, 66, 68, 89–90, 98, 112, 116, 175–196, 199–202, 216, 220, 234, 237–242, 252–254, 259, 265, 269–270
Bologna Process, 7, 77, 98, 102–103, 105, 109, 111, 156, 172, 195, 266

C

Career, 9–10, 12, 15–16, 20, 46, 51, 77, 79, 81–84, 87–90, 103, 106–109, 112, 125–128, 131, 143–145, 155, 166–168, 187–188, 194–195, 210–212, 222–224, 233, 235, 239, 245, 250, 265, 268–269

College
    community, 8–9, 12, 51–52
    district, 219, 221, 231
    engineering, 3, 6–7, 40, 45, 47, 50, 52,
        82, 101, 109, 148, 156–159, 163,
        219–221, 231, 233–234
    health and social, 148, 234
    nursing, 3, 45–47, 50, 52, 54–57, 79, 82,
        187, 201, 219–220, 234, 260
    professional, 3–4, 6–7, 115–119, 121, 124,
        130–131
    regional, 220
    sector, 4, 119, 121, 130, 219–221, 223,
        228, 232–233
    social work, 3, 6, 45, 79, 131, 219, 248,
        260
    state, 82–83, 219–221, 223, 228, 234
    system, 221
    teacher training, 46, 116
    university, 4, 6–7, 25, 28, 36, 38, 50,
        52, 56–57, 68, 70–72, 78, 81, 83,
        97–115, 131, 184, 219–235, 264
Commercialisation, 14, 139
Conflict
    perspective, 48, 252, 260
    theory, *see* Theory
Consultancy, 14, 32–33, 35, 42, 46, 77, 127,
        129, 176, 208, 213, 216, 248
Coordination
    administrative, 226
    market, 250
    national, 47–48, 121, 139, 200–207,
        221–225
    political, 6
    professional, 104, 142–143
    programme, 117–118
    regional, 196
Credentialism, *see* Theory
Curriculum, 9, 27, 37, 39–40, 42, 49, 51–52,
        151, 157, 171, 179, 205, 211–212,
        233, 253
Czech Republic, 3–8, 14, 27, 46, 67–69, 71,
        73–75, 79, 81–83, 85, 88, 115–132,
        259, 261–262, 266–267, 269

D

Decentralisation
    geographical, 234
    institutional, 227
De-differentiation, institutional, 192
De-diversification, 116
Degree
    bachelor's, 98, 107, 156

    doctoral, 10, 70, 118, 124, 126, 210, 233
    master's, 45, 70, 79, 98–99, 107, 135, 140,
        156, 165, 173, 188, 211–212, 220,
        224, 228, 233
    PhD, 99, 105–106, 212, 264
Differentiation
    institutional, 64, 116, 180, 200
    programme, 90, 116, 243, 253
    stakeholder-driven, 26, 204, 219
Diversification, 78, 116
Doctorate, 126, 131, 155, 160, 167, 172, 177,
        179, 187, 200, 210, 217, 223, 227,
        253, 267–268
Drift
    academic, 9, 105, 270
    of ideas, 149
    institutional, 10
    policy, 11
    programme, 10
    sector, 9–12, 20
    staff, 10
    student, 11

E
Education
    engineering, 3, 234
    expertise, 100, 111, 151, 171–172
    health, 6, 45, 146, 175, 220–221, 224, 231,
        234, 240
    nurse, 16, 54–55, 97
    nursing, 56
    practice, 3, 45–58, 234–235
    programme, 45–49, 118
    school, 4, 117, 241, 249
    social work, 3, 79, 219, 260
    teacher training, 3, 45, 47, 50, 52, 55, 58,
        201, 219–220, 234, 248, 260
    technical, 155, 176, 187
Educational
    institutions, 7, 58
    policy, 58, 118, 121–122, 130–131,
        137–139, 142, 159, 176, 203
Efficiency, 64, 176, 191–192, 229
Equality of opportunity, 219, 250, 269
Europe
    Eastern and Central, 4
    Western, 3–4, 164, 168, 184
European framework, 14, 63, 72, 181
European Union (EU), 3, 9, 13–14, 26, 70, 72,
        78, 82, 98, 127, 129, 140–141, 170,
        175, 178, 181, 225, 229, 232
Explanations
    cultural, 132, 139, 147

interest group, 33
    structural, 8, 35, 71, 129, 138–139, 142,
        158–159, 161, 172–174, 181, 183,
        190, 200–202, 263

F
Fachhochschulen, 6, 25, 28, 67, 70, 72, 77,
        84–85, 155, 163, 243
Field
    coupling, 187
Finland, 3–8, 19, 28–29, 46, 48, 67–69, 71–74,
        77, 79–81, 83–85, 88, 90, 135–137,
        140, 143, 145–150, 259, 261–266,
        268
Flanders, 82, 97–113, 269
Fragmented expansion, 238–239, 241

G
Germany, 3–8, 14, 19, 28–29, 46, 48, 62,
        67–70, 72–75, 77, 79, 81, 83–86,
        88–89, 155, 163, 165–166, 168,
        261–262, 264, 267
Greece, 5

H
Harmonisation, 99, 266, 270
Higher education
    institutions, 3–20, 25–26, 31–32, 36, 41,
        45, 62–64, 75, 77, 115–116, 118,
        120–122, 136, 138–140, 147–148,
        151, 156, 203, 220–224, 229, 233,
        237, 239, 259
    sector, 4, 67, 71, 115–121, 123, 131, 181,
        187, 194, 240, 245, 252, 259
    systems
        binary, 3–4, 8, 98, 63, 112, 175–196,
            234, 238, 270
        dual, 4
        stratified, 262
        unified, 4
        university dominated, 3
Homogenisation, 81
Human capital, 27, 29–30, 40, 42, 91, 175
Human resources, 17, 19, 37, 42, 77–91, 103,
        106–109, 121, 125–127, 143–145,
        160, 166–168, 187–188, 194–195,
        200, 202, 210–212, 216, 247,
        249–250, 260, 262

I
Iceland, 4
Identity, 28, 191, 251, 266, 269
Implementation, 5, 64, 109, 137, 149, 152,
        171, 187, 226, 242–243

Industry, 9–14, 19, 25, 27–28, 32, 34–42, 48,
        52, 100–103, 105–106, 111, 132,
        140, 143–147, 156, 159, 161–163,
        165–167, 169, 176, 182–188,
        190–191, 193, 203–205, 207–210,
        212–214, 229, 232–233, 235, 243,
        250, 267
Innovation, 9, 14–15, 25–26, 28, 30–31, 33,
        35–36, 41–42, 48, 54, 66, 71–73,
        77, 87, 91, 121–122, 129, 131,
        138–139, 141–142, 147–148, 157,
        160–161, 163, 172, 179, 182,
        191, 203–205, 207, 209–210, 212,
        215, 219, 221, 223–224, 232–233,
        238–240, 242–243,245, 261, 267
Institutes of technology, 4, 6–7, 25, 27–28,
        77, 176–177, 182, 190, 193, 239,
        268
Integration
    horizontal, 196
    organisational, 264
    programme, 104
    vertical, 9, 196
Intermediary bodies, 124, 215
International, 4, 11, 13, 16–17, 26, 71–72, 78,
        112, 121, 125, 132, 139, 162, 179,
        181, 185, 191–192, 199–201, 204,
        223, 226, 229, 232, 244, 259, 263,
        265–266, 268
Internationalisation, 29, 148–149, 190, 223,
        228, 231–232
Ireland, 3–8, 27, 29, 46, 67–70, 72–73, 77–89,
        175–196, 261–262, 264, 266–267,
        269
Isomorphism
    coercive, 99
    mimetic, 262
    normative, 64, 206, 245, 265, 267

L
Lisbon, 3, 9, 11, 98, 100, 203

M
Merger, 4, 77, 111–112, 139, 191–192,
        219–220, 234, 241, 251, 264
Mobility, upward, 75
Modernisation, 79

N
Netherlands, 3–8, 13, 19, 25–26, 28–30, 33–38,
        41–42, 46–47, 67–70, 72–73, 77,
        79–81, 83–84, 86–90, 99, 200–201,
        207, 209, 259, 261–262, 264,
        266–268

Network
   building, 149
   infrastructural, 149, 215
   Norway, 232
   organisational, 142
   social, 39
New Public Management, 64
Non-university, 6–7, 9, 46, 50, 61–67, 69,
          115–132, 137–138, 141–142,
          147–150, 157, 159–173, 237, 240,
          253, 263–265, 270
Norway, 3–8, 16, 26, 28–29, 35–38, 45–47,
          52, 67–69, 71–75, 78–82, 84–90,
          219–235, 259–264, 266–267,
          269

O
OECD, 4–5, 8–9, 11, 13–14, 25, 30–31, 41,
          46, 49–51, 55, 61, 64, 67, 91, 118,
          131, 136, 145, 153, 175–176, 179,
          191–193, 200, 209, 215, 221–222,
          230, 234, 239–242, 265

P
Patent, 32, 110–111, 127, 130–131, 168–169,
          185–186, 189, 261
PhD, 29, 42, 45, 80–81, 84–87, 90, 99,
          105–107, 109–110, 143–144, 164,
          167, 174, 177–178, 183, 185, 187,
          191, 193, 202, 210, 212, 220,
          225–227, 233, 235, 249–250, 264
Polytechnics, 4, 10, 14, 25, 28, 46, 48, 68–69,
          77, 81, 84–85, 135–153, 239, 259,
          260, 267, 269
Portugal, 5, 77, 79–84, 88–89
Professional
   associations, 10, 12, 46
   colleges, 4, 6–7, 117, 119, 121, 130–131
   courses, 107, 116, 199, 201
   education, 3, 28, 33, 35, 45, 47, 49, 58, 87,
          115–122, 124, 130–131, 199–200,
          202, 208, 210, 215, 234, 238, 240,
          251–252, 263, 266, 269
   expertise, 100, 111, 171–172
   groups, 34, 46, 106
   organisations, 208–209
   practice, 3, 9, 15, 20, 45–58, 78, 107,
          159, 203–205, 207–208, 214, 216,
          221–224, 226, 234–235
   programmes, 3, 15, 45–49, 53–56, 58,
          117–118, 226, 231, 234–235
   schools, 4, 117, 241, 249
   tradition, 10, 57, 151–152, 191, 203
Professionalization, 38

Programme
   bachelor, 34, 45, 118, 124, 128, 131, 220,
          231
   master, 104
   study, 6–7, 9, 45, 48, 123–124, 126–127,
          148, 201, 220–222, 234, 259
Publication, 32, 37, 78, 80, 106, 110–111,
          124, 127, 130–131, 168, 176,
          178, 185–187, 189, 213–214, 225,
          231–233, 245, 260–261
Publishing, 12, 37, 110, 228, 231, 235

Q
Qualifications, 7, 16, 18–19, 33, 49, 74, 80–81,
          87, 126, 131, 159, 167, 172, 177,
          179, 191–192, 194–196, 202, 208,
          210–212, 216, 227–228, 233–234,
          245, 260, 263, 268
Quality, 18, 27, 33, 36, 40, 46–47, 54–56, 58,
          66, 68, 71, 80, 85–87, 113, 121,
          132, 137–139, 157, 165, 176, 182,
          191, 195, 202, 207–208, 211–212,
          214–216, 221, 223–226, 228–229,
          240, 245–246, 252, 263

R
R&D, 5, 13–14, 29, 35, 48, 67, 69–72, 74,
          85, 91, 100–101, 103, 108, 135,
          138–143, 145–153, 155–161,
          163–174, 181, 183, 186, 189,
          191, 206, 221–222, 229–234, 240,
          243–249, 252, 261–262, 264
Regional
   board, 35–36
   community, 26, 30, 42, 111, 147, 170–171,
          214–215, 233–234
   demands, 16, 40
   innovation policy, 242, 267
   interests, 33
   mission, 25, 27–29
   needs, 3, 28, 138, 222, 233
   network, 30, 34, 157, 170, 215
   policy, 38
   relevance, 25–42, 111, 147, 170–171, 190,
          214, 233, 263
   stakeholders, 5, 11, 13, 19, 26, 31, 35, 219,
          233
Regionalisation, 26, 196
Research
   activities, 3–4, 9–11, 15, 17–20, 26–28, 37,
          42, 46, 51, 53, 55–56, 58, 61–75,
          89–90, 123–125, 127, 129, 146,
          152, 168–169, 179, 182, 185–186,
          189, 203–204, 206, 209, 216, 221,

225–226, 228, 233–234, 237–238, 242–247, 249, 251–252, 259–260, 262, 264–267, 269–270

applied, 5, 9, 13, 20, 25, 27–28, 42, 48, 50, 52, 54, 56–57, 62–63, 68, 77, 90, 100, 112, 129, 137, 140, 155, 161, 170, 174, 179, 190, 193, 204, 206–207, 210, 215, 230, 237–254, 261, 268–269

basic, 13, 55–57, 129, 139, 157, 163, 166, 179, 185–186, 204, 220, 230, 240, 242–243, 247

capacity, 17, 37, 77, 85, 91, 119, 100, 150, 163, 184, 208, 211, 233, 261, 263, 266

collaboration, 37, 103, 129, 132, 232

competence, 15, 18–19, 47, 78–81, 89, 222–224, 226, 228, 233, 243, 245, 249, 251, 263–265

contract, 33, 35, 70, 86, 143, 170, 205

cooperation, 139, 226

council, 11, 14, 36–37, 41, 63, 66, 70–72, 104, 179, 181–182, 205, 224–225, 229, 232

and development, 5, 13, 28, 48, 50, 52, 54, 77, 120–123, 129–131, 135–153, 161, 174, 203, 228, 230, 235, 240, 242

drift, 9–12, 20

environment, 13, 40, 79, 82–86, 88, 90, 204, 232

expenditures, 67, 70, 123, 181, 261–262

funding, 15, 62–66, 68–71, 73–75, 79, 84–86, 97, 100, 102, 104–105, 112–113, 120, 122–124, 126–130, 183, 215, 225, 229, 232, 253, 264–265, 267–268

management, 183–184

mission, 5, 11, 13, 17, 19, 28, 36, 62, 127, 146, 179, 219, 221–222, 238, 259, 264, 267, 270

organisation, 66, 74, 128, 131, 260–261

output, 16, 31, 102, 124, 126–127, 129–130, 184, 213, 229, 261

performance, 91, 98, 110–111, 123, 147–150, 168–172, 178, 181, 184, 187, 189–190, 196, 213–215, 219, 228–229

policy, 19, 89–90, 100–102, 120–122, 124–125, 130–131, 179, 182, 221, 223, 225, 240, 243

resources, 13, 18, 103, 111, 200, 221, 223–224, 228, 248, 250, 260, 263

strategy, 14, 16–19, 102, 131, 141–142, 163–168, 182–188, 207–213, 219, 223, 225–228, 269

Resource dependency, 75

S
School
agricultural, 103, 199
nursing, 3, 50, 52, 55–57, 219, 234, 260
private, 7, 177, 220
professional, 4, 117, 241, 249
social work, 219, 240
teacher training, 3, 52, 55, 201–202, 219, 224, 231, 234, 248, 251, 260
technical, 155, 168–169, 176
upper-secondary, 116–117
vocational, 33, 152, 237, 240

Science, 3–4, 6, 19, 25–42, 45, 50, 52, 56, 61–75, 77, 82, 85, 100–101, 103, 122–123, 127, 129, 132, 135, 137, 142, 147–150, 155–174, 176–177, 179–183, 187–188, 193, 195, 199–217, 237–254, 259, 264

Scientific, 9, 45, 48–50, 52–58, 77–78, 80, 82, 90, 97–99, 101, 112–113, 137, 145–146, 155, 158, 167, 169, 171, 176, 190, 203, 212–214, 216, 228, 231, 260

Social
demands, 9
education, see Study programmes
ideology, 135
interests, 247
utility, 203
work, see Study programmes

Societal
needs, 9
stakeholders, 8–9, 12, 20, 49, 265, 267

Spain, 4

Staff, 5, 10–12, 15–19, 25, 27, 29–30, 32–35, 37–40, 42, 45–52, 56–58, 62, 70, 74, 78–91, 99–100, 102, 106–110, 112, 119, 123–128, 130–132, 140–141, 143–148, 150–151, 158–161, 164–171, 178, 180, 184–189, 193–195, 201, 206, 208, 210–213, 215–216, 219–223, 226–235, 249–250, 260–262, 264–265, 269

Standardisation, 81, 156, 168

State authorities, 5, 8–9, 11–15, 20, 47, 131, 219, 221–226, 235, 265, 270

Stjernø Committee, 47

Structure
    formal, 16
    organisational, 18, 78, 128, 200, 219, 239,
        265
    physical, 87
Students, 7–8, 10–12, 14–16, 20, 25, 30–35,
        40, 42, 45–54, 56, 58, 61, 63,
        65, 68–69, 77, 79, 82–84, 87, 90,
        98–99, 102–103, 105, 109, 111
Study programmes
    bachelor, 34, 45, 118, 124, 128, 131, 156,
        220, 231
    economics and business administration,
        219–220
    engineering, 50, 52
    general teacher training, 7, 50
    health and social education, 234
    maritime education, 184
    master, 7, 33–34, 104, 156
    music, 6, 220
    nursing, 52, 57
    PhD, 45, 85–86, 99, 105, 187, 220,
        226–227, 233
    pre-school teacher training, 45, 55
    social work, 3, 6, 220, 231, 260
    teacher training, 3, 7, 50, 55, 58, 260
    vocational teacher training, 10, 77, 82, 87,
        148, 151–152, 187, 221
Supranational organisations, 8–9, 11–13, 20,
        265
Sweden, 5, 52
Switzerland, 3–8, 19, 26, 28–29, 34–38, 41–42,
        46, 61–62, 67–69, 71–74, 80, 84,
        86, 238–240, 248, 259, 261–268

T
Teacher training
    general, 52, 55, 201–202, 219–220, 231,
        248
    pre-school, 45
    vocational, 82, 87, 148, 151–152
Teaching, 5, 9, 12, 15–16, 18, 20, 26–28, 31,
        33, 35, 37, 39–40, 45–53, 55, 58,
        65, 70, 74–75, 78–91, 99–101,
        105–110, 112, 115, 121, 124–127,
        130, 132, 137–140, 142–143,
        145–153, 155, 158–160, 163–169,
        171, 173, 176–177, 180–184, 188,
        193, 195–196, 199–201, 203–213,
        215–216, 220–223, 226–227, 229,
        233–235, 247–248, 251, 259, 260,
        264

Theory
    credentialism, 10
    cultural, 11
    implementation, 242–243
    institutional, 271
    interest group, 33
    network, 30
    reference group, 10
    structural, 138–139

U
UAS, 4–12, 15–16, 18–20, 25–31, 33–42,
        45–46, 54, 56, 61–62, 64–66, 68,
        70–74, 78–83, 85, 88, 91, 155–156,
        158–161, 165, 167, 169–171, 173,
        191, 199–205, 207, 209–211, 213,
        215, 237–238, 240–242, 245–247,
        249–253, 259–268, 270
    sector, 4–12, 15–16, 18–20, 26–29, 35,
        37, 39, 41–42, 45, 54, 56, 65, 68,
        71, 73, 82, 201, 211, 259, 262,
        264–267
United Kingdom (UK), 4, 63–65, 68, 75, 77,
        90–91, 187, 201, 262, 267, 269
Universities of applied sciences, 3–4, 6,
        19, 25–42, 45, 61–75, 77, 135,
        155–174, 199–217, 237–253,
        259
University
    college, 4, 6–7, 25, 28, 36, 38, 50, 52–53,
        56–57, 68, 70–71, 78, 81, 83–84,
        97–113, 131, 184, 219–235, 264
    course, 9, 105, 219–220
    degree, 11, 248–249
    education, 7
    sector, 3–20, 28, 46, 61–67, 81, 89,
        115–117, 119–125, 127–128,
        130–132, 177, 192, 195, 200–201,
        220, 229, 253, 259, 263–267, 270
    status, 7, 116–118, 164, 199, 219–220, 233,
        268–269

V
Vocational
    education, 45, 83, 143, 148, 152, 202,
        239–241, 244
    schools, 33, 152, 237, 240

W
Walloon, 97, 103